"He's seen it all from the inside, and he pulls no punches in showing us the human reality that separates success from failure. This is true wisdom. Learn from the master."

—GEOFF COLVIN, author of *Talent Is Overrated*,
senior editor at large, *Fortune*

"Beware: Noel Tichy's *Succession* may give you nightmares, especially if you are a CEO, CHRO, or board member accountable for a CEO succession. If Tichy succeeds in making people more aware of the risks, opportunities, and nuances of CEO succession, this book will have performed a valuable public service."

—STRATFORD SHERMAN, partner, Accompli;
coauthor of *Control Your Destiny or Someone Else Will*

"If managing a succession is on your horizon or if succession is simply one of your intellectual interests, this book is a page-turner."

—MADELINE HEILMAN,
professor of psychology, New York University

"*Succession* draws on Tichy's decades of experience working with the leaders of Global 100 firms. He goes beyond simplistic recipes and checklists to introduce the reader to both successful transitions and horrifying failures. Succession planning is among the most important functions for boards and CEOs. *Succession* is a crash course in this critical, but too often neglected, responsibility."

—ROBERT KENNEDY, dean and LAWRENCE G. TAPP
Chair in Leadership, Ivey Business School

"The most important question for any institution is Who will lead fearlessly? Tichy's book provides the answer through the rigorous lens of a long-term practitioner and scholar on leadership and succession. Most get succession wrong. This book will help fearless leaders get it right."

—CATHY GREENBERG,
author of *Fearless Leaders: Sharpen Your Focus*.
www.DrCathyGreenberg.com

SUCCESSION

SUCCESSION

MASTERING THE MAKE-OR-BREAK PROCESS OF
LEADERSHIP TRANSITION

NOEL TICHY

PORTFOLIO / PENGUIN

PORTFOLIO / PENGUIN

Published by the Penguin Group
Penguin Group (USA) LLC
375 Hudson Street
New York, New York 10014

USA | Canada | UK | Ireland | Australia | New Zealand | India | South Africa | China
penguin.com
A Penguin Random House Company

First published by Portfolio / Penguin, a member of Penguin Group (USA) LLC, 2014

Copyright © 2014 by Noel M. Tichy
Penguin supports copyright. Copyright fuels creativity, encourages diverse voices,
promotes free speech, and creates a vibrant culture. Thank you for buying an
authorized edition of this book and for complying with copyright laws by
not reproducing, scanning, or distributing any part of it in any form without
permission. You are supporting writers and allowing Penguin to continue to
publish books for every reader.

LIBRARY OF CONGRESS CATALOGING-IN-PUBLICATION DATA
Tichy, Noel M.
Succession : mastering the make or break process of leadership transition /
Noel M. Tichy.
pages cm
Includes bibliographical references and index.
ISBN 978-1-59184-498-3 (hardback)
1. Executive succession. 2. Leadership. 3. Management. 4. Organizational effectiveness.
I. Title.
HD38.2.T53 2014
658.4'0711—dc23
2014022254

Printed in the United States of America
1 3 5 7 9 10 8 6 4 2

Set in Minion Pro
Designed by Elyse Strongin, Neuwirth & Associates, Inc.

*This book is dedicated to the true meaning of succession,
namely, my ten grandchildren, who will, I hope, all find a way
to make the world a little better.*

CONTENTS

INTRODUCTION

Every question about leadership ultimately gets down to development. It's about creating crucible experiences that make others better as a way of making yourself better. It's about focusing on a task you don't think can be done. Where you are rallying people across cultures and functions, where you're challenged ethically, and where your integrity is going to be tested.

In my experience, you don't go searching for those experiences. They tend to find you. The older you get the more you learn that people decisions are the most difficult. They are emotionally difficult, and they are also the best measure of how well you are doing as a leader.

—**James McNerney,**
chairman, president, and CEO, Boeing;
lecture at the University of Michigan's Ross School of Business

Placing a Big Bet on the Long Game

I have known and worked closely with Jim McNerney, the current CEO of Boeing, since early 1985 when as a senior executive at GE Information Services, popularly known as GEIS, he participated in a series of workshops I was facilitating for his unit's top team, of which he was a key member. Later that year, after agreeing to head up GE's famed Leadership Development Center at Crotonville in upstate New York, I got to know Jim even better. Over the more than quarter century since, I have closely tracked his career and had an opportunity to both work with and write about him as he moved through multiple business leadership positions inside GE—including head of Asia Pacific, a senior position in GE Capital, and CEO of both Lighting and Aircraft Engines—before being recruited to serve first as CEO of 3M and then chairman and CEO of Boeing.

McNerney and I are both proud products of and participants in the Jack Welch era at GE, so it is only natural that we share a mutual admiration for Welch as an exemplary leader/teacher who developed more leaders than any CEO in modern business history. This was no happy accident, but rather the result of an elaborate process, framework, and infrastructure of talent development, unique to GE, which has more deeply embedded a culture of leadership in the DNA of that organization—both before and after the Welch era—than any other outfit I know of, whether public or private, for profit or nonprofit. This started with founder Thomas A. Edison, who in 1879 envisioned a company that would light up a nation, through Charles A. Coffin, who started GE on a seemingly permanent path to innovations in technology, management, and leadership and skillfully organized the world's first true industrial conglomerate over his nearly thirty-year reign from 1892 to 1922. While Coffin created a vertical, hierarchical, centralized structure to control the various "GE Works" scattered across the country, he conceived of organizing national sales forces along product lines, and established the nation's first industrial research laboratory under Charles Proteus Steinmetz, widely known as "The Wizard of Schenectady."

But apart from all the patents, inventions, and innovations that GE pioneered—more than any company in the world over time—its most singular contribution to the evolution of modern business has been the intensity of its focus on leadership. By the 1920s under the duo of Coffin's successors Gerard Swope and Owen Young, GE began conducting specialized management retreats in the Thousand Islands area of upstate New York stressing the inculcation of leadership values, the first true corporate leadership curriculum in the world, which served as the precursor to the establishment of the leadership development center at Crotonville in 1956 under then-CEO Ralph Cordiner. The center spearheaded a thirteen-week executive leadership program that would be emulated by Harvard and other leading schools of business as they developed their own leadership programs.

This by-then well-grounded tradition of innovating new business models as well as machines led during the Depression to the foundation of GE Credit (later called GE Capital) to provide struggling householders with the means to buy GE's washing machines, toasters, fans, and other electrical appliances. During that period of the New Deal, as labor relations became a new battlefield, management focused on the adoption of generous pension plans and profit-based bonuses to keep its employees from joining unions. During the post–World War II period of rapid economic expansion, the company continued to develop its core management and leadership curriculum, commissioning such leading lights as the great Austrian-American consultant and theorist Peter F. Drucker to contribute to its famous Bible-like "Blue Books," a series consisting of five volumes of meticulously detailed guidance for GE managers that shaped management theory and practice around the country and the world for decades to come. In the 1960s, GE led the way to strategic planning, while in the 1980s and 1990s under Jack Welch, its warm embrace of such then-cutting-edge leadership development concepts as Work Out, Boundarylessness, and Six Sigma made them an integral part of global management culture.

What I will refer to from here on as the "GE Pipeline" or, in some cases, the "Jack Welch Pipeline," was a marvelous thing not just to behold but to be part of. Its unique design, equipped with multiple redundant systems and an intricate array of checks and balances, was entirely in keeping with the deeply held conviction—adhered to by Welch but also by all GE leaders both before and after his time—that the most important products GE produces aren't aircraft engines or locomotives but great leaders. According to a report in USA Today,[1] author Del Jones noted that the top three companies for producing CEOs of other companies at that time were GE with twenty-six, IBM with eighteen, and McKinsey with sixteen.

The piece openly celebrated the fact that at certain companies, a comparatively small group that includes GE, Procter & Gamble, PepsiCo, and Yum! Brands (all organizations frequently referred to as "academy companies,"[2] which will serve as role models of robust pipeline production in this book), seeing senior executives leave even after decades of investment in their development for presumably greener pastures outside the company is not looked down on or frowned upon, but rather regarded as a high honor, not just for those executives selected for higher office but for the organization that trained, developed, and produced them. When a GE highflier leaves "for a huge external opportunity," executive vice president of executive development Susan Peters—now head of HR at GE—was quoted as saying, "it enhances our employment brand." When *USA Today* e-mailed Procter & Gamble (P&G) a list of 12 alumni, now CEOs of companies with a market cap of $2 billion, P&G faxed back a list of 128 chairmen, CEOs, and CFOs at other companies that it had produced, running in alphabetical order from Fernando Aguirre of Chiquita Brands (CQB) to Sergio Zyman of Zyman Group, a former senior marketing executive at both Coca-Cola and PepsiCo.

The pipeline Jack built—with the help and input of many others, including my own team at Crotonville and its successors—included a number of future stars, many of whom would go on to lead winning teams at other organizations. Just a smattering of the name-brand CEOs turned out by the Jack Welch GE pipeline includes, most notably, former GE vice chairman Lawrence Bossidy, later CEO of AlliedSignal and Honeywell (CEO of the Year, *Chief Exective Magazine*, 1998, and CEO of the Year, *Financial World Magazine,* 1994), whose successor, David Cote, is another GE alum, as is of course former 3M CEO and now Boeing CEO McNerney; Tom Tiller, former CEO of Polaris; Steve Bennett, former CEO of Intuit and later Symantec; Home Depot CEO Frank Blake; former Home Depot and Chrysler CEO Bob Nardelli (along with McNerney a runner-up to Jeff Immelt for Jack Welch's job); and former Siemens CEO Peter Loescher, who was a former senior executive at GE Healthcare before moving to Merck, and then Siemens.

The three finalists—Bob Nardelli, head of Power Systems, Jim McNerney, who led Aircraft Engines, and Jeff Immelt, who led Medical Systems—were all tried and tested in the field under Jack's leadership, and judged by him and the board not just on their innate and conditioned leadership capacity but on their tangible business results. Of those final three, while McNerney went on to become a transformational leader at not one but two iconic companies, 3M and Boeing, Nardelli—sometimes referred to as "Little Jack," in reference to his famous faithfulness to his mentor—didn't handle the political and cultural elements at his new home while attempting a Welch-like transformation at Home Depot nearly as deftly as his mentor Welch might have. He was ultimately forced out at Home Depot, before going on to serve as CEO of Chrysler, which he successfully sold to Fiat. As for Jeff Immelt, winner of the grand prize, who took over the company within days of 9/11, having faced and lived through a nearly decade-long perfect storm of terrorist attacks—which wreaked havoc on the company's aviation and insurance businesses—a technology bust, and a Great Recession and global financial near-collapse deeper and longer than any economic downturn since the Great Depression, it is safe to say that he and the company have withstood and sustained macroeconomic turbulence unprecedented since the outbreak of the Second World War.

During the darkest days of the financial crisis, GE stock dropped to under $7 a share. Immelt felt obliged to cut the company's cherished stock dividend, and faced the loss of its equally cherished triple-A credit bond rating. The simple and undeniable fact is that over the first thirteen years of the Immelt regime, the stock price is down 37 percent (as of mid-2014) below its value when he took over. Yet it is far too early, particularly in the long-term context of GE, to judge his time at the helm, particularly since GE shares soared more than 30 percent in 2013 as he successfully revised the portfolio and continued to promote and drive some impressive initiatives, from Ecomagination to the Industrial Internet to a Guest House at the R&D center that directly connects business leaders to the company's latest technology. Shifting the portfolio is part of the job of every CEO at GE—Welch divested billions in assets and hundreds of businesses, while acquiring others. In short, as of our last status check, even after thirteen years it was still too soon to call.

But one thing we can be sure of is that like all of his predecessors before him, Immelt is thinking long and hard about the selection of his successor. In fact, as *The Wall Street Journal* reported just as this book went to press, Immelt and his fellow directors were conducting high-level "board discussions about shortening the expected tenure for GE's next chief executive to between 10 and 15 years" from what has been widely regarded as a traditional two-decade-long term, despite the fact that Welch's two predecessors, Reginald Jones and Fred Borch, both served at the top for "only" nine years, so the two-decade time frame is scarcely set in stone.

Succeeding at Succession at Crotonville

Just reading that article about CEO succession at GE in the *Journal* took me back more than twenty-five years to the meeting where I was given my first inkling that Jack Welch was seriously committed to blowing up the process that created the pipeline at GE. I had first met Welch in 1978, when as a professor at the Columbia Graduate School of Business I had a team of MBAs do a project with GE on succession planning. At the time, Welch was a sector executive running as hard as he could—and that was hard—in a multihorse race for the top job. After he beat all competitors and was named CEO in 1981 I worked closely with Ted LeVino, GE's longtime head of human resources, running leadership development workshops for senior HR leaders across the company, while also consulting with various units of GE on leadership develop-ment, including GE Information Services, Lighting, and Medical Systems (GEMS).

My next interaction with Welch took place in late 1984 as I was com-pleting my book *The Transformational Leader*.[3] I'd interviewed Chrys-ler's Lee Iacocca, Burroughs's Mike Blumenthal, and other corporate luminaries of the era, and was well aware that leaving out Welch would have been a glaring omission, but he had responded to my first request with the uncharacteristically humble explanation that since his trans-formational revolution remained in its early stages, any insights or re-flections he might have on the subject seemed to him premature. Disappointed as I was by that rejection, I respected him for it. But then, a few months later, on a cold winter's day in January 1985, I was wind-ing down a teaching session at Crotonville on my favorite subject—transformational leadership—when I was handed a message that Welch would be happy to sit down with me to talk about my book, assuming I was available.

Later that afternoon, I found myself sitting with the-then notorious "Neutron Jack"[4] in a small office joyfully brainstorming about the com-plex set of imperatives, challenges, methods, and mechanics of leadership and transformation at a wide range of organizations and institutions, get-ting Welch's comments tape recorded for the book. Throughout our lengthy and wide-ranging discussion, I was, I must admit, blissfully un-aware that Welch was operating with a covert agenda. I thought I was there because I was interviewing him for a book, but he was actually in-terviewing me for a job. All was revealed the following day, when after I'd completed my last session with the executive program and was preparing to head home, I received an urgent summons from Jim Baughman, an ex–Harvard Business School professor who five years before had accepted a strikingly similar offer from Welch to run Crotonville.

Growing more curious by the minute, I was taken aback when, within seconds of my taking a seat in his office, Baughman cut straight to the chase. "I'm being promoted to head of organizational planning and management development," he said. "Jack and I were wondering if you'd like to run Crotonville."

Run Crotonville?

Flattered as I was by the offer, I felt I had no choice but to decline as graciously as I could. As I explained to Baughman, I'd accepted two overseas teaching assignments, half the year at INSEAD in France and the other in Tokyo as a U.S./Japan fellow, that would keep me busy for the next year, on top of a number of other pressing programmatic commitments. Back home in Michigan, I had an International Leadership Development Program and an Advanced Human Research Management Program to run, as well as serving as editor of the journal *Human Resource Management,* none of which could function without me. That said, I told Baughman that I was more than flattered by the offer. I was intrigued—intrigued enough, in fact, to hedge my bets by responding that I'd think about it on an upcoming vacation with my family.

On the con side, if I said yes, my name and reputation would be permanently linked to a man many people, particularly in the press and academia, regarded at the time as a dangerous lunatic, not to mention the quintessence of everything that had gone wrong with American business during the 1980s.[5] On the pro side, if I said no, that meant forgoing not just a rare but a unique opportunity to do something more meaningful (to me, at least) than simply witness, analyze, or observe and consult to Welch's revolution from the comfortable and distant vantage point of an academic, and a long-term consultant.

Saying yes meant, for better or for worse, committing to playing an active, full-time, *leadership* role in one of the most dynamic organizational transformations of the late twentieth century. Ultimately, the prospect of running, and more important, *leading,* Crotonville won out, especially after I was able to convince both Jack and Jim that I could take on the job while keeping my most pressing commitments back at the University of Michigan.

Just a few weeks later, after I accepted his offer, Welch and I met at his office in an old Art Deco tower at Fifty-first Street and Lexington Avenue in midtown Manhattan—this was before GE bought NBC and the company's New York headquarters shifted to 30 Rockefeller Plaza—where he enthusiastically laid out the critical role Crotonville was going to play in driving the revolution he'd been fomenting at GE.

"I want a fucking revolution—and I want it to happen at Crotonville!"

That's just how he put it, in inimitable General of General Electric style, always colorful, always straight to the point, always shooting (as his memoir later put it) straight from the gut. He continued our conversation by explaining in some detail his "80-20 rule," which simply stated that at most 20 percent of leadership development could be conducted in an institutional setting like Crotonville, while a minimum of 80 percent would inevitably take place on the job. As a practical solution to what he evidently regarded as an immutable fact, his direct, unvarnished mandate was for my team to create at Crotonville what Jim McNerney would call "crucible experiences" and what I refer to as "action learning."

Under my leadership and with Welch's strong support, everything at Crotonville was going to change. Our revamped curriculum would require cross-functional teams of executives from across the enterprise to tackle real projects, put their members at real career risk, and end the long-standing practice of sitting around Crotonville's newly revamped campus leisurely reading Harvard Business School case studies and engaging in elaborate intellectual debates about events that had already occurred, more often than not long ago in the past, not even at GE but at other companies. Participants at Crotonville would start spending all of their time there solving real GE challenges while learning business acumen, team building, and organizational transformation. These action learning projects, conducted out in the field for several weeks, would take place in real time, all over the world, and would be designed to frame and tackle a wide range of major strategic challenges facing the company for an equally wide range of businesses, from locomotives to power generation, plastics to credit to health sciences. Others would require us to send teams from Crotonville to Korea, China, or India to explore potential acquisitions or joint venture opportunities. In all cases, these teams—temporary task forces, really—would return to Crotonville prepared to present their recommendations to Welch and a cadre of senior leaders.

As a result of this process, many real decisions would be made at the highest levels, based on team input and clearly stated recommendations, which ultimately determined the strategic direction of both the individual businesses and the organization as a whole. Yet there was a parallel agenda running at "The New Crotonville," which more directly pertained to the construction, destruction, and reconstruction of the time-honored leadership pipeline. Each participant was scrupulously evaluated on his or her performance at these add-on tasks in addition to how well he or she embodied the GE values while taking part in the action learning programs, as well as the more routine evaluations conducted on a regular basis of their performance at their day jobs.

At Welch's behest, my team and I spent nearly two years producing (and publishing in the fall of 1987) a white paper that put all this thinking down. Entitled "Organizational Effectiveness Notes: A Leadership Development Framework," our work laid out in painstaking detail a revised theory of how to construct a leadership development pipeline based not on classroom casework or the results of psychological surveys but on leaders' *consciously cultivated capacity* to exercise best judgment and tackle real business problems. It also concretized the important premise that the best way to pick your next CEO is by building a pipeline that creates real leaders at every level of the company and at every stage in their personal and professional development, from off-campus hires to the vice chairman vying for the CEO job.

———————

Personal Detour: Before continuing with the GE story and my work at GE with Jack Welch, let me provide a little context and background laying out my own professional and leadership journey. Taken in aggregate, these experiences constitute a professional lifetime of preparation for writing this book, as they have spanned a wide range of industrial and economic sectors, from business to health care, and from higher and secondary education to the military, with my military work focusing primarily on advising the leadership of the U.S. Special Operations Forces on how to transform themselves into a fighting machine for a new kind of war.

My journey began when as a PhD student I worked with the new superintendent of schools in East Orange, New Jersey, in 1970 both on his own personal leadership development and on the impact of his appointment as the first black superintendent on the school system as a whole. After becoming an assistant professor at the Columbia Graduate School of Business in 1972, I continued to conduct similar projects with school superintendents in predominantly affluent Westchester, New York. My own work, however, was largely confined to a range of more diverse communities that contained significant working-class and minority populations, including White Plains, New Rochelle, and Mount Vernon. My first book on leadership was rooted in my research into the delivery of health care in an inner-city setting, at a clinic I consulted with called the Martin Luther King Health Center in the South Bronx of New York. At the MLKHC, I collaborated with the top team both on leadership succession and on other, related organizational issues affecting the long-term sustainability of the venture, which continues to flourish today.

Later on in that decade, after becoming a professor at the Graduate School of Business at Columbia, I ran executive programs in leadership and consulted widely on leadership development in the United States and Europe, working with Pehr Gyllenhammar, CEO of Volvo, and Sir John Harvey-Jones, CEO of ICI (Imperial Chemical Industries) in London. The table on the next page represents my clinical database as a practitioner.

As a researcher I have also interviewed and studied hundreds of leaders, ranging from CEOs to heads of school systems, hospitals, not-for-profit agencies, and the military, while as a clinician I have actively worked and collaborated with hundreds of leaders on their own journeys, with the prime goal of producing pipelines designed to sustain the organization from generation to generation, ideally (although not always realistically) in perpetuity. The table highlights the clinical and research background for this book. Like one of my favorite books by Jerome Groopman, *How Doctors Think*, this book is based on both research and clinical practice.

	Organization	Personal Experience: CEO and Leadership Succession	Results
1970s	Ciba Geigy	Advised CEO Don McKinnon on succession planning and selection of successor CEO North America	☺
	Chase Manhattan	Adviser to Fred Hammer, EVP of retail, direct report and potential successor to CEO David Rockefeller	☹
	Appalachian Hospital	Helped save Hazard Family Health Services during a fiscal crisis when hospital system went bankrupt	😐
	Columbia University	Started doctoral program in social psychology in 1968, just prior to the ouster of president Grayson Kirk	☹
	Columbia University	On team of graduate students studying impact of first black school superintendent of East Orange, NJ	☺
	MLK Health Center	Advised former welfare mother/CEO Dolores Smith who earned master's in public health from U. Mich	☺
1980s	U. Michigan	Taught during a succession of successions from Shapiro to Duderstadt to Coleman to Schlissel	☺
	Honeywell	Advised on 1984 succession of CEO Jim Renier, who went on to have a successful run at Honeywell	☺
	Meritor Bank	Worked with former Chase heir apparent Fred Hammer after he became CEO	☹
	Whirlpool	Partnered with Alan Lafley, father of A. G. Lafley, on transition of Dave Whitwam to succeed Jack Sparks	☺
	GE	Ran GE leadership institute at Crotonville under Jack Welch and helped reinvent leadership pipeline	☺
	GM	Advised reorganization led by Bob Stempel, who succeeded Roger Smith as CEO	☹
1990s	Ameritech	Orchestrated simultaneous companywide transformation and leadership succession under CEO Weiss	☺
	Mercedes-Benz	Worked with car group head Helmut Werner and since worked with current CEO, Dieter Zetsche	☺
	Chrysler	Analyzed Iacocca turnaround in *Transformational Leader*, workshops for CEOs Bob Easton and Nardelli	😐
	Ford	Advised CEO Alex Trotman on succession to Jacques Nasser; all of us fired during Firestone tire crisis	☹
	Royal/Dutch Shell	Worked with chairman Cor Herkstroter and CMD on succession system and leadership development	☹
	Honeywell	Worked with CEO/former GE vice chairman Larry Bossidy on establishing GE-style succession process	☺
2000s	Intel	Worked with CEO Paul Otellini on action-learning program; identified current CEO Brian Krzanich	☺
	Intuit	Advised founder Scott Cook, CEO Steve Bennett, and current CEO Brad Smith on succession planning	☺
	Covad	Worked with CEO Bob Knowling before board coup d'etat cost him his job	☹
	Telewares	Continued to work with CEO Bob Knowling on next assignment, resulting in more favorable outcome	☺
	Nomura Securities	Ran leadership development workshop with CEO Yoshihisa Tabuchi; fired for knowledge of bribery	☹
	RBS	Worked on senior leadership development and succession planning when Fred Goodwin was fired	☹
	GE	Culmination of Welch succession process with the appointment of CEO Immelt four days before 9/11	☺
2010s	Grupo Salinas	Worked with Chairman Ricardo Salinas on family and professional leadership succession for six years	☺
	Boys and Girls Clubs	Developed and conducted leadership program for 200 clubs; helped design succession process	☺
	Uplift	Ran leadership development and succession planning program for principals and senior administrators	☺
	Best Buy	Developed leadership institute; advised CEO Anderson on succession; resulted in successor Dunn being fired	☹
	Brunei	Partnered with government in developing leadership program for nationwide school network	☺
	Accenture	Developed internal team to lead leadership institute	☺
	CP Group, Thailand	Partnered with chairman to establish leadership institute; designed and implemented succession planning	☺
	Babson College	Worked with president Len Schlesinger, former Limited exec, since he was my MBA student at Columbia	☺
	IDEA Public Schools	Worked with CEO Tom Torkelson on succession planning and leadership development program	☺

CEO Succession at GE

The second substantive conversation I had with Welch following that first meeting revolved around the topic—as all-consuming for him as it had been for his predecessors and would be for his successor and his successor's successors—of leadership development and succession planning as a core strategic opportunity and challenge for the company. "How I got here," Jack told me, in his characteristically brusque tone, "is totally irrelevant. What I want you to do is work with"—and here he reeled off a long list of names, including then–vice chairman Larry Bossidy, later CEO of AlliedSignal and Honeywell—"on building a real leadership pipeline that will take us into the next century." As I was shortly to learn, Welch didn't think much of the horse race he had won five years before, which had been set up by his predecessor Reginald Jones. The aspect of it that he most strongly detested was that it had compelled him and the two other finalists, all of whom had been promoted to vice chairman, to dedicate several tension-filled years locking horns at corporate headquarters, as opposed to running real businesses in the field. He was determined to avoid that mistake going forward, even as he sought to develop a process firmly grounded in a realistic assessment of the talent and development needs of the organization in the future—even the distant future—as opposed to looking in the rearview mirror at the past.

In the quarter century since we produced that white paper at GE, my leadership team and I at Action Learning Associates have flexibly followed (with any number of significant updates and revisions, of course) many of its fundamental lessons and precepts in the conception and execution of hundreds of leadership development programs and succession plans at companies including the U.S.-based icons IBM, Intuit, Intel, and PepsiCo, as well as global leaders including Royal Dutch Shell and Nokia, to emerging market corporate leaders such as Mexican retail, financial, and communications conglomerate Grupo Salinas and CP Group, one of the largest and most diversified companies in Asia, and now the world.

It is also clearly the case that since imitation and emulation are the finest forms of flattery, literally hundreds of companies both in the United States and around the world have over the past two decades used and adapted what they have been able to derive at a distance from the GE Model as the basis for establishing their own leadership development and training programs, and even in some cases Crotonville-like leadership institutes and academies. But it is important to note for the record that all the bricks-and-mortar and elaborate institutions won't be worth the glass, steel, and bricks they're built with if they lack the right programs and processes to build, assess, evaluate, and create crucible experiences that teach them. And institutions don't matter if the current generation of top leaders, most important the CEO, isn't deeply involved in every stage of the process.

That issue underscores a great fallacy, which over the years has grown into something of a monstrous Mothra, that leads even the most well-meaning of leaders and organizations to slavishly copy and overemphasize the *technical* aspects of the process and virtually ignore, evade, or fatally misunderstand the far subtler, much more difficult, and ultimately far more important determinate of success: the *political* and *cultural* dimensions of succession planning, leadership assessment and evaluation, CEO selection, and executive transition.

As a result, you won't find much in here about trends or citations from statistics, because despite the current preoccupation with big data, I don't believe trends or statistics are meaningful in this context. The analogy that I like to use in all of my work is that I want to observe, work closely with, and ultimately determine what distinguishes the Olympic athletes, and especially the gold medal winners, from the rest of the pack, and in particular from those who never make it to the trials.

I will also be taking an uncomfortably close look at some spectacular failures, the mirror opposites of the Olympic heroes and demigods who adhere to best practices. I've learned the hard way that often the best way to define a best practice is to take a worst practice and turn it upside down. As every true teacher will tell you, teaching is as much about learning as it is about imparting or conveying knowledge you already know. So I conclude by imparting a piece of unsolicited advice based on more than three decades of developing, coaching, teaching, training, and selecting leaders for some of the highest-performing organizations in the world: *This is the most important people judgment call any organization will ever make, and by far the best way to get it dead wrong is by proceeding under the fatal delusion that you've got it all figured out and buttoned up, and just need the right format, framework, and formula to put your plan into action.*

If that commonly held delusion were true, you wouldn't need to read past this point. But since it isn't, I have included—along with the success stories and cautionary tales in this book—ample analytical and clinical procedures to help you guide and frame and navigate through the inherent complexities of the process. In many ways the don'ts are as informative as the dos when it comes to implementing best practices and procedures in this complex and challenging discipline. That said, no process, no matter how well thought out and executed, can ever be perfect or complete. At the most basic level, leadership succession and transition is a continuous process of organizational transformation: a people decision, an organizational decision, and a strategy decision all rolled into one, with not infrequently a crisis call thrown in for good measure. As you will read more than once in this book, leadership succession and transition is simply the most politically and culturally charged, technically challenging, and critical leadership assignment of all the many judgments that business leaders are obliged to make in the course of doing their day jobs. And, for that very reason, it is at least as easy to get it wrong as it is tough to get it right.

CHAPTER 1

GETTING IT WRONG: THE BROKEN CEO SUCCESSION PIPELINE

If it's hard for the IBMs and the GEs, the companies that really pride themselves on building pipelines, it's darn near impossible for all of the rest of us who haven't put that process in place.

—Leonard A. Schlesinger,
Baker Foundation Professor, Harvard Business School;
former president, Babson College; former vice chairman
and COO, Limited Brands; former executive vice president
and COO, Au Bon Pain

KEY ISSUES OF THE BROKEN CEO PIPELINE

TECHNICAL
- Overreliance on the mechanics of succession planning
- Lack of human resource competence and capability

POLITICAL
- Lack of CEO/board/HR alignment and balance of power
- Inability to handle internal infighting of candidates

CULTURAL
- Succession planning as a mechanical exercise
- Dishonest succession planning process

HP, the Poster Child of Failed CEO Successions: Four in a Row

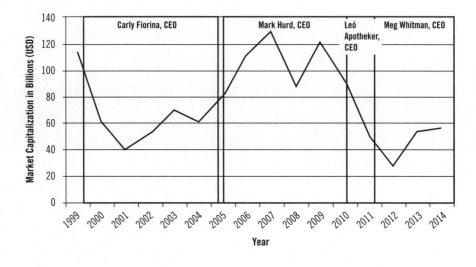

On the morning of September 22, 2011, the board of directors of the computer hardware and software manufacturer Hewlett-Packard[1] announced the resignation, effective immediately, of CEO Léo Apotheker after just eleven months on the job.[2] Simultaneously, it announced that it was passing over a deep bench of long-term insiders to appoint an outsider CEO for the third time in a little more than a decade.[3] The board justified its appointment of failed California gubernatorial candidate, former eBay CEO, and current board member Margaret "Meg" Whitman—who had joined the HP board in January 2011 as part of a board shake-up engineered by Apotheker—without mounting a formal search by noting that since it had conducted a full-scale search less than a year before, it had the results of that search in its hip pocket, if needed. What went without saying was that such an eventuality would only occur if the board's latest pick unexpectedly blew up in their faces, as the selection of Apotheker so damagingly had.

Even by the bland standards of official corporate pronouncements, this one stood out for saying less by saying more. Among the many unanswered questions posed by disturbed HP investors and their surrogates during a conference call with the directors immediately following the announcement was to what degree HP's board, whose fiduciary duty obliged it to represent the interests of shareholders, should have considered it appropriate to express "appreciation" for services rendered to the company by a failed CEO on whose less-than-year watch it had lost an astounding $30 billion in market cap. Certainly, HP's long-suffering shareholders could be forgiven for harboring a sneaking sensation that they had seen this horror show before—in fact three times before, at a staggering cost to their own financial interests, not to mention the hundreds of thousands of employees and their families impacted by the precipitous decline of a once-fabled firm.

The costs directly associated with HP's excessive churn at the top could be tangibly measured by the sharp drop in the company's market capitalization between January 2000, the first year of its first outsider CEO Carly Fiorina's controversial tenure, and December 2011, three months after its third outsider CEO in a row tendered his resignation to a board thickly populated with his own former supporters, who after a year and a half of tragicomic slapstick leadership marked by one mishap after another, reluctantly joined forces in turning against him and ousting him before he could do even more damage.

By contrast, at least from the reeling company's point of view, while HP's market cap had plunged by roughly two thirds over the dozen years between Fiorina's appointment and Apotheker's ouster, from well over $100 billion to well under $30 billion, rival computer firm Apple had entered the decade worth less than $5 billion—5 percent of HP's then market value—and kicked off January 2012 worth well in excess of $400 billion, twenty times that of onetime industry leader HP and more than the net worth of the entire economy of Greece.

So what is the main lesson we should derive from this remarkable turn of events, which prompted former HP director and Silicon Valley venture capital legend Tom Perkins to publicly castigate the group of business brains he had recently served with before resigning in disgust as "the worst board in the world?"[4] As *The New York Times* bluntly put it,

"The mystery isn't why Hewlett-Packard is likely to part ways with its chief executive, Léo Apotheker, after just a year in the job. It's why he was hired in the first place."[5] While it should be noted in all fairness that panning the performance of HP's board requires painting this picture with an unfairly broad brush, since over the years its cast of characters continually shifted, neither can it be denied that regardless of which luminaries served on the board at pivotal points when it arrived at a series of disastrous people, strategy, and crisis decisions, its only true constant was the repetitive nature with which it passed over the company's internal bench and returned to a pool of celebrated outsider CEO candidates to replace outsider CEOs, who miserably and repeatedly failed to deliver the goods, despite ostensibly sterling records and backgrounds.

Am I arguing an open-and-shut case that outsider CEOs are inevitably doomed to failure and should always be ruled out in competition with insider candidates? No. But what I am arguing, unequivocally, is that every time an organization's board needs to reach outside its own ranks for a successor to an incumbent CEO, such a desperate move, even if at the time it may be hailed as a breakthrough, is in fact an unmistakable sign of a broken leadership pipeline, and in my experience, broken leadership pipelines are the primary root cause of broken companies. What the HP story, which unfolded over many quarters of year-after-year earnings declines, confirms is this: of the many factors to which movement of share prices and long-term performance are widely ascribed, the success or failure of senior leadership to drive internal and confront external change is the single most important determinant of long-term success.

Not just at HP but also at virtually every company or organization on the planet, whether run for profit, not-for-profit, public or private, family or shareholder owned, there are two immutable facts about leadership:

1. Leadership matters.
2. Continuity of leadership matters.

The corollary of this thesis is that the defining legacy of any individual's leadership is the quality and outcome of his or her commitment to putting a process in place expressly designed to ensure an orderly transition from present leader to future leader—at any time, for any reason—with minimal disruption and drama. Just Google the old Latin word *interregnum*—literally, "the time between kings"—and you will be treated to a long list, spanning many centuries, of the chaos and conflict that inevitably erupts when a gap—often aptly referred to as a "power vacuum"—opens between the rules of successive monarchs. This has long been a time of danger and risk, typically prompted by succession struggles and ambiguity regarding the legitimacy of various claimants to the throne. The reason the famous phrase "The King [or Queen] is dead; long live the King [or Queen]" is still uttered on the occasion of the death of one king and the seamless ascension of his successor in the United Kingdom is to scrupulously avoid even the slightest implication of the creation of an interregnum between the death or abdication of the present monarch and the announcement of his or her rightful and legitimate heir and successor. Similarly, no leader of any nation or organization ever wants to be a "lame duck"—a term coined in the late nineteenth century to describe a stockbroker on the London exchange who defaulted on his debts, leaving him prey to financial predators, much as a lame duck in real life falls behind the pack, leaving itself unprotected. The "lame duck" phenomenon occurs in business, politics, and organizational dynamics during periods of paralysis and inaction after one person in authority announces his or her departure and the accession of the successor, creating once again a dangerous and in most cases entirely preventable period of indecision detrimental to the organization.

As we shall see time and again in this book, shareholders and investors typically suffer most from fumbled corporate CEO successions, because the ambiguity that inevitably arises during such periods of chaos and uncertainty is deeply detested by serious investors, who tend to punish disruption and discontinuity by dumping the stock and moving on to more stable ground. But employees and other stakeholders, including the communities where companies operate, are just as often severely impacted as well. Whatever the case, the undeniable truth underlying a sad situation is that surprisingly few organizations of any form, structure, region, industrial sector, or nationality get this complex, politicized, emotion-laden job right, either for the first time or the tenth.

But—and this is a big but—how many times have you heard of a winning baseball, football, or any high-performing sports team lose a coach or a star quarterback or pitcher without immediately naming a replacement? If the conductor or first violinist of a world-famous symphony orchestra catches the flu or gets hit by a cab, wouldn't you expect the organization to have a replacement on deck? The same goes with generals. If a commander-in-chief decides to pull a losing general off the battlefield, is he or she likely to wait months or even years to install a successor? Yet at most of our largest and most admired companies, and at many if not most of our largest and most admired academic and other nonprofit institutions, it is more the rule than the exception that if and when an incumbent leader departs the scene, for any number of predictable or unpredictable reasons, the organization all too frequently finds itself in the awkward predicament of lacking an insider candidate or candidates waiting on deck who are ready, willing, eager, and most important, well prepared and able to step up into the top job at a moment's notice and succeed.

I readily concede the fact that many—I would estimate as high a percentage as 80 percent of Fortune 500 companies and an equivalent percentage of academic and other nonprofit institutions—do have formal succession plans in place, but that is not really my point. Because in my experience all too often these formal plans are no more than that—empty formalities, technicalities, and charadelike check-the-box exercises. When push comes to shove, as it nearly always does, such plans and processes ostensibly designed to ensure an orderly, seamless, nondisruptive CEO succession, absent political infighting, cultural confusion, ambiguity, and ambivalence, often break down in practice.

The New Ball Game: CEOs Under the Gun
Due to the Rise of the Activist Investor

CEO tenures have been getting shorter by the day,[6] in large part because activist investors have successfully precipitated and accelerated so many objectively failed CEO departures, when in previous periods more tolerant and cozily incestuous boards might have twiddled their thumbs or fiddled while Rome burned. Today, more responsible and responsive boards, legitimately fearful of incurring reputational and in some extreme cases legal liability, are increasingly willing to quickly pull the plug on any executive the financial analyst community and the market no longer have confidence in, and are just as quick to replace him or her with someone who might be better at it—sooner rather than later—for fear that they will go next out the door. Remember, activist investors don't just demand CEOs' heads on a platter, they demand seats on the board—and these days, are increasingly getting them.

The growing confidence and success of activist investors is from my point of view providing the investment and business communities with yet more confirmation that the fundamental laws of organizational dynamics and the unity of command still apply. Yes, activist investors are making the jobs of some CEOs tougher than ever, but also—when they do win—often more rewarding for shareholders and even managers of a company required under pressure to operate at a higher level, closer to fulfilling its true potential. Activist investors like William Ackman are playing a major, and some would argue outsized, role in the ousters of CEOs and the appointment of handpicked successors. On the one hand Ackman was instrumental in appointing Ron Johnson as CEO of JCPenney and, when it was not working out, quickly firing him. In my view it was a bad judgment call to hire the wrong CEO, followed by a good judgment call of firing him for failing to perform. On the other hand, Ackman made what I consider a bad judgment call at P&G when he orchestrated the ouster of CEO Bob McDonald when still in midstream of strategically repositioning the company for the future. Ackman's bad judgment call in helping to dislodge a good CEO, McDonald, was later rectified by a good judgment call made as this book went to press by President Barack Obama, who had just appointed McDonald to serve as his next secretary of veterans affairs. Good judgments or bad, the reality of today's world is that activist investors have become a significant factor in the CEO succession sweepstakes, and for better or worse are likely to occupy such a role for the foreseeable future.

CEO Succession: The #1 Determinant of Organizational Performance

Activist investors aside, in our 2007 book, *Judgment: How Winning Leaders Make Great Calls*, my longtime friend, colleague, and coauthor Warren Bennis and I contended that "CEO succession in any type of organization—from political, to not for profit, to business or the military—is the key determinant of organizational performance."[7] We further argued that of all the many judgment calls leaders may be obliged to make over the course of their careers—decisions we divided into three buckets: people judgments, strategy judgments, and crisis judgments—people judgments are foundational because without having the right people on your team or the right man or woman driving the bus, it is next to impossible to make sound strategy and/or crisis decisions, which makes a fair part of the leader's job irrelevant.

The Technical, Political, and Cultural (TPC) Context of CEO Succession

Selecting a candidate to be your next leader is the ultimate people judgment call. Ironically, as we shall see shortly, it is a call that essentially amounts to a decision based on an assessment of the candidates' own judgment calls. And as we shall also see, the impartiality and objectivity of those assessments, performed over time, are utterly critical to the integrity of the process. CEO successions that do go awry are nearly always thrown off course or derailed by a series of factors that define the operation of all organizations, which I have also divided into three buckets: the technical, the political, and the cultural.

Thirty years ago I wrote a book entitled *Managing Strategic Change*[8] in which I employed the metaphor of a rope woven from three separate strands to illustrate the division into three dimensions that, in my view, drive all organizational change. The technical strand of the rope includes the rational scientific management precepts of strategic planning, organization design, and human resources that we spend most of our MBA curriculum teaching to our students.

This is only part of the picture, because an organization is a political system, the second strand of the rope. Organizations also have political processes and coalitions that influence what strategies are pursued, and political power is dispersed in organization design, with variations in how centralized power is and how balanced across groups it is. Finally, organizational politics determine how much different groups are paid— this is a political issue, and succession is the most political of all processes, with one political winner getting the CEO slot.

The cultural strand of the rope refers to the values of the organization needed to support the strategy, as well as the organizational challenge of integrating multiple subcultures in an organization to have an overarching corporate or organizational culture, and finally the teaching, reinforcing both rewards and punishments for violating the culture's rules, largely through the human resource systems. When an organization goes through strategic change, a new direction, all three strands need to be rewoven or the result is like rope unraveling and falling apart. Succession throughout this book will be viewed in terms of these technical, political, and cultural strands.

"TPC Theory" applies to the topic of executive transition and CEO succession because one of the primary reasons that organizations fail—which is of course really a euphemism for the people inside those organizations who fail—at this delicate and difficult task is that too many CEOs, boards, and CHROs (chief human resources officers) overly rely on the technical aspects of the process. Succeeding at succession—which at its best re-volves less around selecting one candidate from a pool of finalists in a horse race and more around creating a robust pipeline of future leaders to succeed the present generation of leaders—above and beyond everything else fundamentally requires a deep appreciation of the fact that the tech-nical aspects of the succession dilemma are by far the easiest to solve for, and are therefore most appropriately relegated to secondary and even ter-tiary status in comparison with the political and cultural dimensions. The technical issues, I believe, should at most encompass and demand 20 percent of management emphasis and attention, while something closer to 40 percent of overall investment in refining and perfecting the process should each be apportioned to the far more complex political and cul-tural dimensions of developing leaders to succeed other leaders.

"Management scientists and production engineers," I wrote thirty years ago, "frequently view work and organizational design as essen-tially an engineering or technical problem." Such an overreliance on technique frequently leads to dysfunction as the political and cultural issues remain unacknowledged, misunderstood, and neglected on the surface, only to go underground and undermine the organization. At the same time, "a purely political orientation to organizational life and change is also likely to be dysfunctional, because it can lead to low levels of trust, cynicism, and a prevailing view that all interactions are win/lose bargaining situations." Same for the cultural strand of the rope; it is only meaningful if it supports the technical and political strands.

When I write about the technical dimension of the succession di-lemma, I am mainly referring to what I call the "hard" decisions popu-larly viewed as essential to the CEO role: big-picture goal setting, strategy formation, organizational design, and structural revisions within systems. For the political dimension, I am referring primarily to issues posed by the allocation of power and resources, including the vast majority of personnel issues, including critical promotions, the se-curing of key "stretch" assignments, budget decisions, and the internal power structure of the organization. Cultural factors primarily consist of the values, beliefs, and interpretations of those beliefs ideally shared by every member of the organization. I truly believe that the toughest leadership challenge of all is framing the content of the culture, determining precisely which values need to be shared, achieving alignment as to which objectives are worth collectively striving for, and identifying what beliefs all employees should be committed to.

Having witnessed, lived through, and helped to plan many successions and transitions, based on a virtually lifelong analysis of the intertwined technical, political, and cultural aspects of the puzzle, I have arrived at three inescapable conclusions regarding CEO succession:

1. Successful CEO succession cannot and should not be conducted in a vacuum. It must be about the journey, not the destination; about the process, not the plan. Above all, it must be the culmination of the long-term development of a robust leadership pipeline, based not just on a technical but a cultural and political system designed to assess and promote talent in a disciplined, impartial, objective fashion. This system must be equipped with a series of checks and balances that effectively stack the deck toward picking the best and brightest to reach the pinnacle at the top and to discount, to whatever degree possible, the almost inevitable impact of personal, political, and organizational distortions and biases. For this process to be effective, it needs to be an integral part of a broader, deeper leadership development and human capital strategy, which advances high-potential executives throughout their careers and is conducted at all levels of the organization, from campus hires to vice chairmen. (Except, of course, in crisis situations, where a fresh clean-slate perspective may be desperately needed to save the company and the recruitment of an outsider becomes not just desirable but necessary. See, for example: Louis Gerstner's succession at IBM, Alan Mulally at Ford, James McNerney at Boeing.)

2. There is no perfect, failproof process, but a plan is better than no plan. In cases where no formal succession framework has been formulated, a coherent and rational process must be urgently conceived and authentically implemented that replaces gut instinct and personal favoritism with a strategy focused on the dispassionate evaluation of viable candidates and a clear connection to significant strategic issues facing the company.

3. In too many cases where a plan has been formulated, it ends up turning into an empty annual ritual, like the turning of fall leaves. This is more often than not the result of an excessive and even obsessive focus by the key players (board, CEO, CHRO) on the technical aspects of the process, to the detriment of the political and cultural dimensions.

Defining Success

I define the essential challenge and therefore measure of success all leaders face in today's world as capable of being distilled down to two intertwined tasks:

1. Increasing the value of the assets they were given control over between the day of their arrival and the day of their departure. (In the age of the activist investor, the bar to attain this rare hallmark of success has been heightened. To keep a safe distance from the sharp edge of the activist guillotine, a CEO must increase the value of the assets he or she has been given above a range of benchmark competitors or risk being consigned to the dustbin of corporate history.)

2. Developing and selecting a successor who does the same thing. This is, I admit, a tough benchmark to measure up to. Yet even if only a handful of leaders attain it, I believe it is critical that all leaders aspire to it, to the exclusion of all other benchmarks. The most commonly derived variable expressing this proposition is TRS (total return to shareholders), which in the context of publicly listed corporations is relatively easily determined by doing the math on any one of any number of financial Web sites. With privately held corporations, though the data used for analysis may be more elusive, the overarching concept of TRS nonetheless applies, as all privately held corporations still have investors. Even with nonprofit organizations, though the analysis may be even more difficult, it's not hard to come up with surrogates and proxies for TRS, including the size of the organization's endowment, the quality of its work, and above all its success in meeting precisely defined targets and goals defined by its board.

While I also admit that this is the corporate and organizational equivalent of winning a gold medal at the Olympics, it is an analogy I consider apt because the modern Olympics are a truly global event, attracting the finest athletes from all over the world, while at their inception they were limited to the region of Greece where they were conceived, and up until their revival in the late nineteenth century, strictly limited to nations comprising what we used to call the First World. These days, as in business, the bar to the medal is higher than ever before.

So if, as I say, CEO successions are rarely successful, as the Russian revolutionary Vladimir Lenin once asked, "What is to be done?" A healthy first step would be for more people in high places to continue to read and apply the lessons laid out in this book. Because with more than three decades of consulting to companies and nonprofit organizations large and small, ranging from GE to Merck to Royal Dutch Shell to Intuit, Ford, Chrysler, Nokia, Boeing, 3M, AlliedSignal and Honeywell, Best Buy, CP, Grupo Salinas, and yes, HP, Microsoft, and others under my belt, I can safely say that I have personally witnessed, in many cases from the inside, more troubled and value-destroying leadership successions and transitions than I would care to count. Even in the many nonprofits I've worked with, ranging from the Boys & Girls Clubs to a variety of charter schools, public schools, universities, health care organizations, and foundations, the all-too-human failure to navigate the complexities of executive transition all too frequently spoil "the best-laid schemes of mice and men."

From meddling chairmen and lead directors to domineering CEOs to micromanaging board members to toxic CHROs, from CEOs forced to resign because some, like CEO Harry Stonecipher at Boeing—as I like to put it—couldn't "keep their pecker out of the payroll," to cases in which CEOs die in a plane crash or from a heart attack leaving no qualified or named successor in place, companies, CEOs, and boards certainly have much to contend with. But that is no excuse for boards, CHROs, and CEOs to take the safe and easy way out and duck the issue, on the grounds that it is too complicated, too threatening, too politically charged, too much of a hot potato to handle, because in fact that is the unsafe and far riskier course for CEOs and boards to take.

Over the years I've heard—and you will hear in this book—every excuse there is, ranging from "I don't want to be a lame duck" to "I don't want to run a horse race that will fracture my top leadership team" to "I don't want the losers to resign if I end up picking just one," to, even more commonly, "It's just not an urgent priority, we've got next quarter's results to think about." Needless to say, the list goes on and on. And all are nothing more than pathetic excuses for paralysis and inaction. And, to be frank, errors of omission and commission that are utterly inexcusable for people who, as we well know, are more than adequately compensated for their efforts, or all too often for the lack of them.

The Sorry State of Succession Today

A 2012 Conference Board survey of general counsels and corporate secretaries at more than three hundred publicly traded U.S. companies found that 61 percent of the companies[9] surveyed had no formal succession plan or internal leadership development processes in place. Whether this statistic truly reflects the current state of affairs I'm not entirely sure, but at the very least it leaves nearly 40 percent of publicly traded companies admitting to lacking a formal and clear succession plan in the event of an emergency or even as a longer-range planning framework. A similar survey conducted by the National Association of Directors found additional evidence of the scope and scale of the problem: 67 percent of companies responding reported that they had no succession planning or leadership development process in place. That this is a problem not just of national but global scale is confirmed by a survey conducted by executive search firm Korn Ferry, which found that only 35 percent of respondents disclosed the existence of a formal CEO succession plan, despite the fact that nearly all (98 percent) were willing to admit that CEO succession planning was "an essential ingredient of corporate governance."

I will state right here and now that I am not a big fan of surveys, in part because general trends tend to distract from what matters most: how the Olympic gold medalists are winning on the field. However, the surveys do give us a vague impression that there is something seriously wrong with the picture, an often fatal flaw in our corporate governance processes and best practices that has unnecessarily posed a real risk to companies.

Enter the Feds

In a classic case of closing the gate after the horse has escaped, the U.S. government agency charged with managing these issues did belatedly wake up and smell the coffee, when their noses were plunged into a mess they had for too long conveniently ignored but could no longer because the long-term health of the entire global economic system was at stake. This is in fact no exaggeration, because fundamental leadership flaws led to the risk taking that precipitated the crisis, an excessive indulgence that eventually lopped off the heads of a number of disgraced monarchs of famous financial firms, including E. Stanley O'Neal at Merrill Lynch, Richard Fuld at Lehman Brothers, James Cayne at Bear Stearns, Fred Goodwin at Royal Bank of Scotland, Ken Lewis at Bank of America, and Charles "Chuck" Prince at Citigroup. It wasn't just that these CEOs were kicked to the curb—the real scandal was that after their boards had belatedly handled the job of oversight they should have been doing all along, none of those erstwhile masters of the universe had a viable successor in place prepared to take over in an emergency. In every case, the current regime was so discredited that outsider appointments became the rule, when and if the firms survived the crisis at all.

Before the crisis, boards were permitted by the SEC to consider succession planning an activity "conducted in the ordinary course of business." In practice, that meant that boards of directors were left totally off the hook in this regard, as they were simply able to brush aside shareholder proposals that called for disclosure and discussion of leadership transition and succession plans as being essentially none of their business.

But in October 2009, a month after Bank of America CEO Ken Lewis abruptly tendered his resignation and left his board fumbling to find a successor, the SEC's Division of Corporate Finance finally took a new crack at the case. It clarified a murky and ambiguous issue by publishing a nonbinding ruling that said, in part:

> One of the board's key functions is to provide for succession planning, so that the company is not adversely affected due to a vacancy in leadership. Recent events have underscored the importance of this board function to the governance of the corporation.
>
> We now recognize that CEO succession planning raises a significant policy issue regarding the governance of the corporation that transcends the day-to-day business matter of managing the workforce.
>
> As such, we have reviewed our position on CEO succession planning proposals and have determined to modify our treatment of such proposals. Going forward, we will take the view that a company generally may not rely on [the "ordinary course of business" guideline] to exclude a proposal that focuses on CEO succession planning.[10]

Note that the new rule is nonbinding, and as such, does not rise to the legal standard of fiduciary responsibility or due diligence. As a result of the government's wishy-washy stance on this issue, it may be having less of a practical impact than if it had been imposed on the boards of publicly held corporations. Still, at a minimum, the revised guidance has put CEOs and boards on notice that they cannot, in good conscience or governance, fail to conceive and implement formal succession plans that might cause the company to be "adversely affected due to a vacancy in leadership."

The Failure Factors

Failure Factor #1: SPOTS

The term SPOTS is an acronym for "Succession Plans on Top Shelves," and is a variation on an older, equally dismissive acronym popular with consultants: "Strategic Plans on Top Shelves." Whether the term is used in reference to succession or strategy, the ultimate outcome is the same: the existence of an inoperable or poorly conceived plan can actually hinder the organic evolution of a genuine process designed to develop the next generation of leaders under the intensive and committed guidance of the current one.

Failure Factor #2: Failing the Beer Truck Test— or Not Even Taking It

On Christmas Eve 2012, Microsoft CEO Steven A. Ballmer sat at a Starbucks café on Mercer Island in Seattle's Puget Sound with Ford CEO Alan Mulally, an old friend of his from the days when as a senior Boeing executive Mulally had lived in the Seattle area. On the table between them sat a small pile of personal electronic devices, ranging from smart phones and tablets running Microsoft's Windows software to rival versions produced by competitors Apple, Samsung, Lenovo, Acer, Asus, and others. Ballmer had brought along this assortment of props to provide a tangible backdrop for a candid conversation about Microsoft's increasingly glaring shortcomings in the product innovation department, which were broadly implicated in the company's flagging share price. But he had also invited Mulally to this end-of-the-year powwow with a broader goal in mind: to gain the benefit of the older man's perspective on the medley of strategies, lessons, and tactics he had used to drive a spectacular turnaround at Ford—some of which, he hoped, might be applicable to the wholesale transformation he was attempting to lead at Microsoft.

Over the course of a frank four-hour conversation, Mulally did his best to help Ballmer by putting the tasks facing him into perspective. He stressed the priority he had personally placed at both Boeing and Ford on uniting fractious silos, deploying a unified database even if the results conveyed bad news, and bringing a factionalized company together under one brand as "One Ford." While the latter was a tactic Ballmer would shortly import into his own organization under the imitative rubric "One Microsoft," what doubtless remained unspoken between them was the world of difference between a CEO coming in from the outside armed with a mandate from the board to drive radical change, as Mulally had done at Ford, and a longtime insider trying to do the same thing at a global legacy company he had virtually co-founded four decades before.

In early January 2013, while on a conference call with the board, Microsoft lead director John Thompson, the CEO of technology start-up Virtual Instruments and former CEO of hard-drive producer Seagate, cut short a meandering discourse by Ballmer on the soup-to-nuts transformation he was preparing to drive at Microsoft "once the next version of Windows shipped."

"Hey, dude," he said sharply, shocking his fellow board members with his directness, "let's get on with it. We're in suspended animation mode here."

The urgency and impatience of Thompson's tone clearly conveyed the board's mounting anxiety over the company's strategic drift, which was reflected in its prolonged subpar share price performance. This ongoing sorry state of affairs was prompting one particular shareholder activist to aggressively question the board's seemingly endless tolerance of the mediocrity of Ballmer's regime. At a board retreat in March, Thompson again interrupted a presentation by Ballmer by stating without hesitation that with respect to the changes he was planning to drive at the company, he'd better "get on the bus or get off."

On a trip to London in May, it finally dawned upon the previously oblivious fifty-eight-year-old CEO that "at the end of the day, we needed to break a pattern. Face it: I'm a pattern." Somewhat belatedly, from a TRS point of view, he finally arrived at the inescapable conclusion: "I'm an emblem of an old era, and I have to move on. . . . As much as I love everything about what I'm doing, the best way for Microsoft to enter a new era is under a new leader who will accelerate change."[11]

That was one of the very few strategic decisions Ballmer made that the stock market strongly endorsed. On Friday, August 24, the price of

Microsoft shares jumped 7 percent, their largest one-session gain in more than four years, on the news that Ballmer had decided to step down within a year, giving his board twelve months to select a successor. "No chief executive wants the company's shares to jump sharply on the news that he or she is stepping down," acerbically commented columnist John Gapper in the *Financial Times*. "Pent-up relief, however, was the reaction to Ballmer's decision to retire as Microsoft chief within a year."[12]

"Pent-up relief" was perhaps a charitable term to describe the range of positive emotions with which Microsoft's long-suffering shareholders greeted Ballmer's retirement announcement, for whom news of his impending departure could not have come a moment too soon. A chart published by *The New York Times* on its front page graphically illustrated the slow, steady, agonizing contraction of Microsoft's share price and market capitalization over the course of Ballmer's thirteen years at the helm. Despite a doubling of annual profit, a doubling of revenues, and a doubling of head count, and despite the acquisition of nearly 150 companies at many billions in cost, including the $8.5 billion 2011 acquisition of Skype, between January 23, 2000, the day Ballmer succeeded Bill Gates, and August 23, 2013, the day before the retirement announcement, Microsoft's market cap had dropped an astounding $266 billion, from $555 to $289 billion, on a share price that had fallen from $53.91 to $34.75, or roughly 40 percent over the period.

That $266 billion represented the hefty price Microsoft shareholders had been obliged to pay for the devastating decision made by chairman Bill Gates and his fellow directors in 2000 to elevate Gates's college classmate and friend to the CEO post when Gates retired from his day-to-day operational role at the company to pursue a second career in global philanthropy. It was also the price those same shareholders paid over that prolonged period for the board's daily decision not to kick Ballmer to the curb long after it had become clear that while he might have been a great salesman, as the leader of an incumbent technology company facing disruptive change, he had been a terrible pick.

Role of the Activist Investor in the Microsoft Transition

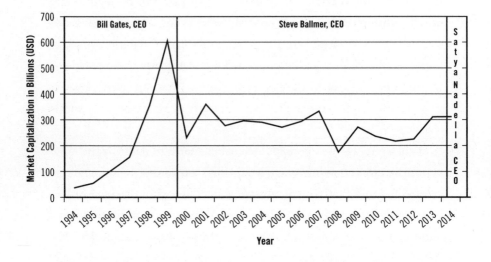

The reason most commonly cited by industry analysts for the abruptness of Ballmer's retirement—since as recently as a few months before he had repeated a long-standing vow to remain at his post until his son graduated from high school, still more than three years away—was that the board had caved in to growing pressure from an activist investor, ValueAct Capital, a $12 billion San Francisco–based hedge fund. After accumulating a nearly 2 percent or $2 billion stake, ValueAct had started agitating behind the scenes for a significant leadership change at the top. What had been mere speculation was confirmed the Friday following the Ballmer retirement announcement, when Microsoft disclosed the signing of a cooperation agreement with ValueAct that called for regular meetings to be held between the thirty-eight-year-old ValueAct president G. Mason Morfit and Microsoft's board and management to "discuss a range of significant business issues." Driving the pressure point home, the Microsoft board further agreed to grant Morfit the option of joining its ranks as a director, which he did in early 2014.

But all the attention being paid to the activist investor angle was, in this case, missing the real point, which was that even if Ballmer cited as his greatest career setback the release of Windows Vista (which badly bombed in the marketplace), and other commentators picked freely from a long list of underperforming acquisitions and ventures including the abandoned $47 billion acquisition of Yahoo, the perplexing purchase of a nearly 20 percent share in Barnes & Noble's troubled Nook tablet division, the $2 billion accounting charge the company took after writing down the takeover of aQuantive, a digital advertising firm that never amounted to anything much in the digital ad space, and the nearly $1 billion write-off of inventory piled up due to slow initial sales of the Surface tablet, I would cite as by far his greatest missed opportunity his ongoing failure—one shared with chairman Bill Gates and the board—to put himself and his legacy on the line, set his own ego aside, and invest the significant time, attention, and resources required to build up a strong bench of internal talent capable of yielding a slate of candidates prepared to replace him at a moment's notice, were he to have been, for any reason whatsoever, bowled over by the proverbial eighteen-wheeler.

Ballmer's "beer truck test" had come barreling along the superhighway of capitalism in the guise of a savvy activist investor who proved surprisingly successful in pushing a passive and complacent board to finally if gently push out the door a failed CEO who actually owned far more stock in the company than it did. (On the day of Ballmer's retirement announcement, ValueAct controlled about $2 billion of Microsoft stock, which was chump change compared with effective cofounder Ballmer's personal stake, worth more than $11 billion.)

Yet we should never forget that with respect to the ultimate leadership requirement of being totally prepared to take the beer truck test at a moment's notice—and not simply when most convenient for the putative test taker—Ballmer and his board were not alone. As the following chart indicates, CEOs and other senior leaders' tenures may and do all too frequently get cut short at any time, often quite unexpectedly, for a variety of reasons ranging from sexual, moral, and ethical indiscretions to financial transgressions to drug and alcohol abuse, unforeseen fatal and near-fatal accidents and unknown or undisclosed serious health issues leading to sudden death or resignation.

Year	Organization	CEO/President	Reason
	Series of Unforeseen CEO Departures, Terminations, Resignations		
2014	Cemex	Lorenzo Zambrano	Heart attack
2014	American Apparel	Dov Charney	Multiple cases sexual misconduct
2013	Citibank	Vikram Pandit	Boardroom coup
2012	Yahoo	Scott Thompson	Padded resume/thyroid cancer
2012	Restoration Hardware	Gary Friedman	Improper relationship with subordinate
2012	CIA	David Petraeus	Improper relationship with biographer
2012	Best Buy	Brian Dunn	Improper relationship with subordinate
2012	Lockheed Martin	Christopher Kubasik	Improper relationship with subordinate
2012	Micron Technologies	Steven Appleton	Crash of experimental aircraft
2012	Stryker	Stephen MacMillan	Improper relationship with former employee
2010	Hewlett-Packard	Mark Hurd	Improper relationship with outside contractor
2010	Sara Lee	Brenda Barnes	Stroke
2010	Sigma-Aldrich	Jai Nagarkatti	Heart attack
2005	Circuit City	Multiple senior leaders	Plane crash
2005	Boeing	Harry Stonecipher	Improper relationship with subordinate
2004	McDonald's	Jim Cantalupo	Heart attack
2004	McDonald's	Charlie Bell	Cancer
2004	Martha Stewart Omnimedia	Martha Stewart	Felony conviction for lying to federal investigators
2003	Boeing	Phil Condit	Hiring/procurement scandal
2003	Dana Corp.	Joseph Magliochetti	Pancreatic cancer
2002	Triangle Pharmaceuticals	David Barry	Heart attack
2002	WorldCom	Bernard Ebbers	Accounting scandal
2001	Enron	Jeffrey Skilling	Accounting scandal
2000	Herbalife	Mark Hughes	Drug overdose
1999	Wendy's International	Gordon Teter	Heart attack
1996	Texas Instruments	Jerry Junkins	Heart attack
1994	McCormick	Bailey Thomas	Heart attack
1993	Household International	Edwin Hoffman	Heart attack

Failure Factor #3: The Domineering CEO Who Won't Let Go

In the Microsoft succession story, you will detect a pattern repeated with sickening frequency again and again in this book. Ballmer's failure to construct and maintain a robust leadership pipeline was largely due, as one commentator put it, to his "larger than life" leadership style, which made it "difficult for [other executives] to really rise up and have a noticeable public role."[13] Among the many talented potential future CEOs who had jumped ship because they either clashed with Ballmer and his outsized personality, or had not felt included in an orderly and transparent succession planning process, were former Windows chief Steven Sinofsky, former VMware CEO Paul Maritz, and former Office chief Stephen Elop. Elop left Microsoft to take the top job at former highflyer Nokia, though following the acquisition of Nokia by Microsoft shortly after the announcement that Ballmer would be leaving, Elop rejoined the company in a special capacity reporting directly to Ballmer. All of these and more—including Ballmer's old friend the sixty-seven-year-old Alan Mulally—would in the weeks and months following Ballmer's retirement announcement be mentioned as potential outsider candidates to replace him. The primary irony being, of course, that if Ballmer had really been on top of his leadership development and succession planning job, that cadre of former seasoned executives would have still been on the inside, prepared to step up when their time came.

Microsoft's February 2014 announcement that the board was appointing an insider and twenty-two-year veteran of the company, Satya Nadella, as its new CEO, coupled with an announcement that founder Bill Gates would step down as chairman—but would retain a seat on the board—does not, in my opinion, let Ballmer, Gates, or the other board members off the hook or immunize them from charges that they bungled their number-one task of ensuring a seamless succession. Not that Nadella is in any way a bad pick. While Nadella's cloud-and-enterprise division had been one of the company's best-performing units, he also oversaw the development and rollout of several consumer cloud products, including Office 365, the Bing search engine, Xbox Live, and Skype. Prior to joining Microsoft, Nadella had worked at Sun Microsystems, owned by Oracle, and was not just a veteran of the company but of the industry.

It is simply that against the backdrop of a sitting CEO's most critical task, particularly when operating in a high-paced, ever-changing industrial environment like information technology, the challenge of nurturing, coaching, developing, and training not just a single individual but an entire pipeline of truly transformational leaders on the inside is not one to be avoided, neglected, or misunderstood. No board should ever have to face the dilemma of staging a rushed succession process after the sitting CEO has either tendered his resignation or announced—as in Ballmer's case—his intention to resign within a fixed period. It is at precisely that point that the endgame of a multiyear or multidecade objective, high-integrity process should be triggered, as opposed to just getting off the ground.

And if announcing the departure of Gates as chairman was clearly intended to assuage the many critics who maintained that his ongoing presence on the board might hamper the autonomy of his successor's successor, the move was seen as largely symbolic by the vast majority of analysts, particularly since he was not only not resigning from the board altogether but sticking around in an ill-defined capacity as self-styled adviser and coach to the new CEO—a role that quite frankly raised more questions than provided answers as to the degree of his future influence.

In so many ways, Microsoft's CEO search was bungled from the start. Having failed to groom an obvious replacement during his thirteen-year tenure as CEO, Ballmer announced his retirement with no successor in place. The CEO search was filled with leaks to the press, many promoting the idea that Ballmer's close friend Alan Mulally sat at the top of a long list of outsiders being hastily interviewed for the job. As to the ongoing roles of both Gates and Ballmer, it remains to be seen how active either of them intends to be in the new management, potentially hampering the new leader's political ability to make changes. This is a prime example of a technical issue, chiefly revolving around arcane matters of corporate structure and governance, becoming a political issue that may undermine the new leader and reduce his freedom of action. As one industry analyst, Rick Sherlund of Nomura Securities, said to CNN, "We question whether it will become necessary for Mr. Ballmer to step aside as a director to facilitate this. We do not think having two previous CEOs on the board to report to as he redirects the business is a good idea."[14]

Failure Factor #4: Superstar Outsider Bias

As anyone who has observed more than one succession train wreck will tell you, probably the hottest, most subject to mythology and ideology, most fiercely contested and misunderstood of all the hot-button issues facing directors and CEOs who have not done their job of developing a pipeline of future internal leaders applies to those embarrassing situations when an incumbent CEO steps down unexpectedly, and the board is faced with a choice: whether to look inside or outside the company for a successor. The selection of an outside candidate to lead a company, I repeat for emphasis, constitutes unimpeachable evidence that the leadership pipeline is broken. For a classic case of a broken leadership pipeline that leads to a broken company, let's turn back to the number-one poster child of CEO successions gone awry, the ever-hapless HP.

The Rise and Fall of Carly Fiorina

I began this chapter describing everything that is wrong with CEO succession with HP. And I will end it with HP. Let's turn the clock back a decade and a half—which is like a century and a half in the computer industry—to July 1999, when as the second millennium loomed and the tech sector boomed, an ebullient HP board announced with a degree of fanfare verging on jubilation the recruitment and appointment of Carly Fiorina, the forty-four-year-old president of AT&T hardware spinoff Lucent Technologies, as its first outside and first female CEO in its history.

At the time of the announcement of her appointment, this stunning move by HP's directors was widely regarded as a maverick and breakthrough maneuver that would—or so it was hoped—set the company back on the right growth track after nearly a decade of stasis. Her outsider status, or so the prevailing mythology went, would be one of her greatest assets as she strove to remake an aging company competing for dominance in a fast-changing industry. "As an outsider, [Carly] is better positioned as the company moves to lose its 'stodgy' reputation than any of the other talented executives who had come up through the organization at HP," was one comment typical of sentiments almost universally expressed at the time.[15]

That optimistic assessment was breezily (if condescendingly) echoed by Fiorina herself in an interview she granted to *Businessweek* within days of her arrival, when she summed up the main challenge facing her as one that primarily entailed her taking a tired old brand and transforming it into one that would "represent the next century rather than the last one."[16]

While the dismissive tone of that line—one that presaged many more dismissive comments to come—should have sent off warning signals right and left, lead director Sam Ginn, CEO of telecom company Vodaphone AirTouch, joined future board chairman Richard Hackborn (who had built up HP's cash cow of a printer business before retiring to a second career in philanthropy) in giddily pronouncing Carly's recruitment as the boardroom victory of the turn of the century. While the board had "looked at" more than three hundred candidates, Ginn explained, including HP's own highly respected enterprise computing chief Ann Livermore (rumored to have been one of four finalists), the search committee had taken a list of twenty key qualities they hoped to see in HP's next CEO, whittled them down to just four, and stacked each of the four finalists against them. "Carly," Ginn said, "clearly stood out as the best. We see her being HP's CEO for a very long time."[17]

Well, I suppose that all depends on what you mean by "a long time." Given Fiorina's long-term track record with regard to the stock, it's surprising in retrospect that she lasted as long as she did, particularly when her nearly six years at the helm were as marked by continual chaos, contention, animosity, fear, and fighting among business leaders, CEO, and ultimately and most destructively, CEO and board as they were. Six years was a long time for her to last, considering that signs of trouble were surfacing within months of her taking the job. There was a pattern of poor leadership judgments along the way, including her purchase of new corporate jets while laying off thirty thousand employees. For Fiorina, her demise was not any single leadership misstep, but a pattern of judgments that alienated her from her HP colleagues and ultimately the board.

I personally experienced a foreshadowing of her demise while my colleague Chris DeRose and I were leading an executive program for high potentials at HP. We launched the program prior to Fiorina's being named CEO. When she was named CEO we had many of the women in the program as well as some of the men share their excitement and enthusiasm for having a female CEO. The women shared with Chris and me that it was about time there was a female role model in the C-suite. Within six months the tide turned on Carly. The women more than the men explained to Chris and me in the workshops and informally outside of class that the greatest turnoffs to Carly were her relentless self-promotion, her autocratic leadership style, and her clear-cut contempt for the culture ingrained by HP's cofounders, Bill Hewlett and Dave Packard. They, in contrast to her distant and remote presentation, freely wandered the halls of the company's headquarters and ate lunch in the company cafeteria. Here I prefer to focus blame on the fatal error of judgment committed by HP's board: misjudging Fiorina's qualifications for the job. To briefly recap, Fiorina had been one of a team of senior executives who had headed Lucent, a company formed from the spinoff of AT&T's former hardware division that emerged from the breakup of the Bell System monopoly in the mid-eighties. Lucent was the manufacturer of switch gear for the phone companies, who were largely captive customers. Carly Fiorina was a successful sales executive who never ran a true profit-and-loss business. Therefore, her first P&L experience was as CEO of HP. In order to land her, the bedazzled HP board agreed to pay her a whopping $65 million as compensation for the stash of Lucent's high-flying stock she would be leaving on the table to jump ship. Compared with the more than $100 billion in annual revenues of a company like Hewlett-Packard, $65 million was pocket change. But let's look at that number by comparison with what the board would have agreed to pay an internal candidate like enterprise chief Ann Livermore—no doubt one tenth of that.

Was Carly worth it? Hell no—but the real meaning of that $65 million the board forked over without batting an eyelash is that outsider CEO selections are not just high risk on the strategic and people fronts, they tend to be exponentially more expensive, and therefore high risk on the financial front, in part because when an incoming CEO is so richly compensated, everyone else's comp needs to be pumped up to keep pace, and face. So what did HPs board and its shareholders get for that $65 million? We shall see. The critical issue here is not that Fiorina was an autocrat, a flashy marketing type lost in an engineering culture, or even that she was a poor leader from so many vantage points. Quite frankly, all that could have been true of an insider candidate who turned out to be a turkey, because as we all know, it does happen—they could very well have promoted someone up through the marketing ranks who lacked the technical skill and knowledge to compete effectively against peers. No, the key point here is that as an outsider candidate, however attractive in so many respects, including the physical (an often-overlooked reality I only point out because I can't tell you how many times I've seen boards half-knowingly appoint candidates CEO because, well, they looked the part), Fiorina was not a known quantity to anyone on the board.

Outsider bias is, in my view, based on a false premise: that a candidate's mere status as an outsider will make it more likely that she or he will inject more of a dose of fresh air into the company's hermetically sealed atmosphere than any insider could.

I refuse to fall into the trap of stating unequivocally that that is never the case, because obviously it can be and has been. No, my real point is that outsider selections, according to my framework and my book, are by definition a sign of defeat and failed leadership, and that they actually pose enormous risks to the future of the enterprise, cost a ton to boot, and more often than not, contrary to myth, fail to pan out as planned.

Failure Factor #5: The Halo Effect

Fiorina's selection by the board was also based to a significant degree on the reputation of the organization she came from, a shockingly popular delusion often referred to as "The Halo Effect." As *Fortune* later revealed too late for HP or its board to do anything about it, Lucent's high-flying stock had been pumped up by phony deals booked as revenue that were being financed by Lucent at artificially low rates. While no legal wrongdoing was ever found or alleged, the revelation of this scam and sham pulled on Lucent shareholders caused its stock to plunge from dizzying heights to under one dollar when it all came out—conveniently for Carly, of course, after she had cashed in her chips with the bank of HP, which paid full freight for her stock at its peak. By the time the Lucent house of cards collapsed (the company was sold for a song to French telecom shop Alcatel in 2006, the same year HP finally kicked her to the curb) the board had long since lost its big bet on Carly.

At GE, Jack Welch took great care to minimize the business cycle halo effect by keeping leaders in charge of businesses as they experienced both up and down cycles. It's too easy, he maintained, to look like a surefire winner when a rising tide is lifting all boats. It's a far more relevant test of a potential leader's judgment capacity to evaluate their success at reviving or sustaining a lousy business.

Failure Factor #6: Assessing CEO Candidates on Traits as Opposed to Experience

When they were evaluating Fiorina as a candidate, the HP board stacked her reputed skills and capabilities against a set of twenty traits they eventually whittled down to four, which they used to put together a test that Carly passed with flying colors. The basic problem with this approach is that it elevates the assessment of traits—an inherently squishy conception—above what at GE and many other "academy" companies is a more rigorous assessment formula based on disciplined "accomplishment analysis." These assessments are so laborious and comprehensive that they are rarely if ever compiled on anyone other than very senior leaders, and often CEO candidates. They read like novels, as they are based on hundreds of interviews, but they are also grounded in a firm foundation of relevant experience and judgments assessed. In Fiorina's case, she had never been in charge of a fully scoped P&L, a dearth of critical experience that in my view would later prove a significant determinant of her failure to thrive in her new environment.

Curtains for Carly

The ultimate test of the success or failure of the leadership of any organization of any size boils down to that leader's ability to artfully and skillfully manage the technical, political, and culture aspects not just of leadership development and succession planning, but of leading his or her organization through a period of significant volatility and change. Volatility and change are certainly nothing new and nothing more than a realistic assessment of the new normal, a perpetually fluctuating state of affairs that has existed for decades and is likely to persist for decades if not centuries to come. In 2005, after spending five lackluster years at the helm during which she racked up quarter after quarter of less than impressive results, Carly threw the classic failed CEO Hail Mary pass by resorting to flogging the tired myth, perpetuated primarily by fee-sucking investment bankers, of the "transformative" merger.

In Carly's case, the merger she successfully pushed for—with fellow and rival hardware maker Compaq—was not just of questionable strategic value, despite her touting it to stakeholders as the miraculous intervention that would save the company. It turned into, for her personally, a political minefield that truly blew her out of the water. What she fatally failed to account for when pushing the merger over the passionate protestations of two highly influential board members—Walter Hewlett, the cofounder's son, and former CEO Lew Platt, who not only remained on the board but was the company's largest individual stockholder, not to mention president of the HP Foundation—was that even if she won the battle, as she eventually did, she could end up losing the war. That is precisely what happened. By early 2006, with the merger completed but the integration of the two companies not yet producing the forecast stellar results, and with the company continuing to trail competitors in a number of key areas, her goose was cooked. Those directors who hadn't liked the deal in the first place garnered enough of their fellow directors' support to kick Carly out. The most vocal of her enemies, who had at one time been the most passionate of her supporters, Lew Platt, had seen the light at last.

It's important to note that, perhaps not surprisingly in light of her personal priorities, over the six years she stayed in the job Fiorina failed to win not just strategically and politically but also culturally, which is the most complex dimension to navigate of all. In the end, her fatal failure was not one of vision but of culture, politics, people, and strategy—which precipitated a corporate crisis. She lacked the technical knowledge and skill to truly grasp the nuances of creating a new cultural reality that would marry what was worth keeping about the old HP with a culture of leadership development that would have yielded a slate of candidates to replace her if and when she hit a brick wall.

After giving Carly the boot the board failed yet again to seriously consider insider candidates but moved quickly to secure the services of a talented turnaround artist, the operational whiz Mark Hurd, who had led the reinvention of yet another AT&T spin-off, NCR. While Hurd presided over a period of relative calm at the board level, and over years of harsh cost-cutting did wonders for HP's sagging stock price, which nearly doubled over the course of his tenure, in a development so incredible it would have seemed unlikely in fiction, in September 2006, a little more than a year after he came to power, *Newsweek* broke the story that HP chairwoman Patricia Dunn—who had been elected to the position on the same day Hurd was hired, not that anyone noticed—had for reasons known only to herself retained the services of a crack team of security experts to track down the source of a leak to a trade publication she had good reason to believe had emanated from somewhere inside the boardroom. Those security experts succeeded at their assigned task, finding the source of the leak, but they did so by employing dubious means to a dubious end. They employed an investigative method known as "pretexting," which required them to pose as HP board members and/or investigative journalists in a ruse to get the telephone company to divulge the records of the suspected board member's calls.

The whole nasty affair ended up blowing up in Dunn's face, and cost her the chairwomanship after the alleged leaker resigned in disgust and the board divided. The sordid affair failed to kill Hurd's makeover, but incredibly enough, scandal at the board level was followed by scandal in the C-suite. In the fall of 2011 the board of HP was advised by an internal investigatory committee that Hurd may or may not have been conducting an inappropriate relationship with an attractive female outside contractor. While the optics didn't look good, what ultimately brought him down was the fact that he had misled the board about the existence of the relationship, and displayed the less than impeccable judgment of putting expenses incurred with her on the company tab.

The board, once again and by now predictably, bitterly divided over Hurd's fate. While some directors argued for a slap on the wrist in light of his good performance, others were so incensed by his behavior that they successfully pushed for him to get the shove. Of the fracas, one beaten-down board member wearily observed, "It's healthy to have differing opinions, but this went too far. It became fractious. There were so many hard feelings. It became difficult to conduct business in a civil manner."[18] But now hear this: when Hurd got hit by his own beer truck in the form of the alleged indiscretion, for the third time in a row the board reached outside for a successor to a fallen outsider.

Executive search firm Spencer Stuart identified four serious insider contenders. But the board found reasons to disqualify each of them on the dubious grounds that the appointment of any one of them would make the three others resign in protest. According to *Fortune*, Hurd didn't make their tough job any easier by telling "three of the internal candidates they were his heir, and then turning around and telling the board that none of them was ready to be CEO."[19] But let's stop right then and there for just a second to assess Hurd's role in this sorry saga. His errors of commission, even if the allegations were true, were not nearly as serious as his errors of omission on the leadership development front. Because what he and the board failed to do, once again, over the course of his five-year tenure was to cooperate and collaborate on developing a slate of internal candidates capable of replacing him if, for whatever reason, the beer truck hit the company's CEO once again. For the board, it should have been twice burned, twice shy—but perhaps they were unfamiliar with the proverb.

Failure Factor #7: In CEO Succession, Winner Takes All

The bogus reason cited by the HP board members for going outside yet again is worthy of further dissection because it is so frequently cited by CEOs and boards resistant to running a proper CEO succession process: setting up any sort of succession "horse race," they maintain with a straight face, will lead to fragmentation and competition among the senior team, many if not all of whom will abandon the company the moment a winner is declared, leaving it in a sorry state. That was, to cite a particularly egregious example, the reason cited by serial financial acquirer Sandy Weill, who, after cobbling together the unruly mess that became Citigroup, installed his former in-house counsel, Charles "Chuck" Prince, which turned into a disaster bet. Prince will be most fondly remembered for going down in flames after proudly declaring that as a bank CEO he had been obliged to "keep dancing until the music stopped." Once Citigroup turned into a synonym for TBTF—"too big to fail"—a scathing article in *Forbes* acutely observed:[20] "CEO succession played an important role in the disaster that is Citigroup—with the creator of the monster, Sandy Weill, having kicked out, undermined, or demoralized just about every decent candidate to succeed him, including, famously, JP Morgan CEO Jamie Dimon." In a 2008 interview with the *Financial Times*, Weill belatedly and ruefully acknowledged that he "certainly had responsibility for working with the board in devising a plan for succession and I would not give myself very good grades on that." In his own defense, he cited as the reason for his screwup his fear that the losers of any horse race he set up would leave once the winner was picked, fatally weakening the company.[21] What happened instead, under Prince's boom-to-bust leadership, was that the bank not only suffered a debilitating hemorrhage of top talent as it edged ever close to the precipice, but it finally went belly-up altogether and had to be bailed out by taxpayers.

So, to recap: as P&G CEO (twice) A. G. Lafley once said to me, "It's always a horse race—get over it." What should be a nonissue is best handled the way Jack Welch did, by insisting (based on his negative experience with his own succession) that it be well understood by all contenders that the losers would be gone the day after the winner was picked. In light of this strict ultimatum, he took special care to keep all the contenders out of staff jobs at corporate headquarters, where they might have been tempted to spend most if not all of their time trying to kill or undermine one another, and instead gave them tough line assignments where they would run independent businesses, the performance of which could be assessed independent of each other—may the best man or woman win.

After Jeffrey Immelt was named winner of the three-way horse race, Welch had essentially already helped the two losers—McNerney and Nardelli—find CEO jobs elsewhere and had them out of there in a matter of days. In my opinion, it is an unnatural act to ask or expect losers to stick around and report to the winner. It's far too easy for the losers still on-site to second-guess their new bosses' decisions, thinking that but for a matter of fate, they would be making the right ones. That unnatural act was in the late fall of 2013 foisted on an excellent insider CEO selection at GM, Mary Barra, who was by all accounts a fine choice. But the board hobbled her by appointing an executive chairman to, in effect, guide her in running the company while retaining the services of the two losers in the horse race as direct reports to her. As I told *Fortune* at the time, it's nothing against Barra to say that she is being saddled with a structural weakness. Only time will tell, of course, if that proves fatal to her future, or that of an extremely troubled company on the upswing.

In the case of HP, only after the internal candidates were ruled out by the board did Spencer Stuart partner James Citrin propose a selection of outsiders. After former Oracle president and future HP lead director Ray Lane turned down the job, Citrin presented the board with a choice so unlikely, so unconventional, so utterly out there, that if they went for it, he assured them, they "would be remembered for making one of the best CEO picks ever."[22] Remarkably enough, the board went for the bait and reached out to a benched CEO who had been tossed out of SAP on account of a pattern of high-handed and erratic behavior, combined with a track record of presiding over multiple quarters of terrible earnings. What on earth were they thinking? As one longtime HP board member wryly recalled, "We had a joke that the code name for the search was Léo Apotheker, because no one had ever heard of the guy."[23]

Even those who had didn't know much more about Apotheker than that his relatively brief career as head of SAP was marred by a suit filed by Oracle asserting that a company acquired by SAP had been downloading Oracle software, tweaking it a bit, and selling it to clients on the cheap. Not surprisingly, when Oracle founder, chairman, and longtime Hurd friend Larry Ellison—who immediately hired Hurd as his next president—learned that the board had gone for Apotheker, his response was predictably derisory: "HP had several good internal candidates [to become CEO] . . . but instead picked a guy who was recently fired because he did such a bad job of running SAP . . . The HP board needs to resign en masse. . . . right away. The madness must stop."[24]

That proclamation topped the one that he made upon hearing the news of Hurd's dismissal for cause, calling the move "the stupidest personnel decision since Apple fired Steve Jobs and replaced him with John Sculley."

But an embattled, fractious board, still traumatized by a contentious merger, yet another failed outsider CEO, and an awkward sexually charged situation, basically rolled over and played dumb.

The most remarkable fact about this search and its weird denouement only emerged after Apotheker was history, when the news broke that while a four-person committee of the board had narrowed the field down to three finalists before picking Apotheker, no one else on the twelve-member board had so much as interviewed those three on the phone, much less met them in person. "I admit it was highly unusual," one board member admitted to *New York Times* columnist James Stewart, "but we were just too exhausted after all the infighting."[25]

And so, for a fourth time in a row, outsider CEO Meg Whitman may also be doomed. In these two cases of CEO transitions drawn from iconic high-tech companies, a series of luminary CEOs and boards packed with other luminary CEOs and big-name business leaders fell down on their two most important jobs: 1. increasing the value of the assets they inherited when first taking power, and 2. picking a successor who did the same.

CHAPTER 2

CULTIVATING TRANSFORMATIONAL LEADERS ON THE INSIDE: THE THEORY OF THE CASE

A company's survival depends on its ability to develop independent leaders below the top who are capable of taking top command themselves, and to devise a system under which succession will be rational and by recognized merit rather than the result of a civil war within the institution and of force, fraud, or favoritism.

—**Peter Drucker,**
Concept of the Corporation, **1946**

CEO succession in any type of organization—from political to not-for-profit to business or military—is the key determinate of organizational success.

—**Noel M. Tichy and Warren G. Bennis,**
Judgment: How Winning Leaders Make Great Calls, **2007**

TECHNICAL

- Formulating the strategy for the organization
- Designing an organization structure to support the strategy
- Designing human resources systems to support strategy and structure

POLITICAL

- Determining who has what power to set strategy
- Distributing power in the organization structure, i.e., how centralized or decentralized
- Managing the politics of succession planning

CULTURAL

- Aligning the culture to support the strategy
- Integrating subcultures in the organization
- Using the human resource systems to shape and reinforce the desired culture

Any and Every Leader's #1 Judgment Call

It is as true in the second decade of the twenty-first century as it was in 2007, when Warren Bennis and I wrote the sentence quoted above, as it was almost seventy ago when Peter Drucker wrote the quote above that, that the development and selection of an organization's next leader by the present generation of leaders is the single most important decision any organization can make. You will note that I specify the plural "leaders" as opposed to a single "leader" when I refer to those responsible for making this critical call, because the single most crucial feature of any process and framework of enterprisewide leadership development, and a prerequisite for it to succeed, is that responsibility for its conception, development, implementation, and execution must be shared (not necessarily equally, but amicably) among the three pivotal points of organizational power:

1. CEO (or the top leader of the not-for-profit organization)
2. CHRO (chief human resources officer) and
3. Board of directors or trustees

As Warren Bennis and I stated in *Judgment*, "The seemingly blindingly obvious premise . . . that CEO succession . . . is the key determinate of organizational success" must be examined in light of the empirical evidence. As the previous chapter pretty well proves, the state of CEO succession even at some of our most admired companies and organizations is and has been nothing less than abysmal, if not catastrophic. Given the gravity and importance of this single judgment—which is the ultimate outcome of a series of judgments made prior to the ultimate selection of a successor—the grade among blue-chip companies is probably no more than a D, as the leaders of so many of them have utterly failed at their number-two task, after raising the value of the assets they inherited when they took over, of selecting a successor who does the same.

If nothing else, the recent global financial crisis along with the hundreds of corporate corpses left floating in its wake validated the old adage, commonly associated with investor Warren Buffett but actually originated by a lesser-known financial figure, "You only learn who has been swimming naked when the tide goes out."[1] In his 2008 letter to Berkshire Hathaway shareholders, Buffett used the phrase to pass the Judgment of Omaha on the competency of a whole series of failed leaders of failed financial institutions, including E. Stanley O'Neal at Merrill Lynch, Chuck Prince at Citigroup, Dick Fuld at Lehman Brothers, James Cayne at Bear Stearns, and Fred Goodwin at RBS, who not merely caused their own organizations to founder on the shores of insolvency but actually exacerbated—one might even say leveraged—their own incompetency by failing to have viable successors prepared to step into their sullied shoes once they themselves were tossed into the dustbin of history.

A Leadership Judgment Framework for Selecting a CEO

The selection of the right successor to a sitting CEO is a judgment that requires those making it to place a high-risk bet on the selected candidate's capacity to make future good judgments. This is a judgment that the CEOs, CHROs, and boards of directors responsible for appointing O'Neal, Prince, Fuld, Cayne, and Goodwin badly bungled. Making the right judgment with such high stakes riding on the outcome requires a careful and disciplined framing of the essential difference between a good and a bad judgment call. In every case, the process is the same. Judgments are not, in fact, single-point-in-time events, but the outcome of a process that can be divided into three distinct phases: 1. preparation phase; 2. call phase; 3. execution phase.

Apart from being divided into three phases along the temporal dimension, all judgments can be further divided into three distinct domains with regard to their subject matter:

1. Judgments about people (who is on the team or off the team)
2. Judgments about strategy (future direction of the organization)
3. Judgments during periods of crisis (unexpected events that threaten the organization)

Operating within these parameters, I consider people calls to be foundational, because the selection of the top team influences all other judgments, both strategy and crisis. Misjudgments in any domain may prove fatal; by far the most damaging to entire organizations and individual careers alike are poor and less than sound judgments regarding the selection or retention of the people on the top team. Only with the right people on board can a leader set the right strategy, which in turn provides a guideline for decision making during the inevitable crises all leaders must face. This is why all board-level reviews of and deliberations about who should be the next CEO, as well as evaluations of the current CEO, *should be explicitly built around the judgment framework.* This framework provides a simple and therefore actionable lens through which to examine a leader's past track record of judgments, as well as providing a practical guide for incumbent leaders to predict how well a particular leader under consideration may do when under pressure to render key judgments in the future.

As the following exhibit shows, several critical factors contribute to a greater or lesser extent in the rendering of good or bad leadership judgments. A leader may make mistakes—but the one mistake that cannot be fixed with a redo loop is selecting the wrong CEO. Every other judgment with a good leader can be fixed and still achieve a good outcome by using redo loops to continuously self-correct a flawed initial judgment. The ultimate test of leadership in this area is not necessarily whether the leader makes the right call initially—because all people are human and no process is ever perfect—but rather how well the leader making the judgment is capable of recognizing flaws in his or her own process and course correcting accordingly. For example, the boards that appointed the failed CEOs highlighted above had ample opportu-

Leadership Judgment Process

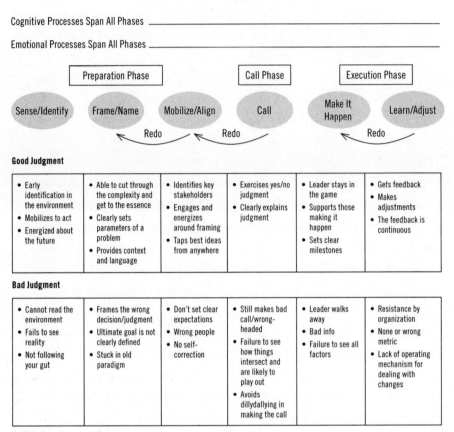

Cognitive Processes Span All Phases _____

Emotional Processes Span All Phases _____

Preparation Phase			Call Phase	Execution Phase	
Sense/Identify	Frame/Name	Mobilize/Align	Call	Make It Happen	Learn/Adjust

Redo   Redo   Redo

Good Judgment

• Early identification in the environment • Mobilizes to act • Energized about the future	• Able to cut through the complexity and get to the essence • Clearly sets parameters of a problem • Provides context and language	• Identifies key stakeholders • Engages and energizes around framing • Taps best ideas from anywhere	• Exercises yes/no judgment • Clearly explains judgment	• Leader stays in the game • Supports those making it happen • Sets clear milestones	• Gets feedback • Makes adjustments • The feedback is continuous

Bad Judgment

• Cannot read the environment • Fails to see reality • Not following your gut	• Frames the wrong decision/judgment • Ultimate goal is not clearly defined • Stuck in old paradigm	• Don't set clear expectations • Wrong people • No self-correction	• Still makes bad call/wrong-headed • Failure to see how things intersect and are likely to play out • Avoids dillydallying in making the call	• Leader walks away • Bad info • Failure to see all factors	• Resistance by organization • None or wrong metric • Lack of operating mechanism for dealing with changes

Not following gut can span all phases

© 2007 from *Judgment: How Winning Leaders Make Great Calls* by Noel M. Tichy and Warren Bennis

nity to correct those misjudgments during annual or biannual reviews of the leadership qualities of their incumbent CEOs. Where these boards fell down on the job was not just in appointing these people in the first place, but in not taking action once they knew the CEO was not up to the task. All too often boards have stuck by CEOs out of either personal loyalty or a sense of obligation to those who engineered their own appointments, thereby saving not just these leaders but the organizations on which hundreds if not thousands of lives and livelihoods depend from going down the tubes with them.

Recognizing the limitations to execution during the judgment process is as vital as possessing intellectual clarity about the conception or implementation of a potentially breakthrough strategy. Similarly, all people judgments rest on whether the people put into key leadership positions are able to do their jobs with integrity and courage as they deliver either outstanding or subpar results.

Hedging the Big Bet

Every successful CEO succession is built on a foundation constructed by the current leadership, chiefly the clear-cut expression of a multifaceted vision of the future strategic direction of the organization. This must be combined with a deep assessment and understanding of the capabilities of all of the candidates to successfully carry that vision forward into the future. A necessary but insufficient first step to the attainment of excellence in the field of leadership is the development and adoption of a clear and actionable teachable point of view (TPOV) about what will lead to future success. The teachable point of view is made up of 1. *ideas,* basically the strategy for organizational success, the way a business leverages its products, services, distribution channels, etc., to make money in the marketplace; 2. *values*: how we want people to behave in support of the ideas; 3. *emotional energy*: how we motivate and align the organization around the ideas and values; and 4. *edge*: how we make the tough yes/no decisions about organizational direction and people (or in not-for-profits it may be decisions about a health system's impact on patient outcomes, for example).

Because CEO succession requires the rendering of a discrete series of technical, political, and cultural decisions as to various candidates' capacity for achieving a successful partnership and teamwork among the three key stakeholders—the sitting CEO, the board, and the head of human resources—judgments made on a last-minute basis by a board under pressure, with a shareholder's gun held to its head, are almost inevitably doomed to failure. As Bennis and I wrote in *Judgment,* all of the current fashionable emphasis on rapid-fire, intuitive, gut decision making doesn't detract from the fact that good judgments are never made in a vacuum. Most if not all of them require many months if not years, in some cases decades, of careful and disciplined preparation in order to achieve the desired outcome.

As Dwight D. Eisenhower once aptly observed, "Plans are worthless, but planning is everything."[2] During the same speech he noted the importance of this distinction, "because when you are planning for an emergency you must start out with this one thing: the very definition of an emergency is that it is unexpected, therefore it is not going to happen the way you are planning." As was amply demonstrated in the last chapter, too many CEO successions turn into embarrassing fire drills and frantic emergencies for precisely the same reason that the man who planned the invasion of Normandy was skeptical of the value of advance planning: a plan is only as good as the person who needs to act upon it. Once again, the people, not the plan, are what counts.

Good CEO succession judgments are best conceived of not as short-term or one-time events but as the ultimate expression of long-term thinking and planning. This is a judgment for which the preparation phase should and in many cases does take years if not decades to plan and execute. As Olympic athletes and artistic geniuses alike will attest, their often fleeting moments of greatness are the result of tireless preparation over many years, which is why when an athlete scores a great shot, pass, or goal, it is common for them to ascribe the success of that move to a lifetime of preparation for that one split-second decision. Jack Welch and the GE board didn't decide to select Jeff Immelt over Bob Nardelli and Jim McNerney a few hours before Thanksgiving in the year 2000—that's just when they made the announcement that was the culmination of a process begun in earnest when I got to Crotonville in 1985, a decade and a half before.

In much the same way, the construction of a powerful pipeline of talent can be considered all part of the preparation phase, before the culminating call and execution. At GE and at nearly all of the organizations where I have worked on leadership development and succession planning, we start by defining the selection and assessment criteria for entry-level off-campus hires, and—as the pipeline gets narrower the further it progresses toward the peak of the pyramid—we just as precisely define the selection and assessment process and framework for first-time leaders, experienced managers, heads of functions, and heads of businesses, all the way up to the contenders for the CEO spot. This is a serious, costly, high-personal-stakes, time-consuming game, but it makes the chances of the big bet paying off infinitely greater.

At each stage of leadership development, the practical and achievable goal of every human resources process must be to create a true meritocracy, where talent moves up the ladder based strictly on performance and potential, not politics, and where those with a more vacuous style who lack demonstrated performance and potential inevitably fall to the wayside. As Peter Drucker brilliantly stated in his groundbreaking *Concept of the Corporation* (1946), a study of the postwar General Motors, the ultimate goal of any succession planning process must be to create "a system under which succession will be rational and by recognized merit rather than the result of a civil war within the institution and of force, fraud, or favoritism." Many years later he elaborated on that statement by reminding his readers that "the CEO places people into key positions. This, in the last analysis, *determines the performance capacity of the institution.*"[3]

Cultivating the Transformational Leader on the Inside

A fundamental assumption underlying CEO succession in the twenty-first century is that across the globe, across industries and sectors, private and public, leaders of every type and stripe will face an urgent, virtually permanent need to radically and continuously transform their organizations. The frameworks laid out in this chapter will be used throughout this book to guide the selection of CEOs and the roles of all the key actors, board, incumbent CEO, HR, and CEO candidates. They will be used as guides to 1. designing the future organization; 2. building the future organization; and 3. making the right judgments and decisions about people, strategy, and crisis as the incumbent leader transforms the organization for success in the future.

Building a Winning Organization

Sound CEO succession planning and process first and foremost requires that the board, incumbent CEO, and CHRO share a mutually synchronized view of how the organization will achieve success in the future. The succession decision must therefore be focused on selecting the candidate at the top of the pipeline judged most able to lead the organization to achieve that precisely defined vision of success. That selection needs, in turn, to be grounded in an explicit framework capable of accurately measuring the capacity of candidates under consideration to internalize knowledge in four areas:

◆ *Self-Knowledge:* Awareness of one's personal values, goals, and aspirations. This includes recognition of when these personal desires may lead to a bias in sensing the need for a judgment or interpreting facts. It also includes the ability to create a mental storyline for how judgments will play out and the results they lead to.

◆ *Social Network Knowledge:* Understanding of the personalities, skills, and judgment track records of those on your team. This includes how they supplement or bias your judgment process.

◆ *Organizational Knowledge:* Knowing how people in the organization will respond, adapt, and execute. This also includes personal networks or mechanisms for learning from leaders at all levels in the organization.

◆ *Contextual Knowledge:* Understanding based on relationships and interactions with stakeholders such as customers, suppliers, government, investors, competitors, or interest groups that may impact the outcome of a judgment. This entails anticipating not only how they will respond directly to a judgment but how they will interact with one another throughout the judgment process.

Successful leaders weave knowledge and insight gleaned from these four domains into a vivid and highly specific storyline describing their vision of the organization's future. They are able to see and foresee how specific actors respond to situations, imagine dialogues, and envision alternate endings. As they learn more and circumstances unfold, leaders must constantly ask how new information could impact and reshape that storyline.

CEOs and leaders in general must increasingly have the awareness of weak signals or environmental changes that trigger the need for a new judgment. During the preparation phase, leaders are evaluating how their new knowledge fits or discomfits their storyline. Acquiring this knowledge requires CEOs to develop networks that extend far beyond formal hierarchical and organizational boundaries. They must be able to tap into those on the front line, as well as experts and analysts who sit at a distance from their organization.

Assessing the Judgment Capacity of CEO Candidates Against the Nine-Cell Template

A key selection screen for the position of CEO is the future leader's judgment capacity and track record, as revealed in a careful and objective audit of the value of his or her past leadership judgments. I have created a technical, political, and cultural (TPC Matrix) nine-cell template that provides a simple, practical screen for conducting just such an audit. It works to align an organization's strategy, structure, and human capital capacity as stacked up against the technical, political, and cultural dimensions of the organization. In a transformation the nine cells are like a dynamic jigsaw puzzle that the leadership must align for the future success of the organization.

For organizational success, the best way—in fact, the only way—for organizations to encourage future high-potential leaders to develop a capacity for making good judgments is through the assignment and structuring of carefully designed real-life, real-risk exercises that carry with them real consequences and real learning along the way. The framework below provides a template for assessing high-potential leaders and their success or failure at these real-life "stretch" or "crucible" assignments. Assessing a leader's capacity and potential against the TPC Matrix starts with evaluating that person's capacity to set a central mission and strategy for the organization, goes on to assess the leader's grasp of the organizational structure and design of critical human resource systems, and tests the leader under consideration with regard to their grasp of key political strategy issues, including the distribution of power among various players to influence mission and strategy and how the politics of that process is handled. The political cell expresses the centralization or decentralization of power against a predictable backdrop of the politics of who gets ahead and how various rewards are divided up. The cultural human resource issues determine, of course, how future and current leaders are rewarded for cultural fit or the lack of it.

	STRATEGY	STRUCTURE	HUMAN RESOURCES
TECHNICAL SYSTEM	Mission and strategy	Organize to implement the strategy	HR infrastructure for hiring, appraising, developing, and rewarding
POLITICAL SYSTEM	Who has how much power in setting strategy	Allocate power up and down the organization (how centralized or decentralized)	Political system promotion and rewards
CULTURAL SYSTEM	Creating a value system to support strategy	Values to support subgroups and simultaneously be part of the overall value system	Use HR systems to screen for values, then teach, appraise, and support strategy

Developing Good Judgment

Organizations skilled at developing leaders with good judgment do so by providing them with carefully structured and scrupulously assessed opportunities and challenges framed by real risk, real success, and real failure. Like an athletic team with a farm league, such organizations literally create positions and assignments designed to expose rising executives and leaders to a breadth of genuine profit-and-loss business unit experience. Any sound succession planning process must rigorously assess and evaluate how rising leaders make judgments, good or bad, achieve success or failure, and most critical of all, their capacity to learn and adjust their strategies in response to changing circumstances.

Creating such opportunities requires deliberate planning not just by the human resources leaders but by the organization's leaders as well. Big manufacturing organizations with large capital investments—like P&G and GE—will even create single P&L businesses to serve as training grounds for future leaders, even if that involves the incurring of short-term costs associated with a considered decision not to achieve economies of scale. Such structural interventions cause difficult judgments to surface like cream rising to the top of a bottle of milk, for the rising leaders to address and the incumbent leaders to evaluate their tackling of the issues. For example, since many large auto companies can offer only a few developmental assignments with true P&L experience, those organizations frequently suffer from the fact that so many people grow up in functional silos and as a result later on experience a dearth of leaders prepared to handle the breadth of judgments required to lead those organizations on an enterprise level.

A CEO Leadership Pipeline Built on Good Judgment: Human Capital Strategy

The cultivation and preparation of good candidates inevitably starts with the creation of human resources systems designed to foster the development of leaders at all levels of the organization. Looking at the recent spate of outside hiring and CEO failures at some of the largest multinational corporations—HP, JCPenney, and Yahoo, to name just three—it is hardly surprising to find that the HR levers in such companies do surprisingly little to develop this critical leadership capability. Succession dialogues in most boardrooms rarely examine the value or quality of the judgments that leaders have made in the past and the conditions under which they made them, as a means of extrapolating on that experience to provide some predictor of future judgment capacity.

True leadership pipelines can only be developed by engaging the board and current CEO with the CHRO to build a multigenerational talent roster, a process that if conducted correctly will typically take years, if not decades. Companies that fail to look seriously at the judgment capability of their leaders today will be hard pressed to find CEO candidates able to cope with the complexity of tomorrow's challenges.

The following chart describes the extent to which HR systems aid in the development of leaders with good judgment.

Using HR Systems to Develop Leadership Judgment

ASSESSING LEADERSHIP JUDGMENT

People	Strategy	Crisis
What judgment calls did the leader make to build his or her team? This may also include judgments about the extended team of business partners or other stakeholders. This area encompasses identifying whether people the leader chooses to work with are capable, trustworthy, and put in the right positions to be successful. Examining hiring, promotion, and outplacement judgments of the leader.	What judgment calls did the leader make to position his or her business area and ultimately the entire company for success with customers in the market? This may include actions taken to enhance the business's offer, its operational effectiveness, or competitive actions.	What judgment calls did the leader make to overcome unexpected difficulties and crises that inevitably happen in all businesses? Remember that a "crisis" will be defined differently at various organizational levels so it can be considered anything that threatened accomplishment of the goals in the leader's area or disrupted normal business operations.

© 2011 Action Learning Associates

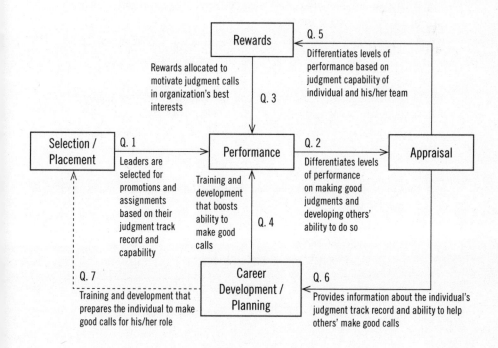

Q. 1. Leaders are selected for promotions and assignments based on their judgment track record and capability.

Little Extent			Moderate		Great Extent	
1	2	3	4	5	6	7

Q. 2. Performance evaluations differentiate levels of performance on making good judgments and developing others' ability to do so.

Little Extent			Moderate		Great Extent	
1	2	3	4	5	6	7

Q. 3. Rewards are allocated to motivate judgment calls in the organization's best interests.

Little Extent			Moderate		Great Extent	
1	2	3	4	5	6	7

Q. 4. Training and development boosts the ability to make good judgment calls.

Little Extent			Moderate		Great Extent	
1	2	3	4	5	6	7

Q. 5. Appraisal differentiates levels of performance based on judgment capability of individual and his/her team.

Little Extent			Moderate		Great Extent	
1	2	3	4	5	6	7

Q6. Career development and planning provides information about the individual's judgment track record and ability to help others make good calls.

Little Extent			Moderate		Great Extent	
1	2	3	4	5	6	7

Q. 7. Career development and planning prepares the individual to make good calls for his/her role.

Little Extent			Moderate		Great Extent	
1	2	3	4	5	6	7

An Action Learning Platform for Succession Planning: Simultaneous Leadership Development and Action Learning

"I just can't find enough leadership talent at GE," Jack Welch announced to me one morning while I was working in my office at Crotonville. "I know you see the leaders in action and can identify the sparklers in the programs. I want to know who they are."

I couldn't resist asking the tough question. "What about the turkeys at the bottom?"

"I could care less," he bluntly shot back. "They'll be discovered in the regular GE appraisal process. It's the high potentials I want you to find."

Welch made it clear that he intended to use my data as a jumping-off point for a deeper analysis of certain high-potential people of interest, employing a systematic "accomplishment analysis," an elaborate project that chiefly consists of a series of evaluators conducting in-depth personal interviews with the candidate under consideration, including his or her current and past bosses as well as subordinates and peers. The qualitative process involving as many as ten in-depth interviews resulted in a ten- to fifteen-page report including past accomplishments, current strengths and weaknesses as a leader, and future potential.

Ever since my Crotonville days ended nearly a quarter of a century ago, I have integrated the rigorous assessment of all participants in every action learning program we have conducted, at Nomura Securities in Japan, Ameritech in the American Midwest, Shell U.S., Mercedes-Benz, Ford, Intel, Intuit, CP in Thailand, and Grupo Salinas in Mexico, all with a view to fostering the development, evaluation, and assessment of the next generation of top leadership, up to and including the chairman and CEO. At PepsiCo I helped CEO Roger Enrico develop his senior program, which he proudly called his "war college," in which he served as sole teacher and coach at a series of five-day off-sites and three-day follow-up workshops, conducted either at his ranch in Montana or hideaway in the Cayman Islands, where he worked closely with his director of executive development, Paul Russell, to carefully assess the ten vice presidents participating in the program at the time, with an eye trained on their potential to succeed him.

Assigning high-potential executives to work on cross-functional and cross-disciplinary teams on projects of true strategic importance to the company provides the organization engaged in the action learning program with a multiplier effect that I have frequently referred to as "1 + 1 = 4." Each team is headed up by a senior leader and coach who meets weekly or biweekly with that team to develop the project and simultaneously coach individuals to tackle the project or challenge. Over the ensuing six months, my consulting team and I gather, compile, and process an enormous volume of observational data, which we carefully review with the internal leadership development staff, during meetings that devote one hour of review to each of the six teams, comprising the final six hours of the last full-day workshop. At these concluding sessions, all of the teams present their projects and their recommendations for solutions and strategy to the chairman and/or CEO and his or her senior top team, during which time the CEO, CHRO, and the top team enter into comprehensive assessment of all the participants, each of whom is clearly screened for their potential to succeed either all the way to the top or tantalizingly near it.

Concluding Meeting Protocol

All coaches, internal leadership development staff, and the members of my team collaborate on the assessment of all the participants against their performance as defined by the performance and values nine-cell matrix.

The program typically concludes with the CEO and the team sponsor and coaches, the CHRO, and members of the leadership development staff all sitting around a conference table facing each participant's nine-cell mounted on the wall. The executive coach takes the cards for

EDGE — Nine Cell

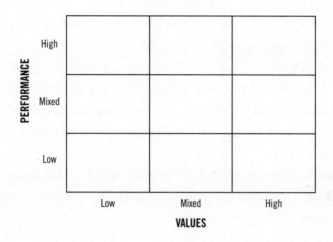

Performance Explanation		Values Explanation	
High:	Regularly exceeded performance expectations and performed above and beyond the expectation level	High:	Regularly exceeded behavioral expectations as a team member (commitment, company values)
Medium:	Performance satisfied/met your expectations	Medium:	Individual's behaviors met your expectations
Low:	Performance did not meet your expectations	Low	Individual's behavior does not align with company values and expectations

all six of the team members and places them on the chart, inside the cell he or she feels they deserve for their performance in the program. He or she then provides a specific rationale for the assessment they delivered, at which point everyone who interacted with this individual during the workshop gives their own views, including the CEO. This collective assessment not infrequently will result in shifting that individual under consideration from one cell to another.

After the group agrees on which cell each individual belongs in, we typically consult a flip chart on the wall, which the group then uses to keep tabs on that individual's performance:

1. Name and project.
2. Which cell in the matrix they were placed in.
3. Why they were placed in that cell—specific feedback—e.g., "lack of effort," "missed meetings," "outstanding help with other team members," "brought global industry input to the group," etc.
4. Areas they need to improve (even if they were high/high).
5. Future potential as an executive in the company, and at what level.

At one workshop we recently conducted, one participant's sponsor and coach rated them high on performance and high on values, but dissent quickly broke out among the rest of the group with regard to the accuracy and validity of this ranking. While a number of other executives provided tangible evidence of this individual's lack of cooperation with the other teams, I watched the CEO and chairman carefully evaluating everyone else's individual assessments, clearly in search of a consensus position as to this person's potential to rise higher in the organization, possibly even to the very top.

Although action learning is no substitute for redundant systems of evaluation and assessment of high-value, high-potential executives, all of the valuable data gathered from those executives' participation in the action learning workshops we conduct is ultimately incorporated into a formal succession planning database, to be drawn upon either by the individual business unit or by the corporate heads of the overall enterprise. We also diligently employ tracking to determine that the assigned follow-up meetings occur, that the designated senior leaders provide appropriate feedback to each participant, and that each participant personally meets with his or her boss to share the results of the program and the feedback, insights, and assessments they received.

The disciplined application of this methodology has on numerous occasions in my experience provided the top team and C-suite executives with the visibility and personal exposure required to surface high-potential executives, even two or three levels deep. These are people they never or rarely would have encountered in the ordinary course of events, which is precisely why action learning is such a valuable tool for leadership development, particularly when carefully combined with the design and implementation of custom-tailored crucible and stretch assignments. The development of leaders to succeed other leaders is every leader's most critical task. When it comes to CEO succession and the development of senior executives, no investment of time, resources, or management attention is ever wasted as long as it is structured to effectively address the technical, political, and cultural aspects of the issue.

At a wide variety of companies and nonprofits ranging from PepsiCo to Intuit, Boys & Girls Clubs to the Special Operations Forces of the United States military, we have seen and participated in the discovery and development of innumerable high-potential leaders who otherwise might have fallen between the cracks, gotten lost in the bureaucratic maze, or been defeated by the political struggle and shuffle of organizational life.

CHAPTER 3

GETTING IT RIGHT: BUILDING A TRANSFORMATIONAL LEADERSHIP PIPELINE

Somebody once said that for succession to work the company has to be ready, the board has to be ready and the CEO has to be ready. If you try to force the process when one of those three is not ready you will end up with angst in the system, nervous energy, doubt, and a lack of confidence.

—**Ivan Seidenberg,**
former chairman and CEO, Verizon

TECHNICAL

- Good succession planning instruction/process
- Systematic monitoring and follow-up process

POLITICAL

- Balance of powers and checks and balances
- Consequences of noncompliance

CULTURAL

- Open, honest, constructive dialogue about people
- Succession planning and leadership development seen as highest priority

Getting It Right at DuPont

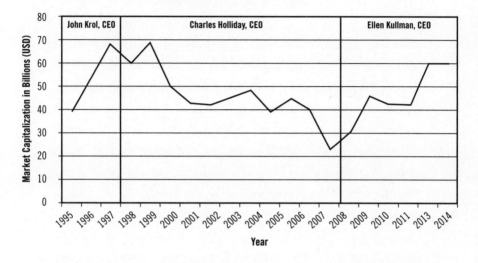

In September 2008, the same month that the over two-hundred-year-old chemical and life sciences company DuPont announced the appointment of fifty-two-year-old executive vice president Ellen J. Kullman to succeed sixty-year-old CEO Charles O. "Chad" Holliday as its next chief executive officer, Lehman Brothers filed for bankruptcy. Three months before, as credit markets froze up worldwide and DuPont's major customers stopped or delayed purchasing its products, the fiercely planning-prone Holliday, with just months to go before turning the reins over to Kullman, had pulled the trigger on a Corporate Crisis Management Plan that hadn't seen the light of day since the dark days after 9/11.

"The whole world," or so it seemed to Kullman, "fell apart"[1] during the fall of 2008. Which made Kullman all the more surprised when she walked into the first board meeting since being named incoming CEO to find that the leading item on the agenda wasn't going to be a debriefing on DuPont's response to the credit crisis, but rather a detailed session devoted to *succession planning.* And not just *any* succession planning, but planning for *her* successor. And, just in case you were wondering, not just planning for a potential replacement in the event of an emergency, but also planning for a successor in the months and years ahead, well beyond the immediate crisis-defined time horizon.

As Kullman later recalled in an interview with me:

> In the first executive session you hear the board say, "We need to talk about who is going to succeed you." My initial response was I just got here, but it was a great interaction and a necessary one on the emergency succession plan. Succession is just that important, and it's not a conversation you can put off until year 5. Over a series of a couple of meetings we got aligned on criteria and talked through candidates. We talked about internal versus external and established a path forward that the corporate secretary has the "letter," and we refresh the emergency succession plan every year.

As she prepared to take office as the company's nineteenth and first female CEO, the "seamlessness of [her] executive transition" earned plaudits from *Bloomberg Businessweek* as a sterling example of how "to do [succession planning] well. Pulling off a CEO transition is never easy," the author approvingly if obviously noted, adding for the record that "DuPont's smooth baton-passing early this year underscores the importance of having a solid plan."[2] This seamless, successful transition from the reign of Holliday to that of Kullman had been meticulously planned and managed over a period of years by Holliday, in close consultation with his senior HR executives and the board. As Holliday remembered:

> I became CEO at 49. So the assumption of the board was that I might be there a few years. I'd say in the first three or four years we didn't focus on the [topic] as much, but then after about three or four years, the board insisted that we build a pipeline of between 15 and 20 people that they wanted to keep their eye on, some of whom were very young and would need several more experiences before they'd be ready to be CEO.[3]

One of those young, comparatively inexperienced, yet nonetheless high-potential future leaders was Ellen J. Kullman, who had caught the future CEO's eye when Holliday was running Asia-Pacific operations, a crucible experience for Holliday that constituted a clear stepping-stone to the top job. At the time, Kullman was a senior manager in the company's electronic imaging unit, pushing products she had first come across at GE Medical Systems on her first visit to Tokyo. Following their first brief yet fateful encounter, Holliday later recalled saying to himself, "There goes a future leader." For her part Kullman remembers being peppered with so many questions by Holliday that he scared her half to death.[4]

Yet those apparently random questions served an intentional purpose, marking the deliberate inception of a long-term mentoring relationship, which Holliday consciously based on his own casual yet critical contacts with the predecessor, to his predecessor, Ed Woolard, the legendary DuPont CEO Irving Shapiro, a former litigator whom Holliday characterized as the company's first "public CEO . . . equally at home in the boardroom, the court room, diplomatic conferences, halls of government, even television talk shows."[5] Shapiro had taken an interest in the congenial Tennessean toward the tail end of his leadership of the company's Asia-Pacific operations, which effectively prepared and positioned him for assuming the CEO role several years later. After becoming CEO, Holliday shared a vivid memory of interacting with Shapiro:

> Irv would attend the annual meeting every year and you would never know he was there. Just sat there quietly. The couple of times I found him in the crowd he had on the perfect poker face. You couldn't tell what he was thinking. But within a month I'd receive a note from Irv with a perfect critique—really honest—of my performance. Things I could do better, things that worked. I got a lot of value out of that.

Holliday's close relations with both Woolard and Shapiro consciously informed his cultivation of Kullman over a period of years. This deliberate and disciplined grooming and coaching process amounted to a faithful following of a nearly century-old tradition at the company of senior members of the current leadership actively mentoring the next generation of leaders. This tradition dated back to a painful period in the company's early history, as at the turn of the twentieth century the founding family nearly lost control of the company when longtime president and family patriarch Eugene du Pont passed away leaving no officially designated successor. In 1902, three du Pont cousins took the risk of stepping into the breach and jointly buying back a controlling share of the company for $12 million. This change restored the company to power and glory and resulted in the creation of a strict policy and legacy of carefully managing its internal leadership transitions, a practice which has survived to the present day.

A risky yet inspired investment in the fledgling General Motors effectively placed GM under Pierre's leadership as chairman in addition to his DuPont explosives and chemical empire. Yet ever mindful that it would be difficult if not impossible for one leader to manage both companies, du Pont recruited the legendary Alfred Sloan, one of the greatest management minds of the century, to grow GM into not just the most technologically innovative car company in the world but also the most capably and innovatively managed. Under Sloan, GM emulated DuPont in investing heavily in leadership development and succession planning, a tradition that in rare cases can have its drawbacks. At GM, this intensive focus on growing internal leaders ultimately contributed to the development of a notoriously insular corporate culture, which over time would precipitate its decline in the latter half of the twentieth century, and would contribute to the sense that the giant company remained deeply out of touch as late as 2014, as under the leadership of freshly appointed internal leader Mary Barra GM wrestled with a crisis sparked by its long-standing failure to adequately monitor and fix safety hazards associated with faulty ignition switches on several models dating back decades before their flaws began hitting the headlines.

Not long after being named DuPont's CEO in 1998, Holliday spent a great deal of his time making sure to his own satisfaction that he was cultivating a strong pool and deep bench of potential successors. He also grasped the finer point that a crucial aspect of their development would require fostering their interactions with board members, who would ultimately select his successor. As he recalled:

> We exposed the board to the [candidates] in multiple ways. Then after I had been in the role for about eight years, there came a point in time when the board started . . . narrowing the pool down to five people or so who we thought were critical and they were ranked [according to] age, skills and capabilities, and we found ways for the board to really get to know those people well.[6]

When he spoke to me about managing his own succession process, Holliday stressed the vital importance of a board's getting appropriate advice and encouragement from the incumbent CEO and lead director as to the urgency and necessity of this task.

> It's important that the CEO and lead director prepare the board and impress upon them that this is serious work and that you need to be constantly doing it no matter where your current CEO is in their stage of life at the job. It's equally important for the CEO to give the board a real sense of the culture of the company and the culture of the industry that the company is in, so that the directors really get a sense of what the critical factors are for a CEO to succeed on the job. And it can take years to do that.

Holliday was also quick to point out the importance of aligning this CEO-, CHRO-, and board-driven process with "the strategic direction of the company." But, uncannily echoing the comment made by Dwight Eisenhower quoted in the previous chapter regarding the limits of planning for an unanticipated crisis or emergency, he hastened to add that this alignment should be with "the strategic direction as opposed to plans, because plans tend to change depending on how the environment shifts. But there is a general direction, market-wise, technology-wise, which the company is headed in. The board needs to understand that, embrace it, and acknowledge the degree to which this sets the criteria for selecting a candidate for CEO who will meet those conditions."

He also stressed that this alignment of board perspective with strategic direction needs to occur prior to the discussion of individual candidates, as a basis for benchmarking internal against potential external successors. "Before I've even talked about a specific candidate yet, it's critical for the board to conduct a good audit of the internal candidates and get a feel for what some of the external candidates might be and how they stack up against the internals."

Chad also took pains to point out that he and the DuPont board went to great lengths not to conduct a typical succession "horse race."

We did not run a GE-like process, not at all. In fact, some would call it the exact opposite. At GE under Welch, they named three people who competed with each other publicly, with all the press associated with that approach. When they were done, one got the job and the other two left. At DuPont, we did something different. We ran an extensive two-year process that was highly confidential. The goal was that not even the candidates would know they were candidates. I gave the candidates various reasons to present before the board so the board could meet them and spend time with them. Our goal was zero rivalry. Rivalry is destructive. We knew we wanted them to work together when it was over.

Holliday also systematically applied a best practice of painstakingly reviewing, with the CHRO and the board, each of the candidates' records on a biannual basis. "Every six months we would review all the candidates in detail, and find out how they are doing, what their assignment was, and even more importantly, what their *next* assignment was." He also was very deliberate about setting up opportunities to review the candidates with himself and the head of HR in the room for a portion of those review sessions. But he also strongly recommends that lead directors then ask the CEO to "step out for a bit so the board gets input directly from the head of HR just to make sure if there is some bias on the part of the CEO, the board can hear that directly from the head of HR."

Chad was equally meticulous about orchestrating and staging crucial opportunities for the board to get to know potential CEO successors by making sure that they made regular presentations to the board, in addition to other exposure to board members.

> We looked for opportunities for the board to travel together with the candidates, either into a major market, a major manufacturing plant, or in some cases one of our laboratories around the world. We would spend multiple hours traveling together and getting to know each other. We would see how they interacted with employees and customers as well as board members. And we would make sure to mix it up, so that multiple board members had a chance to spend time with each candidate. We did that over a two- to three-year period, at the end of which we got to know all of them pretty well.

He and his CHRO kept a systematic database of all of these visits, including the board members' individual reactions and candid and confidential reviews of the candidates. "We kept an absolutely accurate record. We interviewed each of the directors after the trip and asked them what they observed. What was good? What was bad? What could be improved on? What are some of the development items for this particular leader? We kept a close catalogue of what everyone said."

One of those candidates, who wasn't supposed to know that she was a candidate, was Ellen Kullman, who in 1995 had been tasked by Holliday's predecessor Ed Woolard with a high-stakes assignment to assume full P&L responsibility for the company's $2-billion-a-year titanium dioxide business, which produced a commodity product primarily used as a pigment in paints and paper as one of DuPont's long-standing legacy businesses. Despite the fact that Kullman had no experience whatsoever producing or marketing heavy chemicals—her background was in health care—that was precisely the point. Woolard had given her this stretch

assignment and she ran with it, ultimately growing the company's tita-
nium dioxide business into the largest of its kind in the world.

Three years later, after he succeeded John Krol in 1998, Chad Holliday came to Kullman and gave her the challenge and opportunity of
taking on an even more daunting stretch assignment: to establish and
grow an entirely new business almost entirely from scratch, an assignment that would require her to strategically exploit an arcane skill set
that the company had built up over nearly two centuries, from its earliest days as the world's leading producer of high explosives, and turn it
into a major-league profit center. As Kullman later recalled:

> I was just back from vacation one Monday in late August 1998, when
> Chad Holliday called me to his office with an idea about starting a
> consulting business around the company's safety practices. To leave
> an important position to go to nothing wasn't something you did at
> DuPont. This is a company that historically defined importance and
> power with the size of the organization you led. Being asked to take
> on a special project was a way to move somebody out, not to develop
> them. Chad pushed those concerns aside. He made it very clear that
> it was O.K. to say no. Nobody would have ever known.[7]

Blithely brushing aside reservations expressed by her husband Mike,
a senior strategist at the company and fellow GE alum, Kullman took
Holliday's suggestion that she start a new business within DuPont: Du-
Pont Sustainable Solutions. "We had to change our business model
three times before we found the right one," she later recalled, noting for
the record that "there were times when I questioned whether we would
ever get there or not."[8] She hit her final and winning home run when
Holliday asked each of the finalists to give presentations to the board
and senior management on the progress of their respective growth platforms. One highly placed staffer later reported that Kullman's stood out
because "she painted such a compelling picture . . . of how her business
was going to grow,"[9] and by indirection, how she intended to grow the
company. Put another way, this persuasive "visioning exercise" reflected

her development of an increasingly powerful teachable point of view (TPOV), which in my book (and books) is always a prerequisite for any aspiring transformational leader.

In 2004, in a move intended to provide her with even greater exposure to the one experience she would need to acquire outside the company, Holliday engineered an invitation for her to serve on the board of General Motors, a company still close to DuPont despite the fact that the federal government forced it to sell off its controlling interest in 1957 on antitrust grounds. When, four years later, she was finally and officially named Du-Pont's nineteenth CEO, her elevation was greeted virtually across the board, both inside and outside the company, with an appreciative expression of delight and surprise. Because the process had been kept a tightly held secret, and because Holliday and the board announced Kullman's selection significantly earlier than previously planned, both the incumbent CEO and the board had achieved their mutually agreed upon goal not just of selecting the right leader from the next generation to take the company into the future, but of retaining the top talent she would require to face the often bumpy and unpredictable road ahead.

Reflecting on her own journey several years later, she attributed a considerable amount of her success to her acceptance of that stretch assignment from Holliday, and the incalculable wealth of learning and experience she derived not just from taking it on, but from building it into a surprise success.

> I don't know if I would have become CEO if I hadn't done this. When you're an engineer, you learn to go with your head. When you're starting something new, you have to go with your gut, too. We're a 212-year-old company. We won't make it to 300 if we only ask, is my polymer better? Now when I go through strategy reviews, I say: "That's what it is. What could it be?"[10]

As for Holliday, he recalled to me that after staying on as board chair for about a year and a half after Kullman took over, he advised Ellen, "If you ever want to call, you know how to find me, but I'm not going to call you." As a general principle, he agrees with me that with some important exceptions, "I think getting the old folks out is a good idea."

The Political Dimension: Maintaining the Balance of Power and Checks and Balances Between the Three Players, CEO, HR, and Board

As the Holliday to Kullman succession both reveals and confirms, the most critical political aspect of CEO succession planning is the maintenance of a balance of powers—complete with real checks and balances—between the three main players in the game: the CEO, the CHRO, and the board. The key issue here is that the CEO must own and manage the process while not dominating it, undermining it, or in any way compromising its integrity, objectivity, or impartiality. The chief human error undermining the objectivity of the process is inevitably the existence of emotional ties to the various protagonists that cloud the players' best judgment. This means that the board, the CEO, and the CHRO must be tightly aligned on this issue, and defer to the process, which involves setting aside personal agendas and biases. The CHRO is not just permitted but actively encouraged and invited by the CEO and the board to play a central role as the primary owner of the data, despite the fact that from a purely political standpoint, the CHRO clearly swings a smaller bat than either of the two other parties.

In too many companies and organizations, human resources leaders and departments end up being marginalized because they undermine their own best interests by becoming excessively focused on the technical as opposed to the political and cultural dimensions. In fact, human resources strategies when properly formulated always take all three dimensions into account, as HR typically is the guardian of the culture and a critical arbiter of the political dimension. HR processes and systems must be explicitly designed to foster the development of leaders at every level of the company, from the youngest off-campus hires right up through divisional heads and vice chairmen being positioned to succeed the sitting CEO.

As for the board, succession dialogues in too many boardrooms fail to examine and dispassionately evaluate the quality of the judgments that future leaders have made and the conditions under which they made them. And too many boards are content to passively delegate their authority and engagement in the issue to more active managers of the company. But boards that fail to carefully scrutinize the judgment track record and capacity of succession candidates will be hard pressed to find candidates qualified to cope with the complexity of challenges tomorrow. Boards, incumbent CEOs, and CHROs all need to closely collaborate and participate in the protracted and perpetual investment of time, attention, and resources necessary to build high-quality leadership development and appraisal systems that take leadership judgment into account in selecting, appraising, rewarding, and developing leaders at every level of the organization and at every stage of future leaders' careers.

Making the Process Real

Human resources systems and evaluations need to take the reality into account that compensation, promotional, and development opportunities must be intrinsically linked to judgment capacity and related specific criteria, including personal integrity, motivational skill, and contextual knowledge. At GE, Jack Welch and I operated under the assumption that 80 percent of leadership depends on on-the-job training while at most 20 percent is the product of formal leadership training, the challenge becomes to make the 20 percent training element as realistic a simulation of actual top executive experience as possible. My team and I tackle this task by designing action learning projects that are authentic business challenges, which are ultimately developed into real-life, real-time business concepts, tactics, and strategies, the success or failure of which counts against their leadership capacity assessment.

Benchmarking Performance Against External Candidates

Even when focused on succession planning throughout the enterprise, achievement assessments and accomplishment analyses of high-potential executives must be accurately and dispassionately benchmarked against the track records of external candidates for every significant position, as a basis of fostering real competition for every high-level job. This only underscores the fact that while talent development is primarily an internal operation, the search for a truly transformational leader, if it is to be truly rigorous, must involve benchmarking internal candidates with viable external competitors.

Sound succession planning is all about picking the right people for the right jobs at the right stage of their personal and professional development. CEO selection is therefore the ultimate people judgment, which involves people (sitting CEO, CHRO, directors) picking people, in part, on the basis of their past judgments, the most important of which define their own success at picking people, and coaching, training, and developing them to achieve their highest potential. In my experience, successful CEOs, CHROs, and boards all ask the same questions about the people they are evaluating for future leadership positions:

1. How did they do picking their own people?
2. How did those people do after the person being evaluated left the business and moved on?
3. What did the people they picked think of them?
4. How, and in what ways, did they add value to the "soft assets" of the company?

The Cultural Dimension

At every elite and high-performance institution or organization, whether the Navy SEALs, the New York Philharmonic, or Accenture, Bain, or Goldman Sachs, the formative question asked about every new recruit is: will he or she fit into our team? Which is another way of saying, of course, is he or she a good cultural fit? The most powerful shaper of culture is the HR department and the systems it employs to appraise, promote, and reward performance. These are the systems that must be put into place if you are hoping to override powerful personalities and politics. The ultimate goal of any and all leadership institutes, from the U.S. Military Academy at West Point to the Royal Military Academy at Sandhurst in Great Britain, from the IBM leadership institute at the Armonk, New York, headquarters campus to GE's leadership academy at Crotonville, is to indoctrinate the next generation of leaders in the culture of the organization. But as my own professional career suggests, the true trick is to carry out that indoctrination while maintaining the dynamism of transformation and reinvention. Building an effective leadership pipeline in today's world demands the cultivation of transformational leaders, who are able to maintain the continuity of the core culture while continuing to hard-drive internal and adapt to external change.

• • •

Getting It Right at Steelcase

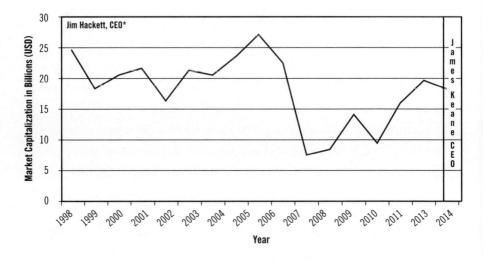

In March 2014, James Hackett, who had served as CEO of office furniture manufacturer Steelcase for twenty years, turned over the leadership of the leading company in his industry to his successor, James Keane. Over the prior two decades, Hackett had spearheaded a fundamental transformation of his organization to make it much more than just an office furniture maker, but a full-fledged, highly innovative workplace design company that created total work environments, integrating furniture with high-tech applications, work space design, and learning environments. The company's award-winning leadership development center, transformed from an old warehouse on the corporate campus, is a model for high-touch and high-tech learning environments that Jim Hackett consciously used as a critical component of his overarching strategy to construct a new creative culture at Steelcase. The leadership center also provides a setting for helping customers create visions of the work spaces they want to create in their own organizations. Influenced by his engineering and product innovation background and experi-

---

*Jim Hackett was CEO beginning in 1994. However, Steelcase did not go public until 1998.

ence, Hackett appropriately enough describes the succession process he crafted in the context of the culture of innovations he has championed at the company for more than two decades:

> I did this job for twenty years so by the time I walked out I will have made a lot of mistakes that I can improve on. So my successor gets to start the tape at a point where they can see the history of things that didn't work and where things did and didn't work. So they don't have to make the same mistakes. That really is a huge advantage for a new CEO.

Early on, Hackett realized that simultaneous transformation and leadership development were the true keys to the kingdom when it came to managing a CEO succession process. I first came to know Hackett as a result of my work with Jack Welch at GE, when he and his team asked for my help building their leadership center. I advised Hackett and his team on the design not just of the center but of the action learning programs. Throughout our association, collaborating on an overall leadership development and succession planning process at the company, Hackett was consistent and clear as to his intention to engineer a more robust succession planning process centered around the rigorous review of top talent in terms of pure performance and values alike. Building the leadership pipeline was the highest of priorities for Hackett, which he regarded as central to his legacy as a CEO. In keeping with that intention, he spent the greater part of five years coaching and grooming his successor, James Keane, to seamlessly transition into his new role when the time came for Hackett to step aside.

Hackett was particularly intent on framing the CEO succession process at Steelcase as a "T-shaped" structure, a term that he intended to describe his aspiration to develop future leaders as people who are "both broad and deep."

> We had to build an inventory of a lot of people with capabilities and a lot of experiences and then it becomes apparent who ought to be in the running for succession.

In addition to assessing their talent, the process looked at how resilient they are and how well they can make adjustments. Hackett spent years working the succession process. He described the development of a pool of potential CEO candidates as follows:

> Because they run a business, which is a complex system, you can see how they've actually made choices and managed it through conflict and handled unexpected events, which is really what you're trying to get your hands on. You're trying to see, how do they manage conflict? How do they manage unexpected events? How do they think in a systems way? And then you give a lot of range, and you don't make the boundaries too tight for the type of personality because you'll tend to pick personalities like yourselves, and that's a big mistake.

Hackett was constantly looking to the future and recognized that he did not want a clone of himself but a leader for tomorrow's work. In his coaching and assessing he was looking for candor, resilience, and the self-confidence to face into problems and recognize one's limitations. He talked about how he observed his leaders working with their teams on problems at Steelcase, and described how he evaluated leaders in the following terms:

> It's the level of frustration that they exhibit when you tell them that they're missing it. Some people are highly resilient to that and say, "You just helped me with something I didn't see." And then you now watch how they're better informed by it and if their strategy just got better. In some cases, the opposite is true and the person just gets highly frustrated.

In a collaborative process, Hackett and his board ultimately agreed they had the leader for the future in James Keane, who took over in March 2014. Building on the legacy of Hackett's work, Keane will get to build his own leadership pipeline.

Building a Transformational Pipeline at PepsiCo

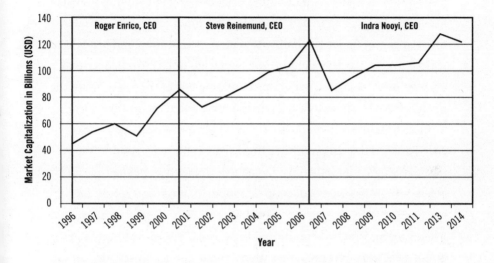

In the late 1970s, when I was doing projects on career planning and succession with my MBA students at Columbia, I entered into a long-term relationship with PepsiCo. It started out with my advising then-CEO Donald Kendall, his top team, and HR executives on the design and implementation of a top-notch leadership development and succession planning infrastructure, an engagement that continued to flourish in the 1980s under Kendall's successor, Wayne Calloway, who after taking the reins in 1986 served on GE's board of directors. After visiting me at Crotonville and seeking my advice on the advancement and refinement of his own program, Calloway and I worked closely together on emulating the GE formula while giving it a real PepsiCo twist.

After Roger Enrico succeeded Calloway in 1996, I continued to advise Roger and his top team on the implementation of a full-fledged action learning leadership program. After he decided to conduct the program by himself, without the assistance of any advisers, I heartily endorsed this decision despite the loss of a long-term engagement, because it reflected the most critical ingredient in the success formula for all such initiatives: the CEO's total, full-hearted commitment to the program. After Roger turned the reins over to Steve Reinemund in 2001, who passed the baton to Indra Nooyi five years later, the program has continued to evolve under Indra's leadership and guidance to reflect her own personal approach, insights, and input. Five decades later, a mission begun under Kendall, articulated by Calloway, and brought to fruition by Enrico, Reinemund, and Nooyi has amply fulfilled Kendall's and Calloway's original mandate: to become one of the finest, if not the finest, global leadership development programs in the world.

In late October 1993, PepsiCo vice chairman Roger Enrico experienced a leadership epiphany in a third-floor conference room at the Hotel Villa Magna in Madrid. With just five weeks to go before the launch of a new high-priority leadership development program, PepsiCo director of executive development Paul Russell was deeply disappointed when Enrico, who had committed to personally spearheading the program, began to express reservations about the promised depth and length of his involvement. The tipping point in their discussion came when Russell asked Enrico to look over a tall stack of books written by a selection of the leading lights of the field, including me. As Russell later recalled, Enrico's passion for personally leading the program visibly faded from his face as he contemplated the prospect of teaching from textbooks.

"Why not just have the B-School professors come in and teach this stuff?" Enrico asked Russell incredulously. Because, an anxious Russell shot back, PepsiCo people didn't want to hear consultants tell stories from other industries—they wanted Enrico's experiences and insights, straight from the source. "The glint in Enrico's eyes returned," Russell remembered, as Enrico "picked up three or four inches of files, including Tichy's, and said—as he dropped everything into the garbage can—'Then I guess we can deep-six this stuff.' We almost literally started from scratch."[11]

This spontaneous decision to "shit can" (as he put it) my books, among others, marked a pivotal point in Enrico's own development into a leader who regarded his primary task as coaching and teaching other, less experienced colleagues to fulfill their potential as leaders. At the time, I admit, I was disappointed that my team and I would, as the result of Enrico's decision, not play a central role in the implementation of the program. Yet I could only fault myself in the sense that mine had been one of the most vocal voices advancing the view that Enrico's deep and personal involvement would be critical to the success of the project.

One reason that PepsiCo lacked GE's deep tradition and framework for systematically developing and growing leaders inside the company was that in its modern incarnation the Purchase, New York–based beverage and snack food giant was the product of a 1965 merger between the original PepsiCo beverage company and snack food giant Frito-Lay, which was itself the product of a merger that had closed just a few years before, when the corn chips company Frito and potato chips producer Lay's themselves came together. Under the leadership of Donald Kendall, who succeeded Lay's founder H. W. Lay in 1971, PepsiCo took on much of its present form and identity as a brash upstart to incumbent Coca-Cola. That also marked the year that the son of a maintenance man at a low-grade iron ore processing plant in Minnesota joined PepsiCo as a twenty-seven-year-old brand manager for a new snack product, the onion-flavored Funyuns. After whizzing through Massachusetts's Babson College in three years and being accepted to business school, Enrico decided at the last minute to join the Navy and see the world, ideally from the helm of a destroyer or aircraft carrier, at the height of the Vietnam War. But his ambition to captain a battleship in action collapsed when he flunked the color-blindness test, so he signed on as an officer in the Supply Corps in South Vietnam to avoid the dread prospect of domestic desk duty. While dodging bullets and bombs in 'Nam he met his first mentor, his commanding officer, whom he would later admiringly compare to Rambo. The leadership trait Enrico most admired in his senior officer was an uncanny capacity to bend the rules to get the job done without ever getting caught or hauled on the carpet for insubordination.

Enrico tried to adopt his former commanding officer's unconventional approach to hierarchy at his first civilian job as a brand manager at General Mills. But he fairly quickly decided that a better fit for his talents was the less tradition-bound PepsiCo, which prided itself on doing things differently. After rising quickly through the ranks as his maverick personality won him friends and influence in high places, Enrico's big break came in 1983, when John Sculley, father of the famed PepsiCo Challenge, accepted a job offer from Apple founder Steve Jobs to succeed him as Apple's president. Taking over from Sculley as chief of marketing for the flagship brand, Enrico signed pop singer Michael Jackson to an unprecedentedly rich multimillion-dollar contract as the face of a new ad campaign that repositioned the brand as "The Choice of a New Generation." But after suffering a heart attack at forty-eight on a dance floor during a trip to Turkey, Enrico decided that what he really wanted to do with the rest of his life was to teach. And what he wanted to teach specifically was leadership, to the next generation of PepsiCo leaders.

That was when Paul Russell asked Enrico to embark on what *Fortune* skeptically described as his "weirdest career move to date." Even Enrico admitted that his mentor Kendall skeptically regarded the undertaking as a bit "flaky." Yet Enrico, who had never earned an MBA himself, felt confident that he could dispense with the conventional case-study method and conduct a personalized "war college" founded on a model of "formally mentoring nine people [at a time] instead of one . . . I try to talk to these people the way [PepsiCo's former CEO Donald] Kendall talked to me—frankly, openly, matter-of-factly. He didn't pontificate; he told stories. I want to make sure people begin to take the top guys off the pedestal. There's no magic to them."[12]

Two years later, the sixty-year-old Calloway asked Enrico to move into the CEO role so that he could step aside and battle the challenge of prostate cancer. When Enrico took over, the company was suffering not insignificant challenges in its core and international businesses, which Enrico decided to personally address not by stepping away from his devotion to coaching and teaching, but by ramping up his involvement in it.

Roger Enrico's leadership program was a three-month learning journey for ten senior executives per class; he ran several classes a year as CEO. Each class participated in a five-day workshop. This was followed by the participants' carrying out sixty-day business growth projects in their part of PepsiCo, which were planned with Roger and the other participants helping. At the end of the sixty days a second three-day follow-up workshop was held by Roger for the leaders to share project results and learnings. Roger Enrico as CEO was the only teacher—no consultants, no professors, no HR staff. The lessons for other CEOs from the PepsiCo benchmark are:

CEO Criteria for Developing Leadership the Roger Enrico Way

1. DO YOU HAVE A TEACHABLE POINT OF VIEW? You must have a teachable point of view on (a) leadership, (b) growing the business, and (c) creating change.

2. WILL YOU SPEND THE TIME? You must be prepared to commit one half to one third of your time to the development program.

3. ARE YOU A VULNERABLE ROLE MODEL AND COACH? You should be a learner open to new ideas and feedback, and a coach who can admit mistakes.

4. CAN YOU CREATE A LEARNING PROGRAM WITH REAL BUSINESS PROJECTS? You need to put people at risk working on business projects that matter.

5. CAN YOU BLEND THE SOFT AND THE HARD? You have to deal simultaneously with people and with hard business issues.

6. CAN YOU ENERGIZE OTHERS AS THEY LEARN? You must create an emotionally engaging process that encourages participants to take risks and learn from their experiences.

As Roger struggled to fix various problems throughout the company, he kept his leadership development eye trained on two promising up-and-comers: Steve Reinemund, a tough-talking and tough-minded former Marine captain who had helped guard the White House during the Ford administration—who became CEO of Frito-Lay's worldwide operations when Enrico was named PepsiCo CEO—and Indra Nooyi, a Yale-educated former consultant at the Boston Consulting Group who had joined PepsiCo in 1994 as a senior strategic consultant. Nooyi had earned a bright spot on Enrico's radar screen when she attended one of his workshops at his ranch in Montana, where her spirited participation, riding horses and serenading her fellow participants around the campfire, provided her with a level of access to the CEO that helped her to drive home her conviction that the company should spin off its floundering fast food division to focus solely on beverages and snacks.

Ironically, that spin-off occurred in 1997 under the leadership of long-time PepsiCo executive David Novak, who had been preparing to teach a workshop at Enrico's "war college" when he was forced to cancel to manage the spin-off. Shortly thereafter, I worked closely with both Enrico and Novak to take PepsiCo's prioritization of leadership and pipeline development over to Yum!, which formed the basis for building its own highly successful leadership pipeline. In the spring of 2001, Enrico put his devotion to pipeline and leadership production to the acid test by naming Steve Reinemund, who had served as COO in preparation for his own elevation, as his successor. On the eve of the next seamless transition, from Reinemund to Nooyi, the transformation that all three CEOs had led in rapid succession was nearing a successful conclusion. "PepsiCo," as one prominent analyst approvingly put it, "isn't really a beverage company anymore: It's a food company that also sells beverages."[13]

Under Nooyi, the leadership pipeline development process has evolved and taken on a new character, influenced by her own personal background and imprinting. Nooyi's "war college" is not referred to as a war college, but is nonetheless a high-profile and high-priority program specifically devoted to off-site team building combined with soul-searching story-sharing sessions in which fifteen selected participants brought in from across the divisions solve real business problems in an informal, cross-functional setting. She personally takes charge of every session, in collaboration with her HR directors, and discusses in depth with both HR and the participants every one of the chosen executives' long-term development plans and goals.

As the only senior executive present at these workshops, Nooyi goes to great lengths to ensure that the interactions are both private and productive. As of August 2013, when I interviewed her, she had led nine groups of fifteen people on these excursions, for a grand total of around 135 future leaders, over a period of roughly two and a half years. Within another year, give or take a few months, she intends to cover and get to know in this intimate setting 300 future leaders. While PepsiCo doesn't formally use off-site participation as a means of accelerating promotions—as high potentials, they are already on an accelerated path—the CEO's heightened awareness of participants' unique skills and capabilities enables her to ask her HR executives in candor and confidence, "Why aren't you looking at so-and-so for this assignment?" "I'm constantly asking them these questions," she cheerfully told me, "based on my personal knowledge of these people." Intimate yet practical knowledge, she needs hardly add, that she could have gained no other way.

"And so," she told me, "as I think about succession, which I started to do the very same day I became CEO, I'm constantly thinking about what kind of a company needs to be shaped and what's the team at the top. That's what I'm always worrying about." Whatever PepsiCo does or does not do under Indra's successor—and true to personal form and company custom she recently elevated, six years into the job, three obvious contenders for her job—the ongoing reinvention of PepsiCo will no doubt continue. Whatever occurs, this dynamic process is being driven and informed by a powerful tradition of transformational leadership development initially launched by Enrico, inspired by Calloway, carried on by Reinemund, and reinvented for a new era by Nooyi. Despite the slings and errors of activist investors, Nooyi's ongoing transformation of the company demonstrates her constant commitment to coaching, developing, and teaching the next generation of leaders in her own unique way.

Indra's teachable point of view regarding talent development at PepsiCo is built on three key principles: 1. future focus—building talent systems and processes that satisfy not only current needs but also future requirements; 2. segmentation mind-set—applying differentiated solutions for different segments of the talent base; and 3. development-centered—ensuring that individual development is embedded into all aspects of its core processes. Indra is also very clear that development is multifaceted and the vast majority occurs over the course of a career from on-the-job experience. PepsiCo has an interesting twist on the GE/Jack Welch 80-20 rule, 80 percent on the job and 20 percent formal development. At PepsiCo, Indra and the leadership team assume that 70 percent is on the job, 20 percent mentoring and coaching, and 10 percent from formal development programs.

Getting It Right at Ameritech

During the summer of 1992, my then colleague and future wife Patricia Stacey and I met with Bill Weiss, the CEO of Ameritech, a company comprising the collected assets and facilities of the former Bell Companies located in five midwestern states, which had been cobbled together to create a new entity in the wake of the dismantling of the Bell Telephone monopoly by federal court order eight years before. Weiss's overwhelming concern, which he openly voiced at our first meeting, was that he was sixty-two years old and would be retiring in three years, when he turned sixty-five. He was determined to lead a head-to-heel transformation at the still bureaucratic, lumbering, and poorly integrated agglomeration of formerly monopoly players, yet he was also determined within the three years remaining before his retirement to select a suitable successor who would be successful at taking that transformation to its next phase.

Stacey and I bluntly advised him that in our opinion, unless he was superhuman, he couldn't possibly manage to accomplish both challenging tasks simultaneously. But to his credit, Weiss insisted not only that he could do it but that he had to do it, because the company couldn't afford to lose the three or four years it was likely to take for his successor to consolidate his or her power so that the revolution would continue. In Weiss's view, such a scenario could be catastrophic, because within five years at most, if Ameritech didn't evolve into something radically different from its current state, it would likely go under in the face of growing competition from other regional "Baby Bells" and combinations, not to mention a horde of new entrants like MCI, WorldCom, and Sprint.

As we analyzed Weiss's dilemma, Stacey and I advised that as we saw it, he had a choice of four of what we called "old way" succession models, any one of which could doom the company:

1. *The Winner Takes All Approach,* characterized by the process set in motion by former Citicorp CEO Walter Wriston, who had a pool of half a dozen senior leaders and had them compete for his favor. The winner was John Reed. All the losing leaders quickly left the institution, but John Reed ultimately lost out himself several years later, when after merging Citigroup with Sanford Weill's Travelers Insurance in 1998, Reed clashed with Weill (who later pushed out his promising protégé, future JPMorgan Chase CEO Jamie Dimon) and himself left the company to become, briefly at least, head of the New York Stock Exchange until he recruited former Goldman Sachs copresident and future Merrill Lynch CEO John Thain to take the job.

2. *The Crown Prince Approach.* This was exemplified by the transition at Exxon from Lawrence Rawl, who appointed his chosen successor Lee Raymond president, before Raymond succeeded Rawl to become CEO in 1993. There was no horse race or bake-off, just the appointment of an heir apparent/crown prince.

3. *The Orchestrated Political Process.* This was the approach favored at GE under Welch predecessor Reginald Jones, who spent years carefully choreographing a succession horse race in which an initial pool of eight candidates was gradually winnowed down to three vice chairmen, one of whom (Welch) eventually emerged as the victor. Jones's stated goal had been to use the succession process as a development opportunity to mold a seasoned leadership team that would stay together following the final selection. Welch, who didn't care for that approach, also conducted

a horse race to select his successor but with one key differentiator from the process that had brought him to power: once Jeff Immelt won the crown, Welch made it his business to find the two other finalists CEO roles at other institutions. Within days of Immelt's ascension shortly before 9/11, Bob Nardelli had accepted the leadership at Home Depot, which he ultimately failed to transform into a company that operated along GE lines, and James McNerney went on to successfully turn 3M around before achieving even greater success at Boeing.

4. Crisis. IBM, General Motors, Digital Equipment (died), Westinghouse (died), American Express, Tenneco, and Kodak (died) are examples of organizations that either died or had near-death experiences due to poor CEO succession.

But as we soberly explained to our new client Bill Weiss, none of these models would help him drive an organizationwide transformation while simultaneously searching for the next best possible leader among the senior echelons of the organization. We encouraged Weiss to regard the transformation he intended to launch as a drama composed of three acts, a metaphor my coauthor and I had developed in *The Transformational Leader* (1986), the book for which I interviewed Jack Welch (who the day after that interview was conducted invited me to join his revolution as the next leader of Crotonville).

The necessary first step of this process, Patti Stacey and I counseled, would be for us to identify a set of potentially transformational leaders within the ranks of his own organization, senior leaders who would in turn be capable of mobilizing the next level down—upwards of several hundred more junior leaders—to jump-start the first act of the drama and first phase of the transformation, which we referred to as the Awakening. The primary protagonists of this narrative, we explained, would be the leaders most deeply committed to setting this revolutionary plot into motion.

Unfortunately—in the short term, but as it turned out fortunately for the long-term future of the company—at the conclusion of a three-day workshop for senior leaders held at the famous North Carolina golf resort at Pinehurst, we had some bad news to deliver. "No one in that room," I told Weiss without hesitation, "is a viable succession candidate for you."

To his credit, Weiss took that harsh judgment in stride and immediately agreed that in search of protagonists for the Awakening, we would need to look beyond the present ranks of senior leaders, all of whom were too deeply invested in safeguarding not just their own positions of power but also the obsolete monopoly management model Weiss was so fiercely intent on discarding and transcending before leaving the company in three years' time.

In February 1993, we convened a much smaller workshop for Ameritech's top thirty executives at the Breakers hotel in Palm Beach. Every day, Stacey and I met with Weiss in his suite to impart our observations and conclusions regarding the participants and their potential to succeed him. On the last morning of the workshop, entirely of his own volition, Weiss made an unexpected and dramatic move. He canceled the customary Monday morning management meeting and instead issued an announcement. He would be calling a new meeting with just four younger leaders, all of whom were officially and nominally junior and subordinate to all of the senior leaders present, who would henceforth lead what Weiss referred to as a transformation team.

The four newly empowered leaders were Dick Notebaert, Dick Brown, Barry Allen, and Gary Drook, to each of whom he assigned a team of thirty high-potential also younger executives to work on strategic initiatives for the future. Much as Chad Holliday had done with his five growth platforms, and Reg Jones and Jack Welch at GE had done by giving their finalists major divisions to run, Weiss was dividing his realm into four distinct domains—the network, customer segments, regulatory, and human resources strategies—and giving one to each of the four finalists to run, clearly in competition with the other three finalists in a classic four-way succession horse race. Notebaert got the network, Drook the customer segmentation, Allen the cultural transformation, and Brown the regulatory reform. The four teams of thirty, 120 executives in all, formed a broader transformation team, which from that moment on represented the future leadership of the company, being officially put to the test.

The most critical component of the process and greatest contributing factor to its ultimate success was Weiss's adroit management of the political dimension from day one right up to the conclusion. He started out the journey by making it abundantly clear to each of the four contenders that he just wouldn't tolerate any attempts, however subtle, to compete for the post by undermining one another or their initiatives. "If I catch any of you undercutting one of your colleagues," he warned, "you're out." The urgency of the need to transform the company while simultaneously focusing on a successor search drove Ameritech through the final two phases of the transformation drama—the Envisioning and the Re-Architecting—with remarkable speed and an equally remarkable total absence of political drama or infighting.

Weiss's most intensive and productive aha moment occurred when he realized that he would need to use the process to resolve an apparent paradox: the next CEO, in his view, would need to be both a team player and a most valuable player all wrapped up into one. As the process gained organic momentum, Weiss's role naturally evolved from strategic thinker to mentor, teacher, and coach, an evolution that helped him to resolve the paradox that ultimately led to the insight that the best combination of team player and most valuable player on the bench was Dick Notebaert, whom Weiss and the board appointed as his successor. In the end, that big bet turned out to have been right on the money. In 1995, two years after the seminal Breakers workshop, Notebaert was appointed CEO and Weiss retired from the company, satisfied that he had put it on the right track, with the right person behind the wheel. Four years after that Notebaert proved the value of Weiss's bet when he sold Ameritech to the Southwestern Bell Corporation (SBC) for $72 billion, having tripled the company's market cap between the day he took over and the day Ameritech passed into history. In the small-world department, SBC was led at the time by future GM CEO Ed Whitacre, who after acquiring the flagging Bell flagship AT&T took the name of its former competitor and went on to face down another agglomeration of former Baby Bells called Verizon for the heavyweight title of the telecom bout in the United States.

The leadership and succession lessons learned from the Bill Weiss-led simultaneous transformation and CEO succession experience at Ameritech include the following principles, which we have applied in other organizations as well:

1. MOBILIZE A CRITICAL MASS OF LEADERS: In large companies, to drive the process of change, from fifty to several hundred leaders must be engaged directly in leading the transformational efforts in the organization. These people must be identified, mobilized, and directed.

2. DEVELOP A CRITICAL MASS OF LEADERS: The organization cannot mobilize leaders it does not have. Therefore, organizations must provide significant developmental experiences and nurture such leaders. Their skills as transformational leaders must be continuously upgraded.

3. PROVIDE A CEO SCREENING AND SUCCESSION PROCESS: In the midst of the transformational effort, a systematic, disciplined process of screening and developing the future CEO must take place. A number of candidates should be put in key leadership positions, tested in various ways, and continuously evaluated throughout the process.

4. DEVELOP THE NEW COMPANY VISION: The key process in continuous revolution is crafting the new vision for the organization. The job of all leaders, including the CEO and the CEO candidates, is to deliver on the new vision. Otherwise, the organization will stall again, waiting for direction to develop.

5. DELIVER FINANCIAL PERFORMANCE: Throughout this transformation process, the numbers must never be missed. To gain control over the organization's destiny, mastering financial performance becomes one of the cardinal rules of transformation.

In forming the framework for a successful succession, I have synthesized virtually everything I have learned, taught, thought about, and written about leadership over the more than forty years that I have been obsessively studying, teaching, consulting, and practicing in the field. In the end, identifying, cultivating, grooming, coaching, and training the right person to lead an organization into the future amounts to a judgment call, a bet-the-farm wager, not on that leader's innate but rather on his or her *cultivated* capacity to learn, teach, coach, motivate, navigate, and inspire future leaders in the next generation to do the same when their time comes.

CHAPTER 4

THE CEO ROLE IN THE SUCCESSION PIPELINE: THE PARADOX OF POWER

What really counts, it's all about performance and leadership. Good leaders must be grounded, be comfortable with themselves, authentic and credible. In other words there's no games, there is self-confidence. There is steadiness and people are treated fairly.

—James McNerney,
chairman, president, and CEO, Boeing

TECHNICAL

- CEO owns the architecture of the process
- CEO takes the lead on integrating strategy with succession

POLITICAL

- CEO drives the process, but is participative/collaborative
- Ensures alignment of CEO role with board, HR, and candidates

CULTURAL

- Role-models open/honest dialogue
- Acts as head coach in the development of succession pipeline

Getting It Right at Verizon: CEO as Architect of the Process

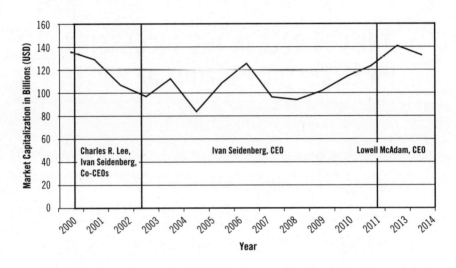

In July 2011, the board of directors of telecom giant Verizon Communications issued an announcement so widely expected it generated only a passing mention in the press. Ivan Seidenberg, who had led Verizon since its founding in 2000 following the merger of GTE and Bell Atlantic—which was itself the product of a previous merger with fellow "Baby Bell" NYNEX, led by Seidenberg, a few years before—would be stepping down as CEO by August 1. After remaining on the board as chairman for a few months to facilitate the transition, he would be retiring permanently at the end of the year, when he turned sixty-five.

On the face of it, the announcement couldn't have been simpler or more straightforward. But the underlying process of which it was the final outcome was prolonged, complex, time-consuming, and laborious, not to mention one of the very few and exceedingly rare examples (even among Fortune 500 companies) of an executive transition *spearheaded* and *architected* by a CEO yet not overly *dominated* by him or her. The naming of Seidenberg's successor, Lowell McAdam, who had led Verizon Wireless (the company's fastest-growing line of business) since 2006, came as no great surprise to anyone who had been following the company closely, because about a year before, Verizon's board had issued a detailed public statement confirming the appointment of McAdam as COO and president of Verizon Communications, the corporate parent, clearly positioning him as Seidenberg's heir apparent. As Seidenberg later recalled in his typically low-key manner, "We appointed [McAdam] COO and named him the designated successor. Most companies create a little drama about once you're COO you're not CEO, but my view was that we just say it."[1]

CEO Succession Rule #1: Great CEO Successions Don't Make Great Copy

☛ **Everything about the Seidenberg-McAdam succession reflected Seidenberg's determination not to "create drama" around the event. An uneventful succession is the clearest indicator of an executive transition's (at least) short-term success.**

Verizon's official announcement of McAdam's succession departed from its genre by focusing not just on the headline of CEO transition, but on clearly laying out the roles and responsibilities of a new incoming top team, saving the next CEO from having to spend valuable time consolidating power by assembling that top team himself. This included the naming of a new CEO of Verizon Wireless to replace McAdam, a new CIO and CFO of Verizon, in addition to the appointment of an entire bench of senior leaders who collectively made up the next generation of top management. In his own personal aside, Seidenberg placed the event of CEO succession in the broader, deeper context of a multiyear, intergenerational transfer of power, which he had deliberately concluded before he departed the scene, saving his successor from tackling that task.

This is a timely, logical next step in our evolution as we put in place an outstanding senior executive team that can carry us into the future. The decision by the board to name these leaders now to such critical positions is a testimony to the depth, flexibility and breadth of Verizon's senior team, the soundness of our operating model, and strength of our culture.

For the last several years, we have focused diligently on preparing these leaders to take on Verizon's most visible and challenging assignments. That diligence and focus is paying off with the development of highly skilled and broadly experienced executives who will ensure that Verizon doesn't skip a beat as we enhance value to customers and shareholders.[2]

CEO Succession Rule #2: The CEO Isn't the Only Game in Town

☛ **The transfer of power from one CEO to the next should not be an isolated event, but the culmination of a disciplined, rigorous process that encompasses the multiyear development and positioning of the top team.**

This quiet, peaceful transfer of power from Seidenberg to McAdam reassured investors not just because it was seamless, but because the two men shared a common heritage as career telecom executives. Both Seidenberg and McAdam departed from Bellhead tradition in one important sense: they had been in the vanguard of traditional telecom leaders who not only embraced the changes sweeping the industry after it was deregulated by federal court order in 1984, but personally thrived by seizing the opportunities deregulation provided savvy operators intent on breaking away from "Ma Bell's" notorious bureaucracy.

The fact that one of McAdam's most daunting challenges following his steady ascent to the top would be negotiating the acquisition of the piece of Verizon's wireless joint venture owned by U.K. phone giant Vodafone spoke to the complexities of competition and growth in a recently globalized industry, in which old-line telecom players like AT&T

and Verizon now openly do battle with fast-growing national cable companies like Comcast and Cox, satellite companies like Dish, content producers and integrated media companies like Time Warner and Sony, and high-tech companies like Apple and Samsung, for ever increasing percentages of fickle consumers' attentions and wallets. But in one key respect, the two men's backgrounds significantly diverged. While the soft-spoken McAdam, raised in a small rural town in upstate New York, was the polished product of Cornell University's undergraduate engineering program, with an MBA from the University of San Diego and six years of service with the U.S. Navy's Seabees' engineering corps under his belt, the Bronx-born Seidenberg was a little rougher around the edges, having entered the industry in 1966 as a cable splicer's assistant, crawling in and out of manholes and up and down telephone poles after returning to New York from a tour of duty in Vietnam. Over the next fourteen years, Seidenberg had earned undergraduate and graduate degrees at New York's Pace University and Lehman College by night while maintaining a meteoric rise through the bureaucratic, hierarchical ranks of the old monopoly Bell System by day.

CEO Succession Rule #3: Process Is Best Served When the CEO Collaborates with the CHRO and the Board

As Seidenberg emphasized in a recent interview with me—which he made a point of conducting in conjunction with his handpicked CHRO Marc Reed—the process that brought not just McAdam but the entire new team to the top had been the product of a close long-term collaboration among himself, the board, and CHRO Marc Reed, who had joined Verizon from predecessor company GTE and served as CHRO of Verizon Wireless before Seidenberg asked him to lead HR for the whole company in 2004. Seidenberg and Reed spoke with one voice about the pride they both took in collaboratively crafting a process that, though by no means perfect, was meticulously engineered to minimize the technical, cultural, and political challenges and disruptions that so often compromise and distort CEO succession sagas at some of our otherwise best-managed companies.

This process wasn't a product of theoretical or abstract thinking but firmly rooted on two opposing sets of formative experiences for Seidenberg. The first consisted of his own tortuous personal odyssey to the top as he skillfully navigated not just his company but himself through a series of megamergers that eventually culminated in the creation of Verizon, of which he was named sole CEO in 2002. While the end result turned out well for him personally, it nonetheless took him six often arduous and difficult years to drive the ball into the end zone. After being appointed CEO of NYNEX (the corporate successor to New York Telephone) in 1994, Seidenberg spent a few years biding his time as second to Bell Atlantic CEO Raymond Smith after Bell Atlantic merged with NYNEX, followed by several more years spent sharing the CEO title and role with former GTE CEO Charles Lee (who also held the title of chairman), following Bell Atlantic's merger with GTE to create Verizon. Even after being appointed Verizon's sole CEO in 2002, he had to wait another year and a half before being named chairman. In designing his successor McAdam's rise to the top, his goal had been to smooth the winning candidate's path to a unified position of power, in part by putting that person and his or her fellow competitors through a rigorous selection process that left precious little to chance or political gamesmanship.

Seidenberg also drew on another set of experiences in mapping the process, which consisted of his years of service on several major corporate boards as they underwent their own succession scenarios, including CVS, Boston Properties, and AlliedSignal as it merged with Honeywell under Larry Bossidy, who recruited fellow former GE exec David Cote from TRW to succeed him. "I'd been through successions at every one of those companies," Seidenberg told me bluntly. "I'd seen what I liked and didn't like firsthand." After comparing the lessons he learned with several succession experiences absorbed by CHRO Reed on his own journey, "we were able," Seidenberg proudly recalled, "to pick the best of what we both had experienced over the course of the previous ten years and present a coherent plan and process to the board, grounded in reality."

CEO Succession Rule #4: Go to the Board with a Plan on Your Own; Don't Make the Board Come to You

☛ *The Paradox of Power:* **Going to the board early before the board comes to you puts the CEO ahead of the curve in preparing the future transition. This is a subtle way for the CEO to influence yet not explicitly control the process by 1. setting a timetable, 2. framing the issue, 3. letting the board know it is an important CEO priority and yet at the same time, 4. giving board members a sense that they have been called into the game early, with ample time for them to provide oversight.**

SEIDENBERG:

Marc Reed and I designed the last five to seven years of my career to give the board the information it needed to begin thinking about my succession in an orderly way. When I turned fifty-eight, which gave me seven years before I turned sixty-five, Marc and I went to the board and said, "We've got a seven-year plan." Why was it seven? It could have been six. It could have been five, but the fact was that it was about the right time to say to the board, "Let's look at this issue over the next five to seven years and let's not focus on just the CEO position but let's make sure we develop the next generation of proxy officers and the next ten or twelve people underneath that."[3]

Let me hit the pause button for just a second to underscore a couple of key points about this approach to the issue.

1. Together, CEO and CHRO presented the board with a *technical* map of the process they envisioned bringing to a culmination many years in the future.

2. By bringing CHRO and board into the loop early and unambiguously, they deftly managed the *political* challenge of ensuring that this would be a genuine three-way collaboration among CEO, CHRO, and board, not a political or personality-driven succession struggle.

3. By confronting this issue head-on while still at his professional and political peak, the CEO was able to integrate the succession process with the ongoing *cultural* evolution of the company.

4. The CEO not only integrated his own succession with succession planning in the broadest sense, but aligned the human capital strategy with the corporate strategy.

CEO Succession Rule #5: Acknowledge and Correct Personal Biases

Seidenberg strongly favored an internal over an external succession, based on the perfectly reasonable supposition that his most important leadership task would be to train and develop the next generation of Verizon leaders to take over after he was gone. He also remained firmly convinced that the board would and should ultimately "select someone who knew the industry, had deep vertical knowledge, had great operating experience, and understood the premium that goes with our brand." While he wasn't shy about letting that bias be known, it made him all the more determined to give CHRO Reed a definite mandate to maintain a viable slate of external competitors for every key position.

Marc's first job was to run the process. But his second job was to make sure he was maintaining a constant surveillance of what was going on outside the company. We need to make sure that we always had a means of comparing our internal candidates against anyone who might be available outside the business, and of keeping that comparison always in front of the board.

On the *technical* side, Seidenberg and Reed focused on creating a process that aligned talent development with the future strategic needs of the company.

MARC REED:

Our first order of business was to synchronize the succession process and make sure it had integrity, legitimacy, and transparency. Part of that meant ensuring that the board didn't view this as a one-off event, but as a process they needed to look at throughout the year. Our next order of business was to develop a model of "commercial leaders." By which we meant people who could look at our business, understand our technology and our operational processes, and then figure out how they could pinpoint external change and then transform our business models to monetize the assets and investments we had made in the company up to that time.

As a means of assessing candidates' potential as future "commercial leaders," Seidenberg and Reed carefully walked the board through two basic questions:

"What are Verizon's global leadership capabilities?"
"What are our leadership requirements for this entity going forward?"

The answers for each candidate formed the basis for the construction of a series of "talent maps," one for each candidate, a high-stakes and rigorous modeling exercise that boiled down to making an authentic assessment of every leader's relevant experiences and/or lack thereof, with regard to four key domains:

1. Who had run large teams?
2. Who had P&L accountability?
3. Who had staff assignments?
4. Who had global experience?

"By the time the plan crescendoed into a full-fledged CEO succession," Reed recalled, "we had a robust process in place whereby directors could see not only that we were moving talented people up to the top, but that we were developing a broader mix of talent across the entire enterprise." As the seven-year process moved into its final phase, Seidenberg and Reed sat down with the directors and presented them with a detailed account and appraisal of the top talent across the board. They conducted a thorough review of the precise nature of the jobs and stretch assignments each candidate had been given to help them to grow and mature, and on their performance in meeting their high expectations. Yet every time a director asked either Reed or Seidenberg to provide a specific report on "how so-and-so was doing" relative to competitors, they took pains to deliberately demur. "We'd say, 'they're all doing great,' or 'they all have to grow,'" Seidenberg recalled with a wry smile, because he felt strongly that for him and Reed to keep their cards close to their chests was critically important to preserving the integrity of the process so as not to betray their own personal views on any one candidate's performance, either through body language or actual language, for fear that to do so might subtly sway a board member, pro or con.

What in the beginning began as a long list of potential external candidates with more than twenty names on it, including a large number of prominent CEOs, was after five or six years winnowed down to a much shorter list, containing only a handful of external candidates to be considered. As Seidenberg recalled to me, reading that list after even a few years down the road made for a disturbing and thought-provoking session, because "over the course of those years, eighty percent of the external names on that list were not eligible or available." In the final phase of this well-planned operation, CEO and CHRO asked all of the remaining candidates to participate in every board meeting, with the idea of directly facilitating directors' personal interaction with each hopeful, so that they could get to know them in informal settings, apart and distinct from polished presentations and canned consultations.

CEO Succession Rule #6: Every Candidate Needs Exposure to the Board

Seidenberg and Reed's carefully coordinated campaign to ensure that every candidate was provided with sufficient exposure to the board was designed to make each director feel confident in their ultimate selection decisions. These decisions would be based in reality, not triviality, politics, or personal connection. On the seemingly trivial side, Seidenberg and Reed took great pains to keep very close tabs on such arcane details as which candidate sat next to which director at which board meeting. All duly noted, they made sure to rotate the candidates' and directors' seating arrangements to "avoid the trap," Seidenberg stressed, "of having certain directors adopt certain candidates just because they'd gotten to know them by sitting next to them several times. 'Oh, I know that person. He's a good person. I like him, because he said something interesting to me six months ago.'" In the end, every thoughtful and deliberate action that Seidenberg and Reed took to manage the process was undertaken with one overarching goal in mind: to minimize any perceived or actual dominance or excessive influence over the process by the CEO—what I often call the death trap of "CEO override."

SEIDENBERG:

One of the main things Marc and I immediately agreed on was that we wanted to take personality out of the process. I'm not saying we were perfect at it, but we worked awfully hard not to have board members or other senior leaders, say, "Oh, I know so-and-so. I sat next to this one. We were on a trip together." I took all of that off the table.

When I asked Ivan to identify the single greatest challenge he and Reed faced managing his succession, Seidenberg didn't hesitate or miss a beat. It was the creation of a leadership *culture* strong enough to withstand even the possibility of a bad decision.

> The hardest issue for me was building a culture and a capacity in the company that was going to be sustainable for two or three years after I left, independent of *whom* we put in the job. I had to stay focused on making sure that there was enough continuity in the company that if we made the right decision everything would be fine. But I also wanted to make sure that if we made the wrong decision, the company wouldn't go to hell in a handbasket in six months and we'd find ourselves with a panic on our hands. I was on some other boards that after one bad quarter there was a lot of nervous energy in the boardroom and in one case the prior CEO was called back.

Fortunately for Seidenberg, his successor McAdam, Marc Reed, and everyone on the incoming top team, three years into the McAdam era every sign points upward and onward. In September 2013, McAdam deftly resolved the greatest question looming over the company's future prospects when he agreed to pay a whopping $130 billion for the 45 percent stake in Verizon Wireless owned by British telecom company Vodafone. In this, the second-largest acquisition in history behind Vodafone's 1999 $172 billion acquisition of Mannesmann, at the height of the tech boom, McAdam's negotiating style was regarded by analysts as successful not just because he was able to cut a fair deal, but because price aside, the acquisition served a cultural purpose. It would consolidate Verizon's control over the biggest wireless operator in the United States, as well as providing further distance from its roots in a bureaucratic, monopolistic past, dominated by a declining legacy landline operation. When asked his opinion of McAdam's performance by a member of the press, Seidenberg surprised no one by declining to comment, stating simply for the record that as far as he was concerned, it was "McAdam's day to shine."

Getting It Right at P&G: A. G. Lafley, the Accidental CEO *Twice*

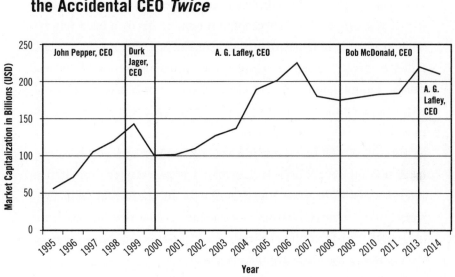

On Tuesday, June 6, 2000, Procter & Gamble veteran A. G. Lafley was preparing to step into a meeting in San Francisco when he took a call from ex-CEO and board member John Pepper, who asked Lafley if he was prepared to replace current CEO Durk Jager, with whom Lafley had been discussing end-of-the-fiscal-year plans as recently as the afternoon before. "Jager resigned," Pepper bluntly disclosed, refusing to go into any more detail on the phone but simply repeating that he needed Lafley's assurance that he was prepared to step into Jager's shoes immediately, if not sooner. After reaffirming his eagerness and willingness to take the job, Lafley followed Pepper's instructions to hop the corporate plane back to Cincinnati and head directly to Pepper's office as soon as he arrived.

On the flight home, Lafley—who had been running the company's flagship North American business as well as the newly formed Global Beauty Business—gave himself a few moments to reflect on the bizarre turn of events that had caused him to ascend to the CEO's seat without more than a moment's warning. The brusque and aggressive Dutch-born Jager was given to issuing statements like "If it ain't broke, break it," as well as threatening to have heads roll if certain sales and production targets weren't met.[4] Unfortunately, after three years of playing second fiddle to Pepper, he mainly succeeded after being handed the top job in breaking his own kneecaps and making his own head roll. His widely touted $2 billion turnaround plan, dubbed "Organization 2005," failed to achieve anything close to the promised results. It instead caused a more than 50 percent loss in P&G's market capitalization between January and June of 2000, amounting to a loss of over $50 billion in enterprise value in a bull market.

Three days after being voted in as CEO by the board, which also decided to bring Pepper back as chairman, Lafley described himself in an interview with *The Wall Street Journal* as an "accidental CEO" who wasn't in the slightest bit shy about sharing his view that the succession process that had put him at the pinnacle of power had been "arguably the poorest in the history of this company."[5]

Practically from his first day in office, Lafley was determined to do better on his watch. While dedicating the first hundred days of his tenure to "improving execution with key customers and suppliers and making a few simple strategic choices that would turn out to be powerful enablers of company performance,"[6] he also devoted considerable time and resources to "strengthening P&G's leadership and management from top to bottom." That involved making a significant commitment to and investment in bolstering P&G's "leadership development and training . . . to produce a cadre of executives who could help P&G regain its leading position in core businesses, expand into new categories and markets, and create a truly global enterprise well positioned for profitable growth."[7]

Next up on his list, and the first topic at hand when he sat down for the first time with chairman Pepper and lead director Norm Augustine, was CEO succession and executive leadership development, a subject that he noticeably put at the top of the list alongside strategic oversight at the corporate level, overall governance, and enterprise risk. The importance of that ranking of priorities at both the CEO and board levels cannot be underestimated. For the CEO, chairman, and lead director of one of the most admired companies on earth that also happened to be in the midst of a crisis to in effect put a stake in the ground that succession and leadership development should sit with strategy, governance, or risk on the priority chart spoke to the depth of passion and commitment Lafley brought to the subject, which at first he had trouble persuading the board was truly an urgent matter. As Lafley later recalled, while "all companies should have a plan for handling the normal transfer of power as well as for dealing with emergencies like health incidents, untimely death, and other unanticipated events.... unfortunately, no such plan was in place when in June 2000, I was suddenly thrust into the role of CEO."[8]

In close collaboration with global HR director Richard Antoine and lead director Norm Augustine, the new CEO embarked on a nearly decade-long journey devoted to carefully formulating, refining, and implementing a thorough, disciplined, rigorous process for selecting and developing a slate of candidates to succeed him as CEO. Over the course of the nine years that he ran P&G, his efforts closely mirrored those of fellow champions Bill Weiss of Ameritech and Ivan Seidenberg of Verizon in deliberately using the succession process—not just at the CEO level but at every level of the organization—as a critical tool in driving a cultural transformation intended to fundamentally rewire and reposition the company to thrive in a new, harsher era. At the end of the game, not only would a hidebound organization ideally become more customer-focused, globally balanced, and innovative both technically and creatively, but it would be managed by a new cadre of seasoned leaders thoroughly prepared to take on whatever challenges might face them in the years ahead, and win in the market.

Much as Seidenberg and Reed did at Verizon during roughly the same period, Lafley and Antoine spent a great deal of time devising the appropriate protocols to increase and enhance each of their high-potential candidates' face time with the people ultimately charged with deciding their fates. "Every director was encouraged to meet at least twice a year with business or functional leaders without any corporate P&G managers present. In addition, we set aside time before and after every board meeting for directors to interact with P&G's senior executives on virtually any subject of their choosing."[9] I will point out here, just for the record, that while Seidenberg and other CEOs and CHROs have done the same thing, Jack Welch went a significant step further at GE in providing his candidates with exposure to the board. He would ask board members to fly out and spend entire days with key business leaders on their own turf, hosting them as they ran through the process of presenting the board members with a full-fledged review of their business practices and overall progress.

Lafley reinforced the message that he was placing the highest possible personal priority on leadership development and succession planning by reserving nearly every Sunday evening for an extensive review in his study at home with CHRO Antoine of the single-page summaries Antoine and team had compiled, not just of the CEO candidates' performance but that of the company's top two hundred people. When a reporter from *Businessweek*[10]caught up with Lafley and Antoine late on a Sunday evening in 2003, three years into this process, he found the two men hunkered down with "stacks of reports on the performance of the company's 200 most senior executives," which the reporter rightly identified as "the boss's signature gesture . . . [one that] shows his determination to nurture talent and serves notice that little escapes his attention. If you worked for P&G, you would have to be both impressed and slightly intimidated by that kind of diligence."[11]

For every senior position, Antoine and Lafley identified three candidates and scrupulously sorted them by generation, level of preparation and readiness, and ultimate leadership potential. Lafley was committed to creating a high-volume as well as high-quality pipeline, rooted in his conviction that his core "responsibility was to develop as many potential CEOs as we could—leaders who would be ready and able at any time to lead P&G under any circumstances we faced in the global economy, the consumer products industry, and our company." As CEO, he regarded his ultimate objective as not just grooming a few horses with the best chances of winning the race, but grooming as many horses as possible to win any race. "I wanted more horses for the race. I wanted horses that could run in all kinds of conditions and on all kinds of tracks. And I wanted the race to be a long one. I wanted the board to be in a position—when it was my turn to hand over the reins—to choose the personnel who best met P&G's standards and best fit the specific needs the company would face over the next decade."[12]

On the technical side, Lafley and Antoine tightly aligned the company's rapidly evolving human capital strategy with its broader corporate strategy. On the basis of a set of core strategic assumptions—"our core household care businesses had ample room for growth, our branded innovation model was still creating significant value, our health, beauty and personal-care businesses would offer additional growth . . . and we still saw major opportunities in the emerging markets of Asia, Latin America and Africa"—Lafley, Antoine, and the P&G board created a "capability map" of P&G's ideal CEO. That individual would come into the job fully equipped with "significant international experience, capable of continuing our rapid expansion into emerging markets and of bringing operating discipline, productivity improvements, and a streamlined approach to our global operations."

As a "catalyst for CEO succession," Lafley defined his role as primarily head "leadership coach. . . . [charged] with the responsibility of identifying, training, and evaluating people with the highest potential."

> In a series of private one-on-one meetings . . . between the potential candidates and me, I learned not only *what* they thought but *how* they thought. I was able to observe firsthand their ability to influence peers not under their direct command. I could discern whether they were comfortable working from principles. I could test how they dealt with ambiguity, change, and pressure. I could get a feel for their self-control and self-awareness. Were they team players? Could they clearly define problems and opportunities? Could they make a call, be decisive, take a stand? Over the course of nine years, hundreds of meetings, and literally thousands of conversations, the ongoing dialogues I had with each individual helped me develop a deep understanding of every potential CEO candidate.[13]

Lafley, Antoine, and Augustine (eventually succeeded by Boeing CEO James McNerney) combined frequent personal interactions with the more typical, technical ongoing scenario planning that virtually all large companies conduct as a matter of course, as well as institutional survival. At Lafley's P&G, the two activities were explicitly designed to mutually reinforce each other, in a process that combined ongoing and rigorous assessments of each candidate's ability to react positively and effectively to a wide range of possible shifts and developments in the global economy. Putting candidates "through their paces" required Lafley and his top team to frame for each individual a series of "crucible" assignments—as both he and McNerney refer to tasks and challenges more popularly known as "stretch" assignments—designed to provide each of the candidates with the particular experience required to win the race for the future. "We challenged them to manage acquisitions. We stretched them with the Gillette integration—the largest, most complex and first really global acquisition P&G had ever done. We asked them to create and test new business models and start new businesses."[14]

Though justifiably skeptical of attempts to distill leadership into a series of characteristics and traits, Lafley did work with Antoine on framing a list of ten personal attributes they agreed would be critical for the next CEO:

1. Character, values, integrity.
2. Proven track record, business, financial, and organizational performance.
3. Capability and capacity builder.
4. High energy and high endurance.
5. Visionary and strategic leader.
6. Inspiring, courageous, compassionate.
7. Productive relationships with colleagues, partners, and other external stakeholders.
8. Embraces change. Leads transformational change.
9. Calm, cool, and resilient in the face of conflict and criticism.

10. Institution builder. Prioritizes greater good and long-term health of the company.[15]

When all was said, done, and delivered, the candidate who most closely fit the bill Lafley had been so carefully and collaboratively composing over the span of nine years was twenty-nine-year company veteran and West Point graduate Robert McDonald. Bob had for good reason ranked high on every list of candidates Lafley and Antoine had compiled over the years, "from the program's inception in 2001 to his election in 2009." Once the selection was made, Lafley scrupulously followed best practice by deliberately and noticeably getting out of the way of the newbie. Before McDonald took over, Lafley quietly removed all of his personal belongings from the CEO's office on the eleventh floor of P&G headquarters and moved into an out-of-the-way hole-in-the-wall nine stories below. Several days into the transition, at a weekly session attended by the top fifteen executives, Lafley arrived early and positioned himself as far as he could from the central ringside seat he had occupied for the better part of the decade. When McDonald entered the room and sat down in Lafley's old chair, all eyes automatically turned toward him. For Lafley, the moment "felt exactly like it was intended to. *The king is dead. Long live the king!*"[16]

A. G. Lafley's Obligatory Redo Loop

Flash forward four years. The quality of the process Lafley spent years bringing to a conclusion ended up being called into question by a surprising turn of events not likely to have been included in even the most far-out succession scenarios. By the spring of 2013, Bob McDonald, deep in the midst of executing on a $10 billion cost-cutting plan, couldn't stop himself from catching heavy flak from activist investor Bill Ackman of Pershing Square Capital Management, who had quietly amassed a stake in P&G worth just under $2 billion, easily enough to ensure that the board would be obliged to listen carefully to just about anything he wanted to say, and what is more, do something about it. What he was saying, to anyone who would listen, was that P&G needed to drive real change at the top and that McDonald wasn't delivering the goods, as defined by the harsh and always unyielding measure of share price performance, although I would argue that what was rotten at the core of Ackman's investment thesis was that his definition of TRS was destructively short-term as opposed to long-term in its logic. While Ackman kept loudly calling for McDonald's head, P&G's results handed him just the ammunition he was looking for to cast McDonald's exertions in a poor light. After sales gains for the first half of the year came in at the bottom end of his own forecasts, McDonald's days were clearly numbered. While McDonald continued to push out lower-priced products designed to woo back customers defecting away from premium brands to cheaper generics, P&G was mainly still "selling BMWs when cash-tight consumers were looking for Kias,"[17] as one analyst cleverly put it.

Despite the fact that P&G stock had risen nearly 50 percent on McDonald's watch, not a shabby performance by virtually any standard except in the eyes of activist investor Ackman, Ackman badgered the board to accept that P&G's price performance had not been keeping pace with that of key category competitors Unilever and Colgate-Palmolive. So did McDonald's resignation—which McDonald and Lafley have been consistent in characterizing as entirely voluntary—cause Lafley's succession process to appear any less robust? After the board decided to call Lafley back from retirement to serve as the successor to his own successor, none of the candidates waiting in the wings struck the board as fully prepared to take charge. After taking the CEO's reins for the second time around as an "accidental CEO," the sixty-six-year-old Lafley made it clear to the public, press, Wall Street, and investors that he would once again put succession planning at the very top of his list of priorities, as he executed a classic "redo loop," a maneuver he had perfected during his previous very successful stint on the job. Within a week of regaining his old job, Lafley announced a reorganization of P&G's leading brands into four separate sectors, each headed by a president who would report directly to him. He also appointed six senior leaders, including the president of global home care, the president of global baby care, the president of global fabric care, and the president of global beauty care, in addition to the presidents of the European and North American businesses, to positions reporting directly to him. This was a move that, not surprisingly, most observers interpreted as strongly sending a signal that now that he was back in the saddle, he was grooming as many horses as possible to run a second race to succeed him—in instant replay.

As for his selection of Bob McDonald four years before, I contend that Bob—whose personal integrity and judgment I grew to admire— fell victim to the agitations of an overly impatient activist investor unwilling to give a CEO in his crosshairs enough runway to execute a well-considered turnaround plan. Yet what Lafley's involuntary redo loop—making him an "accidental CEO" two times running, with a brief few years of retirement in between—did reveal, for better or worse, is that even a meticulously considered process can be upended by the course of unexpected events.

What cannot be taken away from Lafley's impeccable methodology, despite the ambiguous outcome, was that on the *technical* side, he elevated the often-neglected issue of CEO succession to the very highest board and corporate priority, while explicitly linking the succession planning process to the strategic plan for the company. On the *political* side, while assuming ownership of and responsibility for the design of the process, he took every conceivable step to maintain the balance of powers between himself, his CHRO, and the board, critical to its integrity. And last but certainly not least, he successfully located succession planning and leadership training at the very beating heart of a continuous process of *cultural* transformation, reinvention, and renewal.

All three succession sagas, one by Seidenberg, the next two by Lafley, validate Lafley's overarching contention that win or lose, "no other issue demands more candid and open discussion. No other issue demands more collaboration and mutual support between the board and the CEO. No other issue does more to put the greater good and long-term health of the organization ahead of personal or other short-term considerations."[18]

The level of passion and personal commitment A.G. brought to this high-stakes parlor game move was, he admitted to me, strongly informed by the legacy of his father. I had the privilege of getting to know Alan F. Lafley, a pioneer in the field of leadership development, who in mid-career was recruited to Chase by CEO David Rockefeller following many long and influential years as a senior HR leader at GE. "Leadership succession," Alan F. Lafley wrote in a *Journal of Human Resources* that I founded and edited, "is the most critical strategic activity in any organization . . . My own experience confirms that the CEO cannot delegate the overall responsibility for succession planning . . . His leadership and ability to manage the succession planning process is the dominant factor in achieving high quality results."[19]

CHAPTER 5

THE CRITICAL ROLE OF HUMAN RESOURCES IN CEO SUCCESSION

All organizations say routinely "People are our greatest asset." Yet few practice what they preach, let alone truly believe it.

—Peter F. Drucker,
***Managing in a Time of Great Change*, 1995**

It is clear that we are no longer asking the question: Are human resources important? Rather, the question is: How will we integrate human resources into the strategic management of the firm? This new path will require strong leadership on the part of human resources professionals . . . We need a new brand of leader who is able to transform organizations and bring about fundamental change, as opposed to the more status quo–oriented managers of existing systems.

—Anonymous

TECHNICAL

- Provides first draft design of the process
- Develops and monitors the succession planning database
- Conducts accomplishment analysis/top grading

POLITICAL

- Ensures connectivity between technical, political, and cultural
- Navigates balance of power between board, CEO, HR, and candidates

CULTURAL

- Safeguards the integrity and impartiality of both database and process
- Ensures open, honest interactive dialogues between all major players

The Strategic Importance of HR

Over the past thirty years, when I teach MBA classes and conduct workshops around the world on the topic of human resources, I often start out by reading the above "anonymous" passage out loud. I then ask if any of my students or participants have the faintest idea who might have written it, when, or why. Since I've never once had one student or workshop participant correctly identify the author, publication, or year, I pause for a second before dramatically revealing that I wrote that passage in 1983, in the foreword to the first issue of an academic journal I founded (or technically, refounded) called *Human Resource Management.* Then I ask the inevitable follow-on question:

"Do you think anything has changed much over the past thirty years?"

I've never met anyone inside or outside the academy who has responded to that question in the affirmative. My own professional and leadership journey can certainly attest to that fact. Ever since landing a formative summer job during the summer of 1966–67 as an undergraduate at Colgate assisting at a series of leadership development workshops conducted by the Organizational Development (OD) department at the Bankers Trust Company held at the Military Academy at West Point, I have worked closely with human resources professionals both as a consultant and as an academic for the better part of the past fifty years. After joining the faculty of Columbia's Graduate School of Business in 1972, I launched an Advanced Organizational Development and Human Resources Program designed to educate and train the heads of OD departments working at major corporations including Imperial Chemical Industries (ICI), Volvo, Shell, and others throughout the United States and Europe. I then followed up that initiative by founding the first dedicated Human Resource Management concentration at Columbia for MBA students.

But as early as the late seventies, I had come to the somewhat depressing realization that the organizational development leaders I was working with didn't have a real seat at the table, not just from an organizational but from a political perspective, with the senior leaders whose minds and hearts would need to be won over for any real or lasting change in the discipline's organizational role to occur. Even if they might have a firm grasp of the technical and cultural dimensions of the issues most pertinent to their practice, they were so frequently outflanked politically that their capacity to effect change was strictly limited to their own isolated domains, which operated on the margins of these enterprises as an add-on or bolt-on, not a core strategic capacity.

It didn't take much longer to come to the realization that the vast majority of CHROs even at organizations that nominally took the function seriously suffered from what you might call the Rodney Dangerfield syndrome. They didn't get much respect, at least from the people who mattered. Why? Because with rare exceptions like Marc Reed at Verizon under CEO Ivan Seidenberg or Dick Antoine at P&G under CEO A. G. Lafley or Susan Peters at GE under Jeff Immelt, these men and women tended to become overly bureaucratic in their thinking and excessively obsessed with managing the technical aspects of their roles, while neglecting the far more critical political and cultural work that had to be done before the technical issues could have any meaningful impact.

In keeping with the lament I wrote about above, for the most part these well-meaning folks hadn't the faintest idea of how to function politically inside the organization at the highest levels, which meant that they failed to lead the function strategically. An increasingly nagging sense that this professional deficit was holding the discipline back inspired me to establish an Advanced Human Resource Management Program at the Graduate School of Business at the University of Michigan in 1982, shortly after I joined the faculty there, the prime focus of which amounted to a concerted effort to answer the question: *"How does Human Resource Management fit into the strategic management process?"*

As we kicked off the program, I deliberately recruited as visiting professors some true HR leaders whose own careers stood as testimony that HR could be strategic. Apart from a careful selection of Michigan faculty members, I invited the CHROs at major companies, including Chase's Alan F. Lafley (A.G.'s father), GE's Ted LeVino, and T. H. "Scoop" Tiedemann of Exxon, to be sponsors of the program and teach in it. They were CHROs at companies where HR had gone against the professional grain in achieving a genuine strategic role. These were without exception all organizations that regarded themselves as "academy companies," where leadership development was clearly regarded as integral to the strategic competitive advantage of the companies. These are those rare places where two of Peter Drucker's most famous maxims quoted earlier were and still are taken seriously enough for leaders at every level of the enterprise to consistently apply them not just in theory but in practice.

I was hoping to encourage a broad-based shift in the profession from training *transactional managers* to teaching and coaching *transformational leaders* to assert their true potential as change agents in their own right. *"Transactional managers,"* I wrote in 1984, two years after arriving at Michigan, "make only minor adjustments in the organization's mission, structure, and human resource management. [But] *transformational leaders* not only make major changes in these three areas but they also evoke fundamental changes in the basic political and cultural systems of the organization. The revamping of the political and cultural systems is what most distinguishes the transformational leader from the transactional one."[1, 2]

In light of this key distinction, I ask my students and workshop participants the following questions:

1. *Why* are HR professionals at even some of our most widely admired institutions so often accorded second-class status inside their own organizations?

2. *Why* do so few CHROs occupy a seat at the table, enjoy access to the CEO and other senior leaders, or are treated as trusted partners of the CEO and the board, equal to if not superior to the CFO?

These questions pose essential quandaries and dilemmas that lie at the heart of the CEO succession process, because if senior HR leaders are not properly positioned as strategic leaders both in the hierarchy and in the minds of the CEO and the board, HR will never be allowed to transcend the more routine role and responsibility it must shoulder as guardian of the data, keeper of the culture, and astute manager of the political aspects of the task.

Over the years, I've identified the primary causes underlying HR's destructively poor image:

1. Too many HR departments and leaders fit the caricature of managers of bureaucratic organizations filled with drones obsessed with checking boxes and devising complex and intimidating evaluation and self-assessment criteria that they inflict on unsuspecting employees at quarterly intervals. Far too many HR professionals spend 80 percent of their time, energy, and resources focused on the *technical* aspects of leadership training and development as opposed to its political and cultural dimensions.

2. In rare but not sufficiently rare cases, some CHROs can actually perform a negative, soul-sucking, demotivating function, as "toxic" HR professionals.

Why So Few Organizations Get HR Right

As the most political function in any institution, human resources systems and the leaders who devise and implement them must be objective, unbiased, and essentially *impersonal* players in an otherwise emotionally fraught human drama of power, privilege, and politics. This may seem ironic in a system that's all *about* people, but it is precisely because HR is so easily politicized that HR systems must be equipped with enough reliable checks and balances to offset these fun-

damentally personal and political forces buffeting and potentially dis-
torting the process.

Let's take finance as an analogue. Every company or organization of
any size or scale possesses a professional *internal* and *external* audit
staff. Why? Because the leaders of all publicly held companies have an
SEC-mandated fiduciary responsibility, while privately held ones have
comparable fiduciary responsibilities to their shareholders and stakeholders. To keep the SEC and other outside auditors from tearing the
place apart with investigations, every organization worth its salt needs
to have put an array of often *redundant* and *overlapping* checks and balances in place to ensure that human error and frailty don't undermine
and overwhelm the system and to weed out fraud.

The need for these checks and balances is frequently confirmed by
the headlines and press accounts we read virtually every day of the major and minor financial scandals that so often occur at every form of
organization, public or private, for profit or nonprofit. Yet I would contend that HR processes and procedures are at least as easily corrupted
by politics, personalities, and favoritism as financial systems, with the
key difference being that HR corruption tends to be infinitely more
subtle and therefore far more difficult to detect and account for with
countervailing processes and procedures.

So when we read about the accounting scandals that occurred at the
turn of the twentieth century at Enron, ImClone, MCI WorldCom, and
Martha Stewart Living, the more recent accounting scandals and frauds
that occurred within the Mexican subsidiaries of Walmart and Citigroup, that the former head of McKinsey was convicted of committing
insider trading as a board member of Goldman Sachs, or that the second-
largest outsourcing firm in India imploded following the unveiling of a
multiyear accounting fraud, reasonable people are left to conclude that
human beings are prone to cheat, lie, and steal. But what about the human resources systems responsible for putting these flawed leaders into
positions of power? Virtually identical temptations to lie, cheat, and
steal corrupt the trading of human capital assets as well as financial assets, the long history of which goes by names and labels ranging from

nepotism to favoritism, Machiavellian manipulation, and even rampant abuse of power and authority.

One example of the common flaws and loopholes embedded in HR systems large enough to drive a truck through: If you have ever worked at a company or nonprofit organization, I can just about guarantee that your most recent appraisal consisted primarily of what is known in the field as "one-over-one approval." This phrase simply means that your annual performance appraisal is written by your boss and then your boss's boss signs off on it, often in a perfunctory process. Period. End of story. Even at organizations where a 360-degree appraisal process (written assessments of the individual from above, colleagues, and subordinates) has been instituted, few if any negative consequences befall those who fail to get positive feedback. GE, Yum! Brands, PepsiCo, P&G, IBM, DuPont, and others in this book are among a handful of companies and organizations that make participation in the 360 review process mandatory, no excuses accepted. When handled correctly, these are not mere check-the-box exercises, but thoughtfully written, carefully considered quantitative (ratings) and qualitative (written comments) assessments that provide real reasons for why the reviewer is providing the review.

To adopt the financial analogue again, Bernie Madoff's bogus hedge fund had just one outside accountant, a one-man band based in New City, New York. If there was ever a reason for a multibillion-dollar registered hedge fund to rely on a one-over-one system of financial appraisal, it was Bernie Madoff's outfit. Remarkably, the SEC didn't spot that as a red flag, and we see the multibillion-dollar losses that resulted from the agency's failure to provide adequate oversight over one of the most massive frauds in history.

Getting HR Right: The Key Building Blocks

An HR system with *integrity* forms the foundation for the selection system, the appraisal system, the reward and benefits system, and a development system all linked together. The weakest link is generally appraisal. In the absence of honest, rigorous, and impartial appraisal it is not possible to achieve the required integrity in the reward system because the basis upon which who gets more or less is not seen as fair and therefore does not serve as a motivator of performance but rather as a tool for dysfunctional political manipulation. If an appraisal system is weak or in any way compromised, the development system cannot be rooted in rigorous assessment, which makes it unclear who knows what and what any particular leader may still have to learn to advance. Last but not least, if an assessment fails to honestly measure and evaluate the future potential and developmental needs of future leaders, it can't feed proper selection in the succession planning process. In short, organizations lacking a strong and incorruptible HR infrastructure cannot build a viable succession planning process.

For the HR system to support sound succession planning, HR executives must take the lead in designing a system defined by rigorous data and checks and balances. Lacking a rigorously structured, disciplined system of checks and balances, CEO succession becomes a politicized, fragmented, disruptive mess. First and foremost, the board and the CEO need to rely on the integrity of the succession planning database to make their ultimate selection. If that database is in any way compromised, it becomes virtually impossible to make the right choices or to formulate a coherent human capital strategy, because the leaders under consideration haven't been developed according to a coherent and objective plan. Just as would be the case with a fraudulent scientific experiment—and as we know, science is rife with fraudulent experiments, the acid test of which is whether or not they can be readily replicated by peers—if the experimenter has falsified the data, the experiment fails before it has even begun. In the case of HR systems, a failure to keep the processes honest and objective puts the health of the entire organization at risk. Data is a treasure that only HR possesses. If that data is degraded, as is the case in computer science, the result is GIGO: Garbage In, Garbage Out.

Making HR Strategic in Three Not-So-Easy Steps

Step 1: HR helps business leaders prepare the data for review, just as finance does the same on the business side.

Step 2: HR presides over a rigorous review process reflected in open, honest dialogue. The dialogue is marked by a full and nuanced appreciation of the often subtle interplay between technical, political, and cultural elements, with the most important component being the political checks and balances that maintain the system's integrity.

Step 3: Continual review and follow-up.

As is the case with so many statements about people and systems, the steps above may be easy to lay out, but are never easy to put into practice. The most rigorous HR political check-and-balance system I ever encountered was initiated at GE by Alan F. Lafley, where a small HR team in the 1960s created a system that scrupulously separated the organization and staffing (O&S) function from overall human resources. Lafley's group reported directly to the CEO, not through the HR head. Just as audit staffs are kept separate from finance staffs to maintain a check and balance on each other's operations, Alan Lafley kept O&S's role in the HR arena similar to how an audit staff would perform in the financial domain. When succession planning was conducted at GE during the Welch period, and continued in the Immelt era, it happened in all-day meetings led by the CEO and the head of O&S at the business location. As many as twenty full days a year are spent on this by the CEO personally. The roles are very clear, with the CEO of a business at GE along with his/her CHRO for the business presenting their succession planning material to the CEO (Welch or today Immelt) and the corporate HR head in a very open, interactive, candid dialogue.

The results of these all-day meetings impact thousands of careers at GE, including who is promotable, who needs to be removed from the company, and who is a candidate for various other jobs across GE. These succession plans are reviewed by the CEO two other times during the year. One is a video conference follow-up in July with each business CEO and the CEO of GE with the HR leaders involved to check on progress with the career plans discussed in the springtime meetings. The second review is a check on action plans at the annual budget meeting in October where the CEOs of the businesses are asked for an update on their succession plans. The point is, it is not a one-time superficial "check the boxes," or as some companies cynically refer to it, the annual "bios and pictures" meeting with the CEO, often taking only an hour or two to look at succession books with as many as two hundred names, bios, and plans that are superficially examined and hardly discussed.

The Accomplishment Analysis

HR departments that are truly effective and strategic often compile thorough, qualitative portraits of present and high-potential future leaders based on an extensive series of in-depth interviews, known as "accomplishment analyses." These were launched at GE in the 1960s to essentially get better data about key leaders, including their performance history as well as future potential for promotions. These typically start out with the leader under consideration for promotion and advancement discussing and reviewing his or her past accomplishments and aspirations with a series of interviewers initially charged with gathering the subject's own view of their strengths and weaknesses, self-perceived future potential, and what they need to do to become better leaders, which will then be compared with how others who've worked with them see them. The HR auditors then interview former managers, customers, and/or suppliers, superiors, subordinates, and peers, all of which are compiled into an exhaustive assessment often conducted by a certified outside consultant in the field or a certified HR executive from a different business inside the organization. That way, these comprehensive performance reviews and audits remain safely outside that leader's immediate chain of command, a critical check and balance comparable to one that might be implemented in the process of conducting a financial audit of a leader or business unit. Accomplishment analyses serve a valuable function by providing an impartial narrative, which often reads like a novel or a biography, but in truth represents a composite multidimensional review and portrait based not just on one unreliable narrator—the subject himself or herself—but on input and feedback from dozens of other people on the same subject.

Because these reviewers must always be held to the highest standards of moral, ethical, and professional conduct and knowledge, they typically undergo a rigorous process of certification and training conducted by external consultants. Inside some high-capacity, high-resource organizations, a sufficient number of certified HR audit professionals are on hand to train and certify one another and develop their own certification system internally. The industry leader in this field of external consulting, Brad Smart, has developed an elaborate system and methodology based on the GE process that was started years ago by Alan Lafley.

Precisely because no silver bullet or iron-clad guarantee has ever been found in the arena of leadership development, and because the margin of error in assessing human potential is by definition so dramatically wide, the vital importance of creating *a mutually reinforcing collage of overlapping and redundant evaluation, assessment, and development systems* cannot be overstated. At GE, where this discipline frequently rises to the level of an obsession, leaders at all levels grow accustomed to submitting to these rigorous, overlapping, and deliberately redundant evaluation and assessment processes, matrices, benchmarks, yardsticks, and models, and in some cases even grow to like them. They appreciate their value and power as motivators and developers of leadership skills and capacities. In managing their own development, good leaders learn that these systems are often helpful in upping their game and driving their performance to the next level. Not surpris-

ingly, leaders who succeed in being recognized, rewarded, and promoted under such systems tend to regard them as fundamentally fair,
objective, and valuable measures of potential and performance.

This is strategic HR at its best. When they work—and I am the first
to admit they work only rarely—such systems can be truly effective at
producing a culture of leadership that raises the bar for the organization as a whole and sustains it from generation to generation. Jack
Welch was, for lack of a better word, the acknowledged genius at using
these systems to motivate his people to perform to their fullest potential. He would never have dreamed of delivering a bonus to a senior
executive without providing a careful and personal assessment providing the objective rationale for the size of that bonus, but always with his
characteristically rigorous but personal touch. Whatever the size of the
check, it would invariably be accompanied by a handwritten note, under his letterhead, summarizing the accomplishment or performance
analysis on which the bonus had been calculated.

"John," he would write, "you're getting this bonus of __ because you
did X, Y, and Z well and also because here are three things—W, N, and
Q—which in our view you're not doing so well, and we want you to look
carefully at those areas next year."

As you can imagine, receiving a note like that from the CEO can be
a powerful motivator of future performance, starting that very day, going forward.

Structural Development Drivers

At GE, the top leaders had close to two hundred true profit-and-loss
businesses, some of which were tiny, but still functioned as independent
businesses, to draw on strictly for development purposes. At AlliedSignal and Honeywell under Welch protégé Lawrence Bossidy, the CEO
admitted to being willing to consciously exchange efficiency and economies of scale for investing in the long-term development of senior lead-

ers by giving them "farm league" P&Ls to manage and lead as preparation for potential graduation to the major leagues: running the whole enterprise. The leaders of those businesses would have to play what both Bossidy and Welch often referred to as "the complete game." That meant that they had to put budgets together. They were directly in charge of hiring, firing, promoting, and demoting or exchanging and, even more important, developing the top people in their P&L. And they had to take responsibility for that P&L's contribution, or lack of one, to the bottom line. The only thing they didn't have to do that a CEO would was to manage Wall Street or manage the board. In every other respect, these were true CEOs in everything other than name. Executives who, by contrast, rise up through a stovepipe or silo like marketing before being promoted to CEO would lack the key preparation of these "crucible experiences," making the hard trade-offs and the tough people, crisis, and strategy judgments that CEOs make every day, as a matter of course.

Crafting Crucible or Stretch Assignments

HR must be the CEO's partner on this most critical of developmental challenges. There's a business side to this equation, but there's also a people piece. I've got to hire people, I've got to design the organizational structure, I've got to make the railroad operate. It's not the finance leader, it's the HR leader. That's a key part of the succession planning discussion, in the later stages of the game. What cycle is the business in? If Mary Barra has just been named CEO of General Motors and she's come to the job at a point when the pipeline is about to produce a highly desirable new line of cars, that will redound to her benefit. Unfortunately for Barra, she inherited a huge recall crisis instead. But a smart CEO leading a succession and developmental process must ask, did that leader get lucky and her parachute landed at the right time at the right place, right behind enemy lines so she could take out the target? Or was she blown around by the wind and ended up getting tangled in the power wires? Jack Welch consciously slowed down the pace of movement at GE because if the assignment wasn't long enough to last through an entire business cycle, the performance evaluation wasn't nearly as valid. He would ask how well people did with a tailwind and how well with a headwind. Alan Mulally did something similar at Ford. He made sure that Mark Fields, his current heir apparent, stayed for eight years in one job. HR worked closely with Mulally on this succession plan. HR is in the board meetings, right there with the CEO; they're the only leaders who can have the candid and confidential conversations about people with either player behind closed doors.

In the last phases of the CEO succession horse race, HR is critical to creating a structure that gives the finalists a big chunk of the business, ideally an independent P&L if you've got one. Then the process is set up to let each of the finalists duke it out and let the best man or woman win—except that you need to make sure that in the course of competing, they don't do anything to undercut or undermine one another, or undercut or undermine the business to get ahead. The HR person is responsible for 1. crafting the structure to make that horse race fair and honest, and 2. evaluating and measuring the performance of each leader so that it's a little more nuanced than just a totting up of their respective bottom lines.

To recap: as head of HR, you've got a selection of levers to pull on. You've got individual leadership assessment (critical), and you've got the lever of structure. Less well known, structural change in the service of development is one of the most powerful levers. Larry Bossidy played this particular lever like violinist Jascha Heifetz. He literally and deliberately broke down the company into smaller units as a succession planning lever.

Getting It Wrong at Pfizer: The Arrogant and Disengaged CEO

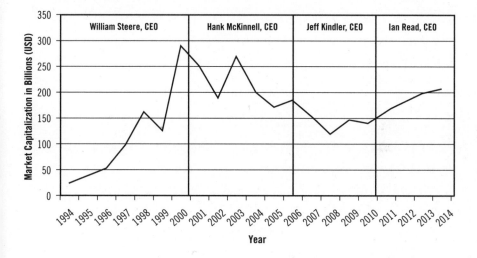

In 2004, I began an engagement with the Global Research & Development division at pharmaceutical giant Pfizer, under the leadership of Dr. Peter Corr, on an ongoing flow of leadership development projects. These included a series of intensive coaching sessions one-on-one with the senior leader, Dr. Corr, followed by a series of two-day off-site workshops where we framed and facilitated a selection of real-life, real-risk, real-reward action learning projects, several of which ended up being successfully implemented by the department and became drivers of innovation during a period when innovation was in desperately short supply, not just at Pfizer but throughout the world of Big Pharma.

Corr is a cardiologist and former professor of medicine at Washington University in St. Louis who had been lured away from the ivory tower in 1994 to become head of R&D at Searle, a middle-tier drug company headquartered in St. Louis, from which he moved up in the world four years later to head up R&D at Warner-Lambert. At the time, being head of R&D at Warner-Lambert was a very big deal, because although it was not anywhere near the largest drug company on earth, its labs had had greater

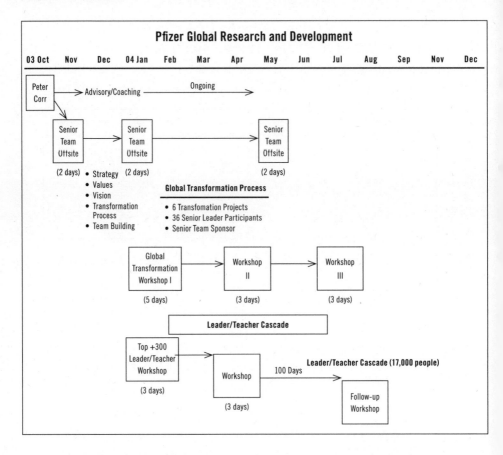

success in developing blockbusters than anyone else in the industry. Viagra and Lipitor, the two biggest blockbusters of the mid-nineties, were both developed at a famous facility in Ann Arbor, Michigan (my hometown), which Dr. Corr just happened to run. The $100 billion Pfizer paid for Warner-Lambert in 2002—the largest pharmaceutical merger ever at that time—was almost entirely driven by Pfizer's insatiable desire to get its hands on the rights to Viagra and Lipitor, both of which it was already distributing, because while it was not the most innovative drug company, its marketing prowess was peerless.

Since the crown jewel of Warner-Lambert was its R&D group, it wasn't surprising that Corr was the only senior Warner-Lambert executive asked to stay on at Pfizer following the merger, nor that he was kept on to succeed Pfizer's longtime R&D chief, Dr. John Niblack, who retired in 2002 after thirty-five years with the company. On his first day on his new job, Corr breezily assured *The New York Times* that from his point of view, "the opportunities have never been greater" to take R&D to a new level at Pfizer. With Wall Street analysts demanding to know what was coming down the pipeline next, the pressure was on not just for Corr but for Pfizer's cerebral, Canadian-born CEO, Henry "Hank" McKinnell, to assure Wall Street and investors that they had a few tricks up their sleeve, and promising drugs in the pipeline, on the R&D development front. All this is to say that when my team and I began working closely with Corr on leadership development for the worldwide R&D organization it was the same mission with which we *always* take on new projects: we would be developing leaders who would in turn develop new ideas and products.

But McKinnell was already signaling to Wall Street that he couldn't wait to see what Corr's division came up with but was intent on hedging his bets by proposing to pay $65 billion for rival drug house Pharmacia, the industry's seventh-largest player, to buy quick and easy access to *its* pipeline of potential blockbusters. While that deal was approved by shareholders and federal regulators, by the time my team and I began consulting with Corr, it was being roundly panned by Wall Street analysts and the market as a case of wildly overpaying for an outfit unlikely to produce the cornucopia of new products McKinnell had unwisely promised Wall Street. Hence, as we began working with Corr, pressure was mounting on him and McKinnell to justify the huge budget R&D had at the company, as well as to instill confidence in the investment community that those billions being spent on internal R&D weren't just a sideshow to the drugs being brought in by M&A. The combined R&D division of the two companies spanned three continents, employed more than 12,000 scientists worldwide, and was overseeing the late-stage development of 160 experimental drugs while conducting research on 300 more in 19 therapeutic areas. The operation's combined budget, initially $7 billion, was quickly cut down to $5 billion. All the same, from the point of view of Wall Street, that was still a huge bet on an outfit that had yet to hit anything close to a home run.

That's the pressure-cooker context under which Dr. Corr invited me and my team to work with him and his team, to see if they could prove the doubters on Wall Street wrong and justify that $5 billion being spent by the shareholders on his group. Fortunately for us, Dr. Corr was so pleased with the results of our work with him that he suggested to CEO Hank McKinnell that the action learning process we had used to help him unify and reinvigorate the innovation culture of the R&D team might be successfully replicated across the company.

I soon found myself meeting with McKinnell at his office in New York, pitching him on what leadership development and action learning could do for his company, its stock price, and therefore for him, provided he truly went with the program. McKinnell was famous for having no patience for protracted meetings—"What's next?" was his trademark line[3]—so I shouldn't have been surprised when he didn't listen to even half of what I had to say and midway through my introductory presentation simply shut me down with a peremptory wave of his hand.

"Oh," he said dismissively, "*action learning*—I know what you're talking about. We're taking care of all that with a six-week program at Harvard Business School."

With all due respect to HBS, I countered with the $64 billion question.

"What's your role in the process?"

When he had the time, he said proudly, he typically presided over a half-day wrap-up session, at which the lessons learned were all neatly tied up with a bow. I was pretty familiar with this drill. As I had been quoted in *Fortune* a few years before, if you want to determine how serious a company is about leadership development, all you need to do is take a good look at the CEO's calendar. At GE Jeff Immelt spends days every month at the Crotonville leadership center, while at Intel the CEO and top team are involved for days in the leadership program's beginning, middle, and end—as is the case with Lafley at P&G and McNerney at Boeing, to name a few examples of how to do it right. I left

McKinnell's office shaking my head and possibly for good measure muttering under my breath.

The gist of my reaction was that *Hank didn't get it*. More to the point, he didn't get that HR and leadership development could be strategic, and might even provide him with, if he were patient, a partial solution to his dire dilemma. Not long after we met, *Fortune* reported:

> In July 2002 [McKinnell] announced the acquisition of Pharmacia, the industry's seventh-largest company, for $60 billion in stock. But even as Pfizer struggled to digest this latest meal, McKinnell seemed to spend less and less time at headquarters, becoming head of industry trade groups, funding an institute in Africa to combat AIDS, even writing a book about reforming health care.[4]

I left McKinnell's office disgusted but not surprised. He was, after all, just another representative of an all-too-common type: *the disengaged and arrogant CEO,* who wasn't just having problems with strategy, but problems with connecting the people piece to the strategic challenges facing the company. From my point of view, cerebral he might have been, but also totally clueless. Not only were we speaking in two different languages, he hadn't the slightest idea that the main reason he was losing the battle on the strategic front, on the innovation front, and by then on the crisis front, was that *there was a direct correlation between the weakness of his leadership pipeline and the weakness of his drug pipeline.* Aware that he was up the creek without a paddle, he gradually and irresponsibly withdrew from the scene.

That left a classic power vacuum that his predecessor, William Campbell Steere, who had led the company through its glory years, kept a seat on the board, and remained a power behind the throne, began quietly maneuvering behind the scenes to take advantage of. Steere persuaded the board to get rid of McKinnell. McKinnell left with a golden parachute worth $83 million in spite of the fact that the stock declined by about 40 percent on his watch. At the annual meeting where he said his crocodile-tear goodbyes, one irate shareholder actually buzzed the building in a small plane towing a sign that said simply, "Give It Back, Hank." Needless to say, the clueless and arrogant leader didn't listen to the shareholders' anger and outrage at their losses and his gains any more than he had listened to me.

What the Arrogant, Disengaged CEO *Never* Gets: The Growing Power of the People

In 1995, roughly a decade before McKinnell and I met and McKinnell shortly thereafter lost his job, the well-known Viennese-born business and leadership analyst Peter Drucker wrote, "All organizations say routinely 'People are our greatest asset.' Yet few practice what they preach, let alone truly believe it." Four years later, he elaborated on that key insight when he wrote the oft-quoted lines, "The most valuable assets of a 20th-century company were its production equipment. [But] the most valuable asset of a 21st-century institution, whether business or non-business, will be its knowledge workers and their productivity."

If you take a closer look at both quotes, I would argue that while Hank McKinnell and others like him might have mouthed platitudes about the importance of people—he knew enough to recognize the value of talent like Peter Corr—he didn't live it, breathe it, or truly believe it. The same holds true for the second Drucker quote. Nothing that McKinnell said to me, or didn't say to me, during our brief meeting dissuaded me from the view that he didn't get it.

So what did McKinnell—and so many others like him—not get?

––––––––––––

As McKinnell began to fade into the woodwork, his predecessor stealthily sprang into action, following a pattern we have seen and will see on multiple occasions throughout this book. While McKinnell's vaunted Harvard-branded leadership development program failed to produce any serious candidates to succeed him, the board was given a second bum Steere in the form of in-house counsel Jeffrey Kindler, who had joined the company only four years before but had spent much of that time courting Steere's favor, a political calculus that in the short term paid off, in that it pushed him ahead of any number of far more experienced and better qualified candidates to become CEO.

Kindler had spent a stint at GE under my old friend and longtime chief counsel Ben Heineman, so I regarded his appointment, at first, as potentially good news for me. But then I found my attempts to speak to Kindler blocked at every turn by a newly installed CRHO and sidekick, one Mary McLeod. She was feared and disliked by many at Pfizer for her role in the company's layoffs. While that was going on, she was viewed in the organization as entirely out of touch with the people, as reflected by the brutal layoffs of ten thousand people from the Pfizer payroll and her abuse of corporate resources, like the company helicopter to ferry her to and from her home in Maryland.

An accurate moniker for Mary McLeod would have been "Typhoid Mary," after the infamous Mary Mallon, an immigrant from Ireland who worked as a cook in the New York area between 1900 and 1907 and who knowingly carried the often fatal germs of typhoid fever from house to house for years until she had to be forcibly hospitalized and then released, only to repeat the process yet again. Unbeknownst to Kindler when he hired her, she had already taken down one CEO in the recent past, and was apparently gunning for another. In 2004, three years before joining Pfizer, she had been fired as VP of human resources at discount brokerage Charles Schwab by CEO David Pottruck, who in the dismissal letter he wrote to her cited "perceptions others have of you around character, integrity and divisiveness . . . There is a perception that you do not tell the truth."[5] Nine days after he fired McLeod, Pottruck was himself out the door, prompted by a board that openly admitted that his convoluted relationship with McLeod had undermined their confidence in his character.

My only interaction with McLeod—to my regret at the time but vast relief later—was her point-blank refusal to let me past her bureaucratic barricade to see the CEO she openly boasted to colleagues she had "under her thumb." After she wrote a very peculiar letter to some colleagues who, not surprisingly, had given her the thumbs-down on her 360 review, the board received an anonymous letter stating that McLeod had "very little interest in the HR function itself, offers little guidance and focuses mainly on the CEO and his needs." Kindler was forced to fire McLeod, but just a few days later he was fired himself. The chief takeaways from the McLeod story can be summed up as follows:

- HR can divide (rather than unite) the people in an organization in ways that no other function can.
- HR is capable of setting a toxic tone that alienates people within the business and the performance of the business in ways that no other function can.

As the *conscience* and *soul* of the organization, HR professionals can't permit this happen.

Getting HR Right: Strategic Human Resources at IBM

Models of Human Resources		
NEGATIVE: Destroys Human Capital	**NEUTRAL: Old-Style Bureaucracy**	**POSITIVE: Trusted Strategic Partner**
■ Machiavellian ■ Low trust ■ Kisses up and kicks downward	■ Form, not substance ■ Reactive, not proactive ■ Knows mechanics of HR	■ A true business partner ■ Confidant of CEO and board on leadership issues ■ Builds a leadership pipeline for CEO succession

In October 2011, the century-old computer hardware, software, and consulting company IBM named the fifty-four-year-old Virginia "Ginni" Rometty as its first female CEO. As of January 1, 2012, she would succeed Sam Palmisano, who at sixty was reaching the customary age for IBM CEOs to retire, on which date he would have served as the company's longest-tenured CEO who didn't carry the founding family's name, Watson. Palmisano's predecessor, Louis V. Gerstner, formerly of American Express, RJR Nabisco, and the private equity firm Kohlberg Kravis Roberts, had served as the poster boy in the early nineties for a profoundly transformative outsider CEO selection. His recruitment in 1992 had certainly been a coup for IBM's board, and his stunning turnaround at IBM would go down in history as one of the twentieth century's more remarkable success stories. However, Gerstner himself counted as his greatest single achievement, as he wrote in his 2002 memoir *Who Says Elephants Can't Dance?*, "If you ask me today what single accomplishment I am most proud of in all my years at IBM, I would tell you it is this—that as I retire, my successor is a longtime IBMer, and so are the heads of all of our major business units."

Gerstner's successor, Sam Palmisano, was just as dedicated as Gerstner was to not just restoring but sustaining the legendary leadership pipeline that had so famously broken down under Gerstner's unfortunate predecessor, IBM lifer John Akers, on whose watch the company nearly cratered and was on the verge of being broken up and the pieces sold off for pocket change to hungry competitors when white knight Gerstner stepped in. As Gerstner had done with him, Palmisano had personally provided Rometty—alongside an entire slate of potential successors—with a steady series of high-risk, high-profile stretch assignments carefully calculated to teach her a medley of tough lessons on the job. Most notable among these was the complex integration of the consulting arm of the big accounting firm PricewaterhouseCoopers into the Big Blue fold, which required her to align people, strategy, and cultural elements to fuse the two entities into a unified whole, a challenge that she rose to with such distinction that it just about sealed her fate as Palmisano's successor. While this was, according to Rometty, "the first and only time a professional services firm of that size has ever been integrated into another large company,"[6] she was also provided along the way with a long list of less momentous yet equally constructive leadership opportunities, many if not all of which were carefully framed by the company's long-serving CHRO Randy MacDonald.

As MacDonald recalled in a recent interview with me, the first time he sat down with Lou Gerstner in May 2000, shortly after his recruitment from GTE—where Verizon CHRO and close confidant of CEO Seidenberg Marc Reed had also earned his stripes—"the topic at the top of his mind was not so much his own succession as all the other lesser successions that would need to occur as a result of his succession." Specifically, Gerstner was thinking out loud about reshaping the company's top team before he stepped down so that his successor wouldn't have to take on the task, and asking for MacDonald's input on the ongoing role of "certain players who were tried and true IBMers, who had been helpful in driving change but going forward may not have been compatible with some of the cultural transformation that still needed to be done." Right off the bat, MacDonald was impressed by the fact that Gerstner clearly considered it "his obligation to make sure that all of the players who remained would be capable of driving the transformation for his successor."[7]

He also understood from experience that he was being charged by the CEO with helping him to align two of the most critical forces playing out in the succession process—the political and the cultural—by evaluating certain key leaders in terms of their commitment and capacity to drive deep cultural change. One of the main reasons that Gerstner and MacDonald's predecessor Tom Bouchard had been so eager to recruit an outsider to succeed Bouchard (who had himself come in at Gerstner's behest from Baby Bell US West) was that certain aspects of the IBM culture that required radical revision would take an outsider's perspective to correct. Gerstner's number-one priority for MacDonald to tackle was a pervasive "culture of entitlement" that had arisen over many decades and that over time had become enshrined in a static set of "Basic Beliefs." While the Basic Beliefs had originally been conceived and then set in stone by the modern IBM's charismatic and paternalistic founder, Thomas Watson Sr., by the time the company nearly collapsed during the Akers era, one of those beliefs, "Respect for the Individual," had devolved over the years into what Gerstner described as a sense "that an IBMer could do pretty much anything he or she wanted to do, with little or no accountability." Terminating an individual for poor performance, or for that matter any reason whatsoever, was tantamount to "not respecting him or her as an individual."

So—here's the question. Was the number-one HR task that Gerstner gave MacDonald strategic or not? I would say yes, especially in the IBM context, because as Gerstner also recalled in his book, at IBM "culture isn't just one aspect of the game—it *is* the game." Gerstner was not only giving MacDonald a seat at the table, he was in effect charging him and his team with being the primary guardian of IBM's ever-evolving corporate culture. And that culture was being entrusted by Gerstner to MacDonald because he, like his predecessor before him, earned that place at the table by being able to understand the business, as opposed to merely the human capital dimension.

MacDonald's primary task as a strategic HR director was to identify and develop the people, the future leaders, best equipped to drive the cultural transformation. As MacDonald put it to me, he needed to "get rid of the entitlement mentality while preserving the core values, something we stood for." Since the key cultural and political task on Gerstner's plate was to turn the company from a collection of warring fiefdoms into an integrated unit, for MacDonald the essential question he needed to ask and answer about every leader he was evaluating was oriented toward business integration: "Were these people focused more on their own business or were they focused more on the ability to manage the whole enterprise?"

But MacDonald had earned—and kept—his seat at the table as confidential adviser to the CEO because he was smart enough and tough enough to seize the opportunity presented to him by the undeniable fact that the CHRO at any organization is the one and only person with whom the CEO can have a candid discussion about people behind closed doors—the corporate equivalent of a priest in a confessional. One of MacDonald's own Basic Beliefs was that "HR leaders need to have the courage of their convictions."

But he also believed—Basic Belief #2—that those convictions need to be realistically rooted in a professional strategy that rigorously divided "core and noncore" activities. To MacDonald, all "noncore" activities fit into the strictly technical realm. In his view, this is where the aspiring transformational CHRO must willfully depart from the negative stereotype of the paper-pushing, box-checking, technically obsessed CHRO. "Administrative responsibilities, such as getting paychecks out on time, are not core," MacDonald once said. "But attracting, retaining, and motivating employees are all core. In HR, we need to focus on what is important and get out in front of issues—not just be reactive. HR should be able to look at the direction of the company and say, 'We need to be here right along with the business.'"[8]

Only when the business leaders understand that the CHRO is in command of the business strategy and comprehends its opportunities and challenges can the CHRO "play a linchpin role in building a performance culture: defining, collecting and analyzing data to understand whether employees are meeting their personal goals. This is about using the technology of 'business analytics' within the workforce, bringing vital statistics to the art of performance reviews. The core of a performance-based culture is more use of analytics. We needed to start in HR by becoming more analytical, using data, defining cause-and-effect relationships, and tying HR activities to business results."[9]

In other words, just as the CFO at any company typically enjoys unfettered access to the top leadership because he or she knows whether the company is making or losing money and what it's making or losing money on, the CHRO needs to employ the database on people—what MacDonald refers to as "the facts on the table"— to enhance his or her own political position inside the hierarchy. If HR leaders are ever going to be taken seriously as change agents as opposed to purely administrative personnel, Randy insists, "We can't be afraid to speak up for change and for what's right or what's wrong about the culture."[10]

A top-notch CHRO must at a minimum "create a succession, assessment, and evaluation process that is grounded in rich facts and rich data, because that gets you entry through the door. You can then allow the emotion and the politics to be part of it, because you've got the data and the facts to back you up."

It's simply naïve, he insists, for anyone involved to believe that it's possible to eliminate emotion and politics from the process entirely, because that would be contrary to human nature. What's most important is to not let the political and personal elements outweigh or overrule the facts, data, and objective criteria that in the end should carry far greater weight in swaying the ultimate decision. Yet he cautions HR professionals not to take any newfound bias toward the analytics to an extreme, because "we should never permit succession to become so formalized that it becomes like producing and packaging aspirin. The pills go in the bottle, they go in the box, they put the instructions in and seal the box and then they're shipped out. That's way too mechanized and technical."

Once again, the skilled CHRO, like the skilled CEO, is able to take the three mutually reinforcing strands of the organization—technical, political, cultural—and synchronize them to achieve the core mission. Those "intangible moments of human interaction," MacDonald says, truly define and influence CEO and board thinking on building a pipeline of succession candidates. "You can think about politics in terms of personal chemistry. Often the person who gets the gig is the one with the best chemistry with his or her predecessor. It always comes down in the end to chemistry at the top. There is a politics to making decisions, so stop making it a dirty word. It's a reality."

So how did Randy MacDonald work hand in hand with Sam Palmisano to engineer the Rometty succession? He credits IBM board member, Boeing CEO, and former 3M chairman and CEO Jim McNerney with advising him to focus on just a handful of critical questions in evaluating her performance as a picker and grower of people:

1. What happened to those people she identified early as leaders?
2. Where did they end up in the organization?
3. How good are they now?
4. How do they feel about her now?
5. How many mentors and mentees did she have on the way up?

6. What do the mentors and mentees think of her now?
7. What happened to the businesses after they left?
8. What businesses did they inherit that were in trouble?
9. What businesses did they inherit that were already growing?
10. What happened to that business when they moved on?
11. What did the people that person left behind think about them?

With the search full on for Palmisano's successor, MacDonald's primary contribution to the process was to "gather as much empirical data as we could on all of the candidates' objective performance. This was very different from the prior period under Gerstner, when we picked Sam. That was more the result of a series of assessments based on qualitative as opposed to quantitative evaluations."

As for the candidates themselves, Randy MacDonald has a few words of advice that he's shared with a number of serious contenders and candidates over the years, including Sam Palmisano and Ginni Rometty: "Perform, don't run." At IBM, he recalls, "if we saw someone running for office we would tell that person to just cut it out. What you've got to focus on," he would advise, "is to create performance that will be recognized. Once people think you can do the job strategically, operationally, and on the leadership front, you'll be tested in all sorts of ways on the cultural and political aspects. If you start running before you've accomplished all that, don't do it because you'll get shot."

On the occasion of his retirement from IBM in 2013, MacDonald had this to say on the subject of making HR a strategic discipline: "In my 42-year career I've witnessed our profession's evolution from an administrative function to one viewed globally as a critical part of the success of the enterprise today. To be part of that evolution, to affect it in some way, has been a great privilege for me personally."[11]

As he later told me, along much the same lines:

I think it's a fundamental, systemic problem of HR in general that most CEOs don't have a lot of respect for HR people. So what they do is they try to put somebody in who can talk the lingo under the guise of "I need somebody who understands the business." Well, what does that mean? Does that mean that HR people are fundamentally stupid and are therefore incapable of understanding the business? Or is it that HR people choose not to learn the business? I think it's the latter.

In a postretirement interview in *Human Resources Executive*, Mac-Donald—whom I've known a long time, since his early days at Ingersoll-Rand—used one of my favorite business metaphors: winning gold, silver, or bronze medals at the Olympics. "If you asked me a decade ago if HR was a competitor in Olympic events, I would respond that the profession never won a medal. Today, I think, more and more, we make it to the platform. I know we haven't won the gold yet; I'd like to think perhaps the silver, certainly the bronze. Winning medals is important, but the ultimate is the gold—and I don't think we're quite there yet."

Partnership Model as HR Model

There's an interesting exception to the 80 or 90 percent of companies that do not do succession planning well. Top-drawer big-league consulting, law, and accounting firms generally take care of this people piece scrupulously because so many still operate on a partnership model. That means that the elevation of any associate to a partnership role can have serious implications for all the others splitting the partnership pie. They are anointed at that point and generally have the equivalent of "lifetime employment." At consulting firms, for every engagement before you make partner, for eight or nine years of your career, HR departments will typically put together a written assessment of how the consultant did on, for example, the IBM engagement, or in the case of a law firm associate, how you did on the Unilever case. Another performance-based succession process occurs at major research universities. They do it well for faculty before they make tenure—typically only one in ten gets tenure at Yale, Harvard, Stanford, or any first-tier research university. The tenure process is an external review by peers in the field on quality of research contributions, often ranking faculty contributions against peers at other universities. In such places, once you put people into partnerships or tenured faculty positions, it is very difficult to get rid of them.

In all high-performance cultures all performers, such as athletes or musicians or trial attorneys, are accustomed to being frequently evaluated. This deliberately keeps barriers to entry high by instituting a rigorous assessment process. If you make tenure at a top-notch university, you will likely stay there until you retire. High-performance institutions can't afford to make too many mistakes in this department or the entire institution suffers. Unfortunately, many publicly traded companies can't claim the same. A shining example of deploying a strategic HR platform that combines action learning with leadership succession is the global consulting firm Accenture, one of the most successful and high-performing consulting organizations on earth.

Getting It Right at Accenture

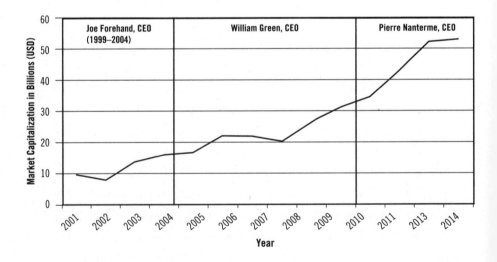

During the millennial summer of 2000, Andersen Consulting officially broke free from accounting giant Arthur Andersen following a rancorous secession that legally separated the world's largest management and technology consulting group with more than $10 billion in annual revenues[12] from its roots in the slower-growth discipline of accounting. This declaration of independence resulted not only in a name change from Andersen Consulting to Accenture (short for "accent on the future") but also in a conversion from a private partnership to a publicly traded company, both of which exercises proved their value in the wake of the 2002 implosion of Arthur Andersen following its corporate conviction on federal charges of obstruction of justice as the result of two partners' ill-fated decision to shred a cache of documents related to the 2001 $100 billion Enron accounting scandal.

Under the leadership of Accenture's first CEO, the Alabama-born twenty-eight-year firm veteran Joe Forehand, the new firm set out to serve its global client base of more than 4,000 companies with 75,000 employees scattered across 110 offices in 46 countries, a set of numbers that has since grown to more than 275,000 employees serving clients in 120 countries and generating nearly $30 billion in revenues.

Right from the outset, Forehand's number-one leadership priority was building up the firm's leadership development program. One of his first appointments was of a chief leadership officer to conceive of and implement a human capital strategy for the firm. He based that critical decision on the thesis that it should be one person's sole responsibility "to manage leadership development and succession planning on a broader basis, so more people [would be] ready to take on more responsibility."[13] This emphasis on developing a coherent human capital strategy was not just a personal value, but a mandate born from decades of experience spent interacting with clients. Every encounter, however minimal, between consultant and client required a combination of leadership skill and business acumen that only the finest leadership development program in the world, he was convinced, could successfully impart to every partner and employee. Forehand summed up his point of view by stating:

I believe that the primary responsibility of a leader today is to become a teacher of future leaders. I've been working with our leadership team to challenge every assumption we've ever made about what it will take to build the workforce and management we'll need over the next decade. We've just created a Chief Leadership Officer who reports directly to me, whose responsibility is management development and succession planning on a broader basis so more people are ready to take on more responsibility.

I first encountered the Accenture model consulting with Mary Tolan, the firm's first global head of leadership development. Our original assignment involved helping Accenture to transform its leadership model from one based on informal apprenticeship and one-on-one mentoring between senior and junior partners to a more strategic approach that placed greater emphasis on positioning its consultants as trusted strategic partners to their clients. The focus of the program shifted from implementation to innovation. Ideas were to come first, implementation and execution second. This revised approach also stressed collaboration and teamwork over the previously dominant star system.

That engagement introduced action learning to the firm. For high-potential managers, we designed a program that framed projects for five teams of five people to work on over a six-month period. These were, as they always are, real-life challenges ranging from evaluating potential acquisition targets to value creation for midsize clients and investment ideas for major clients. The key was for senior leaders to teach and coach junior and high-potential leaders.

That emphasis on leaders creating leaders in a continuous cascade continues under Accenture's current head of global leadership development, Camille Mirshokrai. Her own leadership journey began when her family was driven out of Iran by the 1979 fundamentalist revolution, leaving twelve-year-old Camille, her sister, and her mother to follow her father, who had escaped a few months before over the mountains into Afghanistan. From there they were slowly able to make their way to a new family home in Dallas. With little to go on but shaky English and deep reserves of drive and grit, Camille did surprisingly well at her local high school before earning bachelor's and master's degrees at Texas A&M, followed by an MBA in information technology and HR.

In her Accenture role, Mirshokrai believes that leadership development has "become part of the fabric of Accenture, part of our culture and part of my own legacy. I'm very excited about building the leaders of tomorrow [and] about our diversity of leadership. That diversity is holistic—in terms of geography, gender, and experience."[14] She described her primary assignment as "predicting what the human capital or talent needs of Accenture will be in the future and how we can best prepare our company for the changing talent markets and aligning our mix of talent to our overall business strategy."

Over the tenures of three successful CEOs in succession, Mirshokrai observed, starting with Joe Forehand through his successor Bill Green up through the current CEO Pierre Nanterme, the critical roles of leadership development, succession planning, and talent recruitment and retention have formed a core part of the corporate strategy. No proof of that linkage could be stronger or clearer than the fact that Accenture's current CEO, having served as group chief executive of the financial services division, was asked to take on the dual role of chief leadership development officer in combination with "the planning and executing on Accenture's successful long-term business strategy and the implementation of its global operating model." Marrying these two functions provides a concrete basis for achieving a truly strategic role for human resources in a high-performance firm.

The chief leadership development officer at Accenture is always a senior leader at the company who has run a massive P&L. That way, as Mirshokrai put it to me, "they understand the guts of how Accenture operates but they're also responsible for developing the talent that delivers the business to clients."

The Global Leadership Development team works closely with Accenture's board "to provide the directors with a high-level understanding of the number and quality of the successors we have in the pipeline. We'll take some people's profiles and spotlight them at board meetings. You can imagine how impactful that is on both the board members and the candidates, because we invite all of our board members to participate in leadership development activities and action learning programs."

All of which underscores one of the firm's core values: *stewardship*. "A key part of stewardship," Mirshokrai explains, "requires the leaders of today to help to teach the next generation, so that we can leave Accenture at the end of our time here stronger than we found it."

Charlie Tharp on Strategic HR

Charlie Tharp, executive vice president of the HR Policy Association and co-CEO of its Center on Executive Compensation, has more than a quarter century of corporate experience in senior HR positions under his belt. He's held senior HR positions at GE, PepsiCo, Cigna, and Bristol-Myers Squibb, where he last served as CHRO. Charlie Tharp has long focused on the controversial and greatly misunderstood topic of CEO compensation as it relates to succession. "One of the great unanticipated consequences of screwing up the CEO succession process," he told me, "is that by failing to build up a good leadership pipeline, when you need to go outside you not only raise the risk on the leadership piece, you screw up your whole internal equity and compensation structure as well. What's really driving a good deal of the distortion on the compensation side of this equation, which is generating such public outrage, is the increasing popularity of high-profile external hires, which is in turn raising the cost of internal successors as well, because a rising tide raises all boats."

If an HR department and CHRO are truly strategic, outside hires should be unnecessary, Tharp contends. He has defined four levers that drive and define leadership development: 1. compensation, 2. who sits on what committees, 3. who gets to do what projects, and 4. changing the structure of the organization to promote leadership development. "Moses didn't come down from the mountaintop decreeing that we should organize these functions according to a set structure," he observes. "We make this stuff up as we go along, based largely on trial and error. So the key to success is to pull on all of these levers consciously, keeping the overall context of leadership and talent development at top of mind. I would argue that we have more levers to pull when it comes to leadership development than conventional wisdom would have it."

Echoing Randy MacDonald's assertion, Charlie Tharp contends that above all else, and if anything to maintain their sanity in addition to their credibility, HR professionals need to maintain "the courage of their convictions."

"Things don't tend to work out very well when HR people are too polite," he said to me before signing off. "You want people to be brutally honest, but not brutal in their evaluations of staff. If they're brutal it becomes a painful experience. But if they're brutally honest and putting it all on the table, that's how boards, CEO, and CHRO all work together, strategically, as one team."

CHAPTER 6

THE ROLE OF THE BOARD

The number-one responsibility of a board in terms of its fiduciary obligations is to choose and manage the CEO.

— **Leonard A. Schlesinger,**
Baker Foundation Professor, Harvard Business School;
former president, Babson College; former vice chairman
and COO, Limited Brands; former executive vice president
and COO, Au Bon Pain

TECHNICAL

- Develop the appropriate board structure to support succession
- Create the board processes to make succession its number-one priority

POLITICAL

- Hold CEO accountable for integrity of succession process
- Enforce the balance of power between stakeholder groups

CULTURAL

- Ensure open, honest dialogue with all stakeholders
- Constructive conflict and resolution

Getting It Wrong at Royal Dutch Shell

A few days before Christmas in 1995, I accepted a ride on a Royal Dutch Shell corporate jet from London to The Hague—the twin locations of the Anglo-Dutch energy giant's dual headquarters—from Cornelius Herkströter, chairman of Shell's CMD (Committee of Managing Directors). While I sat with the chairman, popularly known as "Cor," in the front of the plane discussing the transformation I was helping him drive across the company's more than 130 separate operating divisions worldwide, I couldn't help noticing the rear seats of the plane filling up with elegantly dressed couples in their sixties and seventies carrying overstuffed shopping bags from Harrods, Liberty, Fortnum & Mason, and other celebrated London emporia. After we took off and reached cruising altitude Cor introduced me to our fellow passengers, all of whom were members of the company's supervisory board of directors, their wives, and in some cases, their children. That was the first time I'd ever met Shell's directors, or for that matter, thought much about them. Only in retrospect, and after working closely inside the company for several years, did I grasp the extent to which this tightly knit group of older men—in those days, they were all men—exerted a powerful but subtle, semivisible influence over everything Cor and I were hoping to accomplish at the company.

Having a powerful board of directors is not a problem in and of itself. It is a universally acknowledged given in corporate governance circles that a strong, independent board of directors presents a valuable check, balance, and countervailing force against the otherwise unfettered freedom of action of strong-willed CEOs. But I also believe that the lines of political demarcation between CEO and board need to be carefully drawn so as not to hamstring, compromise, or neuter the positive actions of a CEO determined to drive radical and possibly uncomfortable change that may challenge vested interests and threaten long-standing ways of thinking and acting. This inherently complex and often conflicted relationship, with regard to all management matters and in particular the all-important one of CEO succession, is best defined by a phrase Jack Welch often evoked to describe what he regarded as a healthy interaction between opposing forces within an organization: "constructive conflict."

In Shell's case, stuffed shopping bags, holiday presents, freebie travel and perquisites aside, its supervisory board of directors (note the telling title) was not led by an independent lead or outside director but by a small coterie of retired former members and chairmen of the Committee of Managing Directors. In my view and experience, blurring the boundaries between the boardroom and C-suite more often than not spells trouble, particularly for shareholders. In Cor Herkströter's case, while he was officially chairman of the CMD, holding the title of chairman didn't make him a CEO in the most commonly understood sense of the term. He was rather "first among equals" on a committee of representatives drawn from two separate but intertwined companies, the Hague-based Royal Dutch Petroleum and the London-based British Shell Transport and Trading, which had joined forces in 1907 to compete with the rising power of John D. Rockefeller's Standard Oil. More than a century later, the surviving descendant of Standard Oil in the United States, ExxonMobil, continues to battle Royal Dutch Shell for global dominance of the energy landscape. But for decades, Shell's smaller, more tightly managed, consistently more profitable American counterpart has beaten Shell hands down with regard to shareholder value, by a factor of roughly two to one.[1]

In 2012, Exxon still enjoyed a market value roughly twice that of Shell despite the fact that the two companies pulled in roughly equivalent revenues. This marked market cap discrepancy is generally ascribed by experts and industry analysts to the fact that the two companies are managed and structured differently. "Cor Herkströter [was] not in command [of Shell] in the sense that Larry Bossidy [was] in command at AlliedSignal," observed Steve Miller, the sole American on the otherwise exclusively Anglo-Dutch five-member CMD, in 1997.[2] "It matters slightly less who is the CEO of Shell than the CEO of Exxon,"[3] yet another observer explained, a sentiment heartily endorsed by Exxon CEO

Lee Raymond when I called him before my first meeting with Cor to discuss the possibility I might do some consulting work for his global competitor.

During our conversation, Raymond didn't hold back from expressing his feelings about Shell's bizarre governance and ownership structure and what a gift it was to his company, its fiercest competitor. The upshot of our discussion was that if Cor, his team, and mine were unable to put a halt to this destructive diffusion of power at three levels—above the CMD at the board level, on the CMD at the peer level, and beneath the chairman at the divisional level—Lee Raymond ominously predicted that any changes we might be able to achieve on the cultural and strategic fronts wouldn't amount to a hill of beans in Shell's crazy world.

I kept that prophetic warning firmly in mind when I met Herkströter for the first time in person at the St. Regis hotel in New York in the early spring of 1994. It took the two of us only a few minutes to establish an agreement that I would convene an off-site workshop for his top fifty men—in those days, as with the board, all of Shell's senior executives were men—as an exploratory first step in helping him construct a platform and process to drive his transformational agenda across the enterprise. Herkströter was familiar with my work with Philip J. Carroll, CEO of Shell's U.S. subsidiary, on transforming Carroll's strictly domestic organization to meet the rising demands of a new energy era. While Carroll went on to earn high praise for reshaping Shell Oil in the United States, and for pushing a traditionally risk-averse company to take on substantial risks while reaping the rewards of developing large reservoirs of oil and natural gas in the deep waters of the Gulf of Mexico, my team and I began working with Herkströter's team in London and The Hague on setting up a series of leadership development and transformational workshops to take place throughout the year.

In May 1994, we assembled Herkströter's top fifty executives at a seventeenth-century English manor, Hartwell House in Buckinghamshire, to lay out his change agenda and get their buy-in. The decentralized nature of the company hit home for many of us present after it emerged that while most of the participants knew one another, they had never met together as one unified team. That degree of diffusion, we concluded, would have to rank number one on our list of priorities for change, because it had technical, political, and cultural ramifications so profound they would likely determine the success or failure of everything else we were hoping to accomplish with the program.

Herkströter's professional training was in economics, which put him at odds with the majority of his fellow executives, who were mainly trained petroleum engineers. He started out by framing his analysis of the company's challenges from an economic perspective. How was it, he asked, that Shell's *return* on capital typically ran not just *below* its *cost* of capital but typically trailed the 10 percent returns generated on average by Shell's competitors? Since nearly all of those in attendance were petroleum engineers, they didn't have much of a coherent response to that critical question, because they simply didn't think or speak in those terms. The implicit message underscoring Cor's opening question was that it would strongly behoove them to start thinking like businessmen who were in the game to make money, and not just to pump gas and oil at any cost. That, Cor pointed out, was the way Exxon was run, as a financial enterprise that relied on technical expertise to rack up the profits. The results, when measured in total return to shareholders, spoke for themselves.

By the end of that first meeting, a consensus emerged that much of what ailed Shell and accounted for its chronic underperformance could be attributed to an insular corporate culture, whose most negative aspects were exacerbated by an outmoded, unduly complex, cumbersome, and opaque system of governance. In practical terms, any CEO who hoped to act independently or threaten established interests would be constantly second-guessed not only by his peers on the CMD but also by his nominal superiors on the supervisory board, dominated by former peers. At the divisional level the heads of the one-hundred-plus operating companies also were free to push back and resist to an extraordinary degree because their divisions were run as separate fiefdoms with little accountability to each other or the enterprise. This siloed structure, with regional kingpins and potentates, was a structural flaw, pure and simple, not dissimilar to the fragmented situation IBM faced under John Akers, ultimately dismantled by Louis Gerstner in the early nineties, freeing up untold shareholder value. In a doomed attempt to spark a frank discussion of this issue among the group, exploration and production director Robert Sprague put a blank slide up on the overhead projector. "I don't know what to report," he said simply. "This issue is really a mess."[4]

That Shell finished up the year (1994) more than $7 billion bucks in the black, with profits up 33 percent from the previous year, didn't help our case for change much because it removed any sense of urgency it had ever possessed. Fortunately for us and the company, although not for those more directly affected, our case for change was bolstered by two traumatic events that rocked the company from its complacent position the following year. In April 1995, activists from the environmental organization Greenpeace boarded the *Brent Spar*, a nearly five-hundred-foot-tall floating offshore oil platform owned by Shell, to protest the company's carefully communicated plans to decommission it, dismantle it, and sink its parts in the North Sea. Since this plan was in full compliance with all existing U.K. and E.U. environmental laws, and had been explicitly approved by the U.K. environmental ministry, Shell officials in London and at The Hague were, to put it mildly, caught off guard by the massive storm of protests that erupted in the wake of the protest, a campaign expertly fueled and sustained by a sophisticated media campaign mounted by Greenpeace, which cleverly painted the environmental NGO as a brave David locked in combat with Shell's clumsy Goliath. More than fifty Shell gasoline stations were attacked across Europe. Several dozen sustained physical damage. Two were fire-bombed. One was hit by bullets. The depth of the popular rancor was so unexpected that it sparked a renewed bout of soul-searching within the far-flung, historically proud Shell community. Remarkably, even though it knew it had both science and economics on its side—Greenpeace later conceded that its estimates of the effluent and discharge predicted were off by a factor of fifty—the company caved. Pulling a total 180-degree about-face, Shell agreed to pick up the extraordinary cost of having the platform towed to the Norwegian coast, where it was recycled and reconstituted as a long pier.

But while that decision dispelled one firestorm of protest, it couldn't tamp down another, which broke out five months later after the military government of Nigeria announced that it had condemned African tribal activist and author Ken Saro-Wiwa and eight of his compatriots to death on a series of trumped-up murder charges. While the Nigerian government was clearly to blame for this massive miscarriage of justice, a harsh spotlight was trained on Shell's environmental, social, and cultural challenges in the long-restive Ogoni tribal region, where the bulk of the country's oil deposits were located. I was staying with my team during those days of rage at the Amstel Hotel in Amsterdam, preparing to conduct a workshop with the CMD. We were roused in the middle of the night by Shell security officers who advised us that the CMD members would be evacuating the hotel under their guidance, but we were welcome to stay on as we would make highly unlikely targets.

To Herkströter's credit, rather than letting his ambitious change agenda be derailed by this two-pronged public punch to the solar plexus, he cleverly used the public reputation pounding to strengthen the case for change inside the hidebound organization. In the end, and with our help, Shell embarked on a critical first step in an ongoing evolution to become a more responsible global corporate citizen, advancing a cutting-edge CSR (corporate social responsibility) platform that very effectively and plausibly repositioned the company as a responsible party, despite its multiple challenges on the environmental, social, and governance (ESG) fronts, challenges that it fully owned up to in a far-reaching landmark CSR report.

Yet even as we were making substantial headway on the cultural, structural, and strategic issues bogging the company down in bureaucracy and mental inertia, five years into our hoped-for internal revolution, Cor and I were in complete if somewhat disheartened agreement that the company still had a long way to go. In 1998, as he prepared for retirement to make way for fellow CMD member and hand-chosen successor Sir Mark Moody-Stuart, he resolved to take a courageous if potentially futile stab at what he regarded as the company's most intractable problem—its lack of a centralized command at the chairman of the board level. As CMD chairman, his freedom of action had been consistently compromised throughout his tenure by a consensus-driven CMD and a consensus-driven board, which readily assumed the prerogative of endlessly second-guessing and micromanaging the chairman because they were nearly all former CMD members. This top-heavy superstructure only exacerbated the issues created by the decentralized structure of the business units, which gave undue weight and power to regional chieftains and their provincial and parochial concerns at the expense of the organization as a whole.

After Moody-Stuart, former head of the core E&P (Exploration & Production) division, assumed the post of CMD chairman, Cor took an unusual step to break the chain of tradition that in his view was damaging the company's long-term prospects for reinventing itself. He refused to take the customary seat on the supervisory board to which his chairmanship of the CMD unofficially entitled him, and instead retired and stepped away from the company entirely, voluntarily relinquishing the private plane travel, the shopping trips to London, and the other perquisites to which he was by tradition entitled. While he would never have named names, I was well aware of the fact that the gray eminence on the Shell board to whom Herkströter had been constantly forced to justify his every decision was his still powerful predecessor, Lodewijk van Wachem, who had been named president of Shell in 1982, chairman of the CMD in 1985, and clung to the CMD chairmanship for seven long years before nominally retiring in 1992, when he was appointed chairman of the supervisory board and Herkströter took his place as CMD chairman. Incredibly enough, van Wachem didn't retire from the supervisory board until a full decade later, in 2002, after a fifty-year career at the company. At which point, he simply pulled up stakes and took on the chairmanship of Royal Philips Electronics, Holland's other great global company.

By the time a third, by far more serious scandal rocked the company in January 2004, Hersktröter was long gone. Sir Philip Watts, who had succeeded Sir Mark Moody-Stuart as CMD chairman, was caught inflating the stated reserves on the company's books by a factor of 25 percent, contrary to newly drafted SEC guidance. Although it took Watts until March 2005 to formally tender his resignation in the wake of dual investigations by the SEC and the United Kingdom's Financial Services Authority (FSA), the two linked pieces of evidence that sunk his boat were the fact that 1. he had been head of the Exploration & Production (E&P) division at the time the inflation was initiated, and 2. he was the acknowledged recipient of an irate e-mail from his successor as E&P chief, stating plainly that the E&P chief was "sick and tired about lying" about the reserves issues. Shell ended up taking 5 billion barrels of oil and the equivalent off its books—about 23 percent of the total—giving Sir Philip and his E&P chief the boot, paying $150 million in fines to the U.S. and British authorities over the accounting issues, and—most important—at the end of that scandal-plagued year announcing a wide-ranging structural overhaul, which finally combined its two parent companies to form Royal Dutch Shell, and belatedly installed what was described as an "American style" CEO.

Much as I hate to say "I told you so," my colleague Columbia professor Larry Selden and I had seen the scandal coming nearly a decade before. After we watched Watts make a presentation to the CMD that we knew included false data, we aired our suspicions to the members of the CMD. But they (and the board) to their enduring discredit gave Watts a gentlemanly pass on the grounds that he probably didn't *intentionally* misrepresent the data. After Watts was kicked out and sought succor in reinventing himself as an Anglican priest, those of us who had been around Shell long enough to know better diagnosed the issue as in part a character and personality flaw, but more important a structural one, which had permitted a weak personality to succeed when a more rigorous CEO selection and oversight process would have prevented a guy like Watts from gaining power.

Succession at Shell had long been a tradition-bound process, as the post of CMD chairman traditionally (but not always) alternated between British and Dutch men. CMD chairmen were nearly always former chiefs of the core E&P division, and were selected for (diffuse) command not so much for who they were or what they did but for what position in the hierarchy they occupied at various stages in their careers and how well they got along with their colleagues. While the dual ownership structure is history, and Royal Dutch Shell now has independent directors and a real CEO, it takes time for a leopard to change its spots. Even today, the company is still valued at roughly half that of ExxonMobil despite the fact that the two companies consistently pull in roughly equivalent revenues.

On January 1, 2014, the new CEO, Ben van Beurden, took over the role from Peter Voser, who had held that position since 2009. Note that the last two heads of Shell have the more traditional title and role of CEO, not the chairman of the CMD role Cor Herkströter inherited. Mr. van Beurden is setting an agenda to transform the company, saying he wants "better operational discipline." He is very blunt about the underperformance of Shell versus ExxonMobil, which is reflected in a market capitalization of Shell at $230 billion in April 2014 versus ExxonMobil at $430 billion. Both companies have similar total sales and similar operations. One, Shell, is a bloated bureaucracy—which Mr. van Beurden says he is ready to tackle.

Board Dynamics and Succession

I have put this chapter on the role of the board in CEO succession after those portraying and analyzing the roles of the other two key players—CEO and CHRO—because at the end of the day as well as the conclusion of the annual shareholders' meeting, the ultimate responsibility lies with the board. Whether it's a matter of strategic oversight or CEO succession, the board bears responsibility for making the choice. And of the many choices that a board makes, none is more critical than the hiring and firing of the CEO.

In my experience, while directors generally acknowledge—as in pay lip service to—the critical importance of succession planning to the future of the corporations they oversee, for a variety of reasons they frequently bungle or botch the job, or even worse, avoid, delay, or neglect it altogether. The reasons for this reticence aren't too hard to divine: as a rule, directors tend to be hesitant to put reluctant CEOs' feet to the fire because they may owe their seat on the board to them, or hope to remain on collegial and cordial terms with the CEO, and therefore don't feel comfortable broaching subjects that she or he might be inclined to shy away from. What this means in plain language and in real life is that too many directors are willing to tailor their outlooks to their own careers and personal relations, shareholder interests be damned.

No surprise there—the trend is well documented—but this is precisely the opposite approach from best practice, as it clearly amounts to a shirking of the most solemn responsibility any board of directors has to the company's shareholders. As the Shell story vividly illustrates, the paradox of power holds just as true for the board as it does for a CEO: when a board chair or the board as a whole becomes overly dominant in comparison with the other two players, succession struggles and incoherence frequently ensue. But the converse is also true: when a board permits itself to be overly dominated by a single individual—whether chairman, lead director, CEO, or even a persuasive search firm executive—its independence is fatally compromised, at a disservice to shareholders.

Rather than serving as a source of "constructive conflict," it becomes a source of destructive passivity. Pick your poison but keep in mind that an antidote exists: plans, processes, and above all, constructive conflict, thoughtful dialogue, sensible degrees of engagement, and maintaining an open and honest dialogue with both CEO and CHRO.

Surveys like one recently conducted by the Center for Board Leadership (National Association of Company Directors) which reveal that only about half of public and private corporate boards have CEO succession plans in place understate the real problem, in my view, by conveying the notion that just having a plan—or a name in an envelope—is enough to call it a day. Even boards that do plan and claim to have put a process in place are too often caught up in a popular delusion that if and when a leader unexpectedly steps down, having that name in the envelope is enough to let the directors off the hook.

Whether a board fails the beer truck test, or faces a "deterioration in confidence" in the CEO, a far better and braver course is for boards to adhere to a rigorous process rooted in a partnership with the other two key stakeholders, which inevitably requires long-term engagement in development and reviews of internal candidates. Getting these plans and processes down right helps minimize the risks and maximize the rewards of making the most important decision any board can and ever will make. While this is a decision that is inherently collaborative and consensus-driven, it's critical for board members to exercise their independent judgments and offer their candid opinions. After all, if all directors always agreed, there would be no reason for a board to meet at all. On the other side of the equation, CEOs being CEOs, and luminaries in other fields who are just as likely to have strong wills and opinions themselves, a high probability of counterproductive ego- and personality-driven conflict persists, inherent in the board structure. Once again, that is all well and good if those conflicts are constructive, not destructive, and in the end a rational outlook and outcome prevails, built on a carefully constructed consensus informed by data and judgment, not gut and whim.

• • •

Getting It Wrong at Bank of America

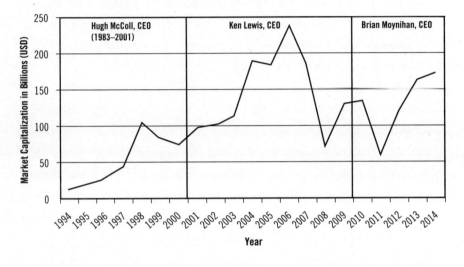

In the fall of 2009, Bank of America CEO Kenneth Doyle Lewis shocked his colleagues on the fifty-eighth floor of the bank's imposing sixty-story headquarters in Charlotte, North Carolina (the tallest building between Philadelphia and Atlanta, locally known as "The Taj Mahal"), by returning to his office after Labor Day weekend sporting a thick, shaggy, unkempt salt-and-pepper beard. His colleagues wondered what was up with Ken. What was up with Ken, they eventually learned, was that after spending a few weeks at his $20 million ranch in the Colorado ski town of Aspen, Lewis had come home to Charlotte determined that 2009 would be the last of the forty years he had spent at the bank, his first thirty-two having been devoted to helping his predecessors Hugh McColl and Tom Storrs relentlessly expand a sleepy regional player into the largest bank in the United States as measured by assets, and the last eight being his own just as expansive and acquisitive years at the helm.

At sixty-two, Lewis had repeatedly stated that he intended to stay on until retiring at sixty-five, or at least until the bank was able to repay the $45 billion in TARP (Troubled Asset Relief Program) funds it had received from the federal government to replenish capital depleted both by the credit crisis and by two massive and controversial takeovers.[5]

In July 2008, the bank had closed on a $4 billion acquisition of troubled mortgage lender Countrywide Financial, which boiled down to a big bet on the long-term stability of the housing market—a wager that ended up $50 billion in the red—followed only two months later by Lewis's September 2008 agreement to lay out $50 billion to acquire the troubled investment bank Merrill Lynch and its as-yet-undisclosed liabilities.

For the bank's restive shareholders, the Merrill merger was one bridge too far. Unnerved by the size of the paper losses widely assumed to be dragging down the bank's books—which had now been transferred to *their* books—irate shareholders overwhelmingly voted to strip Lewis of his chairman's title at the April 2009 shareholder's meeting while permitting him to retain his CEO title and role. Notwithstanding the fact that splitting the CEO and chairman's role is *never* a concrete solution to anything—and does next to nothing, if not worse than nothing, to curb a CEO's excessive risk taking—this stunning rebuke to and repudiation of Lewis's long-standing legacy of leadership was cited by people close to him as the primary factor driving his decision to call it quits five months later, three years earlier than planned.

His widely panned squirmy, sweaty, goggle-eyed performance at the televised congressional hearing early that summer, where he was hauled on the carpet and roundly lambasted for having taken two difficult and controversial decisions at the depths of the crisis, didn't do much to lift his souring mood either. He was in hot water with shareholders and congressmen because he had chosen 1. not to disclose the estimated extent of the Merrill losses prior to the shareholder vote to merge the two companies, and 2. he had granted tacit permission to Merrill Lynch CEO John Thain to pay out billions in bonuses to his top dogs just days before the deal closed. This ill-advised move on both men's parts effectively let Merrill managers further enrich themselves for the massive mistakes made on John Thain's and his predecessor Stan O'Neal's watch, while sticking shareholders with the tab.

The public outcry that resulted, however, was only a whimper compared with the louder howls of protest that broke out after Lewis decided he was going to get out of Dodge sooner rather than later, leaving no successor to take his place. In the wake of his third questionable decision, scorn was heaped equally on him and on the board for passively acquiescing not just to his chronic financial overreaching, but to his evident desire to duck the succession issue and handle the matter by himself, on his own schedule. As one commentator acidly put it:

> When Bank of America CEO Kenneth Lewis said that he was resigning, no one was surprised. Except, it seems, BofA's board of directors. It's been six weeks since the announcement and the company still hasn't named a replacement. Shareholder groups are saying that it's a sign of weakness and unpreparedness on the part of the board, that it didn't have a succession plan in place despite clear signs that Lewis' job was under pressure for months.[6]

Public disquiet over this latest example of boardroom bungling was further deepened by the directors' announcement that they were sending the discredited CEO off into the sunset with a golden parachute conservatively valued at $125 million. Several years later, two well-known consultants and governance experts would connect the dots between Lewis's late September 2009 retirement announcement and the SEC's late October 2009 issuance of revised guidance on the board's responsibility in this key matter. "The tipping point," they wrote, "may well have been the announcement by Ken Lewis . . . on September 30th, 2009, that he would retire by the end of the year [with] no successor in place and would most likely have to bring someone in from outside."[7] Though they offered no direct proof of causality between these two events, it is reasonable to assume that since CEOs and boards were not the only ones taking the heat for failing to see to it that there were viable successors in place when so many famous financial firms failed, and that regulators were taking the heat too, the SEC was eager to deflect criticism by at least loudly closing the barn door after all the horses had escaped. Nevertheless, by issuing an unambiguous ruling that CEO succession had become a "significant issue involving the governance of the corporation, that poor CEO succession planning poses too great a business risk, and that there should be greater transparency and share-holder disclosure about the management of succession," the SEC had at a minimum put all boards on notice that from here on in, CEO succession planning would rank at the top or close to the top of their lists of primary priorities and responsibilities.

Unbeknownst to shareholders and their representatives, the Office of the Comptroller of the Currency (OCC), one of the bank's primary regulators, had also grown concerned about the direction the bank was taking. In confidence, it had expressed that concern to the bank's management by issuing a confidential memo of understanding (MOU) calling for a radical overhaul of the board's structure, composition, management, risk oversight, and governance practices, with an emphasis on boosting the independence of independent directors and cutting the cronyism across the board. In the wake of the April 2009 shareholder vote that stripped Lewis of his chairman's title, that board overhaul began in earnest when the directors for the first time in recent memory chose to defy Lewis's wishes by rejecting his chosen candidate for chairman, North Carolina supporter Temple Sloan, and chose instead to appoint retired Morehouse College president Walter Massey—who had joined the board as a director of the former California-based Bank of America—to that key position, counting on his independence to bolster their own collective reassertion of independence from the controlling CEO.

Even after receiving push-back from his choice of chairman, Lewis attempted to outmaneuver the board and continue to control the selection of his successor by pushing his handpicked candidate, deal maker Greg Curl, into the catbird seat by promoting him to the post of chief risk officer. What had once been a career dead end prior to the crisis had in its aftermath gained new respect, as Lewis belatedly scrambled to make up for nearly a decade of neglect by recruiting some fresh blood into his senior ranks.

Less than a year before, he had squelched the chances to succeed of his most widely touted potential successor, former Merrill Lynch CEO John Thain, by firing him after forcing him to take the blame for paying out billions in bonuses he himself had sanctioned. In a private conversation with Thain several months before, Lewis had conceded that he "had not done a great job of grooming a successor as head of Bank of America"[8] and promised Thain that if he accepted his offer to run the bank's global operations, he would name him president of the bank within a year, making him his successor in all but name.

But several months further on down the road, having just thrown Thain under the bus in a thinly disguised bid to save his own skin, amid conveniently planted leaks that disclosed the outsized cost of Thain's office furniture to minimize sympathy for the victim, Lewis calculatedly compensated by recruiting Wall Street fixture Sallie Krawcheck, who had recently fallen out with newly appointed Citigroup CEO Vikram Pandit, as head of the Merrill Lynch brokerage business. He also promoted former Goldman Sachs partner Tom Montag (whom Thain had recruited to Merrill at a cost upwards of $40 million) to head up the bank's global markets division, and rounded out the pool of potential candidates by appointing one longtime insider, in-house attorney and senior strategist Brian Moynihan, as head of the consumer bank. Lewis went so far as to publicly describe all of these moves as in accordance with a board-sanctioned succession plan: "Working closely with our board, I have decided . . . to bring new talent to the team and add new perspectives. These changes also position a number of senior executives to compete to succeed me at the appropriate time."

Yet all of that effort ended up being worth no more than a plug nickel after Lewis pulled the rug out from under these new recruits by announcing his own departure several months later. That left just the two remaining insider candidates, Moynihan and Curl, to duke it out with each other while facing the prospect of stiff competition from sitting CEOs and former CEOs from outside.

Getting It Right (Finally) at Bank of America

At that point, the reconstituted board, fortunately for the bank, began to assert its new muscle. Newly appointed nonexecutive chairman Walter Massey, operating in close collaboration with the succession committee of the board, retained executive recruiting firm Russell Reynolds to start benchmarking the two remaining internal candidates against a list of external competitors, including former Wachovia chairman and Goldman Sachs partner Robert Steel, BlackRock's highly respected CEO Larry Fink, and Bank of New York Mellon CEO Robert Kelly. But while a fair number of high-profile outsiders turned the job down flat on the grounds that their freedom would be limited by the $45 billion the bank owed to the federal government, which put limits on CEO pay, an avalanche of leaks neutralized the leading outside contender, Kelly, while yet another avalanche of leaks from inside New York attorney general Andrew Cuomo's investigation put a quick end to Curl's candidacy by alleging that Curl might have provided conflicting accounts of critical internal deliberations over the merger to investigators. With the prospect of Curl's being tied up in legal and regulatory hoops for the duration, the balance of power swung sharply toward Moynihan. Aided and abetted by former Fleet chairman Chad Gifford, the board announced on December 16, 2009, that the dark-horse candidate Moynihan would succeed Lewis as of January 1, 2010.

The April 2010 election of former DuPont CEO Charles "Chad" Holliday as nonexecutive chairman marked yet another critical milestone in the bank's slow but steady comeback from popular punching bag into an example of boardroom best practice. As Holliday's adroit management of his own succession to Ellen Kullman attests, the bank at long last enjoyed the benefit of having a real champion of good corporate governance lead a board constituted very differently from the former cozy club model.

Not long after his appointment as CEO, Moynihan promoted two leaders, investment banker Tom Montag and commercial banker David Darnell, to serve as copresidents and leaders of integration among the bank's disparate business units. Although this structural realignment was not explicitly described as in accordance with a formal succession plan, that conclusion isn't very difficult to draw, given the identity of the current chairman.

When I recently asked Holliday, who sits on several boards including those of Royal Dutch Shell and John Deere in addition to chairing the board at Bank of America, how he has adjusted to the role of board member after having been such a strong and hands-on CEO, he stated his philosophy of directorship simply: "It's nose in, fingers out." As a board member, he elaborates, "You get to ask all the questions, and engage in push and shove. But at the end of the day the CEO has got to make the decisions. Once I accepted that fact, I found that I really enjoy being on this side."

The Merrill Lynch Version: Controlling CEO Makes Way for Controlling Lead Director

Those many millions of Merrill Lynch shareholders whose shares had been converted to Bank of America shares at a ratio of roughly one to one in the wake of the Bank of America takeover could be forgiven for having a sneaking feeling that they had been down this road once before. Three years before, in point of fact, in October 2007, Merrill Lynch CEO E. Stanley O'Neal had been pushed out the door by his long-compliant board. The ostensible reason for his ouster, at least as the reports read in the paper, had been that O'Neal had pursued a merger inquiry with rival Wachovia without consulting them first. But in reality he had been asked to fall on his sword because he had unwittingly permitted a very small number of handpicked lieutenants to amass a $30 billion–plus pile of mortgage-backed securities, whose precipitous decline in their dubious value had threatened to torpedo—and ultimately did take down—the prestigious century-old firm.

After peremptorily giving O'Neal the shove, Merrill's directors were forced to confront the fact that they had neglected their core responsibility to hold O'Neal accountable for developing and selecting a successor. "The heart of the problem," as one commentator observed, was that "O'Neal did not choose to build a stable team of talented executives around himself. He promoted and then fired, creating a kind of churn. Obviously, he didn't want any executive to blossom to the point that he or she could become positioned to one day lead the company. That was a bad strategy, and the board members should have called him on it."[9] Yet another pointed out that "O'Neal hand-picked the board members—another violation of best practices that has emerged. Merrill's board members were beholden to O'Neal and therefore unable to challenge him in the right sort of way."[10] Yet another emphasized the fact that O'Neal had been intent on keeping any potential threats to his authority at bay by retaining all the power positions in his own hands. Until the belated promotion, just three months before his fall from grace, of star investment banker Gregory Fleming and the Egyptian-born CFO Ahmass Fakahany, one of his few close confidants, to the posts of copresident, O'Neal had held close to his chest the three most powerful posts and title at the company: president, CEO, and chairman.[11]

Whatever the reason for the board's complacency, O'Neal's precipitous departure sharply narrowed the board's options. Since Fakahany's managerial fingerprints were all over the toxic CEOs, not to mention the selection and promotion of the dubious characters who had produced and warehoused them, his only honorable course of action was to quietly resign, which he did. As for Fleming, while his role in investment banking insulated him from the source of the firm's problems on the trading side, he was still only in his mid-forties and while highly regarded within the bank, had not yet been granted the runway to fulfill his presidential ambitions and prove himself a capable enterprise-wide leader, as he would later do after accepting a senior position running several major businesses at Morgan Stanley.

To buy themselves time, and to deflect the hailstorm of criticism it faced for having no name in the envelope, the Merrill Lynch board did the expedient thing and appointed Fleming interim CEO while announcing its retention of a top-notch executive search firm to help it manage the process of objectively evaluating a wide range of internal and external candidates.

It also elevated one of its own, Italian-born private equity executive Alberto Cribiore, to become head of the CEO search committee and nonexecutive director. That decision proved critical, as Cribiore very quickly swung into action as the kingmaker of Merrill Lynch. His first move was to personally notify Fleming that he was not in the running for the top job, because the board had decided to go in a different direction—to "bring someone in from the outside."[12] That decision, the most important one the board made, was arrived at, to put it mildly, in undue haste. Within the blink of an eye, Cribiore set off on a one-man mission to fast-track the candidacy of his personal pick as Merrill Lynch's white knight, a fifty-two-year-old former Goldman Sachs copresident doing a more than creditable job at transforming the venerable New York Stock Exchange from a cozy boys' club into an efficient global electronic trading platform. John Thain was the veteran of his own fiercely fought succession struggle at Goldman Sachs, where he had spearheaded an insurrection against his former mentor, then CEO and future New Jersey governor Jon Corzine, which had resulted in the elevation of future treasury secretary Hank Paulson as sole CEO.

With that muddy and bloody water under the bridge, the tall, bespectacled former college wrestler and Clark Kent look-alike Thain, who had been recruited to his present position by former Citigroup CEO John Reed (himself the loser of a bitter boardroom battle with archrival Sandy Weill for the top job), informed the supplicant Cribiore that while he was interested in Merrill, he was also being assiduously courted by Citigroup, whose board had recently ousted former in-house counsel and handpicked Sandy Weill protégé Charles "Chuck" Prince without a successor in place. With the market in white knights for failed financial firms heating up fast, Cribiore leaned hard on his fellow directors to make a strong, early, preemptive bid for Thain before losing him to the competition. Cribiore wasn't shy about sitting in on his fellow directors' interviews with his hot prospect, and doing everything within his considerable persuasive power to smooth Thain's passage into the C-suite. At the same time, this frantic maneuvering was occurring at cross-purposes to, or at least independent of, a somewhat less frantic search being managed by executive search firm Spencer Stuart, whose leader Tom Neff was of the opinion that BlackRock CEO Larry Fink, to whom O'Neal had sold his asset management division two years before, was the most qualified external candidate.

While Neff confidentially if erroneously advised Fink he was a shoe-in for the job, Fink learned through other channels that he had lost out to Thain. Less than a year later, after Thain sold out to Ken Lewis and was subsequently fired, many mourning Merrill Lynch insiders were left to ponder two different what-ifs: if the board had picked either Fleming or Fink, the strong feeling was, a century-old legend of Wall Street (to Main Street) might well have survived.

Boardroom Groupthink

What happened to the boards of Bank of America and Merrill Lynch? These were not, after all, groups of uninformed, malintentioned, ne-glectful, or callous individuals—if anything, quite the contrary. What happened, in my view, at both boards was the eruption of a well-documented group psychological phenomenon first identified by social psychologist Irving Janis in the early seventies, which he memorably labeled "groupthink."[13] This all-too-common dynamic occurs within groups faced with making an urgent consensus-based decision, as was the case with both boards. Citing prominent examples from history, ranging from the ill-fated decision to press ahead with the Bay of Pigs invasion of Cuba to the *Challenger* space shuttle disaster, Janis identi-fied a number of cases where sound decision making was, in effect, un-consciously circumvented by an overriding mutual concern that the group needed to preserve unity and cohesion at just about any cost. This priority overrides rationality and reinforces faulty or unexamined premises, creating conspicuous disconnects from reality, particularly if that hard-to-face reality is uncomfortable or potentially divisive. A col-lective drive for consensus suppresses disagreements that might lead to opposing conclusions. The groupthink phenomenon prevents the objective appraisal of rational alternatives.

Organizations regarded as particularly susceptible to groupthink tend to be insular, composed of insiders drawn from the same social class, often from similar ethnic or religious backgrounds and tightly circumscribed ranges of experience. Private clubs and fraternities, religious groups, and homogenous corporate managements are all examples of closed societies prone to groupthink. Few organizations with which I am familiar are as insular, composed of people of the same social class and perspective, and as professionally incestuous as the boards of major corporations. Certainly both the Bank of America and Merrill Lynch boards can be characterized as mainly made up of "insiders," despite the fact that both boards contained women, academics, and people of color—Stan O'Neal, for example, was the grandson of a former slave. Despite decades of on-again, off-again progress toward greater diversity of races, genders, social classes, industry sectors, and points of view, any expert on boards and their composition will tell you that these groups continue to remain overwhelmingly dominated by older white men who have gained positions of power in their fields due to similar backgrounds, attendance at similarly exclusive schools, and similar formative experiences and notions of achievement and credentials. Despite best efforts and good intentions, too many boards go off the rails by inadvertently seeking the comfort and validation of a herd mentality. My hypothesis is that Merrill's board exchanged one example of groupthink for another, trading in undue submission to a strong-willed CEO for undue submission to a strong-willed lead director/ nonexecutive chairman. In late 2007, the illustrious Merrill Lynch board included a retired rear admiral of the U.S. Pacific Fleet, a former commissioner of the IRS, the sitting CEO of the prestigious Chubb Insurance company, the former CFO of ITT, and the president of Smith College. This was hardly a collection of losers or weaklings, yet in this one critical respect, operating under great pressure and a sense of acute embarrassment at failing to fulfill one of their most important fiduciary duties, they appear to have done what they were told, not just by one but by two powerful people.

Board Succession Planning Best Practice #1: Accept This as a Priority

So what *is* a board to do? For some fresh and original answers to those questions, as well as to bolster my own empirical evidence, I turned to an informal panel of experts in the field, all people I have known for a very long time and have extensive experience both serving on boards and working closely with them, as CEOs or CHROs. I will be delving into their personal points of view on some key questions in due course. But first, I will offer up my short punch list of dos and don'ts, some of which may strike you as total no-brainers, except that some surprisingly brainy people fail to follow through on them when push comes to shove, in practice as well as in theory.

Board Succession Planning Best Practice #2: Tackle the Political and Cultural Issues Head-On

As the quote from Harvard Business School professor, former university president, and former COO of both Limited Brands and Au Bon Pain Len Schlesinger, with which I kicked off this chapter simply states, "The number one responsibility of a board in terms of its fiduciary obligations is to choose and manage the CEO." This is widely admitted to be true, except that in too many cases, even highly experienced directors—even sitting or former CEOs themselves—don't accept this proposition as a given, or do so with sufficient sincerity to actually act on it in practice. As I have stated more than once in this book, many directors will engage in only the technical piece, because the cultural and political dimensions of the issue are too awkward to navigate.

Board Succession Planning Best Practice #3: Operate from the Assumption That All Organizations Need Leaders at All Levels

While many readers—and nonreaders—of this book might intellectually agree with the proposition that organizations need leaders to lead at all levels, remarkably few leaders in fact lead in accordance with this immutable best practice. What needing leaders at all levels of the organization means in reality is that boards and directors who want to *lead* as opposed to *follow* need to intuitively grasp one essential follow-on fact: their number-one priority is to oversee the actions of the current CEO and help that CEO develop and select a suitable pipeline of future leaders.

Board Succession Planning Best Practice #4: Develop Transformational Leaders on the Inside

This will not come as news to anyone who has read closely this far, but boards must ground every decision they make as directors in the conviction that going inside is preferable to going outside except in the case of certain anomalies. Outsider selections are unimpeachable evidence that the board, the CHRO, and the CEO have failed at their core obligation to develop future leaders on the inside. As such, it is critical for directors to avoid being outmaneuvered by a CEO who feels threatened by internal leadership development—a surprisingly common occurrence despite the fact that you will never hear a CEO admit it to anyone's face. A direct corollary to this is that it is critical to resist, whenever possible, the seductive allure of the superstar outsider. I will be dealing with this issue in greater depth in the next chapter, but suffice it to say that a critical pitfall to avoid for *any* board is not to fall prey to "The Halo Effect."[14] This phrase, popularized by Phil Rosenzweig, a professor at IMD in Lausanne, Switzerland, accurately and whimsically skewers much business writing and analysis as hopelessly mired in a common human failing, the compulsion to weave stories that reinforce our preconceptions and unchallenged assumptions, and marshal evidence to that effect. In few areas of human endeavor does the Halo Effect operate more insidiously than when boards of directors of companies in crisis throw what is always a risky and costly Hail Mary pass to rope in a superstar outsider, with the often unfulfilled hope of saving the day, just as the quarterback hopes to win the game in the final seconds by hurling the ball over half the field into the end zone.

As I will demonstrate in the next chapter, occasionally the Hail Mary pass hits. That's why quarterbacks, companies, and embarrassed directors throw them. But no one in their right mind would argue that a Hail Mary pass is anything but an admission of failure that the playbook hasn't panned out. Beware the allure of the Halo Effect—which captured and dazzled the directors of Merrill Lynch with Thain, HP with Fiorina, Hurd, Apotheker, Whitman, and Johnson at JCPenney, and countless others.

Board Succession Planning Best Practice #5: Benchmark Against Both Internal and External Candidates

Directors need to have had deep, long, thoughtful exposure to senior management in order to make a sound and responsible selection of a successor from a pool of insider candidates. Though this would seem to be yet another no-brainer, it's shocking how infrequently such exposure is effectively provided, free of personal bias, politics, and distortion. The CEO, board, and CHRO must closely collaborate on creating conditions for candidate exposure that showcase potential future leaders' strengths and weaknessess. Boards needs to benchmark just as CHROs and CEOs do. Directors, in particular, need to get to know the senior leadership through presentations in the boardroom, regular meetings outside it, and quality time spent in the field where the candidates are running their businesses in real time. CEOs cannot be the sole conduit to the board on talent management. The board needs to be close to the CHRO and to the development processes devoted to producing a pipeline of future leaders. To do this correctly, boards need to have access to reams of well-collated data and clearly vetted information about potential successors without the need to approach executives directly. Benchmarking provides boards with in-depth profiles of potential leaders, putting them in a better position to quickly assemble a list of potential candidates.

As Verizon's Ivan Seidenberg told me: "We gave our board the names of the top candidates, and after a while, someone on the board would say, 'I don't think that one can do it. And I don't think that one can do it.' So I said to them, 'How do you know? Why don't you just watch?' And you want to know what? They did—closely."

Board Succession Planning Best Practice #6: Look Out the Windshield, Not the Rearview Mirror

Don't focus on inside or outside as much as from past to future. This is often referred to as looking out the windshield, not the rearview mirror. Most important, looking to the future means not picking a clone of the current CEO but a maverick, a rogue gene, who will transform the organization without turning it upside down and sideways, as so many outsider CEOs do. The need here is for open dialogue around a strategic consensus on the board about future growth and a vision of where the company should be in three to five years.

Board Succession Planning Best Practice #7: Maintain Continual Review

Update plans, profiles, and data sets on a continual basis. Part of not looking in the rearview mirror involves continually updating reviews with knowledge gained from looking forward, out the windshield, into the driving snow. With all due credit to my old friend and colleague Ram Charan, I am including here a series of excellent and critical suggestions from his and colleagues' recent work on the appropriate role for boards in CEO and leadership selection.[15]

Ten Principles for Finding the Right CEO

1. *People set strategy.* Directors and executives who know where the company should be going will be best equipped to guide it there.

2. *Implement an evaluation methodology.* Use an evaluation system that links the company's strategic requirements with the prospects' individual capacities and performance, with the latter focusing on integrity and ethics, team building, execution excellence, shareholder return, personal gravitas, and ability to work in the boardroom.

3. *Include in the current CEO's evaluation an assessment of how well the company is doing at building a succession plan for the next generation of company leaders.*

4. *Place the board leader in charge.* By tackling the job in partnership with a still-effective chief executive, the board leader can help root the process deeply in the company's management development, preventing succession from becoming an event-driven crisis.

5. *Retain a high-performing chief executive, but also work to keep capable successors.*

6. *Seek candid comparative data on insider candidates from those who worked with them.*

7. *Make direct contact with both sources and candidates to verify information.* Directors should personally check references, which can sometimes reveal limited inside information and even false information.

8. *Ensure that outside consultants do not pose conflicts of interest.*

9. *Maintain confidentiality.*

10. *Embed succession planning in the culture.*

Adapted from *Boards That Lead: When to Take Charge, When to Partner, and When to Stay Out of the Way,* Ram Charan, Dennis Carey, and Michael Useem, Harvard Business Press, 2014.

Boardroom Dos and Don'ts

My good friend Bob Knowling, who served on the board of HP after Carly Fiorina was hired and left after she was fired, has been serving on numerous corporate and nonprofit boards for nearly thirty years, ever since he agreed to become a director of his local Blue Cross and Blue Shield affiliate in Indiana, after which he joined the board of Royal Dutch Shell subsidiary Shell Oil Exploration. He currently serves on the boards of executive search firm Heidrick & Struggles, the industrial conglomerate Roper Industries, and network solutions provider Ariba. As CEO of high-flying telecom company Covad, Bob helped build its board and ultimately clashed on a number of critical strategy issues with his directors, leading finally to his resignation. He later went on to lead the New York Board of Education's innovative Leadership Academy under Bloomberg appointee Joel Klein, and is currently involved with a wide range of high-profile consultancies and assignments, on some of which he works with me and my team.

Recently, I sat down with Knowling to learn more of what, in his opinion, makes boards succeed or fail at their assigned mission of selecting leaders. Is it truly a mission impossible? Most of us who have worked on or with boards would agree with one definition of the board's ideal role proposed by Sir John Harvey-Jones, the former chairman of Britain's ICI (Imperial Chemical Industries), whom many referred to as the English Jack Welch. Whether the comparison to Welch is an apt one or not is not for me to say, but I do like his definition of a board's real role, which is "to create tomorrow's company out of today's." Another useful definition is provided by his friend Sir Adrian Cadbury:

> Boards are in place to *direct* but not to *manage*. They have the task of defining the purpose of the enterprise and of agreeing on a strategy for achieving that purpose. They are responsible for appointing the chief executive . . . and if necessary, replacing [him or her]. Above all, boards are there to provide leadership.[16]

A straightforward enough task, one might think, when so simply described. But as the stories in this chapter confirm, it isn't easy to execute. So why do so many board members blow it on CEO succession, and what can they do to improve their track records?

Don't #1: Don't Not *Have a Name in the Envelope*

The most awkward predicament any board can get itself into, which occurs just the same with alarming frequency, lately accelerated by the rise of activist investors and ratcheting pressures on boards and CEOs to deliver better performance, is for a sitting CEO to abruptly step down and leave the board with no name to pull out of the envelope. Time and again this occurs, and time and again, cooler and more rational minds are left to scratch their heads and wonder: *What on earth were they thinking?* Don't they know about the beer-truck test? Don't they know that the beer truck can come hurtling toward you at any time, at any speed, without warning, in the form of so many factors from health issues to ethical lapses to criminal behavior to subpar performance to . . . you know the drill. An emergency succession plan is the corporate equivalent of carrying a first aid kit and a spare tire in the trunk of your car. It is commonsense business continuity planning, but by one account, up to 40 percent of directors surveyed admitted that they were "not prepared for an emergency succession in the event of a sudden, unexpected, or unplanned departure of their company's leader."[17]

To which my response is: come on, you have got to be kidding. This is the source of the dreaded interregnum, and what gets boards of directors laughed at on business talk shows. The solution to this problem is really quite simple: As the Boy Scout motto puts it, "Be Prepared!"

Don't #2: Don't Have a SPOTS Paper Plan

The most frequent result of having a strong-willed CEO and a reticent board, despite the egregious examples cited above, is not that the issue of succession planning is formally neglected, but that the plan, such as it is, isn't worth the paper it's printed on. This is the SPOTS ("Succession Plans on Top Shelves") issue that many years ago my longtime colleague and friend Ram Charan and I framed as a variant on a cynical old consultant's term, "Strategic Plans on Top Shelves."

BOB KNOWLING:

What you get when it's all just on paper, when it's mainly a matter of going through the motions, is a sterile review of the CEO's direct reports, a quick peek at the performance appraisals, a cursory discussion of who has what potential and who doesn't. You perform this empty exercise as meaningless ritual once a year. And you never go any deeper, you never get real visibility into the organization, and what you get when the company hits its next crisis is that the process quickly deteriorates into a death march.

"Most boards," Bob adds,

fail miserably in the area of succession planning because while everyone agrees *in principle* that succession planning is right at the top of the list, right up there with fiduciary oversight, most boards end up with a paper plan, which in turn culminates in a fire drill exercise, which in turn precipitates a crisis when a CEO is asked to leave the business. Typically, even if they do have a good process in place on paper, they may not have been doing a good job of sourcing internal candidates and keeping up with their external scans. Boards that end up in that position will be forced, if required, to execute lengthy searches of six to nine to twelve months. Conversely, I've seen boards go through the gymnastics of appointing interim CEOs by putting a member of the board in the slot temporarily. Whenever I see a board appoint one of their own to replace an outgoing CEO, I will invariably interpret that as a sign that they have failed at their number-one responsibility: CEO succession planning.

Why, I wondered, does this happen so often?

"I've been on some boards where succession planning has been pursued as a real science in terms of rigor and discipline of the process and planning," Knowling replied. "But I've also been on boards—and I'm not naming any names here—where it didn't work out so well, despite the fact that we should have known better."

Don't #3: Don't Be Afraid of Alienating a Successful CEO

Knowling also points out that in his experience, boards of directors frequently shy away from forcing the issue on a CEO when the CEO is riding high—see, for example, both Ken Lewis and Stan O'Neal.

> This reticence on the part of even well-intentioned directors all too often boils down to a situation when you've got a strong-willed CEO who's got some real momentum in terms of quarterly earnings and the stock price is doing well. This makes directors a little reticent to take on the CEO and force the discipline around succession planning. Ninety-nine-point-nine percent of the situations when this happens is when you've got a very strong-willed CEO. I mean, I was a CEO for fifteen years and I've been a board member for thirty, and I can tell you from personal experience, most CEOs are egomaniacs. That's how they get there in the first place.

He recalled one egregious incident where he sat in on an executive session of the board and made a sincere attempt to personally press the issue on a reluctant CEO who was achieving demigod status based purely on his financial results. Was he putting in the time developing the next generation of leaders? Hell no—he was focused on the quarterly earnings, which were producing a different form of Halo Effect that was dazzling the board, making them unable to see that they were both failing, fast.

> KNOWLING: "We've got to get more serious about this and push the envelope."
>
> RELUCTANT CEO: "There really are no credible internal candidates."

KNOWLING: *"Okay, let's take the best ones you've got and put some development plans around them and see how they do."*

RELUCTANT CEO: *"Absolutely, great idea, Bob. I'll see what we can do."*

In the end, nothing happened, of course. Even after the CEO kept obviously stonewalling, Knowling gained no support from his fellow board members.

Why?

Knowling knows the answer: "The CEO had all the leverage. Two years before the stock was at 39 bucks and it had risen over 130 by then."

Don't #4: Don't Split the Role

With all this talk of overweening CEOs the fashionable solution to a very real problem is for boards to split the role of chairman and CEO. In theory, the idea of having a nonexecutive chairman as a counterweight to a CEO makes a certain amount of sense, except that in my experience it doesn't work in practice. Because in reality, organizations are better off with one leader, not two, or three—as in the case of Google. Shareholder proposals are constantly calling for this. It has so far worked out at Bank of America, but Chad Holliday is, as we have seen, a pretty exceptional leader, and this may be the exception that proves the rule. If the resolution had passed in 2013 to strip JPMorgan Chase CEO Jamie Dimon of the chairman's title, his response would have been exactly that of Ken Lewis's—to take his money and run. Not a good outcome, if the CEO is any good. And if they are not, dump them and get a new CEO; don't do a pussyfooting wishy-washy thing and take half the power away, as if neutering were a solution.

Do #1: Prepare for a Deep, Long, Constructive Engagement

"There's one board I can think of, which I sit on," Knowling recalled, "where in all modesty we were really, totally on our game."

He spelled out for me what they did right in seven easy steps:

1. We all agreed, right off the bat, that this was our most important job.

2. We conducted in-depth succession reviews biannually, looking deep inside the organization.

3. We carved out enough time to do it right, because we knew from experience that's what it takes.

4. We went through the internal candidates at the direct CEO report level but also dug deeper, a level or two down, to understand where the talent really was inside the organization. We wanted visibility and we got it.

5. We benchmarked internal candidates with external ones, because we believed we'd be better positioned to understand the development needs of the internal candidates if we kept our eye on the external comparison. We retained a search firm and we did an external comparative scan on them all.

6. We created aggressive plans to expose any candidate who had not yet achieved but clearly possessed CEO potential to the three or four things we decided that those particular candidates needed to know if they were going to grow into viable candidates.

7. Through a process of focused, intentional interventions over a period of three or four years, we got all of those internal candidates to the point where we had unanimous consent on the board that if the CEO ever wanted to go off and play golf for the rest of his life, we had a couple of good internal candidates teed up, thoroughly vetted, and put through their paces. This was a case where we couldn't have been more pleased with the sitting CEO's performance, by the way. We just knew we needed to do this because—who can predict the future?

Do #2: Coach the Candidates

Boards may arrange for an outside consultant from a premier firm to work closely with a candidate on their business, strategic, and leadership development plans. Not only will that consultant be able to provide the candidate with the benefit of his thirty-five years of industry knowledge, but after the consultant reports back to the board, the directors will enjoy the benefit of a more accurate, more nuanced, more in-depth sense of the candidate's qualifications than they would have by any other means.

KNOWLING:

I'm a big believer in assigning the leading internal candidates executive coaches. In every board that I serve on I try to push the agenda of providing the CEO candidate with coaches, because I believe that coaching is the key to personal and professional development.

Do #3: Ensure Fair and Equal Exposure for All Candidates

As Ivan Seidenberg showed in partnership with Verizon CHRO Marc Reed, success at succession requires the board's active and thoughtful involvement. All players need to collaborate on the creation of an active and dynamic environment, or series of environments, designed to provide the board members with genuine, authentic exposure to the candidates, as they run businesses and in informal settings. The key here is to ensure that all of the candidates get fair and equal exposure to the board, because working closely and constructively with the board, as Carly Fiorina learned to her dismay, is probably the most important single job a CEO has, followed by communicating and working with Wall Street—all critical learning experiences.

Whether the method is to hold formal or informal dinners on the first night of the board or committee meeting, it's crucial to ensure that the entire slate of CEO succession candidates gain appropriate exposure in an informal setting. Interaction at a three-hour board dinner is different from seeing the same person in the context of a formal presentation. Directors are smart: they can pick a lot of things up when casually sitting around, enjoying some wine, having dinner. As Knowling told me, "We would never let the same executive sit next to the same director too many times because directors end up adopting somebody. They say, 'Well, I know that person. He's good, I like that person.' So we consciously used to keep score. We used to watch this very closely."

Do #4: Get Succession Candidates on Other Companies' Boards

Wining and dining and convening in a casual or intimate setting isn't enough or the right kind of exposure for directors to make thoughtful judgments about the most important decision they'll make as board members. It's also critical for board members to discuss in detail with the CEO and the head of HR whether a certain candidate would benefit from getting more deeply involved with a part of the business they've never experienced. It's important for board members to make a detailed, planned intervention that is carefully constructed with regard to every stage of the candidates' development and careers. It's equally important for directors to help succession candidates go on boards themselves to gain additional experience and exposure outside the walls. Just being around other talented executives, other CEOs, other companies, other environments, can be critical to a candidate's development.

Do #5: Expose Directors to Candidates on Their Own Turf

At Ford under Jacques Nasser, my team and I would arrange for board members to come in a day early and for them to spend extended periods of time at close quarters with the different candidates, engaging them with a deep review of their action plans, and actually allowing them to get the board members' input. Both the candidates and board members enjoyed the reality and the novelty of it. They got to roll up their sleeves, engage with the candidates on real current business strategies, in an intimate setting, then follow up with a casual lunch meeting with the entire board. We'd get a report from the board members on their views of the various candidates, and they, in turn, would be provided with an unusual setting in which to check out the talent.

The World According to Tharp and Murphy

The second of my informal panel of experts was Charles Tharp, who spoke from more than twenty-five years of corporate experience, starting with human resources positions at GE (where I first got to know him), PepsiCo, Pillsbury, Cigna, and Bristol-Myers Squibb, where he served as senior vice president of human resources—in other words, CHRO. According to Tharp, the most important piece of this puzzle is "to have the whole board in the game. That means *everybody on the board.*"

According to Tharp, it's critical not to hive this important task off to a subcommittee, whose conclusions end up being passively rubber-stamped by the rest of the board. "This is really too important to delegate entirely to a committee," he cautions. "Unless the committee's role is carefully defined as preparing the total board to make the decision, if you isolate a group of three or four directors and nominate them as the few that handle succession, that can be pretty dangerous. The whole board has to be in the game, and that means everybody on the board."

Tharp's "vision of the perfect selection process" is to carefully limit the task of the subcommittee to "pulling together and vetting the relevant information provided by the CHRO." But then the critical next step is to spark "a candid and ongoing dialogue back and forth with everyone in the boardroom. Whoever takes the lead in the process goes around the room saying, 'Would you make this person CEO? Why or why not?' And if the answer is yes, the next question becomes: 'What are you going to do to make them succeed?' The ultimate question," Tharp says, "is 'How does the board get the right information so they can express an informed judgment not just about the candidate but about what that candidate needs to grow?'"

Once again, that information needs not to be of the arid and sterile sort that one typically finds typed up on a piece of paper. It needs to be up close, personal, and real. As we saw in the first chapter, when HP's board, weary of infighting, left the essential decision of selecting a replacement for Mark Hurd in one hell of a hurry, the directors didn't even meet the leading candidate in person. They rubber-stamped the selection of a subcommittee, most of whom mainly talked to the ill-fated Léo Apotheker on the phone. If that is egregious bad practice, what is its mirror opposite?

In short, how to create the right conditions for fair and authentic exposure for all of the candidates?

Tharp recommends "inviting the candidates to board meetings, board dinners, and board luncheons, having them sit with directors, having them meet with different directors at different times." He also recommends at some point relatively late in the process to "have board members unencumbered by the CEO or anybody else either visit the business or have one-on-one discussions with the people you think are the leading candidates, preferably in an informal business setting."

David Murphy, my third expert CHRO at Ford under Jacques Nasser, where we worked closely together on leadership development and succession planning (he went on to become CHRO at McGraw-Hill after we were all fired in tandem with Nasser), concurs that the key is for the board not just to get *more* exposure to the candidates but the right sort of exposure. He is not a fan of having candidates "make presentations in board meetings because some people are great at making presentations, but that doesn't make them great leaders. Attending a dinner and politely talking about whatever," he insists, really doesn't hold water either. He mentioned one company he is aware of, which for obvious reasons will remain nameless, where the board picked a new CEO after "talking to him on the phone a couple of times." Could that have been HP? Unfortunately, such negligence is not limited to a case of one. As Murphy said with a sigh, "Then you go into their organization and see them at work and you think oh, my god, what was I thinking?"

In the end, Murphy distills the best practices and best processes, from the board point of view, down to a few critical nonnegotiable points:

A clearly defined process, maximum transparency, a carefully tasked board committee, rigorous assessment and relentless coaching of all the potential candidates by the entire board, not just relying on the committee, close and constant collaboration with the CEO and CHRO, and when the time comes, a willingness to accept expert help.

CHAPTER 7

THE INSIDER/OUTSIDER DILEMMA

The rationale for selecting internal candidates is simple: you know their personalities and capabilities better than you can ever know someone from outside.

—**Ellen Kullman, chair and CEO of DuPont**

TECHNICAL

- Framing the future strategic needs of the company
- Developing a rigorous assessment process for the candidates, benchmarking internal candidates versus external candidates

POLITICAL

- Carefully planning how to avoid "organ rejection" of outside CEO
- Building a supportive coalition

CULTURAL

- Integrating new cultural DNA brought in by the external CEO
- Rebuilding a new leadership team and pipeline

Getting It Wrong at JCPenney

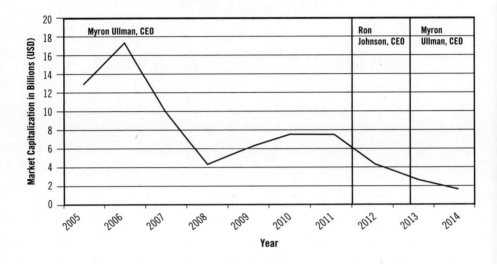

On May 1, 2013, the iconic but struggling mid-market department store chain JCPenney posted a contrite video on Facebook, which also appeared on YouTube and broadcast networks around the country. It featured classic soothing images of families happily shopping at JCPenney stores from the 1960s, accompanied by a friendly female voiceover proclaiming that "what matters with mistakes is what we learn. We learned a very simple lesson—to listen to you."[1]

The mistakes to which the video obliquely referred, from dumping store coupons to ending variable discount pricing and promotions, all of which could be blamed on a catastrophic failure to listen to core customers, had been committed during the short but turbulent reign of recently ousted Penney CEO Ron Johnson. In the spring of 2011, activist investor Bill Ackman of Pershing Square Capital Management, who had amassed a nearly 20 percent stake in the company in the hope of driving and profiting from a turnaround, had personally recruited Johnson, the former head of Apple's retail division, as a replacement for CEO Myron "Mike" Ullman, who had led the chain for seven years. Ackman had not only pushed the board hard to reel Johnson in, but had sanctioned a payout estimated at well over $50 million to do it. Seventeen months later, after retail sales had dropped by 25 percent, the stock had sunk by roughly half,[2] and a deeply embarrassed Ackman had been obliged to acknowledge that his high-profile selection of Johnson "had been something very close to a disaster,"[3] it was not just reasonable but obvious for people to say: *"What on earth had they been thinking?"*

But they—and by "they" I would include not just Ackman and the Penney board but the untold number of investors and analysts who had cheered Johnson's recruitment, driving Penney's long-stagnant stock up a staggering 19 percent in one day[4]—had based their assessment of Penney's new leader's potential to pull off a dramatic turnaround on what I would argue is a false premise. When an organization is in trouble, the best way to fix what ails it is to bring in a visionary, transformational leader from the outside to clean out the conceptual cobwebs, shake the place up, and in some cases, even blow the place up—or so the smart money often believes. That last part Johnson certainly took care of, but not quite in the way his recruiters had envisioned. As Mark Cohen, a former CEO of Sears Canada and now a Columbia professor, caustically observed to *The New Yorker:* "Penney had been run into a ditch when he took it over. But rather than getting it back on the road, he essentially set it on fire."[5]

The theory that outsiders do Schumpeterian "creative destruction" better than insiders is not a new one, although it has taken on greater salience in recent years, as the notion of "glass breaking" transformational CEOs has gained traction among such influential stakeholders as stock market analysts, activist investors, and many among the academic business community. I will be the first to admit that this theory has a certain logic to recommend it, and that it sometimes is (but rarely) the case that outsider CEOs imported into troubled organizations have brought with them an injection of fresh perspective and a set of skills that have resulted in genuine, dramatic, and even spectacular turnarounds.

But that said, an overwhelming preponderance of evidence supports a contrary view, which is that these few exceptions do not prove or make a rule to be slavishly followed as a matter of dogma or doctrine. The fact that a handful of highly talented outsiders, as we shall see in this chapter, have pulled off this remarkable feat is no reason to ignore the more salient fact, which is that in the vast majority of cases, outsider selections and recruitments are riskier, costlier, and far more disruptive to the fabric of the organization than insider selections. A perfect if distressing case in point: Ron Johnson at Penney's.

Recruiting an outsider, any outsider, is by definition a Hail Mary pass, which in my book and in this book reflects a clear-cut and utterly unnecessary failure. The solution to companies' and organizations' growing stale, stuffy, stodgy, and outmoded—as Penney's undoubtedly was and may well still be—is to grow transformational leaders on the inside, forming a pipeline that reinvents and repopulates the senior ranks of the organization with a constant flow of talented and well-prepared insiders. But since, as I will be the first to admit, so few leaders and organizations know how to do that, all too frequently we get the opposite result from the vast majority of executive transitions and CEO selections: inertia, entropy, and decline.

JCPenney was certainly sliding rapidly downhill—its revenues had been on the downswing for three years[6]—when Pershing Square's Bill Ackman offered Apple's senior vice president of retail operations Ron Johnson the shot of a lifetime to turn a floundering retail icon around. At the time, Johnson's reputation as a maverick genius of retail was riding high based on his extraordinary success over the previous decade at pioneering the concept of Apple's retail stores and, in particular, the Genius Bar, under the leadership of the quintessential control-freak maverick CEO Steve Jobs. Before Apple, Johnson had been vice president of merchandising at Target, and the man deemed largely responsible for conceiving and implementing that chain's innovative and extraordinarily successful "affordable chic" high-design, low-cost merchandising and marketing strategy that so many of its peers have since sought to emulate, with varying degrees of success. Before heading for Target, the Stanford University and Harvard Business School graduate had turned down a lucrative offer from Goldman Sachs to take a less glamorous job in the menswear department at Mervyns, a mid-level department store chain later acquired by Dayton-Hudson, the predecessor company to Target, before being sold off to a private equity firm that shuttered its doors in 2008.

Johnson had taken a low-level sales job at Mervyns, he later maintained, because he "wanted to run a whole company some day," and needed to "learn the business from the ground up."[7] That was precisely the opportunity Ackman and the Penney board provided him with on the strength of his role in developing a 325-store mall-based empire of Apple stores that grossed an average of nearly $6,000 per square foot, more than twice Tiffany's take, and exponentially outpacing department and general stores like Penney's ($156), Kohl's ($194), and Macy's ($171).

When Jobs had first discussed the idea of launching a retail presence with trusted advisers both inside and outside the company, nearly everyone he spoke to predicted failure based on the doomed efforts of other computing companies before him, including Gateway. In an era when consumer electronics were increasingly regarded as a commodity category likely to migrate online, a computer company like Apple, not a big-box retailer like Best Buy, ended up proving the smart money wrong.

By the time Ackman came calling, Johnson had reaped a rich reward of tens of millions of dollars for purportedly spearheading Apple's entire retail strategy and implementation. In numerous interviews he personally took credit for dreaming up the Genius Bar, a centerpiece of Apple's unique retail environment. Yet when Johnson informed an ailing Steve Jobs that he would be leaving Apple for the Plano, Texas–based Penney's, Jobs was incredulous, curtly commenting that Penney's was at best "a B-minus or C company with B-minus people."[8] In the wake of Jobs's death, precisely what role Johnson played in the success of Apple stores in the malls remained murky, at best. Whatever the truth, the ambitious Johnson shrugged off Jobs's derisory comments and embraced Penney's egalitarian ethos. He became so enthralled with his purported power to work wonders at the troubled chain that he put up $50 million of his own cash to invest in Penney's stock—in the form of warrants—"as a demonstration of his confidence in J. C. Penney's long-term potential."

In classic outsider glass-breaking CEO style, Johnson employed a by-now predictable revolutionary rhetoric to position himself as truly transformative. His high-end A-team, recruited like himself from outside, would reinvent retail for the twenty-first century and create a new entity, to be known simply as JCP, that would be bolder, crisper, cleaner, simpler to understand, and chicly contemporary in a Target-esque sort of way.

The cost of those outsider recruitments, including his own, could be measured not just in dollars but in the incalculable cost of declining morale that blowing up the existing hierarchy in the name of transformation rang up on the chain's internal registers. Johnson seemed to take a perverse pleasure in trashing the legacy locals by blowing an astounding $170 million in "executive transition costs" on the installation of himself and his top three lieutenants while simultaneously sending a message that he was too good to spend much time in down-market Plano, Texas, preferring to commute to Penney headquarters by corporate jet from his "real home" in cooler California.

Culturally, he also played all his cards wrong, failing to realize that he had to carefully bring his people along on the change path, not scare the bejesus out of them. As one commentator later put it:

> On a deeper level, while Johnson transformed the look and feel of the stores, he failed to transform the company *culture* needed to support his vision. He tried to replicate Apple's culture and practices, replacing executives with Apple veterans, for example, but those alums reportedly sequestered themselves away, working in an Apple-like bubble and failing to communicate with the rest of the company. Morale also dropped with each layoff, and not even sales floor staff—the front lines to the customer—could keep up with the changes in philosophies and policies.[9]

After just a few months, when the vaunted revolution failed to deliver the goods, Johnson waved off the naysayers by citing his prior successes at confounding conventional wisdom with radical innovation on the floor. "What you can't do is chicken out," he informed *Fortune*. "If you had looked at the data on the Genius Bar after a year and a half, we should have taken it out of the store. But it was something I believed in with every bone in my body . . . There's no reason to sell an idea short. The only risk would be to not fulfill the dream."[10]

By midsummer, however, ever widening cracks were creasing the sleek Johnson façade, prompting even former staunch supporter Bill Ackman to take a brief break from his ultimately successful campaign to unseat the CEO at P&G and dash off a quasi-contrite letter to the investors in his fund stating that while he had "complete confidence in Ron Johnson and the new management team he has assembled to execute a total transformation of this iconic U.S. retailer," he could not deny the fact that "the execution has not . . . been flawless."[11] By the close of Johnson's first full year in office, even that lukewarm defense was revealed as wishful thinking as the guilty verdict rolled in. After the company reported a $985 million annual loss for the year on revenues that had declined 25 percent from the previous year to $13 billion, prompting a 50 percent decline in the stock under Johnson's erratic leadership, the JCP commercials began running admitting that yes, Penney's had "made a mistake" by not listening to its customers, while neglecting to mention the far greater mistake made by Ackman and Penney's board for placing such blind faith in their superstar recruit in the first place.

In the ultimate rebuke of both Ackman and Johnson, a deeply fractured board voted to throw in the towel on Johnson's activist-led revolution by making a much safer bet, and getting down on bended knee to beg Myron "I Told You So" Ullman, who had been brusquely pushed out to make way for Johnson, to return as the successor to his successor. After continuing to tussle with the board over the decision to bring Ullman back, Ackman capitulated and sold his remaining shares in Penney's to Citigroup at a deep discount, reporting a $400 million loss on his run at the company.

So let's take a minute to look back on where the Penney board and Ackman had gone wrong in throwing the Hail Mary pass to Johnson.

First and foremost, after dismissing Ullman, they apparently didn't even consider drawing on Penney's existing pipeline for a replacement. Instead, just as the HP board had done when recruiting Fiorina a dozen years earlier, the board had fallen prey to the Halo Effect. Just as Fiorina's halo had been due to the glamour that surrounded the Wall Street success of AT&T spin-off firm Lucent, Johnson's genius had mainly been the genius of Jobs, and Johnson was subsequently revealed as Apple's Wizard of Oz.

While the majority of postmortems focused on Johnson's tragedy of errors, Columbia's Mark Cohen correctly flagged the board's cardinal errors as central to the catastrophe. Pure and simple, the board had fatally misjudged the quality of Johnson's credentials and the relevance of his prior experience. As Cohen correctly said, "He had never been a C.E.O., never mounted or managed a turnaround, had limited fashion-apparel experience, and had no experience in the middle-market space."[12] But while all that was undoubtedly the case, the vast majority of technical, political, and cultural errors Johnson had gotten wrong at Penney's could be chalked up to his outsider status. Yes, he had never run a company on his own or a fully scoped P&L in the way that divisional heads at P&G or GE might have. Yes, he had never managed a turnaround of a failing brand, but had helped goose and burnish brands that were already strong. Yes, he had been out of tune with his customers, out of touch with his own people, and utterly tone deaf when it came to the optics and effect on morale of half the changes he was seeking to drive. He had condescended to his own customers by advising them, on Oscar night no less, that they "deserved to look better," as if to suggest that they looked pretty bad in the present, and possibly even worse in the past.[13]

He had managed to fail the organization and its stakeholders and shareholders—including himself—along all three dimensions. On the technical side, his radical repricing strategy had been based on gut instinct and hunches that had worked for him at Target and Apple but washed out in a mid-market outfit like Penney's. On the political side, he failed to motivate his long-serving managers and instead utterly demoralized them by bringing in an inner cadre of former executives at exorbitant cost. Johnson, the savior outsider, a highflier at Apple and Target, was a misfit in this new environment. No one, it seems, was more surprised at this unlikely turn of events than Johnson himself.

The Insider Versus Outsider Debate

Few subjects related to CEO succession arouse the intensity of interest or fuel such passionate and rancorous debate as the insider versus outsider dilemma. At the risk of repeating myself, the case for an insider selection cannot be overstated. The insider knows the company, knows the industry, knows the people, knows the networks, knows the subtle and shifting alliances, knows the existing strategy and—for better or worse, knows where many of the existing flaws and faults lie and where all the skeletons are buried and where the dirt has been carefully swept under the rug. Most important, to employ another common but useful cliché, the insider is likely to be more sensitive to the cost of throwing the baby out with the bath water.

Yet all that said, in special situations—as when an organization is in deep distress, its core strategy and business model are no longer working, and/or its current leadership, meaning the entire top team, has been fairly or unfairly tinged with the outgoing CEO's tar brush, an outsider selection may be not only justifiable but advisable, even inevitable. Yet make no mistake about it: no matter how successful that outsider may ultimately be, his or her recruitment by definition is the result of failure.

When I say that a *leadership pipeline is broken,* I should emphasize that a pipeline may be broken even when a formal succession plan has been agreed to by the CEO and board, even when that plan has been worked out months or even years in advance of an impending transition, and even when there are qualified candidates inside the company who might be able to take on the job. Where the break often occurs is not so much in the training or development of the next generation of leaders, per se, as in the lack of a system for evaluating those upcoming leaders' developmental opportunities and for giving those leaders the relevant experience that will truly prepare them to succeed, if and when the day comes.

When an existential crisis facing an organization can be plausibly attributed to bad people, strategy, or crisis decisions made by the CEO and his or her entire senior management team, it's not uncommon for industry analysts, activist investors, investor advocates, and other influential stakeholders to openly agitate or apply pressure on the board to bring in a high-profile outsider with a proven track record of radical reinvention. Such wholesale house cleanings typically include not just the flawed strategies that led the company to a pretty pass, but the entire senior team deemed responsible for just about tanking the place. In rare cases, far rarer than the advocates of the outsider-as-change-agent doctrine would like to admit, that analysis of the situation may be correct. That is precisely what occurred in late 1992, when the IBM board did the unthinkable and reached outside for the first time in the company's history to bring in a white knight they hoped against hope could and would pull the organization back from the precipice.

Getting It Right at IBM (After Getting It Wrong)

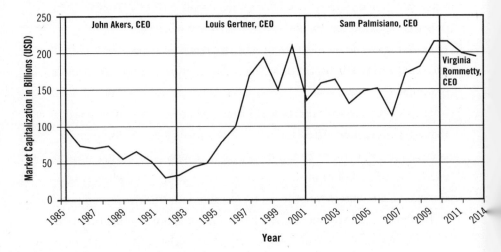

One evening in December 1992, Louis V. Gerstner Jr., a former divisional head at American Express serving as CEO of food and tobacco giant RJR Nabisco, returned home from a charity dinner to his Fifth Avenue New York apartment to the sound of the telephone ringing in his living room. It was a call from the concierge in the lobby, advising Gerstner that "Mr. Burke wants to see you as soon as possible this evening." When Gerstner asked which Mr. Burke he was referring to, because there were two in the building, the concierge replied that it was his upstairs neighbor James Burke, former CEO of pharmaceutical titan Johnson & Johnson.

Gerstner phoned Burke, who cut to the chase by stating that he had heard through the grapevine that Gerstner might be considering returning to American Express as CEO. Gerstner replied that that wasn't true, at which point Burke asked Gerstner to consider taking on a tougher task: turning around IBM. An avid follower of the business press whose brother had worked at IBM in a senior role for decades, Gerstner was aware of the dire straits IBM was in at the tail end of 1992. But as he later recalled to *Fortune,* IBM "looked like it was going into a death spiral. I wasn't convinced it was solvable."[14]

Dire as the situation was, Gerstner was not alone in making that assessment. I had had the misfortune to be an eyewitness to IBM's precipitous decline in the early nineties, having frequently conducted leadership development workshops at the company since the seventies and remained on close terms with IBM CHRO Walton Burdick, who taught at the Human Resources Program I launched at Columbia and moved out to Michigan in 1981. After leaving Crotonville in 1987, I worked closely with Burdick and his staff on a number of tough cultural issues facing the company, including its long-cherished policy of lifetime employment, long considered among one of its greatest strengths. But much as had occurred on Jack Welch's watch at GE, a key values-based policy had turned into an albatross in a company that was no longer a complacent monopoly, but just another player in what had become a truly competitive industry.

IBM circa 1992 was facing even greater challenges to transform itself than GE faced circa 1981. Not surprisingly, Gerstner immediately looked to the Welch Revolution as an example for him to emulate, as nearly every CEO of a legacy iconic company facing competitive challenges driven by advancing technology and globalization did in those days.

Before Gerstner arrived as the new CEO, I had spent several years at IBM in the late 1980s until Akers was let go on January 25, 1993, trying unsuccessfully to help with his transformation of the company. This included running a two-thousand-person workshop with Akers at the Waldorf Astoria to mobilize his leaders to teach more than twenty thousand IBMers to take on projects to transform IBM. The most telling foreshadowing of Akers's demise came in a workshop I was leading in Belgium at the IBM La Hulpe leadership center for Europe with all the IBM presidents of the Europe community. I had to stop an insurrection in the classroom as the heads of the various IBM countries started bashing John Akers. I called a time-out and said I was there to help them and IBM, not trash the CEO. At that time, it was a clear indication to me that Akers had lost the battle and the leaders had turned on him.

But as Gerstner—among others—strongly suspected, changing IBM would just possibly pose an even tougher job than changing GE, with the one bright spot being that in Gerstner's case he would have no trouble constructing a "burning platform for change," because it was widely acknowledged both within and outside the company that radical change was required to save the company. In the early eighties, by stark contrast, Welch had struggled internally and externally to make the case that GE's situation was equally dire.

The extent of IBM's crisis could easily be measured by consulting a historical share price chart depicting the 25 percent drop in the company's market value over the five years that John Akers had been in office to the more than 200 percent rise in the Dow over the same period. That IBM was facing a political as well as a cultural and financial crisis was driven home to me less than a year before Gerstner's recruitment, when I conducted the workshop for the presidents of IBM in Europe, all of whom were more than willing to state, if not for the record, that from their point of view, the company was going to hell in a handbasket. Little did they know that their futures as independent regional chieftains would be among the first targets put on the line for elimination.

In January 1993, just a few weeks after Burke made that first call to Gerstner, IBM's annual financial statement proved the pessimists right, as the company announced a $5 billion annual loss, the largest in U.S. corporate history up to that time. After dropping that financial bombshell, the concurrent announcement that CEO John Akers would be "retiring" immediately—which the board insisted for the record had been a completely voluntary departure—struck most observers as no more than a foregone conclusion. But what was decidedly not a foregone conclusion was the new direction the board was turning to in search of a savior successor. For the first time since the founding of the modern IBM in 1911 as the Computing Tabulating Recording Company, which Thomas Watson Sr. was recruited from rival National Cash Register by the financier who owned it to run (rebranded International Business Machines in 1924), the board, still dominated by former CEOs, had decided to look outside the company.

Within days of that stunning announcement, the names on the list of outsiders began to leak, including such leading lights of the industrial and tech firmaments as Jack Welch, former GE vice chairman, and current AlliedSignal CEO Lawrence Bossidy, EDS founder and former presidential candidate H. Ross Perot, ex–Apple head John Sculley, Eckhard Pfeiffer of Compaq, George Fisher of Motorola, and even Bill Gates of Microsoft. When comparing his own record with those of the names being bandied about, Gerstner didn't take the board's flirtation with his candidacy seriously, particularly since, in his own mind, his lack of technical background and expertise disqualified him from the start. The committee even went so far as to seek input from IBM's toughest competitors, with Sun Microsystems founder Scott McNealy helpfully offering the suggestion that the IBM board should do him a favor and hire "somebody lousy."

Not unlike the position other boards have felt obliged to take when push came to shove, the IBM board's controversial decision to look outside for its next CEO to drag it out of the doldrums constituted an explicit admission that the status quo could no longer be tolerated. By giving Akers the push four years before the official CEO retirement age of sixty at IBM, the board was also paying at least tacit recognition to the fact that the deeply embedded aspects of IBM's stultifying and static paternalistic culture might make it harder for an insider than an outsider to drive radical cultural and political change. In my book, however, it wasn't Akers's "insiderness" that doomed him to fail, but rather that for all IBM's self-conscious devotion to leadership training in the abstract sense, it wasn't structurally, politically, or culturally positioned to offer its rising stars the relevant experience to prepare them for the top job at a point when the company's long-cherished monopoly of mainframe computing was threatened. Not because the mainframe was dead as a dodo, as some maintained, but because the high-technology universe was seismically shifting around it, a fact of life to which many IBM lifers appeared blithely oblivious. As someone who had risen through the marketing ranks for much of his career, Akers was surprisingly tone deaf to the "voice of the customer." The ultimate computer marketer Steve Jobs once dismissed Akers as "a smart, eloquent, fantastic salesperson [who] didn't know anything about product."

Not unlike Bob Stempel at General Motors, a similarly doomed leader of another iconic company, Akers had never run a fully scoped P&L, although after succeeding at a series of marketing positions he had been named president of the Data Processing Division, IBM's largest domestic marketing unit, in 1974 at age thirty-nine. Like Cor Herkströter at Royal Dutch Shell, Akers's political capacity to mobilize the resources to drive deep substantive change had also been hampered by the looming presence of two former CEOs—Frank Cary (CEO 1973–81) and John Opel (CEO 1981–85) on the board, in addition to the founder's son, Thomas Watson Jr., who after stepping down from the board in 1985, remained an important touchstone for the company until his death in 1993. By the end of the Akers era of desultory downsizing, even CHRO Walton Burdick's staff had been cut to shreds, taking a real toll of leadership development and training, having shrunk 90 percent from a peak of four hundred in 1987 to forty in 1992.[15] Poor Akers would frequently call Jack Welch for his advice on how to dispense with the lifetime employment promise, which had become an albatross around his neck, but to hear Welch tell it the ex-CEOs on the board and Thomas Watson Jr. wouldn't hear of it.

But after IBM board members Capital Cities CEO Tom Murphy and former J&J chairman James Burke reached out to Gerstner again, they made it clear that they viewed his relative lack of technical and industry knowledge as an asset, not a liability. What IBM needed most, they stated emphatically, was to be shaken out of its complacency from top to bottom. In tackling this task, his outsider status—not just at the company but within the industry—was in their view a success factor. While it posed significant risks, keeping Akers in the job or appointing an internal successor would pose an even greater risk to the long-term survival of the enterprise.

Let's take a closer look at how that Hail Mary pass ended up being caught in the end zone, turning into the corporate equivalent of a Super Bowl win in the final five seconds. As my old friend and colleague Ram Charan and his coauthors Dennis Carey and Michael Useem point out in their insightful book *Boards That Lead*, the insurgents on the IBM board were successful in forging a consensus on a solution that would have been heretical in prior years.[16] They then created a special committee that deliberately drew on Murphy's and Burke's capabilities in framing a new set of capabilities that made Gerstner their first pick: among the new criteria for the next CEO they decided to stress 1. customer orientation (*check*), 2. business savvy (*check*), and 3. *an ability to execute the changes to reverse the decline.* Most important, they downgraded the key criteria that would have prevented Gerstner from rising to the top: industry and technical background, knowledge, and experience. Intent on restoring IBM to the customer-centricity that had distinguished it during its first seven decades, the board chose to focus its attention on what I would call the candidate's teachable point of view on the enterprise. Gerstner, most critically, went into his new job meticulously vetted as to his TPOV on IBM, on which he was able to execute promptly and effectively, in record time.

Making Judgments Along the Technical/Strategic Dimension

The first strategic question facing IBM in 1993 was whether to keep the company intact or break it up into lots of little "Baby Blues," much as the federal court order of 1984 had broken up the Bell Company's monopoly on telephony into a cluster of Baby Bells. While the phone breakup was regarded as quite successful in opening up competition in the telecommunications field by the early nineties, IBM's case was not exactly parallel, although that divestiture had been the core of Akers's lifeboat strategy, a decision that may well have cost him his job, since many board members, rightly or wrongly, regarded the breakup of the company as a case of killing the patient to cure the disease. While IBM had been the target of one of the longest-running antitrust suits in U.S. history, finally dropped in the mid-eighties under the pro-business Reagan administration, it was Akers who decided on this radical remedy in response to its loss of monopoly, and the threat of competition from such new entrants as Sun, Oracle, and Compaq. While Akers had invited teams of investment bankers to pore over the divisional books, after consulting with a number of experienced IBM managers, including his own brother (who if not for health issues forcing an early retirement might well have been sitting in Louis's seat), Gerstner quickly rendered the most critical decision of his career: to keep the behemoth intact. He based that decision not on any deep industry or technical knowledge but on his experience as a major IBM customer, as the head of a division of American Express that relied on integrated packages of IBM hardware, software, and services to succeed.

His second most important strategic decision, also rooted in a technical issue, was whether to dial down or exit the company's historic reliance on the mainframe. There was a certain logic to this, as IBM was overrun with "Big Iron Bigots," whose allegiance to the mainframe was far more important to them than their allegiance to the future of the enterprise. Much as Intel, HP, and Microsoft would face the apparent decline of the PC in 2013, IBM faced the apparent decline of its core product, the mainframe, twenty years earlier. With next to no technical experience, Gerstner's greatest technical judgment call was to keep the mainframe, but to use it in the new era as a hub from which to compose tightly integrated solutions that played to IBM's strength as a one-stop shop for hardware, software, and services. Under Gerstner, IBM's Software Group, formerly the ugly duckling of the brood, grew into one of the largest software enterprises in the world, second only to Microsoft, while the percentage of revenues generated by hardware seismically shifted in favor of software and services.

Political Judgments

Gerstner would never have committed the cardinal outsider error that Ron Johnson did at JCPenney: coming in like a conquering general and alienating the legacy leadership by callously importing high-priced talent from outside. He would never, he later recalled, have been so naïve or impetuous as to contemplate "coming into a company as complex as IBM with a plan to import a band of outsiders to somehow magically run the place better than the people who were there in the first place."[17] Based on his extensive organizational experience, he scoured the existing structure and hierarchy in search of like-minded souls, "teammates ready to try to do things a different way." That political decision was of course also a cultural one, because the crux of that search involved putting people into positions to drive internal change. It was in the course of that search, in fact, that he found his own successor: Sam Palmisano, Akers's executive assistant through much of the turmoil, an experience that prepared his rise through the ranks in a different, more open era.

Gerstner also decided that the greatest political threat to his revolution was the company's long-standing division into powerful regional units, each run by a local potentate whose interests didn't necessarily tightly align with the enterprise. As had been the case at Royal Dutch Shell during the Herkströter era, going back decades before, Gerstner would later recall openly "declaring war on [IBM's] geographic fiefdoms," and mounting a campaign to replace the rigid regional command-and-control structure with a more globally integrated, more customer-centric organizational matrix made up of business units tailored to serve different customer segments and needs, organized by sector—banking, government, insurance, distribution, manufacturing, and others.

Making Cultural Judgment Calls

Gerstner wisely tackled the more complex cultural questions only after having definitively settled the technical and political issues. He knew the powerful impact that leadership development could play in driving the transition. The hopelessly convoluted array of silos and categories that had grown up at the company like branches on an untrimmed tree didn't provide rising executives with the opportunity to function autonomously as virtual CEOs, as they might have at a truly diversified conglomerate like GE. Jobs's assessment that Akers had been a "smart, eloquent, fantastic salesperson, who didn't know anything about product" could be combined with the fact that his prior experience hadn't prepared him to run a global tech giant like IBM not in the monopoly landscape it had long enjoyed, but in the far more competitive environment of the last decade of the twentieth century.

Perhaps the greatest surprise Gerstner experienced during his tenure at IBM was his realization that "everything at IBM came down to culture." But he wielded a scalpel as opposed to a sledgehammer in slicing away the unwanted fat while retaining muscle and strengthening the bones. He never attempted to blow up the whole complex wholesale, as Ron Johnson had done at Penney's, with deleterious results. Instead, he moved prudently, trimming the tree one branch at a time, revamping the pay policy to link pay to performance, as discussed in the HR chapter in the passage describing Randy MacDonald's role in dialing back on the Basic Belief "Respect for the Individual," long used to justify clinging to the anachronism of lifetime employment, performance be damned. He overhauled the stock option program to make IBMers "think and act more like long-term shareholders." And he disposed of the platinum-plated health benefits, on-campus country clubs, and unwritten lifetime employment contracts that IBM lifers regarded as sacred cows, as opposed to oxen to be gored. He even took on the company's famously staid white shirt and black suit dress code, but cleverly framed the symbolic change as a conservative move. Tom Watson Sr., he explained, had simply requested that his sales staff dress more like their clients, to make them comfortable dealing with IBM salespeople as peers and equals. Half a century later, since the company's customers and clients dressed very differently at the office, Gerstner was simply updating the old Watson policy for a new era.

Rebuilding the IBM Pipeline

"If you asked me today to name the single greatest accomplishment I am most proud of in all my years at IBM, I would tell you it is this—that as I retire, my successor is a longtime IBMer, and so are the heads of all of our major business units." That single sentence, drawn from his memoir, encapsulates Gerstner's determination to rebuild the leadership pipeline that had broken down, seemingly irreparably, under Akers. This is not to say that under Akers the company ever stopped training, coaching, or evaluating its people with respect to their potential to assume leadership roles at some point in their future careers. It is simply that the pipeline under Akers and the lackluster team around him produced no one who could have accomplished what Gerstner did—an indictment of all the effort, resources, and thought expended on teaching development at IBM's version of Crotonville. That simple fact, that the pipeline had broken, forced the board's hand, prompting Murphy and Burke to go outside in search of a change agent. But Gerstner's most enduring legacy-defining decision was to expend an incalculable amount of time, money, and effort rebuilding the pipeline, so no IBM board would have to face that painful and risk-ridden dilemma again. From Sam Palmisano to Virginia Rometty, executive transitions at IBM post-Gerstner have been seamless and undramatic. Nearly going bankrupt was enough drama for even one very big company to take.

Getting It Right at Ford (Finally!)

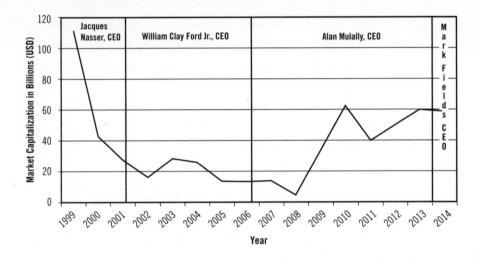

On a Tuesday morning in September 2006, Ford Motor Company executive chairman William Clay Ford Jr., the forty-nine-year-old great grandson of founder Henry Ford, sat on a stage at Ford headquarters in Dearborn, Michigan, twenty miles west of Detroit. To his right sat a beaming Alan Mulally, the sixty-one-year-old former senior vice president of Boeing and head of its wildly successful commercial aviation division, who in a surprise move had been appointed CEO (but not chairman) by a Ford board still heavily influenced by members of the founding family, which controlled and still controls 40 percent of the vote through its ownership of special super-voting Class B shares.

For all the celebratory nature of the occasion, behind the flashbulb-frozen smiles, the staged-for-the-cameras handshakes, and the self-congratulatory rhetoric about a new age dawning at faltering Ford, a reporter for *The New York Times* observantly noted that "Mr. Ford [kept] nervously twisting his wedding ring, while his tired eyes showed the toll that Ford's travails had taken on his runner's frame. No wonder he was uncomfortable. In bringing on Mr. Mulally, a former executive at Boeing, Mr. Ford was conceding, bravely and publicly, that he could not run the place by himself."[18]

Yet to give credit where credit is due, William Ford Jr.'s high-minded decision—one shared with the board, several members of which had been deeply engaged in Mulally's recruitment—to turn over day-to-day management of the company not just to a *family* outsider but to an *industry* outsider earned virtually universal plaudits from analysts. "I have a lot of myself invested in this company, but not my ego," Bill Ford self-effacingly insisted to *The Wall Street Journal*. "I just want the company to do well. It's not about me."[19] As a well-known industry analyst put it, "You have to give Bill Ford credit for putting his pride and his ego aside and reaching outside the company to bring in somebody of Alan Mulally's stature."[20] On that key point, I most wholeheartedly agree.

Yet on another point the board, the CEO, and the chairman had every reason to feel apprehensive, in part because in my view splitting the CEO's and chairman's role is never advisable under any circumstances, but more critically because the Ford Motor Company had quite a lengthy history of contention and disruption on this very issue. Eight years before, practically to the day, I had watched a similar press conference, one strikingly confident in tone, starring the very same but much younger Bill Ford and a newly appointed CEO with whom he was said to be sharing control of the company.

In the fall of 1998, William Clay Ford Jr. had celebrated his ascension to the chairmanship of the Ford board in conjunction with the appointment of Ford veteran Jacques Nasser, an Australian of Lebanese descent, as CEO. On that occasion, Ford had spoken with great confidence of a warm, casual power-sharing arrangement between the two men, one that would be defined by a tendency for them to "just wander in and out" of each other's offices to discuss the business decisions of the day.[21] But just three years later, that warm and confidential relationship had irretrievably broken down, as Jacques Nasser was pushed out the door at the behest of a coterie of insiders who had never cared for the change agenda Nasser was pushing, much of which was strongly influenced by me and my team. In the wake of the Firestone tire/Ford Explorer fatal rollover crisis, Nasser's internal enemies had seen their opportunity to undermine and dislodge him.

Smart and experienced as he was, Nasser played his political cards badly, starting out by ignoring my advice and that of his predecessor, the British-born Alex Trotman, who had pushed hard with the Ford family as he prepared to retire in the fall of 1998 to give Nasser the same titles and responsibilities he had been given when he took the top job: CEO, president, and chairman. But after losing that battle, Trotman had retired, leaving Nasser with the poor choice of hoping to equally partner with the man whose name was on the building, or quit. Not surprisingly, he chose the former. Following Ford's appointment as chairman, Trotman, a former RAF fighter pilot who reportedly possessed a strong antimonarchical streak based on his working-class roots, had been gutsy enough to angrily address the new chairman of the board. "Now Prince William," he sneered, "you have your monarchy." A few months later, he resigned, though, ironically, he had been knighted in 1996 and would become a baron in 1999.

Killing off nonfamily CEOs is something of a Ford family tradition, dating back decades even before the Lee Iacocca era, when Henry Ford II raised the dark art to a new level. As a *Fortune* writer once wrote, the process of management succession at Ford was similar to the use of "firing squads in a South American banana republic."[22] In 1978, superstar Ford president Lee Iacocca, buoyed by the recent success of the Mustang, had been summarily fired by Henry Ford II in the basement executive parking lot as they were entering the building to start work that day. It was a very brief discussion. Iacocca reported that Ford, not so affectionately known as "Hank the Deuce," told him, "You know, sometimes you just don't like someone." So ended Iacocca's tenure at Ford.

Three decades later, a reportedly chastened William Clay Ford Jr. had learned his lesson the hard way: that he simply did not, as *The New York*

Times noted, have what it took to run the family firm all by his lonesome. "After nearly 40 years at Boeing," *The Economist* observed, "Mr. Mulally knows a lot about production lines, suppliers and manufacturing efficiently. But it remains unclear whether Mr. Ford, who remains executive chairman and whose family controls roughly 40% of the votes with only 5% of the shares will give him the independence to get on with the job."

But as opposed to Trotman or Iacocca, Mulally, the new CEO, had been handed a much stronger deck, by virtue of the fact that Ford had just lost a whopping $1.3 billion in the first half of 2006 alone, with Ford's share of the hard-fought domestic market having slipped from 25 percent to 17 percent on William's watch. Even though Mulally wasn't coming in with the titular power of chairman and CEO, he was clearly arriving with a mandate to shake the place up and set it to rights. As auto-industry analyst John Casesa told a reporter from *The New York Times,* "Ford needs a genuine transformation of its business model, and it's pretty hard to achieve such a transformation from the inside."[23]

Technical Judgments

Mulally's most urgent technical mission would be to push forward with a bold recapitalization plan that Bill Ford and his team had been working on but had not yet sold to fickle Wall Street. As Mulally later recalled,

> We were on track to lose $17 billion when I came in 2006. The business was slowing down, fuel prices were going up, and a lot of people were reducing their investment in new products. We needed to decide on a new strategy and then immediately get the financing to do it. We could have asked the banks for just enough money to restructure the business. But we also wanted to accelerate new products to develop a complete family of vehicles and have extra money in case the economy slowed down. It meant adding $23.5 billion in debt as

profits were going down. That was a really hard decision. I knew we'd be generating less profit, but I couldn't let the economy get in the way of what we needed to do. We needed to invest in our product line.[24]

This critical decision to mortgage the company to raise nearly $25 billion in cash would later be credited with providing Ford with the wherewithal to qualify as the only one of the Big Three U.S. automakers to avoid going hat in hand to Uncle Sam for a bailout. With the company adequately capitalized to hold strong in the storm, Mulally's background and experience in the aviation industry gave him the confidence to go in and repair what needed to be fixed about Ford's hidebound and insular engineering culture. "A car might have 10,000 parts and an airplane 4 million," Mulally observed, "but both deal with very complex engineering solutions, with thousands of people working on them around the world."[25]

The Cultural Dimension

Mulally has credited his own Road to Damascus conversion to a data-driven, open, and transparent culture to a formative near-death experience Boeing had suffered nearly a decade before, in 1997, after its commercial division suffered a communications breakdown that caused the divisional leaders to incorrectly match production to falling demand. The result had been a last-minute decision to shut two assembly lines down for a month, forcing the company to take a $2.7 billion charge on the lost income. After being promoted to CEO of the commercial plane division two years later, Mulally had instituted a weekly series of business plan review meetings, during which he carefully grilled all of his senior lieutenants on progress or obstacles they were experiencing delivering against clearly defined targets, as indicated in a red, yellow, or green code. He expected candor, not obfuscation, and took whatever steps he felt were required to get it.

He had been at Ford for only a few weeks when at a meeting of senior lieutenants he went around the table in a conference room, asking tough and probing questions to which he received only the vaguest, flagrantly upbeat responses. Since he knew that the company was projecting a loss from its automotive operations alone of a staggering $17 billion for the year, he wasn't sure where the disconnect lay, but after completing the conference table circuit, a lone hand went up, waving a telltale bright red warning flag. A faulty tailgate latch, the manager in charge of that business explained, was causing serious delays in the production of the Edge sport utility vehicle, forcing his division to restate its annual sales projections for the model, generating a probable loss for the fiscal year. As an embarrassed silence fell in the room, Mulally—to general consternation and surprise—began to enthusiastically applaud. "Great visibility, Mark," Mulally said to the one man in the room brave enough to flash a red flag. "Is there any way we can help you?"

The Mark waving the red flag was Mark Fields, chief of the company's North American division, who had previously run Mazda before taking charge of Ford South America, Ford Europe, and the Premier Auto Group, comprising luxury brands Jaguar, Volvo, and Land Rover. With that one candid admission, Mulally had found his likely successor. True to form, six years later, in November 2012, Mulally and chairman Bill Ford officially appointed Mark Fields chief operating officer. Most telling of all, Mulally asked Fields to run his sacred Thursday morning weekly review meetings, stating for the record that he would be stepping aside from the day-to-day action to "mentor Mark" and keep an eye on broad strategic positioning.

Like Gerstner and other successful outsider CEOs before him, Mulally has made it plain that he is determined not to let the company fall into the dire position of having to call on an outsider like him again, at least not on his watch. He effectively repaired Ford's long-compromised leadership pipeline by decisively putting an end to an ancient Ford custom of frequently shuttling executives in and out of senior positions, never letting them stay in one position for long enough to see through a full business cycle. Fields had held four jobs in the four years prior to Mulally's arrival, yet for six years after that, he stayed in one position as the leader responsible for Ford North America. In 2012, Fields repaid

Mulally's confidence in him by leading his division to an $8.3 billion profit,[26] paving the way for his succession to president. Mulally officially retired on July 1, 2014, and Fields is currently the CEO.

"The speed with which Mulally transformed Ford into a more nimble and healthy operation has been one of the more impressive jobs I've seen," observed veteran industry analyst John Casesa after Mulally had dramatically pulled Ford back from the brink. "It probably would have been game over for Ford already but for the changes he brought."[27]

Getting It Right at Boeing

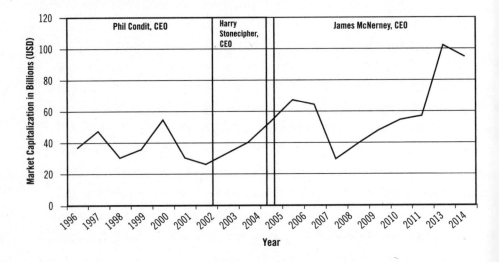

In June of 2005, a little more than a year before Mulally left Boeing to lead Ford, Boeing's board had passed over the one shining star in its own pipeline and named one of its own members as CEO to replace outgoing CEO Harry C. Stonecipher. After serving in the top job for five years between 1997 and 2002, Condit had passed the baton to Stonecipher, whose truncated term of just sixteen months was marked by a seemingly endless series of moral and ethical lapses, not committed by him but committed on his watch, including the firing of chief financial officer Michael Sears after it emerged that he had engaged in illegal hiring discussions with an Air Force procurement officer, Darleen Druyun, before she was hired by Boeing in exchange for steering Air Force contracts to the company. Following their convictions both Sears and Druyun had been sentenced to long prison terms, followed by the additional indignity of seeing Boeing barred from bidding on $1 billion in Air Force rocket launching contracts after a few of its employees were found to have made off with thousands of proprietary documents from archrival Lockheed Martin in an attempt to learn more about their rival's bid.

In the wake of that reputational catastrophe, Condit was pushed out, and the Boeing board resorted to the all-too-familiar crisis tactic of reaching out to a former executive, Stonecipher, to stabilize the ship. Remarkably, the tactic failed after Stonecipher himself was forced to resign in the spring of 2005, after less than a year and a half on the job, following the revelation of an inappropriate relationship with a female employee. All of these shenanigans and skulduggery prompted board chairman Lew Platt—yes, the same Lew Platt who promoted the succession of Carly Fiorina at HP—to reach outside the company for a successor. Except in this case, and to the board's credit, former GE executive and then 3M CEO Jim McNerney had served on the Boeing board since 2001, and was therefore an insider outsider in the context of the aviation giants.

Fortunately, McNerney—whom I have known since he ran GE's Mobile Communications division for Jack Welch, after which he ran Information Services, Financial Services, Electrical Distribution and Control, Asia-Pacific, Lighting, and finally, his true love, Aircraft Engines—jumped to Boeing from 3M with a high degree of confidence that the most vexing technical and strategic issues at the company were in pretty good shape and really didn't need much tinkering from him. But it was also the case that his significant stint at GE Aircraft had given him a strong taste of the aviation business to add to his extraordinary experience moving through the celebrated Welch leadership pipeline. McNerney's own development and growth, he is more than ready to admit, is in large part a by-product of Welch's genius at the game. As he recently told me, it was this wealth of experience more than anything else that set him up for that rare outsider success at both 3M and Boeing.

> I think my career may highlight one aspect of leadership development, which is the volume of different jobs and how all that volume can add up to relevant experience. I was always willing to take on new assignments and always liked the changing landscape at GE. My story is probably that diversity of experience does count, and is important.

Boeing's technical prowess appeared to be taking care of itself, as expressed in the looming rollout of the long-awaited 787 Dreamliner—ironically developed under the leadership of Ford's Mulally—which was widely acknowledged to be the most fuel-efficient, technologically advanced commercial airliner of its generation. One of its most innovative design features, apart from an unprecedented use of lightweight carbon-fiber composites and an outsourcing model that farmed out far more of the manufacturing around the world than had been customary at the company, was its reliance on lightweight lithium-ion batteries for power. Seven years after he signed on, a series of mysterious explosions and fires from those batteries would trigger the greatest crisis of McNerney's career.

A graduate of Yale and Harvard Business School who starred on his high school ice hockey team and played on the same varsity baseball team at Yale as future president George W. Bush, McNerney is the oldest of six siblings and the son of a respected professor of management at Northwestern's Kellogg School of Business who spent his early years in Michigan while his father taught at the University before moving on to Northwestern. After Yale and Harvard, he took his first corporate job as a brand manager at Procter & Gamble, followed by a seven-year stint at McKinsey, followed by a remarkable twenty-three-year career at General Electric, where he ran seven major GE divisions. By 2001, McNerney was one of three finalists in the bake-off to succeed Welch, along with Bob Nardelli, head of Power Systems, and Jeff Immelt, head of Medical Systems, popularly referred to as "GEMS." At five in the afternoon on the Friday after Thanksgiving in 2000, Welch officially named Jeff Immelt his successor, while announcing that he would be postponing his long-planned retirement for a few months to see through what he then hoped would be the capstone of his career.

Unfortunately, while GE's acquisition of electronics leader Honeywell was ultimately foiled by European Union regulators on antitrust grounds, Welch in remarkably short order succeeded in spiriting the two finalists, Nardelli and McNerney, who lost the horse race to Immelt, into CEO jobs at what might charitably be considered lesser yet still outstanding companies. Two weeks after the Immelt announcement, the board of 3M (Minnesota Mining and Manufacturing) announced that it was reaching outside the company for the first time in its ninety-eight-year history to name McNerney its new CEO, passing over six insiders. McNerney's appointment went over well with the analyst community, who were nearly unanimous in their opinion that the old-line manufacturing company was in real need of what one referred to as "an infusion of GE dynamism."[28] That was precisely what McNerney delivered. As he later told *Businessweek*,

> It's easy to make the speech about leadership and then disappear into a backroom grading everybody . . . [But] we spent a year debating what leadership is. I made speeches on the subject and solicited input from everybody. So when we hammered it out, it was the company's leadership goals we were aspiring to—not the CEO's, not some consultant's, not what we read in a book last week . . .[29]

After landing at Boeing, he was careful not to further destabilize a reeling company but at the same time careful to radically address some seemingly insurmountable cultural, as opposed to strictly technical, challenges. His first symbolic/cultural move was to shift the annual senior leaders' three-day retreat from its customary setting at an elegant resort in Palm Springs, California, to a nondescript Hyatt Regency in

Orlando, Florida, and cut it down to a day and a half of sober and sobering meetings and presentations, in contrast to the famously wild parties in Palm Springs. The first two presentations set a bracing new tone of candor and were deliberately designed for maximum Richter-scale impact.

McNerney roundly castigated the company's senior management for having "gotten carried away with itself," for relying on a massive bureaucracy as "a place to hide" (shades of Jack Welch), and, most important, for "failing to develop the best leadership." General counsel Doug Bain then took over the podium to deliver a sermon railing against the company's "culture of silence." To drive his point home, Bain showed a slide with a series of numbers. "Those aren't zip codes," he barked, but the prison numbers of the two jailed former Boeing employees. Bain completed his presentation on a decidedly down note. Many prosecutors, Bain insisted, regarded "Boeing as rotten to the core."[30]

This was a knock-down drag-out cultural war, and McNerney was determined to win it. Yet another key challenge to Boeing's revival was political, as McNerney learned soon after his first meeting with senior staff, where he detected a strong whiff of internal rivalry and tension, the legacy of the previous leadership's failure to fully integrate Boeing employees with those of its former rival, McDonnell Douglas, acquired nearly a decade earlier, in 1997. This was why, he later told me, he set out to tackle the "soft issues" of values and culture first and left the business and technical strategies for the later innings. On January 7, 2013, all of those cultural and political dynamics were put to the test when the sixty-two-year-old McNerney learned that one of the revolutionary, lightweight, cutting-edge lithium-ion batteries powering a Japan Airlines Dreamliner had caught fire on a runway at Boston's Logan Airport, prompting the emergency evacuation of all of its passengers.

McNerney called upon his chief technology officer to provide him with an independent channel of information apart from the data coming directly from the directors of the 787 program,[31] not because he didn't trust the program's managers but because he knew that in managing complex technical and industrial projects, redundant knowledge and information is as important as redundant technology—it's a way to manage risk. He assigned more than 250 managers and engineers from across the company to an around-the-clock investigation of the causes of the battery fire, while simultaneously opening direct lines of communications with his board of directors and government officials, with particular focus on senior officials at the Federal Aviation Administration (FAA).

The news a week later that the pilots of an All Nippon Airways 787 had been forced to make an emergency landing after receiving a battery-fault warning in Japan reinforced a growing suspicion that the Boston battery fire was not an isolated incident. Within ten days of the Boston fire, all fifty 787s in operation worldwide were grounded for what would turn out to be a four-month trial by fire, not only of the innovative and cost-effective new airplane, but of McNerney's leadership.

In a November 2012 interview, conducted two months before the onset of the battery issue, I asked McNerney—whom I have known since the eighties—what he considered to be his greatest accomplishment both at 3M and Boeing. He immediately spoke of distilling the values of leadership down to its core elements.

> When we finally got down to the leadership attributes we were finally able to say, "This is what we're going to be, this is what a good leader is." And then the really tough job became tying these values back to the business challenge. Because the single most important part of developing a leadership pipeline is to create a culture of performance. That may sound so simple, but cultures can support so many things other than performance. And then you end up with a culture that values things that aren't important to your customers. If you don't have a culture of performance you'll develop an inauthentic pipeline. You'll have one that's not ready for the future because it hasn't performed today.[32]

Getting It Right at AlliedSignal

In July 1991, longtime GE vice chairman Lawrence Bossidy, who had occasionally asked Welch to promote him to the presidency, to no avail, finally got his own company to run. The New Jersey–based AlliedSignal Corporation, a sprawling aerospace, automotive components, chemicals, engineered materials, and technology conglomerate, had been gamely cobbled together by the fiercely acquisitive Edward L. Hennessy Jr. from the former Allied Chemical Company. On the day Bossidy took over, its outstanding debt ran to more than 40 percent of capital on hand, cash was flowing out instead of in, and morale at every level of the organization was hitting new lows prompted by rumors of imminent mass layoffs and restructuring.

On his first day on the job, after a senior executive showed Bossidy a freshly hatched internal forecast that predicted a negative cash flow of $435 million for 1991 and an additional $336 million in 1992, he was handed yet another chart reflecting the results of an employee satisfaction survey that plainly revealed a level of morale that, he later told *Fortune,* was "the worst I'd ever seen."[33] His first order of business was to cut capital spending, cut the annual dividend, cut eight divisions, cut 6,200 jobs, and combine ten data-processing centers into two. But even when tackling that technical task, he never forgot that this radical restructuring possessed a strong cultural component. The "infusion of GE dynamism" into a reluctant host culture required the importation of new DNA into the organism, as he later reflected on during an interview that Ram Charan and I conducted with him, published in the *Harvard Business Review.*[34] "We had 58 business units, each guarding its own turf. It was an inner-directed company, focused mainly on itself. Management made all the decisions, and employees' ideas were rarely solicited and therefore rarely offered," Bossidy recalled. This political structure constituted a cultural handicap, so his next step was to spend two days hunkered down with the top leaders of the company defining the values that they could all agree on as guides to provide direction for the path ahead. Then, and only then, did he turn to the people piece. As he later recounted in his own *Harvard Business Review* article,

> I devoted what some people considered an inordinate amount of emotional energy and time—perhaps between 30% and 40% of my day for the first two years—to hiring and developing leaders. That's a huge amount of time for a CEO to devote to any single task. . . . But I knew it was essential. I'm convinced that AlliedSignal's success was due in large part to the amount of time and emotional commitment I devoted to leadership development.[35]

By 1994, the dramatic turnaround executed by the then fifty-nine-year-old Bossidy earned him more than just praise from a grateful board, which doubled his salary and awarded him a compensation package worth up to $47 million over six years. With its stock up 110 percent, earnings up 97 percent, and its market value more than doubled from $4 billion to $10 billion, the salary and stock awards he reaped certainly seemed like a bargain.

In late 1999, in what was clearly intended to mark a milestone in the company's stunning transformation, Bossidy spent nearly $15 billion in cash acquiring Honeywell. What was initially billed as a merger of equals didn't mesh the two companies' cultures. A year later, Jack Welch learned that United Technologies, whose Pratt & Whitney division manufactured jet engines and directly competed with GE in that category, had hatched a plan to buy Honeywell. From his car phone, Welch urgently reached out to every member of the GE board, and within minutes gained their support to make a counteroffer that Honeywell, he knew, would find nearly impossible to refuse.[36]

It took Welch only two days to snag Honeywell in what was billed as the largest merger between two industrial companies in history. But the plan of the century hatched by the manager of the century was dealt a fatal setback after Mario Monti, the future prime minister of Italy, then overseeing competition for the European Commission, torpedoed the merger on antitrust grounds.

The collapse of the merger prompted Honeywell's board to ask Bossidy to step back into his old job following the ouster of Honeywell's former CEO, Michael Bonsignore. The sixty-six-year-old Bossidy brought in an outsider, the newly appointed CEO of the Cleveland-based industrial giant TRW and former head of GE Appliances, David Cote, as his successor.

Getting It Right at Honeywell

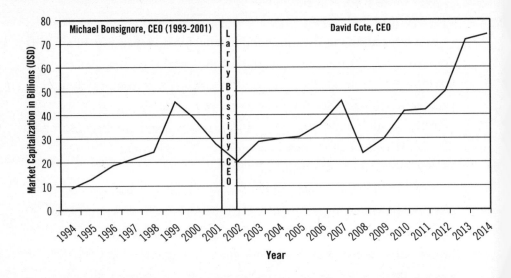

As Bossidy told *The New York Times,* he had been "scouring corporate America for a successor. I didn't care if he or she was quiet or loud, or came from finance or marketing or someplace else. I just wanted someone with passion for the job, who would have the gas and energy for the next 10 years."[37, 38] David Cote's first task was political, unifying a company that included people from three factions: legacy Honeywell, legacy AlliedSignal, and legacy Pittway, a recently acquired fire and safety systems manufacturer. Like Gerstner and Mulally before him, he had powerful, fiercely independent regional chieftains to contend with, win over, or let go, as symbolized by the fact that when he convened a meeting for regional heads in Europe, only a few of them even bothered to show up to meet him. Over the decade that Cote has run Honeywell, the turnaround has been little short of spectacular. Following eighty-three acquisitions and fifty-eight sold businesses, the portfolio today is organized around a coherent cluster of central themes: energy efficiency, clean energy generation, safety and security, and globalization. The scale of Cote's achievement is best measured by metrics any GE alum would value: Between the end of 2003 and April 2014, Honeywell's stock increased 174 percent from $33.43 to $93.09. Measured by total return to shareholders, during that period investors earned returns of 249 percent, which put Honeywell in second place among industrial conglomerates—just behind Danaher and ahead of United Technologies, not to mention GE, which returned less than 10 percent over the same period, while the S&P returned 88 percent.

Whether it's Gerstner at IBM, Mulally at Ford, McNerney at Boeing, Bossidy at AlliedSignal, or Cote at Honeywell, successful outsiders work equally hard to strike the right balance among dramatically different and often competing priorities: resolving the organization's technical and political challenges while rejuvenating often distorted and outmoded cultures. Last but not least, the ultimate gauge of their success was the restoration of the ruptured leadership pipelines that brought them into the mix in the first place. As outsiders they knew how important it was to nurture insiders, so white knights like themselves would never be needed again. This critical distinction between outsiders and insiders and their respective assets and liabilities has been most insightfully articulated by Harvard Business School professor Joseph L. Bower:

> Both insider and outsider CEOs have strengths and weaknesses when they begin. Insiders know the company and its people but are often blind to the need for radical change—they've drunk the Kool-Aid. Outsiders see the need for a new approach but can't foster change

because they don't know the company or industry sector well enough. What organizations need, then, is to find a way to nurture what I call *inside-outsiders*—that is, internal candidates who have outside perspective. For some companies, that may look like mission impossible. But the succession crisis will only get worse if companies don't tackle the problem.[39]

CHAPTER 8

BUILDING A SUCCESSION PIPELINE IN FAMILY ORGANIZATIONS

Unless you're willing to take a risk of failing with your own children, they will never be able to demonstrate what it is that they are capable of doing. —**Ivan Lansberg, Lansberg, Gersick and Associates**

It is much cheaper to pay a lazy nephew not to come to work than to keep him on the payroll.

—**Peter F. Drucker, "How to Save a Family Business"**

He that spareth his rod hateth his son: but he that loveth him chasteneth him betimes. —**King James Bible, Book of Proverbs, 13:24**

Princes who come to their position by good fortune do so with little exertion on their part, but subsequently, they maintain their position only through considerable exertion. [But] those who become rulers by prowess acquire their principalities with difficulty but hold them with ease.

—**Niccolò Machiavelli, *The Prince***

TECHNICAL

- Carving out a career path for family members
- Integrating professional management pipeline with family pipeline

POLITICAL

- Productively managing potential conflicts between family and nonfamily professional managers
- Designing appropriate board and governance structure for sustaining family enterprise

CULTURAL

- Enforcing culture of performance, not entitlement
- Ensuring that the family culture is unifying, not divisive, and productive to the enterprise

Fast Facts About Family Businesses

Family businesses comprise 90 percent of all business enterprises in North America, and 62 percent of total U.S. employment.

Sixty percent of current worldwide enterprises are family-owned, generating from 40 to 60 percent of the world's GNP.[1]

Only 30 percent of family businesses in America will pass the reins to the next generation, although close to 70 percent would like to keep the business in the family.

By the third generation, only 12 percent of family businesses in the United States are typically still viable. Only 3 percent of family businesses survive the fourth generation and beyond.

The environment for innovation in family businesses improves when more generations of the owning family are actively involved in the business.

Return on investment is greater in family businesses, averaging a 6.65 percent greater return than nonfamily firms.

The average life span of a family-owned business is twenty-four years.

Between 10 percent and 15 percent of U.S. family firms are managed by nonfamily executives.

In nearly half (47.7 percent) of all family-owned business collapses in the United States, the failure of the business was precipitated by the founder's death, or in 29.8 percent of the cases, the owner's unexpected death. Only in relatively few instances (16.4 percent) did the business failure follow an orderly transition, and in situations where the owner was forced to retire, the figure drops to 6.1 percent

[SOURCES: Small Business Administration; Peakfamilybusiness.com; *Family Business Review*; *Family Business Magazine*; ffi.org; familybusinesscenter.com; Barclays Wealth and The Economist Intelligence Unit; University of Connecticut Family Business Program; as provided in Cindy Krischer Goodman, "Three-Generation Family Businesses Share Their Secrets of Success," *Miami Herald*, Jan. 20, 2013.]

A Tale of Two Cities

Getting It Wrong at Anheuser-Busch

In 2008, the forty-seven-year-old beer baron August "Augie" Busch IV, familiarly known to family and friends as "The Fourth," reluctantly acceded to the $52 billion takeover by Belgian beverage conglomerate InBev of the 151-year-old beer company founded by his great-great-great-grandfather Adolphus Busch in 1857, the longtime spirit of St. Louis, Anheuser-Busch. Within months of the sale, the family scion who had presided over the dizzying fall of the "House of Busch" spiraled into a deep depression, divorced his wife, left his family, and shacked up with a former waitress at Hooters twenty years his junior, who would later die from a drug overdose in a disheveled back bedroom of his six-thousand-square-foot mansion set on four wooded acres in suburban St. Louis.

After the world-famous beer company with the world-touring Clydesdale horses succumbed to an irresistible bid from a foreign conglomerate, it's not surprising that the fourth-generation heir felt the loss deeply and personally, regarding it as a failure to family, community, and legacy. Yet there were still plenty of people in St. Louis old enough to recall that during Prohibition, when the company wasn't permitted to sell beer and narrowly survived by selling yeast and other beer-making ingredients to distributors, the Busches had dug into their suddenly shallower pockets to keep more than two thousand otherwise unemployable people on the payroll until the good times began rolling again. For seven decades after Prohibition was repealed, Anheuser-Busch dominated the American beer market, until by the first decade of the twenty-first century, it suddenly did not. Around the Busches' hometown, the sardonic saying went that while it had taken four generations to build the House of Busch, it had taken just one to tear it down.

Getting It Wrong at Seagram

In June 2000, the occasional songwriter, would-be music mogul, and flamboyant film producer Edgar Bronfman Jr., the handsome scion of the Bronfman family of Montreal, the majority owners and founders of the liquor and entertainment colossus Seagram, confided in Jean-Marie Messier, a self-styled visionary hell-bent on transforming the sleepy French water utility Compagnie Générale des Eaux into a $51 billion global media conglomerate, that he was haunted by an old saying about family businesses: "The first generation builds, the second becomes wealthy and the third generation loses everything."[2] This ancient folk adage, various versions of which can be heard around the world, was all too familiar to Edgar Jr.'s grandfather Sam Bronfman, a Russian immigrant who had succeeded in acquiring the venerable Canadian distiller Seagram in 1928 and prospered by selling licit Canadian whiskey into the illicit American market at the height of Prohibition, just as the Busches to the south were having a hard time of it staying afloat. Old man Sam had conceded as much in a 1966 interview with *Fortune*, glumly and prophetically observing: "You've heard about shirtsleeves to shirtsleeves in three generations? I'm worried about the third generation. Empires have come and gone."

Thirty-four years later, Sam's grandson Edgar Jr. and his son Edgar Sr. shared in the widespread jubilation that Messier and Vivendi International's highball $77-a-share offer for the whole company brought to the founding family, as it represented a whopping 45 percent premium over the company's then market price. To the much-maligned Edgar Jr., who had quietly endured a decade of harsh criticism from, among others, his uncle Charles, a noted Canadian philanthropist, the deal was sweet vindication, as on paper, at least, his 1995 decision, backed to the hilt by his father, to sell Seagram's 25 percent stake in chemical and life sciences giant DuPont to raise cash to buy MCA Universal and Polygram seemed to have panned out precisely as planned.

While neither business had generated the handsome and consistent returns that the DuPont stake would have if they had passively held on to it, since the stake had soared in value after DuPont gladly bought it back from Seagram's at a steep discount—the $34 billion windfall for Seagram's, of which the family's take was roughly $6 billion, appeared to have further reaffirmed Edgar Sr.'s controversial selection of Edgar Jr. as CEO and successor, at least for a time.

Yet as the long-running soap opera title famously put it, as the world turns. . . . Less than a year after the Bronfmans closed their landmark merger with Vivendi, the dot-com boom burst, and the globe-spanning house of cards that the messianic and manic Messier had assembled at a dizzying pace, in part with cash raised from the sale of Seagram's core liquor business to two spirits distributors, collapsed in the harsh winds of reality. By the time Messier's $70 billion–plus shopping spree came to a screeching halt, the bulk of his purchases landed squarely on Vivendi's shaky books, saddling the flailing mirage of a media conglomerate with a hefty $20 billion in debt and cutting the residual value of the Bronfman family holdings in the hulking colossus that remained by half, from $6 to $3 billion.

But more than the monetary losses, the loss of face and prestige both Bronfmans, father and son, suffered, on top of the damage the soured deal had done to relations with the Canadian branch of the family, hurt more. Within a matter of months, the father-son tag team of deal makers went from looking like business geniuses on a par with the dearly departed "Mr. Sam" to looking more like a pair of greenhorns sold the Brooklyn Bridge by a smooth-talking Frenchman who had quietly picked their pockets over a fancy French lunch.

The Family Firm: Built to Last?

These back-to-back stories about billionaire brats blowing their family fortunes represent an all-too-common truth about multigenerational family businesses, one aptly summed up by that ancient and haunting phrase, "rags to riches to rags in three generations." Predicting the inevitability of generational decline in family enterprises dates back at least to the late nineteenth-century claim by the Scottish-born American steel robber baron Andrew Carnegie that "there are but three generations in America from shirt sleeves to shirt sleeves. Under such conditions an aristocracy of wealth is impossible."[3]

In those heady industrial days, when only workingmen wore "shirtsleeves" to their jobs, while upper- and middle-class gentlemen wouldn't have been caught dead in their offices without their status-affirming dark suits and ties, the "shirtsleeves to shirtsleeves" image not only caught the public's imagination, it tended to deflect the broader society's attention from the wealth being amassed by first-generation entrepreneurs, many of whom—including Carnegie, J. P. Morgan, John D. Rockefeller, and others of their Gilded Age ilk—vowed to give away much of their vast fortunes to charity, even as they took great pains to sustain their family fortunes for future generations, which for the most part they successfully did.

Current statistics support the folklore. In the United States, close to 70 percent of the proprietors of family enterprises *say* they would like to keep their businesses in the family, but only 30 percent *succeed* in passing the reins on to a second generation. Only 12 percent in fact succeed in passing their wealth on to a third generation, while a paltry 3 percent of family businesses manage to survive into the fourth. The founders, proprietors, and heirs of family businesses, however, should take comfort in the fact that the only thing such statistics truly tell us is that trends are based on averages. As I have observed in prior pages, the problem with averages is that they reveal next to nothing about superior and subpar performance, which are the only examples from which real-life actual, actionable lessons can be drawn for the rest of us.

Statistics aside, the one true inheritance and legacy that firm-founding self-made parents can never pass on to their kids, no matter how much they wish to, is their own pride, satisfaction, and delight at having built up a great business from scratch. In the absence of what must be considered a largely psychological legacy, entrepreneurial founder parents are left hoping to inculcate in their offspring a similar sense of pride and achievement in their own accomplishments. Yet the obvious fact is that the accomplishments and achievements of the vast majority of second-, third-, and even fourth-generation heirs must inevitably feel compromised by the sense of privilege that significant inheritance brings.

The only solution to this issue that has ever proved practical is for parents to take special care to permit their offspring to *take real risks in search of real rewards.* Just as they themselves overcame and faced down the prospect of failure, successors and heirs to family businesses must operate in an environment where they can do the same—succeed or fail on their own merits or demerits.

The number-one lesson for all family founders: just as all good leaders provide their rising next-generation potential successors with crucible experiences designed for them to assume the responsibility of taking on real risk in the future, all crucible experiences designed by incumbent leaders of family business to develop heirs into leaders must entail real risk and real reward. Not surprisingly, as would be the case for most parents, who are often deathly afraid that their kids won't be as driven or successful as they are, this can be a very tough lesson to absorb and to follow. Yet experience has shown, and the cautionary tales of the Busches and Bronfmans vividly illustrate, the perils of ignoring this rock-bottom truth: the key to the preservation of family wealth and enterprise over the course of future generations is no different from the developmental challenges all leaders face in passing the baton to the next generation. *How do we, the current generation of leaders, mentor, teach, coach, and provide our potential successors with the right crucible experiences that will truly prepare them to make good business decisions in all three key judgment areas: people, strategy, and crisis?*

The Parent Trap

In this context of designing good or not-so-good crucible experiences for heirs, it is instructive to note the wide world of difference between how Edgar Bronfman Sr. was raised by his curmudgeonly, cantankerous, entrepreneurial father and how he chose to raise his own son to take over from him, ironically because Edgar Sr. suffered dearly at the hands of the controlling Sam, an experience he hoped to spare Edgar Jr. The first task that old man Sam assigned his son after he graduated from college—first Williams, then McGill—was to spend his formative years working at Seagram's Montreal headquarters as a clerk in the accounts payable and receivable department. After painstakingly learning the financial side of the business from the ground up, young Edgar was then tasked by his tough-love dad with spending another few years working on the floor of Seagram's original plant, learning the ins and outs and the fine arts of blending spirits. After that task was completed to the discerning Sam's satisfaction, the future CEO-in-training spent yet another multiyear stint working outside the family fold, learning the ropes of mergers and acquisitions at a small investment bank that specialized in arranging creative financing for oil companies. In short, by the time Edgar Sr. was finally invited to return to Seagram's as a senior executive, he was a veteran of countless deals in which he had not had the privilege of leaning back on his family fortune to pull them off. If anything, he had been carefully hardened by crucible experiences more tasking and challenging than those of many of the other senior executives who had climbed up the ladder at the family firm.

By the time he took over from his father as Seagram's CEO, Edgar was knowledgeable enough about finances and deal making to confidently embark on a diversification strategy based largely on his experience as a banker to the oil industry. Starting out with a modest $65 million investment in Texas Pacific Coal and Oil, he moved on to pick up other stakes in other oil companies at attractive prices, all in keeping with a carefully conceived long-range strategy that culminated in his 1981 decision to make a run at oil giant Conoco and then, after being beaten to the punch by DuPont, masterfully trading the stake he had built up in Conoco for a 25 percent share in the chemicals and life sciences colossus. Over the course of his twenty-three years as Seagram CEO, Edgar Sr. nearly quintupled sales from $1.5 to $5.2 billion, and more significant, held on to that share in DuPont as it gradually grew to an $8 billion pile that threw off as much in annual dividends as it had cost to buy. At $300 million plus in free cash flow per year, the DuPont holding significantly outpaced profits from the core spirits business.

It was that symbolic stake, widely regarded within the family as its crown jewel, which Edgar Jr. decided to liquidate in 1995, after he took over from his father at age forty-seven. While his uncle Charles was deeply upset about this seismic shift to Hollywood, music, and movies, he didn't try to block the strategy because, he later maintained, he was intent on preserving family unity even at the potential cost of the family fortune. It's worth noting that by steadfastly refusing to second-guess his son's strategic decisions as his father had continually done to him, Edgar Sr. was in so many respects sincerely "doing the right thing." Unfortunately for all concerned, with the possible exception of Messier, Edgar Sr.'s decision to give his son and CEO free rein ultimately led to their embarking on a disastrous course, foreshadowed by founder Sam's gloomy prediction of eventual failure several decades before.

The true tragedy of the Bronfman saga is not that the family lost a ton of money, because if you have a few billion left, it's always possible to make those billions back. It is that a proud and doting father, hoping to avoid causing the pain to his son that his father had caused him, ended up actually failing his son by indulging him in his every whim, inadvertently setting him up for precisely the failure that would define his checkered career. The lesson here is pretty simple, and can be summed up with another folk adage based on a quote from the King James Bible: "Spare the rod, and spoil the child."

In 2003, ten years before he died in 2013, Edgar Sr. waxed philosophical over that loss, insisting that perhaps it was better for his descendants, including twenty-two grandchildren, not to be burdened with the heavy obligation he and his son had grown up with to preserve and grow the family fortune as their lives' work.

> I'm glad that there isn't any Seagram to leave to them [because] this whole question of entitlement and that they're the Seagram Bronfmans or whatever is not a good thing. People have to go and fend for themselves. I don't know who the hell would run it. There would be family fights. It's much better not to have that as a legacy.[4]

Edgar Jr., for his part, revealed a profound ambivalence about having accepted his father's offer—more like a command—to take over from him at the tender age of forty-seven. "It was the family legacy," he said, "My father wanted to turn it over to the third generation. I felt I couldn't really say no."[5]

All in the Family

Not for nothing is that overused term "Shakespearean" so frequently invoked by observers and commentators when attempting to relate, analyze, and describe these never-ending and seemingly never-resolved dynastic dramas, dynamics, and dilemmas. We can often detect distinct echoes of *King Lear, Macbeth, Hamlet,* and the royal history plays—in particular the two parts of *Henry IV* starring the playboy Prince Hal, boozing and partying with Falstaff, who matures into a brilliant military strategist following the epic battle of Agincourt on St. Crispin's Day before reigning wisely over his subjects as King Henry V—when mulling over the the demonic dance of succession surrounding the aging Lear-like Rupert Murdoch, the crusty media patriarch, who at various times has treated all three of his offspring by his first marriage as likely and potential successors or outcasts, depending on whim, fate, and circumstance.

Who can forget the riveting cliff-hanger succession drama—still unresolved—of yet another aging media mogul, Viacom and CBS Corp chairman Sumner Redstone, who after famously falling out with his daughter Shari in 2008 led the whole world to believe that he would be naming his nonfamily CEO Philippe Dauman his successor. In late September 2012, he unequivocally told *The New York Times,* "I can't say what will happen after I'm gone—which will be never. But everyone understands, I think, that Philippe [Dauman] will be my successor."[6] But less than a month later, in October, he capriciously announced in an interview with *The Wall Street Journal* that he remained undecided. "Philippe," he cagily confided, "knows that Shari might be my successor and that it's not a competitive race between them. We just have to see what happens."[7]

Family Businesses Aren't Anachronisms:
They Dominate the Global and U.S. Economies

Whether we're talking about the global engineering and construction conglomerate Bechtel, the Ford Motor Company, the energy giant Koch Industries, the $23 billion food and candy company Mars, the $9 billion household products company S. C. Johnson & Son, the agricultural combine Cargill, the hospital giant HCA Holdings, the cable giant Comcast, or the leading chip producer Qualcomm, family businesses account for a staggering 50 percent of the gross domestic product in the United States, and 60 percent of all employment and 78 percent of new jobs created here. According to a 2010 McKinsey study,[8] one third of all companies in the S&P 500 index and 40 percent of the 250 largest companies in France and Germany are family-owned, which the authors define as any businesses in which a single family owns a significant share and can influence important decisions, in particular *the selection of the chairman and CEO.* The McKinsey study also uncovered a revealing fact: from 1997 to 2009 a broad index of publicly traded family firms in the United States and Western Europe achieved total returns to shareholders (TRS) *two to three percentage points higher* than those of the MSCI World, the S&P 500, and the MSCI Europe indexes. The study also determined that during downturns and financial crises, privately held family firms often prosper because they are able to opportunistically seize on the opportunity to invest in assets at temporarily depressed prices, while their publicly traded brethren are constrained by shareholder sentiment and anxiety from spending their money during a period of economic contraction—which is precisely when they should be spending it.

Yet another study,[9] based on an analysis of 150 publicly traded family-controlled businesses with revenues of more than $1 billion based in the United States, Canada, France, Spain, Portugal, Italy, and Mexico, found a direct correlation between the superior performance of family-run companies during bad economic times and their long-term view of financial performance. The authors maintain that "family businesses focus on resilience more than performance, and forgo the excess returns available during good times in order to increase their odds of survival during bad times." Executives of family businesses, they found, often invest with a ten- or twenty-year horizon, "concentrating on what they can do now to benefit the next generation. They also tend to manage their downside more than their upside, in contrast with the CEOs of publicly-traded firms, who are obliged to make their mark through outperformance."

While it is widely recognized that family firms are the most common type of business organization worldwide (the Spanish Instituto de la Empresa Familiar [IEF] estimates that 60 percent of current worldwide enterprises are family-owned, generating from 40 to 60 percent of the world's GNP[10]), since the 1950s a growing body of research has focused on the inevitable conflicts between nonfamily and family managers, particularly with regard to leadership transition and succession. But what all of the research in the world would find nearly impossible to quantify is the degree to which family firms possess a unique form of intellectual and human capital, comprising the knowledge gained through the life experiences of each family member, as well as what those family members know about the business and the relationships they have built up over years to achieve that success. Apart from a balance sheet, family businesses and their preservation are about shared values expressed in the form of long-held traditions and culture, and business acumen transmitted to their employees, who are often treated like extensions of the founding family. These are the legacies that drive family firms, and while their loss can be a source of great pain, their possession can be a source of great joy for a family that pulls together through thick and thin to preserve not just the dynasty, or the fortune, but the far more intangible legacy and mission. A case in point is the Sulzberger family, owners of *The New York Times*, which has over generations and centuries defined its mission as preserving an asset that is of unique benefit to a free society.

Seven Best Practices for Handling Succession in Family Businesses

(from founding editor of *Family Business*, professor, and consultant Ivan Lansberg)

1. Create interest in the company while the kids are growing up—often kids shy away from going into the business.

2. Parents should model enthusiasm for the business, talk about the company around the dining room table, design internships, expose children to business, who may pick up the bug.

3. Let children know that even if they express interest in the business there are no guarantees of easy entry; there are still certain things you have to do: get a good education, possibly work for another company, build your own business before entering the family firm.

4. When and if they do enter, they need a real job, with real accountability, with real performance criteria, with real rigorous assessment and feedback, and with real risks of failure.

5. Some forms of protection are needed for the assessors of the children so that they are free to speak their mind honestly about the kids' development and progress.

6. Get consensus from the family on the ground rules for assessing the children, and see to it that the children understand that they will need to submit to those mechanisms and that the family needs to tolerate the turbulence of this honest assessment process.

7. Family businesses often require two boards: one a solid professional board and a second that constitutes a forum where the family can come together and have the big picture discussion: Why is the business in our family? What does it mean to us? What are our core values and how do we want to do things in the business? The discussion needs to continuously address the urgent question of why the family is good for the business long term.

The Lansberg Family Formula

To gain some additional insight into the complex dynamics of CEO succession and leadership transition in multigenerational family-owned enterprises, I sat down with my old friend and colleague Ivan Lansberg, a senior partner at the New Haven, Connecticut–based research and con-

sulting company Lansberg, Gersick and Associates, to discuss and explore the special circumstances that make leadership transition and
succession and "passing the baton" in family-owned companies even
more complex, emotionally fraught, and potentially politicizing and polarizing than in publicly held or private nonfamily enterprises. In the
spirit of full disclosure, I have known Ivan since I met him many years
ago in Caracas, Venezuela, where his family owned a successful reinsur-
ance business, at which time he was attending a British boarding school
and contemplating his future education and professional career. With my
encouragement, Ivan received his PhD in social psychology from Columbia, and has spent the vast majority of the years since pondering the
special issues, challenges, and opportunities that uniquely affect family
companies, while advising family proprietors on how to preserve their
assets over time while simultaneously preserving their sanity.

Lansberg began our discussion by pointing out that the word *nepotism* is derived from the Italian word *nepotismo,* based on the Latin root
nepos, for "nephew." In the Middle Ages, he cheerily explained, some
less than scrupulously ethical Catholic popes, cardinals, bishops, and
other princes of the Church, who had taken vows of chastity and as a
result possessed no legitimate offspring, frequently gave to their supposed "nephews" positions of preference and power, in some cases because they were not in fact their nephews at all but illegitimate sons,
whose true paternity was artfully concealed by ascribing their parent-
age to their real father's siblings.

The term *nepotism,* Ivan continued, is actually central to the welter of
issues surrounding family legacies and ownership, because the word
clearly carries so many negative connotations and associations, some of
which are justified, but many of which are often not. The freer and more
meritocratic a society aspires to be or become, Ivan stressed, the less fair it
seems to the rest of us that certain people should get ahead simply by virtue of the fact that they have been born with the last name Ford, Murdoch,
Koch, Rockefeller, or for that matter Tata in India or Aldi in Germany.

Lansberg's main point is that while the unfairness of nepotism is well
understood and accepted by virtually all of us, a more invisible and

therefore far more insidious prejudice lurks beneath every casual use of the term to negatively define the circumstances of what might be another perfectly capable heir. Because no matter how talented, well prepared, or experienced heirs and family members may be, or how hard they may work, their every achievement, their talents, their intellectual capacities, stamina, and drive are continually called into question by those inclined to ascribe their successes or failures to the fact that they were born, as the old phrase has it, with silver spoons in their mouths. The notion that those raised in wealth, privilege, and preferment are unfairly endowed with advantages is not easy to dispel under the most benign of circumstances, and even in situations where family members have taken great pains to modify their dynastic ambitions in favor of fairness when stacked up against the more uncertain prospects of non-family professional leaders and managers.

As Lansberg once wrote in a trenchant article published in the *Harvard Business Review,* "As a scion moves to center stage, stakeholders naturally dissect his or her intellectual, emotional and physical capacity at every turn . . . Being a member of the family in a family business can actually be a handicap for successors, since the widespread assumption is that they got to where they are because of family connections" as opposed to intrinsic leadership, capacity, or hard work. To illustrate the timelessness of this bias, he quotes from Machiavelli's *The Prince,* which I borrowed to serve as an epigraph for the opening of this chapter: "Princes who come to their position by good fortune do so with little exertion on their part, but subsequently, they maintain their position only through considerable exertion. [But] those who become rulers by prowess acquire their principalities with difficulty but hold them with ease."

The Meritocratic Solution

Lansberg's solution to this problem faced by entrepreneurial parents hoping to develop their offspring into authentic, self-confident, and legitimate leaders is for them to be scrupulous, meticulous, and fearlessly objective in "designing an entry and assessment policy and process for family members that is patently *more rigorous* than for non-family members." In other words, it is not merely necessary for the process to *be* more rigorous for the *nepots*, but for it to be perceived as such by nonfamily members and less well bloodline-endowed competitors. This tough-love approach effectively defines the difference between how Sam Bronfman raised his son Edgar Bronfman Sr. and how Edgar Sr. raised his son Edgar Jr.

"Even before you come and knock at the door you need to have met certain criteria, including having gained a good education in a relevant area," is how Lansberg puts it. "You need to have worked outside the family firm for a period of two to three years or more, ideally in a company that's bigger and better than your own family company. Some really rigorous family policies," he points out, "firmly stipulate that the kids have received a couple of real promotions outside the firm before they qualify for entry."

Some families establish a policy dictating that family members may not even come knocking at the door but must only respond to an express invitation issued by a family member, committee, or board. Still other families have been known to institute an "up and out" system comparable to those found in partnerships like law and consulting firms, where if an associate fails to rise to a certain level within a stipulated period of time, they are gently invited to look elsewhere for employment, and may even have their outward-bound path eased through family connections and recommendations.

The real issue here is to avoid parents' being overly protective with regard to preventing their kids from failing. The ultimate goal, once again, is to provide offspring with crucible experiences and training programs that above all carry real risks and real rewards. Even the most well-meaning attempt by hovering helicopter parents to protect their offspring from failure, or even the fear of failure, will in fact backfire, serving only to undermine their children's and potential heirs' often fragile self-esteem, in which they typically suffer from the fact that they recognize how hard it may be to live up to the high expectations placed upon them to succeed by their self-made entrepreneurial parents.

Offspring who, with all the best of intentions, end up being steered by their parents to "low-risk staff jobs where nobody knows quite what it is that they do" represent, Lansberg insists, a circumstance that may have a "deeply corrosive effect on the kids' ability to demonstrate what it is that they are capable of doing."

The overall objective that Lansberg and others advise family founders to recognize and embrace is *to turn family membership from a liability into an asset.* The only way to do that is for family members to work harder than their nonfamily peers to succeed. And the best way to do that is to avoid situations like those he has seen at some multinational family-owned companies, where the HR files of nonfamily members are "chock full of data, with all of the 360-degree performance reviews, and all of the negative and positive comments from bosses, laid out like a diagram," but the equivalent files for family members are revealingly empty, or even worse, never even compiled.

Why? The reason for this deeply destructive dual-track system is simple: "The otherwise objective assessors are afraid, and with good reason, that if they are critical of family members, there will be negative repercussions for them." Imagine the head of HR preparing a file on James, Elisabeth, or Lachlan Murdoch for presentation to the board, of which their old man is chairman. Case closed.

One solution to this all-too-common problem of gutted HR is for families to create a separate committee, council, or board of directors, where the progression and development of family members can be confidentially discussed by the CHRO on its own terms and in the appropriate context. "You ask your independent directors, CHRO, and chairman to sit on that committee," Lansberg explains, "because it isn't enough to develop policy. The explicit purpose must be to consciously manage the relationship between the family and the business. Families need to create an ongoing institutional mechanism to actively monitor how these family policies are being implemented across the enterprise."

Politically, such organizations need to be structured so that family and nonfamily members complement one another, and that the relationship between them is constructive and mutually productive as opposed to destructive, politicized, and polarizing. In a seminal essay on the subject, "How to Save a Family Business," Peter F. Drucker goes Lansberg a step further by advising that "the issue of management succession be entrusted to someone neither part of the family nor part of the business." Since Drucker's insights are always worth listening to, I will leave him with the final word on that subject.

A TALE OF THREE CITIES: MUMBAI, MEXICO CITY, BANGKOK

In stark if welcome contrast to the "Tale of Two Cities" with which I began this discussion, I'd like to conclude it on a more positive note with a "Tale of Three Cities." The stories that follow of three successful, well-managed, and historic family enterprises and their patriarchs' well-considered efforts to avoid the mistakes so frequently committed by their wealthy and successful peers are instructive for all family firm proprietors of every size, scope, and scale. The fact that all three dynastic corporations are headquartered in developing economies is only relevant to the extent that in the developing world, the tendency for family firms to dominate the economic landscape is well documented, as are such firms' ongoing efforts to maintain a competitive edge in a globalized playing field by deftly negotiating between the rights and responsibilities of family and nonfamily members.

Getting It Right at Tata Industries

Tata Group Overview

- Privately held company
- Founded in 1868 by Jamsetji Tata
- Chairman Cyrus Pallonji Mistry
- Headquarters in Mumbai, Maharashtra, India
- 455,947 employees, serves worldwide area
- Revenue: $100 billion US in 2012–13
- Products: Airline, automotive, steel, IT, electricity generation, chemicals, beverages, telecom, hospitality, retail, consumer goods, engineering, construction, financial services

I first met Ratan Tata, then chairman of the Tata Group, India's most valuable, prestigious, important, and diversified conglomerate, in 1987, when I was just completing the second year of my two-year stint running Crotonville and he was on the lookout for a model for revamping the Tata Management Training Centre (TMTC) in Pune. Much as I had helped Jack Welch reinvigorate Crotonville to adapt to a rapidly changing commercial environment, I was fortunate to be able to provide Ratan with some timely advice on his ongoing project. In the early nineties I connected him and the Confederation of Indian Industries that Jack Welch chaired as GE endeavored to expand its already sizable presence in India. In addition, Tata met with the international teams I had assembled in conjunction with the University of Michigan Business School's Global Leadership Program to conduct business opportunity assessments and multiweek benchmarking workshops across the Indian subcontinent. I have also conducted a number of workshops with the Confederation of Indian Industries (CII) in India, where Ratan kindly paid us the honor of generously stopping by to share his perspectives on leadership, management, and globalization.

As is the case with most leaders of great family enterprises, Ratan's own personal story cannot be separated from that of Tata & Sons, a remarkable dynastic enterprise officially founded in 1868 by Jamsetji Tata, a member of an affluent priestly family of Parsis, followers of one of the oldest religions in the world. Zoroastrianism, which originated in Persia in the seventh or eighth century BC, is currently practiced by fewer than 100,000 Parsis residing in India today, all of whom are descended from refugees from Persia (hence the name Parsi) who fled to India in the tenth century CE to escape persecution of their tiny but wealthy and influential sect by Arabian tribes and clans.

No less an authority than Mahatma Gandhi observed that he was proud of his country for "producing this splendid Zoroastrian stock, in numbers beneath contempt but in charity and philanthropy, perhaps unequaled, certainly unsurpassed." The unique combination of a dualistic entrepreneurial-philanthropic spirit motivated the firm's founder, Jamsetji Tata, to dramatically expand his father's local export trading firm in Bombay with branches in Japan, China, the United Kingdom, and the United States, all with the view not just toward expanding the fortunes of his own family or family enterprise, but of invigorating and rejuvenating the Indian economy as a whole, which at the time was virtually held hostage to British colonial interests, which conspired to keep Indian industry in a state of dependency and infancy. By the late 1870s Tata textile factories were churning out vast volumes of fine cotton and silk textiles that vied with the best British imports, proving to the world that India could establish its own indigenous industries and potentially rescue its technologically backward agricultural economy from the British colonial yoke. One can see the roots of Gandhi's later campaign for Indian self-sufficiency and the ending of the local economy's destructive reliance on British imperial industry in Tata's visions of a truly domestic industrial base.

In 1991, Ratan Tata, whose father Naval Tata, a son of a relative who had been adopted by the widow of Sir Ratan Tata, was a dark-horse candidate to succeed his uncle J. R. D. Tata, the then leading light of Indian industry who among other remarkable exploits had become India's first licensed commercial pilot and founder of Tata Airlines, the corporate predecessor of Air India. After being summoned back home by his ailing father to join Tata & Sons as an unpaid apprentice in 1925, Ratan was elected chairman of the firm in 1938, succeeding his uncle Nowroji Saklatwala. After expanding the Tata Group's diversified assets from fourteen enterprises into a sprawling conglomerate of ninety-five Tata-branded companies by the time he stepped down after fifty years at the helm, it is something of an understatement to say that the flamboyant and charismatic "J.R.D." was a hard act to follow, particularly for the media-shy Ratan, a serious student with a B.S. in structural engineering from Cornell and a management degree from Harvard Business School, who had been seriously considering taking a job with IBM in the United States when he was summoned back home to serve not as a senior executive but as a lowly shop floor hand, shoveling limestone and manually feeding the blast furnace on the factory floor at Tata Iron & Steel. Over the succeeding three decades, while he successfully expanded and turned around a number of key Tata companies, he was never regarded as a political power at Bombay House, the holding company's magnificent group headquarters building in downtown Mumbai. In the eyes of the powerful "satraps," as they were aptly known—a term used to describe regional chieftains and grandees under the Persian Empire—J.R.D.'s inexplicable decision to pass them over to put Ratan in charge was a deep disappointment. Few of them understood before it was too late that J.R.D. had put Tata into the job as a means of establishing greater central control over the enterprise and clipping the wings of the satraps.

In a subsequent interview Ratan recalled that "J.R.D. Tata had around him a team of senior managers, all of them people of substantial standing in their respective spheres. While they may have acceded to his wish that I take over the chairmanship—and this happened suddenly—I must confess that I did not feel any sense of joyousness on their part, because some of them had aspirations to have the job themselves."[11]

After spending the ensuing five years "quelling the satraps," Ratan boldly exited a number of traditional businesses including cement, textiles, and cosmetics to raise a war chest for investing heavily in what he rightly regarded as Tata Industries' future: software, telecommunications, finance, retail, and high-tech consulting. The recent acquisitions of Tetley Tea, iconic British car maker Jaguar Land Rover, and the spearheading of the innovative Nano world-car, which grew out of a radical innovation program Ratan pioneered, are all worthwhile achievements. But Ratan has been quite clear that in his own eyes, a far more significant accomplishment against which even the most illustrious acquisitions fail was his success at reestablishing the overarching Tata identity and brand as reflective of an "organization [structured] in a more cohesive way than it had been in the past," permitting it to "identify itself more as a group" than as a cluster of companies.

When planning his own succession and imminent retirement, Ratan Tata carefully approached the selection of his successor with a view toward sparing whoever the board picked the tumult and turmoil he had faced, marked by years of sparring with defiant subordinates. For better or worse, he was not obliged to pick among his own children, because he didn't have any, while the first public statement he made regarding the succession planning process he would be instituting was that his successor did not, in his view, have to be a family member, or a Parsi, or even a longtime Tata insider. The one awkward interpersonal aspect of the process was the widespread belief that the leading candidate was his half brother Noel, then fifty-five, when in fact he was intent on the five-person committee he appointed to oversee the selection to seriously consider a wide range of outsider candidates, including—so it was said—such luminaries of the Indian diaspora as Deutsche Bank cohead Anshu Jain, former Vodafone chief Arun Sarin, and curiously enough, former Merrill Lynch CEO John Thain, in addition to a passel of internal candidates including the CFO and the former head of Tata Steel.

In the end, the panel surprised itself, although not Ratan, by appointing one of its own members, the forty-three-year-old Cyrus Mistry, son of the octogenarian billionaire Pallonji Shapoorji Mistry, Tata's largest individual shareholder with a nearly 20 percent stake in the company, a board member for the past five years, and the brother-in-law of Ratan's half brother Noel. So in a sense, he was a family member and also a nonfamily member—the perfect balance to strike between the two. After being sounded out for the job by his fellow committee members, Cyrus promptly excused himself from the proceedings and gamely submitted to the same rigorous review process he had up until then been conducting with regard to now competing candidates. After the selection was announced, its rationale was clear. One of our three city tales is a hybrid, family but not close family, an outsider and an insider; nevertheless, at the end of the day clearly part of the larger Tata family.

Getting It Right in Mexico City: Ricardo Salinas and Grupo Salinas

Grupo Salinas Overview

- Private, family-owned company
- Founded in 1906
- CEO Ricardo Salinas Pliego
- Headquarters in Mexico City, Mexico
- 68,000 employees
- Revenue: $57.4 billion US in 2008
- Businesses: TV Azteca, Azteca América, Grupo Elektra, Banco Azteca, Afore Azteca, Seguros Azteca, Iusacell, Azteca Internet, GS Motors, Italika, and the Asociación del Empresario Azteca

Over six years ago, I was contacted by a young HR professional, Danthe Escamilla from Grupo Salinas, who was given the assignment to check me out as a possible resource to help work with Grupo Salinas on change and leadership development. I invited him to a three-day workshop I was conducting in Silicon Valley for companies in that region on "The Cycle of Leadership," to help leaders develop their teachable point of view and learn how to be leader/teachers. Danthe went back to Mexico City and invited me to come for a two-day visit to explore working together. I ran a short workshop for some of the HR professionals and met with several senior managers before sitting down with Ricardo Salinas Pliego, chairman of Grupo Salinas, a multibusiness company made up of Grupo Elektra (at one time around four thousand points of sale throughout Mexico—furniture, electronics, motorcycles, appliances, etc.), Banco Azteca (a financial arm that mostly extends credit given in the stores), Azteca (a major television network with subsidiaries in the United States), Iusacell (a mobile phone business with retail stores), as well as a number of other smaller businesses in Mexico, the United States, and South America. Banco Azteca, a subsidiary of Grupo Elektra, is Mexico's only multinational bank, with operations in seven different countries.

Ricardo and I had a great meeting, sharing my work with Jack Welch, my approach to working globally with Royal Dutch Shell and Nomura Securities, and my work in Russia, China, India, and Brazil. We agreed to see how we might collaborate. My team of Patti Stacey and Chris DeRose and I would do a two-day workshop with about ten of his senior leaders, heads of the businesses and staff heads, as well as his three children (Ninfa, Benjamín, and Hugo). We ran this session in Cancún at Ricardo's condominium. By the second day Ricardo and my team had great chemistry and he asked if we could come to his workshop on Friday and Saturday with the top three hundred leaders in Grupo Salinas, being held right there in Cancún. We helped him run the session, we taught in the session, and we decided to partner on a journey to build his leadership pipeline and help transform the company.

At the Cancún session, the subject of succession was never raised, yet the presence of the next generation at the workshop spoke volumes. Ricardo was and remains intensely interested in developing the next generation of leaders for the enterprise, and though they are still young, he is consciously creating a pipeline for the future family leaders parallel to the pipeline for nonfamily executives.

As is the case with Ratan Tata and many other patriarchs of family enterprises, Ricardo's own personal story cannot be separated from that of his family firm. The origins of Grupo Salinas date back to the founding in 1906 of a small furniture retail and manufacturing company, Salinas & Rocha, by Ricardo's great-grandfather, Benjamín Salinas Westrup, in the industrial city of Monterrey in northern Mexico. After Benjamín Salinas's death, two branches of the family separated, and in 1952, Ricardo's grandfather, Hugo SalinasRocha, founded Grupo Elektra, a chain of furniture and consumer electronics stores targeted at the mass market, while yet another branch of the family continued to expand its retail presence under the Salinas y Rocha brand, aimed at a more affluent clientele.

In 1987, the thirty-two-year-old Ricardo Salinas Pliego, who had a bachelor's degree in accounting from a prestigious technical institute in Monterrey and an MBA from Tulane, took over the helm of Grupo Elektra following the retirement of his father, Hugo Salinas Price. His father couldn't have picked a worse—or better—time to retire, as Ricardo's succession coincided with a sharp Mexican currency devaluation that had touched off a national economic crisis, which had effectively bankrupted the company. In a classic trial by fire, a true crucible experience, Ricardo wasted no time completely restructuring Elektra's operations and reinventing the enterprise from the bottom up, based on a new business model that emphasized low profit margins, strict cash-and-carry policies, and disciplined management of what little credit he had to extend. Several years later, in 1993, having stabilized Elektra, Ricardo headed up a group of investors that purchased a package of TV licenses and some crippled broadcasting equipment from the government and established Azteca, which soon captured 40 percent of Mexico's commercial viewing audience. Six years later, after spending several years focused on getting Azteca off the ground, Ricardo went up against Mexico's richest man, Carlos Slim Helú, bidding at a bank auction to purchase the assets of the bankrupt furniture chain Salinas y Rocha, which his great-grandfather had founded in Monterrey but which had been hard hit by fierce competition from, among other new entrants, JCPenney. After prevailing over Slim Helú, Ricardo used the combined entity to recover an asset and a legacy he intended to pass on to future generations, while launching a dramatic expansion beyond the core appliances, electronics, and furniture business into financial services, including banking and insurance, tightly targeted at a vast new consumer market fueled by the rise of a lower-middle-income consumer willing to purchase big-ticket items on credit.

Whenever I talk to Ricardo about leadership development and succession planning, we talk about the sustainability of human capital and of human capacity, with the ultimate goal of creating a process that will help maintain the viability of the enterprise across the upcoming decades. We speak of two kinds of leadership, leading businesses and leading people. Leadership 20/20: what sort of knowledge and what sort of leaders do you need to succeed and grow a decade from now? With Grupo Salinas, as with many family companies, we are developing two separate and distinct pipeline processes: one for the family and one for the nonfamily members. At Grupo Salinas, two sons are currently running their own independent start-ups, which are all-importantly fully scoped P&Ls, where the prospect of failure is very real and where the challenges of meeting a payroll, making trade-offs, picking the right people, and making the right judgments of strategy and in crisis are their daily toil—precisely the sort of "tough love" process that will prepare them to lead when the time comes.

Hugo Salinas Sada is the CEO of Tiendas Neto, a grocery hard discount retailer with more than five hundred stores located in the central states of Mexico. Benjamín Salinas Sada, who runs Grupo Sago, has participated in industries as diverse as fiber-optic network construction, thermal paper production and distribution, electronics, and television production.

Salinas's oldest daughter, Ninfa Salinas Sada, is by contrast a public servant, a senator. She worked in Grupo Salinas in a variety of staff positions for a decade, but her major career is in government. She is a member of the Ecologist Green Party of Mexico and one of the youngest women ever to hold public office in Mexico. As a federal deputy in the legislature and president of the Environment Committee of the Chamber of Deputies, she was able to increase federal appropriations dedicated to environmental preservation, climate change mitigation, land management programs, and environmental education. Then there are three very young children under the age of seven, thus long-term participants in the business.

Getting It Right in Bangkok

CP Group Overview

- Private, family-owned company

- Founded in 1921

- Chairman and CEO, Dhanin Chearavanont

- Headquarters in Bangkok, Thailand

- 300,000+ employees

- Revenue: $46.5 billion USD in 2014

- Products: Meat, Ready-to-Eat Meals, Fixed and Mobile Telephone Service, Internet and Cable-TV service provider, Cash & Carry and Hyper Supermarkets, Convenience stores, Financial services, Plastics, etc.

In 1921, during the reign of the illustrious and long-lived King Rama VI of Siam (the colonial-era name for present-day Thailand), two Chinese immigrant brothers, Chia Ek Chor and Chia Siew Whooy, started a seed store they named Chia Tai Chueng in the crooked and bustling streets of Bangkok's Chinatown. They imported their seeds and vegetables from China, and exported pigs and eggs to Hong Kong. Under Ek Chor's two elder sons, Jaran Chiaravanont and Montri Jiaravanont, the company increased its scope under the second generation of ownership from selling vegetable seeds to the production of animal feed, while in the third generation, under the leadership of the present chairman,

Dhanin Chearavanont, the enterprise that has since become known worldwide as "CP" (for Charoen Pokphand) further integrated its business to include livestock farming, marketing, and distribution. By the 1970s, the company was the major player in the production of chicken and eggs in Thailand, and was unique in the field for following a strict policy of vertical integration that required it to further expand into a number of adjacent business lines, adding breeding farms, slaughterhouses, processed foods production, and, later, its own chain of restaurants. By 1972, CP had expanded internationally as well as vertically, launching operations throughout Asia, including feed mills in Indonesia, the export of chickens to Japan, and opening branches of the business in Singapore.

In the 1980s, as mainland China opened up to foreign investments, CP became the first foreign company to establish itself in the newly created Shenzhen free trade zone by partnering with the U.S. grain company Continental Grain. By the early 1990s, CP had launched some two hundred subsidiaries in China. CP's massive investment in four joint ventures in the petrochemical business with Belgium's Solvay had entered into a partnership with the U.S. telecommunications firm of NYNEX to launch TelecomAsia (TA) and had begun the constructions of its own fiber-optic telephone network.

In the wake of the Asian financial crisis in 1997, CP consolidated into three business lines, agro-industry and food (CP Foods), retail (CP All), and telecommunications (True). In 2013, CP acquired the Cash & Carry Siam Makro and a stake in China's Ping An Insurance. With CP in Thailand, issues arose relating to the holding company structure of the organization, which was highly decentralized across geographical and business lines. The head of CP Foods, for example, is in charge of an organization of eighty thousand. Each of these businesses runs its own talent development and succession planning processes, independent of centralized corporate control. As long as the business leaders deliver the numbers to the chairman, there has been only a limited appetite for or interest in more centralized talent development or HR function. At CP in Bangkok we are five years into a process of building the leadership pipeline for a three-hundred-thousand-plus organization that is in a rapid globalization process from a base in sixteen countries, which include Thailand and China but are moving into the United States, Europe, Africa, Brazil, and Japan. The leadership pipeline needs to be much more global and must groom CEOs for the major businesses, food, 7-Eleven convenience stores, mobile phones, hypermarkets, and retail stores in China as well as a number of smaller business units.

There will be a blend of family and professional leadership, with the family maintaining five of the top leadership positions, and the three sons being prepared for leadership positions in the future.

S. C. Johnson & Son: The Gold Standard for Family Businesses

S. C. Johnson Overview

- Privately held company
- Founded in 1886
- Chairman and CEO, Herbert Fisk Johnson III
- Headquarters in Racine, Wisconsin, USA
- 12,000 employees
- Revenue: $11.75 billion US in 2013
- Products: Shout, Windex, Mr. Muscle, Ziploc, Glade, Brise, Raid, OFF!, Kabikiller, Pledge, Scrubbing Bubbles

"This We Believe" explains S. C. Johnson's values in relation to the five groups of stakeholders to whom it is responsible and whose trust it has to earn:

Employees

We believe that the fundamental vitality and strength of our worldwide company lies in our people.

Consumers and Users

We believe in earning the enduring goodwill of consumers and users of our products and services.

General Public

We believe in being a responsible leader within the free market community.

Neighbors and Hosts

We believe in contributing to the well-being of the countries and communities where we conduct business.

World Community

We believe in improving international understanding.

We Understand Family, Because We Are Family

Not a squabbling-in-the-backseat kind of family. (Well, not usually.) But a glad-we're-in-this-together kind of family. So we understand the joys and strains you feel every day. Dig in and discover tips to help any family, and special ways to celebrate yours.

Integrity Is Part of Our DNA

It's not a fad or a phase. It's been our family way since 1886. From the ingredients in our products, to the way we run our factories, we're committed to working every day to do what's right for people, the planet and generations to come.

We Know What Home Means to You

It's where you kick off your shoes and gather your friends. It's a reflection of you and a gift to your family. That's why we've spent over a century making products that help make your home cleaner and better.

Samuel Curtis (S. C.) Johnson was nearly fifty years old when he and his family moved to Racine, Wisconsin, on the shores of Lake Michigan, in 1882 to make a fresh start after his previous two entrepreneurial ventures, helping to build a new railway and running a book and stationery store in Kenosha, Wisconsin, failed. Always determined to be his own boss, after taking a job as a salesman of fine wood parquet flooring with the Racine Hardware Manufacturing Co., within four years he had purchased the flooring business from the company and a few years after that, established his own factory to manufacture floor waxes and wood finishes, which he sold to commercial and residential contractors as the Johnson's Prepared Paste Wax Company. While one secret to S. C. Johnson's ultimate success was the hard work he put in as the firm's chief salesman, bookkeeper, and business manager, the real money that eventually flowed in didn't come from the flooring itself, which was essentially a commodity business, but from the cans of Johnson's Prepared Paste Wax that came with every order, which Johnson had invented by experimenting at home in the evenings and on weekends mixing up batches of wax formulations in the family bathtub.

By 1898, sales of floor wax, finishes, and wood fillers exceeded those of flooring, and a highly profitable specialty business was born. By 1906, S. C. Johnson's son, Herbert F. Johnson, had joined the company, and to celebrate the passage of the enterprise to the second generation, the company was officially renamed S. C. Johnson & Son. But passing on a profitable and sustainable business to future generations was in some ways a comparatively small part of S. C. Johnson's personal legacy, because he also laid down and passed on a set of values and a set of beliefs about the importance of giving back to the community and to society that has defined the company ever since as a very special sort of operation. Until his death in 1919, S. C. Johnson gave 10 percent of his personal income back to his community, primarily to programs that supported the development of young people into civic and business leaders. Nearly a century after S. C. Johnson's death, while the global company he founded boasts operations in seventy-two countries, its world-famous brands of household products including Windex, Pledge,

Glade, Shout, Saran, Ziploc, Kiwi, Scrubbing Bubbles, and Raid are sold in more than one hundred countries. The Household Products piece of the business is merely the largest component of a diversified multisector Johnson Family Enterprises with more than thirteen thousand employees worldwide and nearly $10 billion in annual revenues. The most remarkable thing about this fifth-generation family company, number thirty-six on the *Forbes* list of "America's Largest Family Companies," is that in so many important respects it has remained very much the same sort of friendly, intimate, environmentally conscious, socially responsible company that the founder established in 1886. Being a family company is critical to its brand, its identity, and its value proposition. As the family itself put it on page 264. "We understand family, because we are family." It is still a family selling to families from its family home in Racine, Wisconsin. As the company itself says on its Web site—where the slogan "A Family Company" is prominently displayed—it is the founder's "commitment to community, along with his perseverance, which are the most enduring" qualities that continue to define and differentiate the company more than a century after his death, even as it competes with P&G, Unilever, Colgate-Palmolive, and others, none of which are family-owned and are some of the best-managed and most admired enterprises on the planet. It is the family that gives S. C. Johnson not just an identity, a focus, and a mission, but an authentic competitive edge.

The task that Herbert F. Johnson Sr., the second-generation leader, assigned to himself to sustain the enterprise and his father's image of its responsible expansion was to broaden the geographic and regional range in which the family's products would be distributed nationally and internationally. On a trip to England in 1912, he called on a little hardware shop in London wearing—as the family history proudly puts it—"his trademark white flannel suit."

"This product will not only clean your floor," H. F. Johnson promised, "it'll polish it so shiny that you could drag me across the floor and not see any dirt on the seat of my pants." As the proper British shopkeeper looked on in disbelief, the president of the company got down on his knees, rolled up his sleeves, polished the floor and then sat down on it to be dragged about on its surface on his backside. When he stood up and proudly displayed the pure white flannel seat of his pants as clean as it was before he sat on the floor and wriggled about, the deal was sealed. That was how Herbert established the family's first beachhead in Europe, with Australia and Canada soon to follow. Connecting to people was Herbert's "thing," and while that included customers and business partners, he was most interested in making his own people more than merely employees, but members of a larger family that would in turn maintain close connections to its surrounding community. In 1917, two years before his father's death, Herbert started one of the first profit-sharing programs. A decade later, a few months before he died in 1927, H.F. Senior explained his underlying philosophy to employees:

> When all is said and done, this business is nothing but a symbol. And when we translate this, we find that it means a great many people think well of its products, and that a great multitude has faith in the integrity of the people who make this product. In a very short time, the machines that are now so lively will soon become obsolete. And the big buildings, for all their solidity, must someday be replaced.
>
> But a business which symbolizes can live so long as there are human beings alive . . . for it is not built of such flimsy materials as steel and concrete. It is built of human opinions, which may be made to live forever. The goodwill of people is the only enduring thing in any business. It is the sole substance. The rest is shadow.

His son, H. F. Johnson Jr., was just twenty-eight years old when his father died, a few months after speaking those prophetic and enduring words to his employees. It was left to the third generation to steer the company, with three hundred employees and $5 million in annual revenues, through the Great Depression without laying off any of its people. In 1935, in the depths of the depression, H.F. Junior, an early environmentalist, set off for Brazil in search of the native source of the carnauba palm, called the "tree of life" by the indigenous people of the Amazon rain forest, whose remarkable wax protected it from droughts; its trunk and leaves could be used as building materials, its roots were used to make medicine, and its fruit was edible—a symbol of the enduring and sustainable values the company represented. It was H.F. Junior's global view, not yet common among U.S. businessmen, that made the company's products known worldwide through national and international advertising, and it was his vision of a sustainable enterprise that prompted him to commission from the legendary organic architect Frank Lloyd Wright the most beautiful and enduring corporate headquarters on earth. "Anybody can build a typical building," he said. "I wanted to build the best office building in the world, and the only way to do that was to get the greatest architect in the world."

Over the next forty-five years, under the leadership of H. F. Johnson Jr.'s son Sam, the company grew from a $150 million wax business into a $6 billion family of companies with operations in sixty-five countries and products sold on six continents. In 1975, Sam shocked the chemical industry by taking a leadership position in support of the elimination of chlorofluorocarbons, or CFCs, which harm the earth's ozone layer, from all the company's aerosol products worldwide. This was before there were any legal protocols against their use—it was simply, he said, good for the planet. When asked why he put people before profits, and when other chemical industry executives accused him of being reckless and irresponsible, and even of trying to destroy the entire chemical industry, he said: "Am I an environmentalist? Yes. Am I a businessman? Yes. But what I am more than anything else is a grandfather who wants his grandchildren to have the same kind of place to live and grow up in as I did."

Today, under the leadership of the fifth generation, with Fisk Johnson at the helm, the company has taken its founder's original values and sustained them by partnering with local entrepreneurs to create new and successful enterprises, from pyrethrum farmers in Rwanda whose crop is used in organic pesticides to others around the world. The company's goal is to make money, yes, to sustain the family fortune, yes, but ultimately, as it says itself, right there on its Web site, its real mission remains the same: "To continue to grow and flourish so we can achieve our ultimate goal of making the world a better place. What matters most [to Fisk Johnson] is the legacy he can leave as a parent." Those previous four generations would be proud, because it's all in the family.

CHAPTER 9

BUILDING A SUCCESSION PIPELINE FOR NONPROFIT ORGANIZATIONS

The notion that organizations, independent of their tax status, shouldn't be focused on the development and succession of their leadership, especially at the top, strikes me as patently absurd . . . There is no reason that institutions in the not-for-profit sector shouldn't be held accountable for the development of the next generation of leadership.

—Leonard Schlesinger,
Baker Foundation Professor, Harvard Business School; former COO of
Au Bon Pain and The Limited; former president, Babson College

---

TECHNICAL
- Impact social and health status of constituencies
- Negotiate mix of managerial and professional roles
- Fund-raise from disparate sources: fees, tuition, gifts, grants, appropriations

POLITICAL
- Juggle multiple and decentralized nodes of power: in universities, administration and faculty; in hospitals and health care, administrators and physicians; in the military, civilian political and military chain of command
- Negotiate continually between disparate stakeholders
- Place strict limitations on command-and-control hierarchical decision making
- Manage transition challenges in new regimes and between sectors

CULTURAL
- Ensure the integrity and objectivity of the succession process
- Handle multiple diverse subcultures: administrative, professional, idealistic, pragmatic

With both nonprofits and for-profits, the same basic elements and pre-requisites apply when planning good leadership transitions and leadership successions:

1. Complete CEO ownership and involvement
2. Strong HR partner collaborating with the process
3. A board that is determined to hold the CEO and HR account-able for getting it right and paying attention
4. Developing the right tools (performance and values assess-ments) for the pipeline to produce accountability for succes-sion at all levels of the organization.

Having lived and worked inside colleges and universities since I entered Colgate University in upstate New York as a freshman nearly half a century ago, I will for the first time share my lessons learned along the way about how to lead in nonprofit organizations. As a full-time professor at the business schools of both Columbia and Michigan over the past forty years, I have lived and taught though the tenures of eight university presidents and at least as many deans, and have learned about the challenges and opportunities of creating a viable succession plan and leading nonprofit institutions from both inside and out.

Starting out in the early seventies, I began actively consulting on leadership issues in the nonprofit health care field, working first with the Martin Luther King Health Center in the South Bronx of New York, where I gained valuable experience that I captured in my first book, *Organization Design for Primary Health Care: The Case of the Dr. Martin Luther King, Jr. Health Center.* Shortly thereafter, I segued into working with the rural equivalent of the MLK Center located in impoverished Hazard, Kentucky, a clinic whose primary funder was the Robert Wood Johnson Foundation, the leader of which asked me to move down to Hazard in 1977 to lead a massive internal transformation while on a year's leave of absence from Columbia.

The crucible experience of leading Crotonville for two years under Jack Welch served, in turn, as a natural springboard to a sequence of multiyear engagements developing succession and leadership systems for secondary schools, including the pioneering Leadership Academy for principals in New York established by Chancellor Joel Klein under a mandate from Mayor Michael Bloomberg. I've since gone on to help local teams develop leadership pipelines at a network of charter schools in Texas, and more recently, the national secondary school system established by the Sultan of Brunei.

At all of these nonprofit organizations, I have applied my always evolving leadership philosophy and methodology, conducting workshops for senior leaders, principals, and other high-ranking administrators at more than a dozen major medical centers and hospital systems, the Boys and Girls Clubs of America, and—as a core multidecade personal commitment—Focus: HOPE, a celebrated nonprofit located in inner-city Detroit whose goal and mission is to provide "practical solutions to racism and poverty" through a medley of food programs, a top-notch nursery school, and community housing, in addition to award-winning programs in machinist training, IT training, and an engineering bachelor's degree program.

And last but not least, starting out in the late 1990s I have spent considerable time and effort working with several generations of leaders of the United States Special Operations Forces (SOF) including Army Rangers, Navy SEALs, and Air Force, designing, developing, and implementing leadership development systems and programs inspired by the example of then retired and since deceased four-star general Wayne Downing, the first SOF leader to lead the transformation of this elite cadre of warriors into a network of crack units capable of operating in the radically different context of late twentieth- and early twenty-first-century global turbulence, terrorism, and asymmetrical conflict.

Profit Versus Nonprofit Leadership Development

In every case and at every institution, a key element of our efforts has been to create a viable succession planning process. So what, you may ask, are the essential differences between profit-making and non-profit-making institutions and organizations with regard to leadership development, succession planning, and transition? First and foremost, the most obvious differentiator is that nonprofit leaders and future leaders have with virtually no exceptions signed on to a mission—a term with both religious and military connotations—as opposed to pursuing a set of goals primarily dominated by financial considerations. In all not-for-profit organizations, a higher-order technical mission (healing patients, teaching children, protecting our freedom, or empowering and training a specific population) is typically coupled with widely varying political considerations and challenges, which are in turn magnified and exacerbated by cultural forces that are frequently defined by legacy and tradition, particularly when these institutions are long-standing fixtures of society, as is the case with many leading universities and the military as a whole. In the Special Operations Forces, for example, an unusually clear chain of command is paradoxically highly participative: frontline SEALs and Rangers are granted considerable autonomy by their leaders to make split-second, high-risk, potentially fatal decisions out in the field, since they typically operate out of touch with and out of range of communication with senior commanders.

In universities, by contrast, power tends to be highly dispersed, but for different reasons and based on a different history unique to academic enterprises. By deliberate design, universities are fragmented lack-of-command structures dominated by multiple stakeholders each of which wields substantial political power over their own domains and turfs, whether those stakeholders are tenured faculty, major funders and donors, the student body, or campus administrators.

My focus here is on nonprofit large research universities, which differ dramatically, both politically and culturally, from small liberal arts colleges. At major research universities, unlike colleges, faculty members tend to be focused almost entirely on pursuing research projects and publications, whereas in most colleges the scale is tilted toward teaching. The eminent sociologist and student of university life Alvin Gouldner divided faculty members into two distinct groups: "locals" and "cosmopolitans." While "locals" were in his view more oriented toward classroom instruction and internal institutional management, "cosmopolitans" remained focused on the external academic community and publications in their respective fields, eschewing any but the most minimal involvement and interest in teaching and governance.

Hospital medical staffs, especially the superstars, resemble university faculty cosmopolitans in that they typically make a great deal of money both for themselves and their institutions, a state of affairs that inevitably confers upon them considerable power, prestige, and perquisites, as well as autonomy from what they might regard as undue interference from hapless administrators, who possess remarkably little power and leverage as a result over the nominal "employees." And speaking of "employees," you'll note that the term is rarely used in the nonprofit universe, as it is widely regarded as needlessly emphasizing the hierarchy over the shared vision and culture that binds every member of these institutions into a tightly knit web of beliefs. Culturally, all not-for-profits are organized according to a framework that places critical importance on the pursuit of a "higher calling" defined by a distinct set of values, whether oriented toward saving lives (health care), educating the young (secondary schools), or conducting research and preparing high-performing students for academic and nonacademic careers (universities). All of these institutions are grounded in an acknowledged need to address a wide range of societal causes and challenges, from empowering inner-city minorities and underprivileged citizens (Focus: HOPE, Boys and Girls Clubs, etc.) to protecting the nation and safeguarding our freedom (the Special Operations Forces).

Universities as Organized Anarchy

In 1974, Michael D. Cohen, a professor of information and public policy at the University of Michigan, and James G. Marsh, a professor of education at Stanford, published *Leadership and Ambiguity: The American College President,*[1] a book that effectively skewered and cleverly defined the unique and unusual leadership challenge facing university presidents in the modern era. Whenever my colleagues in business who interact with nonprofit institutions either as donors or trustees express frustration at the idiosyncrasies of their nonprofit counterparts, because they tend to assume the existence of considerably more command-and-control authority, I always point them toward Cohen and Marsh, who coined the eloquent term "organized anarchy" to describe the political structure of these unique institutions. In my experience, as well as that of my colleagues, the concept of command-and-control authority simply doesn't exist.

For example, a university president, by Cohen and Marsh's definition, is part arbitrator, part bureaucrat, part manager, part administrator, part fund-raiser, part coach, part faculty scourge, part politician. But no matter how many parts or roles the president fills, at the end of the day he or she is no more than a symbolic figurehead nominally in charge of a hydra-headed structure of distributed power so intensely convoluted that only an inherently paradoxical term like "organized anarchy" can be used to describe it. The defining feature of organized anarchies, Cohen and Marsh contend, is *ambiguity*—ambiguity of mission, strategy, power, and constituent relationships, and above all, ambiguity of assessment, measurement, evaluation, performance, and most critical of all, definition of success.

As in all organizational contexts, rendering a fair and objective assessment of performance—both for candidates and incumbents—is critical to the integrity of the succession process. "What are the objectives of leadership?" Cohen and Marsh asked. "Does a college president see himself as a military commander or a mayor? As a clergyman or a foreman? As a mediator or a business executive?"[2] "University presidents," they wrote, "live in an ambiguous world, in which success is as difficult to define as it is to achieve." These questions are critical for leaders assessing other leaders as they climb up the ranks—and thus central to the concept of leadership development and succession planning, which at nearly all universities remains at best a study in organized anarchy, and at its worst, a human resources disaster at least as pathetic as the far more extensively documented leadership crisis afflicting the for-profit sector.

Yet I would humbly submit that there are and always have been an accepted set of objective measures of success that constitute legitimate yardsticks and benchmarks to rank universities. I would include among these key performance indicators (KPIs) the quality and prestige of 1. professional schools and graduate departments by profession and discipline; 2. the quality and prestige of different undergraduate programs, and quality of admitted students as defined by selective admissions policies; 3. faculty publications and contributions to their respective fields of study; 4. alumni career success; and 5. the relative growth or decline of the institution's endowment. Note that despite being a long-time faculty member at the University of Michigan, which takes success in sports very seriously, I do not include the success of sports teams as a measure of achievement. How could I, having spent fourteen years of my career at Columbia University, where the football team never won more than a handful of games?

Dwight D. Eisenhower, President of Columbia University

On the evening of April 2, 1946, Dwight D. Eisenhower, the fifty-six-year-old former commanding general of the American forces in Europe and supreme commander of the Allied Expeditionary Force during World War II, gave a speech at the Metropolitan Museum of Art in New York. After the speech, Thomas Watson Sr., the seventy-two-year-old CEO and founder of the modern IBM and head of the presidential selection committee of Columbia University's board, offered the five-star general his first civilian job since graduating from high school in Abilene, Kansas, before attending the Military Academy at West Point: the presidency of Columbia University.

The succession challenge facing Watson and his fellow trustees was to land a suitable successor to the legendary Nicholas Murray Butler,

Columbia's twelfth and longest-serving president, who had reluctantly resigned the year before, at age eighty-three and nearly blind, after spending the previous forty-three years transforming a parochial college for the New York City elite into an institution of international esteem and renown. Watson was convinced that only one man on the national scene—despite his complete lack of academic and scholarly credentials and university administrative experience—fit the bill: the savior of the Western Alliance, Dwight D. Eisenhower.

Not until eighteen months later, however, when Watson sounded out Eisenhower for a second time, and after the future president had fulfilled his promise to President Truman to serve as Army Chief of Staff, did he learn that in the interim, his target recruit had grown tired of Pentagon politics and of dismantling the magnificent army he had helped to build up in wartime. He was also intrigued by the offer because, as he conceded to his brother Milton, Watson "painted the rosiest picture of what I would be offered in the way of conveniences, expenses, remuneration and so on."

Ike's Employees at Columbia

After agonizing for some months over what he would later describe as "the first decision I ever had to make in my life that was directly concerned with myself," the five-star general dashed off a letter to Watson provisionally accepting his offer, and formally agreed to take up his duties as Columbia's thirteenth president in May 1948. Not long after establishing a provisional beachhead on Columbia's classical campus, the general on alien territory committed a cardinal cultural error. Toward the end of a speech celebrating the lifetime achievement of Dr. Isidor Isaac Rabi, the discoverer of nuclear magnetic imaging and winner of the 1944 Nobel Prize in Physics, the retired old soldier casually commented that as a university president, it was gratifying to see "an employee" of the university achieve such universal recognition and renown.

At hearing the word "employee," the honoree stood up and to the assembled audience's astonishment, openly contradicted his once and future president. "Excuse me, sir," Rabi defiantly declared, "but the faculty of this university are not *employees* of this university! The faculty *are* the university!" This defiant and confrontational remark delighted Rabi's fellow faculty members as a courageous blow against the nonacademic interloper president, a former general. That story was still making the rounds of the faculty lounges a quarter of a century later in 1972, when I joined the Columbia faculty as an assistant professor of organization behavior at the Graduate School of Business. If we look more closely at this cautionary tale of how the greatest business leader of his generation recruited the greatest military leader of his generation to succeed one of the greatest educational leaders of his generation, we see just another example of a starry-eyed board member being dazzled by the credentials of a superstar outsider. We also see an example of an otherwise great leader—Watson—falling prey to the popular delusion that shining success in one sector or field of endeavor necessarily translates into similar success in a different sector. Leadership, in this misguided view, is essentially a fungible trait, a quality so versatile it translates into every arena. A university president, as Eisenhower learned, is not a general or a CEO but a figure of real ambiguity attempting to govern a system of "organized anarchy" as set forth by Cohen and Marsh in the box below.

Cohen and Marsh Rules for Managing in an Organized Anarchy

1. SPEND TIME: Universities have a chronic shortage of decision-making energy, because as a general rule tenured faculty are not motivated (because they have no incentive) to invest valuable time in managing the university. As a result energy being a scarce resource on campus, if one is in a position to devote time to decision-making activities . . . he or she can make considerable claims on the system.

2. PERSIST: It is a mistake to assume that if a particular proposal has been rejected today, it will be rejected tomorrow. Different sets of people and concerns may show up at the next meeting, with different results.

3. EXCHANGE STATUS FOR SUBSTANCE: Faculty are less interested in substance than they are in the implications of the outcome of any decision as it reflects their own sense of self-esteem, status, and recognition. Smart leaders use this to their advantage.

4. FACILITATE OPPOSITION PARTICIPATION: Remain focused on the reality instead of stated beliefs regarding the feasibility of planned projects in order to keep dissident groups fully engaged.

5. OVERLOAD THE SYSTEM: Universities are energy-poor organizations, which means that accomplishing institutional overload is easy, which enables the leadership to do what they want, sometimes for better, sometimes for worse.

6. PROVIDE GARBAGE CANS: Skillful university leaders create "garbage can" issues for everyone to throw their "garbage" in, which distract them from the more significant issues and challenges and provides the leader with air cover and freedom to make decisions as they see fit.

7. MANAGE UNOBTRUSIVELY: Let the system go where it wants to go with only minor and select interventions, since the institution can only accept a limited degree of change at any one time.

8. CREATE YOUR OWN REVISIONIST HISTORY: Because faculty meetings and involvement are never consistent, i.e. missing meetings, leaving early and arriving late—information about meetings is poorly maintained, which makes it laughably easy to control history by writing the minutes sufficiently long enough after the event so that no one can remember, legitimizing the reality of forgetfulness.

On the evening of April 5, 1950, having spent a desultory two years on the job, Eisenhower privately confided to his diary the realization that compared with wrangling a posse of egotistical generals like Douglas MacArthur during World War II, running a great and venerable university was, from a power perspective, a mess.

There is probably no more complicated business in the world than that of picking a new dean within a university. Faculties, including the retiring dean, feel an almost religious fervor in insisting upon acceptance of their particular views. These are as varied as there are individuals involved, and every man's opinion is voiced in terms of urgency. The result is complete confusion and I cannot see why universities have followed such a custom. I'll be damned glad when we have a new dean of engineering and the fuss, fury and hysteria have died down.[3]

That was a lesson that Eisenhower's handpicked successor, Dr. Grayson Kirk—who served as provost and acting head of the university during Eisenhower's extended absences from campus to serve, among other outside duties, as the first leader of NATO forces in Europe—learned the hard way. After Kirk took over within days of the newly elected president's departure for the White House in 1953, he served with distinction for another fifteen years, until his highly centralized command-and-control style of leadership clashed with the faculty, students, and surrounding community during the student uprising of 1968, which I personally witnessed as a newly arrived graduate student in social psychology. I observed the otherwise capable Kirk tragically lose his footing, his reputation, and his position of authority by paradoxically exerting his authority, calling in the New York City police to suppress the protests and eject student occupiers from the university's administrative facilities, including his own office. In so doing, he not only revealed the flaws of the university's succession planning process, which relied on a board that rubber-stamped Eisenhower's selection, but also undermined his own chosen successor, popular professor and vice president David Truman. In the wake of the riots and the bloody aftermath of their violent suppression, both Truman and Kirk were forced to resign. Though the university ultimately recovered, the succession plan put into place by the man who planned D-Day was jeopardized by leaders' inability to keep pace with the course of human events. This was a pattern that time and again I would witness in institutional settings, as best-laid plans were waylaid by unpredictable occurrences, from the decline of the mainframe computer to the advent of the Internet, seismic shifts in consumer behavior, or in the case of financial institutions, systemic collapses that brought not just firms but the leaders who led them into the abyss.

The University of Michigan Leadership Pipeline and Succession

In the discussion of leadership succession at the University of Michigan, I will attempt to frame the technical, political, and cultural challenges of leadership at a significant and globally esteemed research university. The technical challenges consist of setting the context for the subparts of the university, including a welter of different schools, institutes, and a medical center, ensuring that all are provided with sufficient resources, with regard to both human and financial capital, to remain at the top of their class. Politically, I have previously identified universities as organized anarchies hampered by a highly specific set of processes and constituencies that lead to either the success or the downfall of university presidents. The political—with a capital "P"—is hugely important and unique to these institutions. The cultural component also contains an unpredictable and often volatile mixture of values not always closely aligned among the various power centers, but which all ideally revolve around such lofty ideals as the pursuit of knowledge, the education of the next generation of leaders to succeed in a changing world, combined with enhancing the success and prestige of the institution at a time when universities, like companies, are competing on a global playing field to attract the best talent, whether they be students, professors, or administrators.

At Michigan, starting on July 1, 2014, I will experience my fifth president since 1981 (Harold Shapiro, Jim Duderstadt, Lee Bollinger, Mary Sue Coleman, and Mark Schlissel). Before that at Columbia University, between 1968 and 1981 I lived and taught through four presidents (Grayson Kirk, and Andrew Cordier, William McGill, and Michael Sovern). I will begin with Michigan, where I interviewed three generations of leaders for this book, starting with a past president, Jim Duderstadt (1988–96), a transitioning president, Mary Sue Coleman (2002–14), and a new president, Mark Schlissel (July 2014–), who has recently taken the helm at a university that has nineteen schools and colleges on its Ann Arbor campus alone, serving twenty-eight thousand under-graduates, fifteen thousand graduate and professional school students, has two regional campuses in Dearborn and Flint, has ninety-nine graduate programs ranked in the top ten by *U.S. News & World Report,* and in 2012 was ranked number one in research spending among public universities at $1.3 billion per annum.

In a recent discussion with me, Duderstadt framed the job of university president at such an august institution with regard to leadership and talent development:

> One of the most critical roles a president can play is to make sure that they serve as chief headhunter, to identify talent and make sure it advances at the right pace through the system. At Michigan, we don't have a more structured approach to this task the way many companies do, and we don't get a chance to move people around as we might do at a public company. But we do keep an eye out for talent. At Michigan our experience has been historically we go inside or outside about fifty percent of the time.

I first met Mary Sue Coleman shortly after she arrived as the president of the University of Michigan in 1981. Right away I invited her to visit Focus: HOPE in inner-city Detroit, a longtime partner with the university with a mission of "intelligent and practical solutions to racism and poverty." I specifically wanted her to meet the cofounder Eleanor Josaitis, who served on the business school advisory board and regularly involved Michigan students in Focus: HOPE efforts. That same year she helped me host then 3M CEO James McNerney as a keynote speaker for our MBAs. Over the years I have met with Coleman a number of times to discuss global citizenship efforts at Michigan and, most recently, her views on succession in universities. She helped frame my thinking regarding the leadership challenges for a university president with their multiple constituencies: students, faculty, staff, alumni, donors, politicians, and employees. When she stepped down

as president she received many well-deserved accolades for her accomplishments as president. Her successor, Mark Schlissel, took over
on July 1, 2014.

I had the opportunity to discuss succession with Schlissel (previously provost of Brown) a few months before he officially took the baton
from Coleman. During our conversation, Schlissel remained intently
and intentionally focused on distinguishing and defining the boundaries between the respective domains of faculty and administration.

> The faculty owns the issue of setting academic standards and cur-
> ricular content in the different disciplines, including what consti-
> tutes an academic degree in a certain area, and how to assess and
> measure and hold ourselves to certain very specific standards of ex-
> cellence. However, the administrative leadership of the university
> bears sole responsibility for sustaining the enterprise as a business,
> and strategically determining the balance of investments—both hu-
> man and financial capital—across the breadth of the enterprise.

All three of these highly experienced university leaders have adopted
a multi-institutional, multisector perspective on what it takes to successfully lead a university. Each sector, business, nonprofit, or military
branch possesses, for better or for worse, unique political and cultural
elements. In my extensive experience, universities are by far the most
difficult institutions for business executives to fathom because they are
the most complex and challenging institutions to govern, a cross-sector
disconnect which, in the case of General Eisenhower at Columbia, can
sometimes have tragic consequences, since corporate executives so frequently serve as trustees of universities, just as Thomas Watson Sr. did
at Columbia. Business executives all too often operate under the errone-
ous and occasionally fatal assumption that presidents and deans are
able to make reasonably unfettered and unconstrained command decisions, just like senior executives in a for-profit institution or a general in
a military hierarchy. Yet as Schlissel so aptly points out, college and

university administrators may not, and therefore should not, even attempt to behave like a general or a traditional CEO if they know what is good for them. That is a lesson that the greatest general of the twentieth century learned the hard way.

As Jim Duderstadt points out, Michigan tends to select internal or external presidents in approximately equal proportion. He himself was an internal selection, as was his immediate predecessor, Harold Shapiro, who in turn passed the torch to internal candidate Lee Bollinger, who left Ann Arbor after three years to become president of Columbia, thereby setting the stage for the recruitment of Mary Sue Coleman from the University of Iowa, who has lately been followed by another outsider, Mark Schlissel, formerly of Brown, Berkeley, and Johns Hopkins. Duderstadt couldn't have been clearer to me with regard to the fact that a university president does not and cannot exert as much power as a Fortune 500 CEO when selecting his or her successor:

> The best thing that a university president can do is to make sure that talent is widely spread across the institution . . . and make sure that the power and therefore the future of the institution is broadly distributed to where the talent is and should be.

"There is not a lot else that a sitting president can do," he adds, "to prepare the way for the next person other than to populate the university with a lot of talent and protect it if the board is unstable." Duderstadt shared this piece of unsolicited advice from his predecessor, Shapiro, with Coleman with regard to navigating the transition to newcomer Schlissel: "Just walk out the door."

When discussing the new president, Mark Schlissel, Duderstadt remains highly optimistic about his capacity and potential for leadership in the complex environment of a vast university many times the size of Brown. He told me:

> I like what I see about this guy. He's smart, he's honest, he listens, and he gets it . . . I can support this guy to the hilt because he understands

the medical side of the equation from his time at Hopkins. He understands not simply academic quality but the importance of faculty governance from his time at Berkeley and his two years at Brown, which also gave him an understanding of innovative undergraduate education—Brown's strong suit. He's got the right set of experiences, background, and characterizations—so let's see if we can't make him a great president.

Michigan's most distinctive institutional feature is its unique combination of "quality, intellectual breadth, scale, and spirit of risk taking," in Duderstadt's view. "Every once in a while Michigan does something that changes the world, including its critical role in the launch of the Internet, and its long-standing leadership position in the quantitative social sciences."

Duderstadt's advice for any new leader attempting to negotiate the transition in such a diverse institution is to draw on the experiences of those people already on campus who can form, as he puts it, an informal "kitchen cabinet."

Coming into a big, complex place like Michigan, with its unique culture, he will need to determine who will be in his kitchen cabinet. The only way to do that is by talking to people who have been around for a while and getting a sense of whom you can trust, and whom do you have to stay away from.

To succeed as a university president at this unique institution, Duderstadt shared with me a list that lays out the leadership challenges in three sections: 1. how the University of Michigan is organized and managed, 2. how faculty gets things done, and 3. some operating rules for academic leaders.

Jim Duderstadt's Handy-Dandy Guide to Leadership at Michigan

How Is the University of Michigan Organized and Managed?

1. The University is a "loosely coupled, adaptive system," with a growing complexity, and its entrepreneurial character has made it remarkably adaptive and resilient.

2. Faculty is free and encouraged to move toward personal goals in highly flexible ways, almost as a type of holding company of faculty entrepreneurs, who drive the evolution of the university.

3. The university administration sets some general ground rules and regulations, acts as an arbiter, raises money for the enterprise, and tries to keep activities roughly coordinated.

4. Budget authority is delegated to the lowest level where assets are acquired and costs are incurred, typically at the level of deans and directors.

5. Academic priorities come from the deans. Every effort should be made to encourage the deans and provost to function as a true team.

6. Faculty governance is most effective at the level of department, school, and college executive committees, which are generally comprised of UM's strongest faculty.

7. The free flow of information is absolutely critical to the success of the loosely coupled character of the University. Attempts to keep bad news in confidence and promote only good news will seriously harm the University over the long term.

How Does the Faculty Get Things Done Around Here?

Rule 1: NEVER accept "no" for the answer to a request. In a highly decentralized organization, there are lots of folks who may have the capacity to say "yes."

Rule 2: The most important play in the Michigan playbook is the "end run" . . . around chairs to deans, around deans to provosts, around presidents to Regents, and around the University to Lansing, Washington, or donors. Administrators should never try to block this, since the University would soon cease to function as an entrepreneurial organization.

Rule 3: It is usually better to seek forgiveness than ask permission.

Rule 4: Under no circumstances should faculty (or academic leaders) allow themselves to be constrained by staff in areas unrelated to core activities (e.g., development, communications, public relations, government relations). These individuals work to support the academic units, not to constrain them.

Some Operating Rules for Academic Leaders
1. In simplest terms, the president's job is to raise the money, the provost's job is to determine how to spend it, and the CFO's job is to make certain folks spend it the way the provost wants them to. In hierarchy, the president trumps the provost, and the provost trumps everybody else.
2. It is critical that any administrators with major authority have strong backgrounds in higher education . . . or at least supervisors with such backgrounds.
3. To reaffirm the role of the provost, both the Committee on Budget Administration and the Budget Priorities Committee should be reinstituted and chaired by the provost.
4. Because of the decentralization of the University, every effort must be made to benchmark all operations against best practices at other institutions (e.g., funding, staffing, achievements). In a similar sense, a rigorous audit operation (both external and internal) is critical.

The incoming president Mark Schlissel shared why he was attracted to Michigan:

What attracted me to Michigan is its public character, the quality and impact of its academic programs, and its commitment to serve the public good through education and research. And what I hope to accomplish during however much time I am really blessed with the privilege of leadership of such an outstanding institution is to continue to promote academic excellence, to maintain and enhance affordability and access to a Michigan education at all levels regardless of where a person's coming from in our society, and to focus the university's research portfolio on things of value to the public that it's serving, both locally and nationally and globally.

He has a very clear teachable point of view when it comes to how a university operates, which he has experienced as faculty at Johns Hopkins, biological science dean, and head of the Health Sciences Initiative for the campus. Similar to the earlier Duderstadt quote, Schlissel shares many of the same beliefs regarding the role of faculty governance and the role of administration and the regents. In his own words:

There are aspects of university governance that are quite completely owned by the faculty. The faculty own the issues of what academic standards are, what curricula content is in different disciplines, what constitutes an academic degree in a certain area, how to assess and measure and hold ourselves to standards of excellence. Those are all issues owned by the faculty. However, the leadership, the administrative leadership of the university has responsibility for the enterprise as a business and has responsibility for strategically determining the balance of investments across the breadth of the enterprise. That's owned by senior administration and trustees or regents. So this concept of faculty governance is certainly true and extends across a significant fraction of the enterprise but not across the entire enterprise.

With his PhD and MD with a research background, Schlissel spoke of taking an almost scientific method approach to learning about an institution:

What you get to do of course is to try to learn the culture of the institution at the same time you're trying to wrap your hands around the levers that allow you to exert a positive influence. And all the while I'm testing new observations against prior experience. So there's much more in common amongst academic institutions than there are differences, even though each is unique. So I've been able to rely a lot on my Berkeley experience.

According to Schlissel, his prior experiences at Brown and Berkeley taught him that when you enter a complex political environment like a university with its multiple power bases and many key leaders wondering if they will make the cut on the new leadership team, or thinking about whether they even want to be part of the team, the political element in the the TPC equation needs to be carefully orchestrated by the leader for the overall and long-range good of the institution.

When you first come in, everyone on the senior leadership staff realizes that, you're going to be playing a role in determining their future, so they all want to get off to a good start with you.

Consistent with his academic background as a research scientist focused on the developmental biology of the immunological system, Schlissel approached his impending transition in a characteristically systematic fashion. Prior to officially taking on his new role as of July 1, 2014, he and his wife decided to travel across the entire state, conducting an informal yet objective assessment of the political and cultural landscape in addition to its physical and topographical layout. After taking up his new role, he intended to clearly address two vital agenda items: first, developing constructive working relationships with the staff he is inheriting, followed by a thorough assessment of their leadership potential. He intends to enter into this process operating under "the presumption that everybody's good at their job and functioning at a high level. And I will then test that presumption." Again his scientific hypothesis test mind-set rises to the fore as he contemplates the second most important item on his agenda: "To develop a properly healthy relationship with the regents . . . it's very important for me to work on both the personal aspects of the relationship but also the structural aspects of the relationship between my board and the university right from the beginning."

With regard to planning his own succession, Schlissel fully intends to get started on tackling the challenge of building a leadership pipeline at his new home immediately. He articulated his desire to emulate Harvard and Yale, where the rate of internal promotion to president is far higher and greater than at comparable institutions around the country and around the world.

In fact, the only university in the United States that does takes internal leadership pipeline building as seriously as GE is the oldest one in the country. Since its founding in 1636, Harvard has had only had three presidents who did not receive a Harvard degree, with current president

Dr. Drew Gilpin Faust, a direct descendant of the Puritan divine Jonathan Edwards, being not just the first female president of Harvard but the second who does not hold either an undergraduate or graduate degree from the university since 1672.

My longtime friend Leonard Schlesinger, the current Baker Foundation Professor of Business Administration at Harvard Business School who has also served as the president of Babson College, as well as chief operating officer at both the restaurant chain Au Bon Pain and the fashion retailer The Limited, is one of those rare creatures who, like myself, has moved from academic to corporate environments and back to academia with unusual finesse and ease. According to Schlesinger, while he attempted to develop a leadership pipeline at Babson, Harvard leads every other great institution of higher learning in the nation when it comes to having put processes in place to produce a robust pipeline. Schlesinger, in fact, holds not just the university at large but the business school in particular up as a model of being an "academy academy" virtually unique in the land:

> The Harvard Business School is the only one that I know of that has ever truly been serious about ensuring that the faculty leadership really does play a critical role in the development of the institution and provides an array of roles and process in which to accomplish that goal. Regardless of whether they elect to go inside or outside for deans, there has never during my years here been a shortage of potential leaders for the institution. Since I started here in the 1970s the school has measured the amount of time the faculty leadership spends in coordinating roles inside the institution, as well as the length of time faculty leaders spend in those roles as part of the overall staffing model. I am not talking about faculty meetings, which as we all know are mere conversations. I'm talking about the entire tenured faculty sitting on the appointments committee, which decides who gets promoted and who gets tenure and in effect makes all of the key executive decisions of the university.

The sad commentary is that Harvard appears to be unique in promoting leadership development, organizational transformation, and change among universities. Harvard's example at least provides a model to follow and a benchmark against which to measure rivals' performance in this long-neglected arena.

Leadership Development and Succession in K–12 Schools

In this section the focus is on another very different set of schools from universities, namely the kindergarten through high school levels which are the feeders to colleges and universities. I have developed leadership academies for school principals in New York City (more than 1,400 schools and principals) and leadership and succession planning processes for 20 Uplift charter schools in Dallas; for 30 IDEA charter schools in the Rio Grande Valley of Texas; and for 200 schools in Brunei and dozens more in Laos, Cambodia, Singapore, and Malaysia. The technical challenges in these schools connect with those in universities, namely, they exist to educate students to prepare them for higher education or a career right out of high school. There are curriculum and other issues with parallels at both levels. The real differences emerge when we look at the political and cultural challenges for schools.

Whether we are dealing with the largest school system in the United States, in New York, or a small charter school system like IDEA in Texas, they share many of the same political challenges of aligning a school board, a parent population, teachers, principals, and the surrounding community to support the vision and agenda of the school head (chancellor in New York City, president of IDEA). New York, like virtually every other big urban system from Detroit to Philadelphia, faces the added political and cultural challenge of needing to negotiate with very strong unions, one for the teachers and one for the principals;

one of the political advantages that charter schools like IDEA enjoy is that their staff is not unionized.

My introduction to building leadership pipelines and working on succession planning in public school systems dates back to 1980, when as a graduate student at Columbia I worked on a project that examined the impact on the broader system of the appointment of the first black superintendent to oversee the predominantly minority-populated Newark suburb of East Orange, New Jersey. After joining the faculty at Columbia in 1972, I advised public school systems in communities across the New York suburbs of Westchester County, including New Rochelle, White Plains, and Mount Vernon. And more recently, I teamed up with Jack Welch, my good friend and colleague Bob Knowling, Carolyn Kennedy, and others to establish a Leadership Academy for principals in New York under the leadership of then-mayor Michael Bloomberg and schools chancellor Joel Klein.

A working-class kid who grew up in Queens and graduated from Columbia and Harvard Law School, Klein was a highly successful attorney in both the public and private sectors and the former U.S. CEO of the German-based global media conglomerate Bertelsmann when his friend Michael Bloomberg tapped him for what is arguably the toughest and most politically contentious job in the entire public school system in the country. As would have been true if we had been working with any number of large public companies that had been carved up into independent fiefdoms—think GE, Ford, GM, etc.—we had our work cut out for us attempting to establish a modicum of centralized control over the development of leaders throughout this highly bureaucratized and dysfunctional system. At Klein's invitation, a wide range of business and civic leaders supported the effort, ranging from Bill Gates to Carolyn Kennedy and Jack Welch, who rolled up his sleeves and energetically pitched in because he believed so fervently in our cause. Welch even offered us GE's Crotonville as a setting for the opening workshop we conducted for ten regional superintendents and dozens of high-potential principals. As the author of an article in the business magazine *Strategy + Business* noted, "New York is declaring that principals, though rarely thought of as managers—at least not in the conventional sense—have the same need for managerial and leadership development as rising corporate executives."[4]

From East Orange, New Jersey, to New York City to the Sultanate of Brunei, all of our work with public school systems is founded on the same principles. All of it consists of helping the current generation of leaders build robust leadership pipelines that select high-potential future leaders from the next generation based on an objective assessment of their skills, motivation, and drive to lead and succeed. Our overarching objective, no matter where the system may be located or what sort of political environment it may be operating in, is to create a clear and rational career path from classroom teacher to department head to assistant principal to principal to assistant superintendent or central office leader, all the way up to candidates for head of the system. We create an infrastructure that prepares the next generation of leadership to confront and cope with whatever challenges may lie ahead for the organization. Wherever we work, we make sure to train and develop sufficient internal talent on the human resources side so that even when we are long gone the infrastructure and development remain intact and survive with integrity.

One of our more recent engagements, with the esteemed IDEA Public Schools network of thirty-six charter schools scattered across Texas, serves as a role model for succession planning and building a leadership pipeline in a school environment. Over the past five years, I have worked with IDEA Public Schools CEO Tom Torkelson and chief of schools and cofounder JoAnn Gama to help their team build a strong and enduring leadership pipeline that will ensure the longevity of the enterprise for decades to come. One of the most remarkable aspects of this ongoing project is that while IDEA is a young organization, its leadership is deeply committed to investing whatever it takes to evolve a systematic approach to talent and leadership development, starting from entry-level teachers through department heads to assistant principals, all the way up the ladder to potential successors for Torkelson and Gama.

A graduate of Georgetown with a degree in economics, Torkelson served a formative three-year stint after graduating from college teaching fourth-graders in tiny Donna, Texas, under the auspices of the groundbreaking program Teach for America with fellow cofounder JoAnn Gama. After launching the IDEA Academy in 2000 and serving as the organization's first board president and founding principal at the tender age of twenty-four, Tom became not only Texas's youngest-ever charter school founder but head of a system that quickly blossomed into a national leader in the movement to reform secondary education, particularly in lower-income school districts. Starting out in the historically impoverished and largely Hispanic Rio Grande Valley, IDEA now encompasses a statewide network of thirty-six schools, with campuses in the capital city of Austin and other Texas cities that teach thirteen thousand students, with close to 100 percent of graduates going on to colleges and universities, where they continue to receive support and guidance from IDEA. In 2009, *U.S. News & World Report* ranked IDEA College Preparatory the thirteenth-best high school system overall and the second-best charter high school in the nation. That same year Tom was featured in *Time* magazine and received the prestigious Peter Jennings Award for Civic Leadership.

Torkelson described the leadership development process that he, Gama, and their top team have instituted through their fast-growing system as follows:

> What we try to do is to think three leaders out and three levels deep. So we're always projecting into the future. So if we know how many schools we're going to be launching over the next three years out and we keep looking three levels deep into the organization, that makes it possible for us to figure out who can take over a school or lead one of those schools with enough of a runway so we can start developing those candidates now.
>
> First and foremost, we start with our principals, objectively assessing their capabilities, preparation, and potential to take on bigger, more complex roles in the organization. This first step is an abso-

lute prerequisite organizationally, because we're growing so quickly. On the campus level, when a principal comes on our radar screen whom we recognize as somebody who has a lot of potential to be running a bigger section of the organization, we ask that principal to start their assessments of the people two layers underneath them. What do their assistant principals look like? What do their rising teacher leaders look like? We craft a process that enables us to collect these high-potential talented leaders from their respective campuses, and take steps to ensure that all of the principals are being very thoughtful about cultivating those people most likely to step into their position if we promote them to a higher level of leadership.

Working closely together, Torkelson and Gama take great pains to remain extremely systematic and to personally play a very powerful role in the process. For example, both senior leaders routinely inform their most high-value principals and assistant principals that they are working within a system based on an ongoing process of evaluation and assessment that is not only fair and transparent, but designed to develop them to their fullest personal and professional potential.

After spending three or four hours evaluating the talent of all of the teachers on a particular campus, we make sure to ask the leaders to place themselves on a nine cell, and to think for themselves what some areas for coaching or improvement might be, or what particular stretch assignments might be the right ones to help them grow to the next level.

After completing the talent assessment and pipeline production for all thirty-six schools, Torkelson, Gama, and their senior leadership team take their second big step: reporting back to the board. As Torkelson explains:

When I get my board into a closed-door session, I'll say to my directors, "All right, guys, here are my most senior leaders. Here is the first person I would nominate to replace me. Here is the second person in line to replace me. This is what they would need to do my job well and this is how I'm helping them get those different experiences." So we just do it all the way up through the organization. The last thing is you're doing succession planning not because you're leaving the organization but we want to get you ready for that promotion. If you want to lead our Qatar school or open up a new region in north Texas or to a new state, then you have to have your successor ready. So this isn't about getting ready for retirement or leaving the organization or getting fired, this is about a promotion that you want down the line perhaps.

The box below is based on supporting materials that IDEA uses for its succession planning process, representing a best-practice example and one that Torkelson is actually using today to make sure that he and his organization are prepared to pass the "beer truck test" at any time.

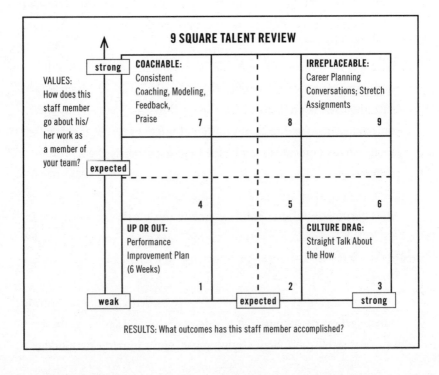

9 SQUARE TALENT REVIEW

VALUES: How does this staff member go about his/her work as a member of your team?

	weak	expected	strong
strong	COACHABLE: Consistent Coaching, Modeling, Feedback, Praise — 7	8	IRREPLACEABLE: Career Planning Conversations; Stretch Assignments — 9
expected	4	5	6
	UP OR OUT: Performance Improvement Plan (6 Weeks) — 1	2	CULTURE DRAG: Straight Talk About the How — 3

RESULTS: What outcomes has this staff member accomplished?

Schools in Brunei

The same leadership development process and succession planning process that we developed for IDEA and the New York City Leadership Academy was recently implemented in the Sultanate of Brunei after my colleagues and I spent four years replicating our New York City experience with two hundred schools in this small country with a predominantly Muslim population of just four hundred thousand, or less than one sixteenth the population of New York City. Each school principal arrived at the leadership academy with two assistant principals and participated in a six-month, three-workshop process. We provide each team with hands-on projects to improve numeracy and literacy for the entire system. We also implement succession planning processes to fill both principal roles in the future as well as the leadership of the ministry of education.

We have successfully adapted every activity and exercise initially developed in the United States to a wide variety of cultures around the world, including a number of teams from nations scattered throughout the ASEAN (Association of Southeast Asian Nations) region, including Singapore, Vietnam, and Cambodia. The main lesson I've learned after conducting action learning and succession planning workshops for a wide range of institutions in countries as diverse as Japan, China, India, Germany, Mexico, and Brazil is that the the underlying methodology applies because the human fundamentals and organizational dynamics are sufficiently similar, despite the fact that cultural and leadership styles may vary from region to region and nation to nation.

Boys & Girls Clubs

Boys & Girls Clubs of America (BGCA) is a federation of local youth-service organizations that was founded in 1906. Today, more than eleven hundred Boys & Girls Club organizations operating as independent 501c3 nonprofits manage more than four thousand club sites nationwide and on U.S. military installations worldwide. Every local organization is governed by a local board of directors and is responsible for raising its own funds and developing staff. BGCA oversees the federation and provides vital support to local clubs in the form of programs, services, and leadership development and succession-planning support.

For much of the last decade, I have worked closely with BGCA to develop leadership programs and succession-planning strategies—much the same way I worked with the schools in New York City and Brunei. Leadership teams of six each attended a workshop with five other clubs. Each team worked to enhance its management skills, create organizational improvement plans, and develop a succession-planning process. The same nine cell assessments (performance and values) were conducted with each club's leadership. Plans were then put in place to determine who could replace the CEO on both a short- and long-term basis.

At the national level, BGCA promotes leaders from the field; namely, those who demonstrate exemplary performance by successfully operating and expanding a local club organization. Promoting from within the federation encourages seamless and harmonious successions and helps national leadership to stay grounded in the local experience—a critical part of being a successful leader in a mission-driven organization. BGCA president and CEO, Jim Clark, for example, previously served in the same capacities for the Boys & Girls Clubs of Greater Milwaukee.

When possible, succession plans are made known well in advance. For example, BGCA formally announced Clark would succeed past-president Roxanne Spillett more than six months before the formal transition took place. This in turn allowed Clark to ensure the seamless transition of leadership at the Boys & Girls Clubs of Greater Milwaukee.

Leadership Succession in Health Care

My personal introduction to the politics of succession planning and leadership development in nonprofit health care institutions occurred as I was just starting out as an assistant professor at the Graduate School of Business at Columbia. At this watershed moment in my own professional development, I had decided that the only legitimate objective of studying social psychology in depth would be to arm myself with the intellectual and experiential resources to become an active change agent. Determined to spend as much time as I could outside the ivory tower and in the communities with which universities like Columbia had so long neglected to engage, I embarked on an intensive field research and action learning project at the Dr. Martin Luther King Jr. Health Center in the South Bronx, one of 144 neighborhood health centers created nationally as part of the Johnson-era "war on poverty," which boasted a total staff of five hundred, including physicians practicing internal medicine, pediatrics, and family proactive care, nurses and nurse practitioners, and other health care professionals. Nearly all of the doctors were from Montefiore's Albert Einstein Medical Center and residents in Montefiore's department of social medicine, which specialized in training physicians intent on serving society. As a pro-bono consultant to the residents, I was responsible for providing them with behavioral science training while simultaneously serving as a consultant to the center's executive management team on leadership development and succession planning for the institution.

At the Center, I devoted much of my time to helping the then current generation of leaders reframe the organization's structure and design to promote a culture of accountability and leadership as opposed to management and status quo. In keeping with that mission, I ran a series of off-site workshops with the director, Delores Smith, and her team on a quarterly basis over a period of several years and visited the Center at least every other week, often getting my Columbia University MBA and PhD students involved in projects. One important output was a succession planning process that resulted in Delores Smith's being promoted to a senior executive role at Montefiore and a new and capable CEO appointed as her successor as the Center's director. An additional positive output was the publication of my first book, *Organization Design for Primary Health Care: The Case of the Dr. Martin Luther King Jr. Health Center* (Praeger, 1977).

The Martin Luther King Health Center's most significant supporter was the Robert Wood Johnson Foundation, one of the leaders of which, Tom Maloney—who coincidentally had been a classmate of mine at Colgate—called me in late 1974 to ask if I might be interested in doing some consulting for the rural equivalent of the urban MLKHC. The Hazard Family Health Services, located (not surprisingly, given its name) in Hazard, Kentucky, in the most rugged, mountainous, and impoverished area of a state dominated by the Appalachian Mountains, was an innovative health care venture launched by an idealistic, creative young pediatrician, Dr. Gregory Culley, who on a shoestring and a dream had set out to organize an interdisciplinary team of more than twenty-five health care providers, including nurse practitioners, nutritionists, social and family health workers, whose mission impossible—which they had chosen to accept—was to provide prenatal and postnatal care to rural Kentucky women and families, in an attempt to positively impact the appallingly high infant mortality rate in those isolated hills and "hollers" of Appalachia.

Culley was young, charismatic, and committed, but he was not—nor, to his credit, did he profess to be—any sort of professional manager, much less an expert in making an organization function as a viable enterprise. Having observed and supported my work coaching, mentoring, and setting up the leadership pipeline in the South Bronx, Maloney offered me the opportunity to consult with Culley and team to help them to get more clearly aligned around tightly defined goals and roles, and rationalize the organization's decision-making and conflict resolution framework. While continuing to teach full-time at Columbia, I started flying on a monthly basis down to Lexington, Kentucky, and would then drive three hours on rural roads to Hazard. After two years of successful consulting under the assumption that we would have national health insurance which would reimburse the outreach services, the reality sank in that this would be a long time in the future. Maloney and I agreed that I needed to spend at least a full year full-time in Hazard to change the model from outreach services to services delivered in the clinic.

By then I had established an executive program in Advanced Organization Development and Human Resources Management at Columbia, and was busy teaching MBAs and PhD students and in charge of the MBA/MSW and MBA/MPH programs there. But Maloney was nothing if not persistent, and virtually begged me to help the foundation recover from what we all agreed was a "miscalculation" regarding national health insurance.

Since that didn't happen—and only recently has happened four decades later, and only to a very limited and controversial degree—my sole recourse to save the place from going under was to take on the leadership task myself. In June 1977, I moved down with my family to Hazard and arrived just in time to learn that the Appalachian Regional Hospitals (ARH) system, with which the clinic was associated, was on the verge of declaring bankruptcy because the United Mine Workers union had cut back on their health benefits and the ARH, as a result, did not have money to meet the payroll or other financial obligations.

My mission immediately morphed from a management-organizational-orientation focus into an urgent need to develop a strategy that might keep not just the clinic but the entire hospital system financially viable. I immediately enrolled the president of the hospital chain in my executive management program at Columbia, hoping to bring him up to speed on the latest developments in the field. I also initiated a series of meetings with HEW officials, hoping that we might be able to work out some sort of realistic solution. What I ultimately realized during my traumatic stint in the Appalachians was that while I had been focusing on a technical solution to the organizational dilemma, the political challenges were far more insurmountable, and would as a result effectively neutralize any technical changes we succeeded in instituting. At

the end of the day, the executive director of the hospital chain was de-
posed and the clinic itself developed—at my behest—a new leader. As
acting manager, I found my successor soon enough, in the form of Les-
lie Rogers the assistant manager, whom I was able to develop into a
leader who could run the place once I was back in New York.

I had come to the inescapable conclusion that—as I later wrote, "Theory didn't help; all of my change tools had been useless in this endeavor . . . I had to rethink the nature of nonprofit organizations and the
problems they faced. I had been missing a strand, the *political* strand
[which required] me to integrate the political dimension into my evolving theory of organizational change."[5] I not only learned a lot about the
politics of health care, I also successfully implemented my own CEO
succession by mentoring and coaching my successor as CEO to succeed
in the job.

Health Care Leadership Consortium

All health care institutions share certain technical, political, and cultural features with other nonprofit institutions, in that they are variations on "organized anarchy." Medical doctors, for example, resemble
tenured university faculty members in forming their own independent
power base which, much like faculty, cannot be treated like soldiers or
"employees." Other political constituencies unique to the politics of
health care include the patients, the insurers, and major employers in
the surrounding community. For several years I ran a University of
Michigan–sponsored leadership development and succession program
for a number of major medical centers, including Alina, Catholic West,
St. Joseph System, the Cleveland Clinic, Memphis Baptist, Baylor, and
the Manipal System in India, which attempted to take all of these disparate factors into account. The program primarily consisted of six-month
action learning programs, combined with consulting work between the
workshops designed to improve the functioning of the institution,
qualitatively and quantitatively, in addition to developing viable succes-

sion pipelines. These teams were typically made up of the CEO, the head of medicine, and the respective heads of the nursing department, as well as selected key administrators.

Two graduates of that program have since gone on to serve as excellent CEO role models at major medical centers. Nancy Schlichting is chief executive officer of the Henry Ford Health System, a nationally recognized $4.6 billion health care organization with twenty-three thousand employees. A hallmark of Schlichting's career has been working with community, legislative, and business leaders to improve health services while providing affordable care to the residents of downtown Detroit. Combined with satellite branches scattered throughout the Detroit suburbs, the Henry Ford multihospital system has annual revenue of $4.46 billion and serves more than one million patients. Schlicting was part of my Healthcare Leadership Program and successfully implemented much of what she was taught there. The result is that she and her team have developed their own leadership development programs combined with a systematic succession process. As she recently related to me, she is crystal clear about her people priorities. "My basic job is to create an atmosphere where every person can reach their full potential. I view the world as being all about leadership. I believe leaders can make or break a group of people. One leader can be so toxic as to make a team fail. I've watched it in action too many times." As a result of her core beliefs she has developed a clear and teachable point of view on the subject of developing her successor. The fundamentals required of that role going forward, she insists, will be "strategic thinking skills, the ability to get people to do hard things, things they wouldn't normally do—that's what leadership is all about. They have to take risks in real-life risky situations to grow. Sometimes we protect people too much."

As an example of this development philosophy, Schlicting hired Kathy Oswald as her head of human resources and gives her ample credit for helping her build a robust leadership development and succession process despite the political and cultural complexities of the nonprofit environment.

Half of my discussions with direct reports in regular meetings revolve around the topic of executive succession. We have cross learning about talent because one of the cool things about a system of our size and scale is that we are able to move talent as a means of encouraging that talent to grow. The only way we're going to prepare people to take on these senior-level jobs is if they work in more than one business unit, and learn how to apply the skills that they learn to a variety of organizational settings.

As the leaders responsible for constructing a CEO developmental pipeline, Schlicting and Oswald design developmental experiences for high-potential candidates. "We put them on boards. We put them in leadership teams. We put together unusual suspects to solve problems, which is what I've done myself from the very beginning of my tenure. I've put the head of the health plan and the head of the medical group working together on a problem that allowed them to understand each other." Schlichting assures me that she gets triple mileage out of these task forces: first, they produce divergent thinking and perspectives which lead to better results; second, they develop individuals as leaders; and third, they provide her team with a reliable assessment tool for benchmarking the potential of future leaders and their qualification for promotion to more senior roles in the organization, up to and including CEO.

Wellmont Health System

I first met Denny DeNarvaez when she was serving as CEO of one of the hospitals in the Minneapolis-based Alina Health System, a consortium that comprises a network of eight hospitals with more than 1,300 beds, revenue of $2.4 billion, and a staff of 7,000. Having served in a variety of health care leadership roles, she recently commented on the appropriate relationship between CEOs, CHROs, and boards with regard to managing the governance of these large and complex institutions.

Most board members understand the need for succession planning in large health care institutions, but most health executives don't. While board members have been waiting for this a long time, every executive who comes into the job claims that they are going to do it, but every executive has failed.

A couple of reasons for why those executives have failed include a certain degree of insecurity on their part about creating an heir and a spare. This ultimately boils down to the question of if they institute a plan and a process for their succession, what on earth is going to happen to them? That's always the elephant in the room, in my experience. While in other cases, it is simply the fact that good succession planning takes a lot of work and discipline and so they put if off for another day, and then another. They fail to see the magic of what it is going to produce for the future. On too many occasions I've seen otherwise good and talented CEOs not hold their HR executives accountable for making sure everybody is meeting their deadlines throughout the organization on planning for their own successions.

To avoid succumbing to those failures herself, DeNarvaez works closely with her staff to teach them the process and then just as closely monitors that process's timely and effective execution. At Wellmont Health System, she has consciously built a culture where all of her people at every level are held accountable for developing talent—including their own. She has overseen the construction of a pipeline designed to allow her to execute a smooth transition to the next CEO from an internal pipeline developed from within the system. She reinforces this conviction with teeth: "I don't advance anyone if they don't have a bench built up behind them that allows me to responsibly promote them . . . folks that fail to create an heir and a spare put themselves at great risk of not being able to get the next opportunity."

At Wellmont Health, she has, she says,

taken a very formalized process to hold all of our people accountable so that they are constantly thinking about succession. I use the nine-cell that Noel Tichy has taught me—"performance—low, medium, and high; values—low, medium, and high"—in order to produce my replacement when the time comes.

At the end of the day, both Schlichting and DeNarvaez have learned from experience that no single element of a succession system produces a process that perfectly selects for the next CEO. In both universities and health care systems, organizations tend to be riddled with powerful interest groups and internal constituencies that don't always share common interests, such as powerful physician groups and individuals with independent power bases, equally or even more powerful board members who are, in effect, part-time volunteers with their own complex and often conflicting agendas, community leaders, patient advocates, and other groups that make administrative control inherently challenging. Operating in this complex environment, Schlichting and DeNarvaez represent a tiny minority, who on a national level have their counterparts in excellence at such a small handful of prestigious institutions that take leadership development and succession planning seriously, including the Mayo Clinic, the Cleveland Clinic, Johns Hopkins, and my own University of Michigan Medical System.

The Gold Standard for Nonprofits: The U.S. Special Operations Forces

The most cleanly and clearly aligned nonprofit organization I have personally worked with is the Special Operations Command of the United States armed forces, an elite group within the larger military establishment that has over the years developed a highly systematic internal "succession from within" process that essentially dictates that the importation of a four-star general or admiral to lead SOF without having grown up and risen up the ranks from within the organization would be nothing short of out-and-out blasphemy. In this mission-critical sense, the Special Operations Forces, comprising the Army Rangers, the Army aviation regiment known as the Night Stalkers, the Green Berets, the Navy SEALs, and the Air Force SOF squadrons, are the antithesis of the far more cripplingly politicized and bureaucratized Army, Navy, and Air Force command-and-control, old-school, hidebound hierarchies. The many leaders of the SOF with whom I have worked over the past twenty years have virtually without exception prided themselves on living and breathing outside the stereotypical military political and cultural system, precisely that cumbersome military-industrial complex that Dwight Eisenhower so roundly denounced in his farewell speech to the nation in 1960, before John F. Kennedy succeeded him as president.

SOF leaders are, in stark contrast to their bemedaled brethren at the Pentagon, insistently antihierarchical, antibureaucratic, fast-moving, fast decision-making mavericks. The epitome of this characterological type was my longtime and close friend Wayne Downing, now deceased, who when I first met him was a four-star general, a former Green Beret, a proud graduate of West Point, and the acknowledged father and founder of the modern Special Operations Forces, which he led from the end of the cold war until the dawn of the twenty-first-century age of terrorism and asymmetrical warfare. A true American hero, General Downing personally spearheaded a radical transformation of the SOF from a force primarily equipped to duel with the Soviets and their nuclear arsenal to the tension-filled world of today. The success of the high-risk, high-stakes mission conducted by the U.S. Navy SEALs to find and kill Osama bin Laden in Pakistan was in many respects the ultimate outcome of the hard work that Downing and his successors have done over the course of several decades to develop a unique cadre of fighting forces unmatched in their capabilities to protect the United States and its allies abroad from acts of terrorism around the world.

Downing was not just a world-class leader and teacher himself, he was truly the model of the modern major general, who built a succession pipeline that stands out as defining the gold standard for any organization. An example of how he led his team is exemplified in the stack of plastic cards he used to hand out to all his SOF leaders. One was called a "reinventing license."

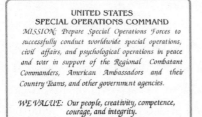

UNITED STATES
SPECIAL OPERATIONS COMMAND

MISSION: Prepare Special Operations Forces to successfully conduct worldwide special operations, civil affairs, and psychological operations in peace and war in support of the Regional Combatant Commanders, American Ambassadors and their Country Teams, and other government agencies.

WE VALUE: Our people, creativity, competence, courage, and integrity.

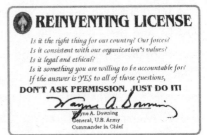

REINVENTING LICENSE

Is it the right thing for our country? Our forces?
Is it consistent with our organization's values?
Is it legal and ethical?
Is it something you are willing to be accountable for?
If the answer is YES to all of those questions,
DON'T ASK PERMISSION, JUST DO IT!

Wayne A. Downing
General, U.S. Army
Commander in Chief

These cards provided an especially powerful symbol to their possessors that the world is rife with paradoxes, and that the SOF troops will succeed by living with them and by them. The best members of the SOF follow orders—except when their other values tell them to do something else.

For several years after he retired from the Army as head of the SOF, General Downing taught in my leadership program at the University of Michigan and also worked with me in numerous workshops with business executives. I have also had more than 120 Special Operations officers participate in my leadership judgment program at the University of Michigan and I regularly run special leadership workshops for the Special Operations Forces. As a strong advocate for their way of life and their esprit de corps, I have had the privilege of helping the SOF develop a leadership development and succession planning process which, I contend, is second to none not just in the military, but in organizations as a whole.

SOF Leadership Pipeline

Wayne Downing as leader/teacher built the modern leadership pipeline for the SOF. It started with a very clear teachable point of view about the SOF and the future leadership needed to succeed in tomorrow's world. His teachable point of view is a template for building the leadership pipeline and for selecting the next leader of the SOF.

Downing developed the ideas component of his teachable point of view to help leaders and future leaders—from soldiers on the ground to generals commanding divisions and battalions—to deal with an ambiguous new world of fragmented terrorism far removed from the cold war environment that he grew up in himself. As Downing had said many times in my presence and more times when not, we all live in a world where "people, not technology" matter most and he was for many years the military's most eloquent and outspoken exponent of that essential yet little-known and underappreciated fact. He was as fierce a hater of bureaucracy as Jack Welch, who included "our systems must defeat Bureaucracy"—with a capital "B"—in every one of his presentations both to the powers that be and to the rank and file. To a large extent, of course, he was indirectly referring to his bosses and holders of the privy purse inside the Pentagon. Until the day he died he was adamant about the fact that in order to win, he and the SOF would need to "exercise unique powers for budget and acquisitions," which he creatively performed by frequently and blithely bypassing the normal military acquisition bureaucracy, and even famously buying some much-needed weapons for his crack troops from sporting goods stores.

But he also understood the practical political realities of the mission he had signed on for, which frequently demanded that he woo politicians, so that the SOF to which he was so deeply devoted would be provided with the resources it needed to maintain the standard of excellence he not only personally demanded but truly believed was necessary to protect our country and our unique way of life. Downing proudly shared one of his trips when other passengers were mainly senators and congressmen. They were both deeply taken aback and deeply impressed when unbeknownst to them, the SEALs parachuted out of the plane so that when the plane landed, they were standing on the tarmac saluting the congressmen as they disembarked. Downing's message was clear: these silent warriors were damn impressive.

In the values component of his teachable point of view, Downing reiterated his conviction that the "primacy of the mission" is critical and that nothing else matters in the end. And for that mission to be accomplished, "people [must] value environment, recruitment, assessment/selections, train[ing] and re-training." Downing invested most of his personal time on people, in keeping with his deeply held values of "creativity, integrity, courage, competence and simplicity."

He had a passion for wielding a remarkable degree of emotional energy. He commanded by motivating and energizing more than sixty thousand SOF members throughout his decades of transformational service. His teachable point of view was both simple and clear: "to be an energy pump not a sump; show people you care, manage by walking around, make visits to the field, never pass up an opportunity to talk to the troops, and above all, you need victories as benchmarks—it is never too early to start winning and kicking ass."

When it came to edge, making the yes/no decisions, Downing was equally clear about the importance of "walking the talk, honest—no naked emperors, trust your gut, make tough calls, bold, decisive actions, like a chain—as strong as the weakest link, if you walk by a substandard performance you have just set a new standard, reinventing license" (presented above).

Since Downing's retirement the culture he created has carried on and there have been seven successful transitions including the one upcoming when Admiral Bill McRaven retires in July 2014. In each succession case, the teachable point of view of the current leader has been slightly modified to fit the needs of the SOF in their current environment. This remarkable and unique organization, unlike any other organization in the world, either military or civilian, is the gold standard for leaders developing leaders. We will always need more like Wayne Downing, and most remarkably of all, long after he has passed away he has ensured that we will have them.

CHAPTER 10

LEADERSHIP 20/20: FRAMING AND FACING THE FUTURE

There are no facts about the future.

—**Peter Drucker**

TECHNICAL

- Putting a technically sophisticated, forward-looking, flexible succession planning process in place that:
  1. Develops transformational leaders at all levels
  2. Frames the assessment, development, and CEO selection process to ensure adaptability to four future trends
  3. Integrates political and cultural organizational dimensions so that the technical component doesn't obliterate the political and cultural.

POLITICAL

- Maintaining and sustaining the paradox of power: combining unity of command at the top with high-integrity political alignment between CEO, board, and HR
- Political power is balanced and coordinated to meet the challenges of future trends

CULTURAL

- Articulating a set of values that support where the organization is headed in the future
- Creating mechanisms for teaching and enforcing the values

Getting It Right at Intuit: The Past, Present, and Future of Silicon Valley

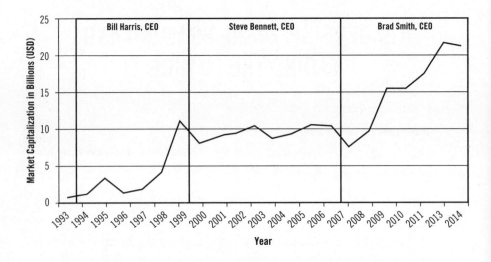

In October 2013, I took fifteen executive MBA students from Asia (Korea, Japan, China, Taiwan, and Thailand) enrolled in our Global MBA program at the University of Michigan's Ross School of Business on a trip to Silicon Valley. Our goal was to benchmark a select group of high-technology companies, both stalwarts and start-ups, as a means of observing, exploring, and learning about the strategic, organizational, and leadership challenges and opportunities that all companies everywhere, of all shapes, sizes, and ages, face every day as they look to win and lead in their respective sectors in the future.

All these bright, eager, capable students were high-potential mid-career executives working at large multinational companies including Panasonic, Sony, Korea Telecom (now KT Corporation), Shinsei Bank, and Fujitsu, among others. The degree to which the senior managements of these well-established organizations considered these rising executives worthy of serious and significant investment was evidenced by the fact that they had chosen to keep these students on full salary for two years while they earned their MBAs in the United States, after which they would return to their home countries and companies bringing back with them the presumed benefits of their extensive classroom and hands-on learning and experience.

As a longtime proponent of action learning in the real world outside the classroom, I intended this multiday benchmarking trip to provide our high-potential students with actionable insights that they would commit to bring back to their companies and implement. Among the high-tech, high-performance organizations we visited in Silicon Valley were:

+ Qualcomm: the world's largest fabless semiconductor producer and wireless chipset provider;

+ eSilicon: a fourteen-year-old fabless semiconductor company and key supplier to Apple;

+ Ikanos Communications: which develops and produces high-performance semiconductor and software products;

+ Solazyme: a start-up whose sustainable technology transforms low-cost plant sugars into high-value renewable vegetable oils capable of replacing fossil fuels in a wide range of applications;

+ Xero: which developed and produces financial software for small businesses, accountants, and households;

+ Intuit: whose flagship financial software products include Quick-Books, TurboTax, and Quicken, on which millions of individuals, households, and small businesses worldwide rely to meet their financial accounting needs;

+ IDEO: the iconic research and development group partnered with many global companies to develop both new products and IT applications;

+ Stanford University Design Lab.

Intuit is the venerable Silicon Valley stalwart whose first product, Quicken, revolutionized personal finance management. While many legendary start-ups began in a garage, Intuit got its start at a kitchen table, where Scott Cook, a former Procter & Gamble marketer and Bain consultant, watched his highly educated wife struggle to balance the family checkbook. Cook intuitively realized—hence the name—that he could work collaboratively with a team of developers to create a software program that would help not just his wife, but also people all over the world manage their household finances more conveniently and rationally.

We spent several hours with current CEO Brad Smith discussing how the company has successfully framed and implemented a series of three successions and leadership transitions that resulted in his being named as the company's fifth CEO in January 2008. Over the course of more than three decades, Intuit has never become complacent while defending its leadership position in the face of new entrants rising up to challenge its dominance of a still fast-growing category.

Under Smith's leadership, Intuit has cultivated an agile experimentation culture that defies the much-derided valley trend of companies' following the laws of Newtonian physics by falling fast in the wake of their rise. Smith views the company as a thirty-year-old start-up, retaining a scrappy mind-set across multiple businesses and product lines. This approach requires Intuit to continually reinvent and transform itself by sustaining a culture that prizes innovation and aggressively keeps abreast of this century's swiftly shape-shifting social, mobile, media, and global trends.

Our conversation with Smith focused on Intuit's uncanny ability to maintain a tight connection and alignment between leadership development, executive transition, and succession planning. Having conducted countless workshops on these topics at the company over many years, Smith reflected on the degree to which every successive leader has worked diligently to maintain the scrappy culture and mind-set that founder Cook initially instilled and has entrusted to his successors to sustain.

Several years ago, Cook realized that the key to sustaining a culture of innovation would be to instill a culture of experimentation among senior leaders, as opposed to the old-fashioned twentieth-century command-and-control model. In a personal transformation that echoes the development of legendary Army General Wayne Downing into a leadership-at-all-levels advocate, Cook has ceaselessly proselytized around the world for organizations to reframe their conception of leadership from one that stresses the leader-as-general, command-and-control model to one that casts the leader in the role of chief coach, adviser, and yes, in the Silicon Valley high-tech context, "Chief Innovator."

Cook explained his evolving philosophy of leadership in the Information Age, which is, as we know, a turbulent period of fast-paced technological and social disruption,

> My father learned leadership in the U.S. military in the Second World War. To him, in his time, leaders were those who framed the options, made the decisions, and told people what to do. Very much like Eisenhower planning D-Day. That worked in his day.
>
> My view is that in our day, and our children's day, inspiration will be more along the lines of Thomas Edison. Because the new skill in leadership is leadership by experiment, decisions made by having a hypothesis that you then test.[1]

During our visit, Brad Smith generously observed:

> We take very seriously the thinking that Noel brought to us, which was a method of taking our *implicit* leadership philosophy and turning it into an *explicit* set of frameworks and principles that others can then use to move beyond building *individual* capability to building *organizational* capability.

"It's our responsibility to leave this company stronger for the next generation. So we try to put those things in place. So I owe a lot to Noel still talk about him regularly and all the stuff that he introduced many years ago are still in our culture."

In his discussions with the students, Smith stressed the importance of establishing a succession plan that could seamlessly transfer the essential DNA of the company—that experimental "from Eisenhower to Edison" leadership and cultural model—from one generation to the next. Nurturing and safeguarding this DNA is as vitally important to Intuit in the business world as it is in the outside world, where DNA informs the regeneration of every living thing to retain something unique and essential that survives long after the original progenitor has passed on.

As chairman of Intuit's executive committee, Scott still plays a major role there, helping fan the spark of innovation throughout the company. Yet early in his career, he made a conscious decision to turn over the reins of the day-to-day decision making to a series of successful successors. This disciplined devotion to succession planning in the highest sense, I would argue, has put Intuit on a path to become the GE of Silicon Valley, if it isn't already there.

The parallels are striking: GE continues to thrive and reinvent itself through decades of change, and through ups and downs in the business cycle and changes in leadership at the top. At the same time, it retains that fundamentally experimental culture even as it continuously battles, due to its scale, the ongoing threat of bureaucratic inertia.

As Smith explained to my increasingly rapt students, succession planning at Intuit can be described as a brief history of four exemplary leaders passing the baton prior to their own ascension, in each case ensuring that the original spark and culture established by the founder Cook wasn't lost in translation, as it so often is.

Our process of leadership succession started with Scott Cook, our founder, followed by the second CEO, Bill Campbell, who is our current chairman of the board. Campbell began his career as a football coach at Columbia and has since become more widely known as the coach of Silicon Valley, advising leaders in great companies ranging from Apple, Google, Twitter, and Square in addition to his continued coaching of Intuit executives.

Our third CEO, Bill Harris, was a serial entrepreneur and served a short stint as Intuit's CEO before leaving to become one of the original investors in PayPal. Our fourth CEO was Steve Bennett, formerly of GE, who led the company for eight years before passing the torch to me.

Over the course of thirty years we've had just five CEOs, with all but one having a fairly long tenure. But much more important than the length of time that they spent in the job was the key fact that *each of them has taken very seriously Scott Cook's philosophy that the role of the CEO at Intuit is not a genius with thousands of helpers, but rather cultivating an environment where inspiration and innovation come from every level of the organization.*

Our leadership philosophy is more informed by the observation of a great investor who once said that he looks for companies with such strong business models that even a monkey could run the company, because—as he put it—one day a monkey will. So Intuit's been testing that theory for the last six years during my tenure, and so far the business model is stronger than the monkey.

Smith explained that he contributes to the ongoing and continually self-sustaining succession-planning process by investing more than one third of his time nurturing and coaching leaders at all levels in the organization. Building on the cultures of GE and P&G, he stress tests upcoming leaders with crucible experiences that will challenge their leadership capabilities and skills by offering them opportunities to fail, as well as succeed.

We seek to grow individuals by moving them between business units and functional roles, challenging them to become less relentless on their craft and the answers they have, and instead nurture their intellectual curiosity and the questions they ask. They participate in one or two action learning projects each year, so they are exposed to the rest of the company and become increasingly aware of the operations of the entire company.

He also ensures that leaders get visibility in front of the Intuit board at the quarterly meetings where succession planning and leadership development are at the top of every agenda.

We conduct High Performance Organization Reviews, or HPOR, for all eight thousand employees every year. In each case, we review performance rating versus their goals for the year. We evaluate their promotional potential, determine if and when they can be promoted within the next year, and then we look at the effect on the company if they got recruited away from here tomorrow. We call that their "retention value."

We place all those employees on a nine-square grid based upon their current performance, their future potential, and their retention value. All are developed and placed in roles to receive the greatest personal development while having the biggest impact on the company.

Based on this process, we have several candidates we believe have the runway and growth trajectory to potentially run this company. We have also identified an emergency successor who could run the company if I couldn't show up for whatever reason. While this is an evergreen process that evolves and changes over time, it is something we actively talk about and manage each quarter with the board.

The Four Trends to Which All Future CEOs Will Need to Adapt to Thrive

As a student of organizational and social change for more than forty years, I have long been intent on studying and analyzing what are often referred to as "megatrends" as a means of framing the leadership challenges any and all organizations' rising stars will be likely to face in the future. Why? Because perhaps more critical to determining their probability of achieving success or suffering failure in the top job will be their capacity to anticipate, adapt to, and get out in front of these trends—or sit helplessly back on their laurels while upstart competitors eat them for lunch.

Sometimes I have been right and sometimes wrong, and my intellectual hero Peter Drucker's quote at the top of this chapter—"There are no facts about the future"—helps to explain why we all tend to be at best indifferent clairvoyants. Yet Drucker was also quite adept at identifying future trends throughout his career, to some degree belying the dim view he took of futurism as a discipline. As I look to the future, the following four trends will not alter the CEO succession game, the fundamentals of which have truly not altered substantially throughout history, but their likely acceleration will simply make what is already a tough job tougher, faster, and more exciting for the winners and more punishing for the losers. The metaphor I typically use to describe how I see the entire framework and process of CEO succession and executive transition from the perspective of current and prospective senior leaders is trying to change a tire on a car while it is speeding down the highway at sixty miles per hour, or even one hundred and sixty.

1. More globalization of everything—businesses, medical treatment, education, and all other services.

2. Even greater acceleration of the more-than-a-century-old technological revolution, continuing to disrupt industry after industry, creating many new companies and destroying old ones, while in a phenomenon much more germane to the topic of this book, creating just as many brilliant new careers while destroying and ending old ones—like those of John Akers at IBM or Grayson Kirk at Columbia— who fail to keep pace with change, and end up being consigned to the dustbin of history as a result.

3. Corporate investment in global citizenship activities, environmental and human capital investments, with money and volunteerism, continues to accelerate and deepen as more and more organizations orient themselves toward a customer and client focus, away from an inside-out approach to an outside-in approach.

4. Activist investors will play an even more prominent role in executive transition and CEO succession by demanding even better performance and leadership, with the inevitable result being that churn at the top will increase as CEOs falter and fail, while increasingly less tolerant, more capably governed, and more diverse boards increase their due diligence, responding to the ratcheting up of pressure from all sides to hold CEOs accountable for doing their primary job: *raising the value of the assets they inherited while simultaneously transforming the company and developing, coaching, and picking a successor capable of doing the same.*

Trend 1: Increasing Globalization

Since the 1970s I have been working with and studying global companies, and have repeatedly witnessed the tragic outcomes and consequences of haphazard and poorly planned CEO successions, as excruciatingly detailed in the first chapter and to some degree throughout the preceding chapters of this book. Witnessing the demise and near-demise of countless once-great companies and organizations, from Westinghouse to the near-collapse of IBM, the issue of failure and success at leadership has never been far from the top of my mind.

In fact, I have often reflected on the demise of the once-great company that rapidly rose in tandem with archrival GE, but then fell into a deep ditch and was sold off to CBS for less than the price of its parts just as Jack Welch was right-sizing and reviving GE. Founded by inventor George Westinghouse, who famously defeated Edison in a "Battle of the Currents" between Edison's DC—direct current—and Westinghouse's AC—alternating current—electrical distribution systems, Westinghouse was for most of its history run by engineers and scientists who typically got the benefits of technology while missing precisely the discipline that GE perfected: the "human science" of rigorous leadership development and business management, which are in many ways really one and the same thing. Westinghouse was ultimately brought low by the collapse of Westinghouse Credit, the counterpart to GE Credit, the failure of which sucked $6 billion out of the corporation in the early 1980s, just as Jack Welch and Gary Wendt were breathing new life into their financial services subsidiary, which they turned into a powerhouse. Westinghouse's final four CEOs each lasted for an average term of less than four years, while GE during the same period had only one leader, Welch, at the top during the same fourteen-year span.

Looking ahead, even six weeks ahead, it has been patently obvious for decades by now that you can't possibly qualify as a great leader of a global enterprise without understanding, at a deep level, the increasingly geopolitical backdrop and context of global capitalism. Great leaders today and for the foreseeable future will first and foremost need to be vetted by predecessors and boards for their ability to move effectively across cultural boundaries, build cross-cultural teams, and demonstrate firmly grounded knowledge of how to make money anywhere on the globe relevant to that particular business.

In 2014 my colleagues and I are working with Chinese, Indian, and U.S. companies to help them with one emerging area of globalization, how China, India, and the United States will compete and cooperate going forward. The next generation of CEOs in global companies will need the capacity to continually assess the global playing field for business opportunities. For example, farmer Yum! CEO David Novak recently described his long-term vision of leadership in the twenty-first century in the following terms:

We have one global culture, and we have one global standard for our people. We think that these key characteristics are universal. I think the people that will have the biggest jobs in the future will be people who embrace global, who love going to different countries and learning to adapt to different cultures, who like learning about different business situations and how they differentiate around the world, and who are good at making themselves fit in while still having their own unique and personal point of view wherever they go and wherever they happen to be at any one point in time. I think that those executives most likely to do extremely well in the future will be those who have those capabilities basically embedded in their bones.

From the Novak perspective, as the leader of a truly global company doing business in more than 120 countries that has prospered in Asia more than just about any other Western company, the CEO of 2020 will need:

1. A global mind-set with the ability to understand the macro geopolitical context of business as the backdrop for developing a global strategy for the organization's success.

2. Cross-cultural leadership skills for building global networks and teams to support organizational success—developing winning strategies and execution platforms.

3. The ability to develop the next generation of leaders who are truly global, thus ensuring a successful 2020 leadership pipeline.

As Novak explained just a few months before publicly announcing his own succession plan, his overarching goal has been to develop his next CEO to build on the global legacy he intends to leave behind.

I don't think my job is done yet, if you want to know the truth. I feel like what I'm passionate about is wanting to create a truly great company, one that's admired by everybody in the world. The vision that I shared with the organization is for Yum! Brands to be the defining global company that feeds the world. We want to set the standard for what it takes to become a truly great multinational company. To us this means developing a famous recognition culture in which everybody counts, building vibrant dynamic brands wherever we do business, and being a company with a huge heart, demonstrating compassion by building awareness and attacking the hunger issue of 1 billion people going to bed hungry every night. With three global brands, 1.4 million people in more than 125 countries, we have the platform to lead the way. Our people are excited about going for greatness.

This is the global organizational platform that Novak intends to hand over to his successor Greg Creed, who after January 1, 2015, will partner with Novak—who will retain the role of nonexecutive chairman—in building the Yum! global organization and developing the leadership pipeline that will sustain the company into the next generation, as all great companies do. As Novak described Creed in a public statement, "He is a breakthrough thinker . . . who has a passion for our global business, rooted with international positions at Unilever and at KFC and Pizza Hut in Australia and New Zealand." Further ensuring the continued global nature of the institution, Novak established as a key component of the executive transition process an Office of the Chairman, the only member of which apart from himself and his successor Creed will be Sam Su, an outstanding executive and leader whom my colleagues and I have worked closely with over many years. In Novak's estimation, Su will "continue to build leading brands in China and share best practices with other emerging market general managers system-wide. Greg, Sam, and I look forward to partnering together in the coming years to continue to build the defining global company that feeds the world."

Trend 2: Start-ups and Old-Line Company Paradoxes

In my view, the coming decade will see a surprising convergence of what it takes to lead a successful old company like GE and a new company like Google. The paradox is that the leaders of older and more established incumbent and legacy firms will need to both think and act more like the leaders of start-ups with regard to their capacity to adapt to the speed, informality, and continuous disruptions in the set ways of doing things brought on by technological and social change. Yet the leaders of newer companies will conversely be continually called upon to manage their increasing scale and size without becoming overly bureaucratic, drawing upon a set of skills and insights perfected by the transformational leaders of legacy companies like Jack Welch, David Novak, Chad Holliday, Roger Enrico, and Indra Nooyi, and other outstanding leaders-as-coaches whom we have admiringly featured in this book as exemplifying the commitment to leadership development that will make both old and new companies win in the marketplace, however it may shift or evolve on the surface.

In this critical sense, the essence of leadership doesn't ever change, and truly hasn't changed in certain respects from the age of Julius Caesar or Alexander the Great to the present era. All great leaders anticipate and embrace change. But as the future unfolds, the leaders of both old and new organizations and institutions will only succeed to the extent that they continue to be learners and teachers creating what I have termed "virtuous teaching cycles." These are organizational models strictly designed to foster mutual learning from the leader and the followers, a phenomenon guaranteed to manifest itself in a variety of means and methods, ranging from the deployment of action learning platforms and teams to the development of new leaders who are, in turn, capable of developing new strategies for the company which not infrequently will be anchored and grounded in sophisticated human capital strategies.

In announcing his own succession, David Novak stressed the continuity of the virtuous teaching cycle he and his former chairman developed and sustained since the company's 1997 spin-off from PepsiCo. "As executive chairman, I will lead the board of directors and focus on mentoring Greg [Creed] as our new CEO. Our late founding chairman, Andy Pearson, did the same for me when I was appointed CEO in 1999, and I found his experience and counsel to be enormously beneficial to both me and to the company. I will spend my time supporting Greg on corporate strategy, innovative business and brand building ideas, and leadership development."

Trend 3: Increasing Corporate Investment in Global Citizenship and Corporate Social Responsibility

For more than two decades, I have led an orientation session of the onboarding program that every incoming MBA student at the University of Michigan undergoes, centered on their participation in several days of immersive community service in local communities. Given the convenient but sometimes jarring proximity of bucolic and affluent Ann Arbor to perennially challenged inner-city Detroit, those of us who help lead the university's business school have been in some vaguely paradoxical way privileged to be able to expose these future leaders of businesses and organizations to the harsh realities of communities and neighborhoods situated less than an hour's drive from the campus, but which might as well be located on a different planet.

Given the duration of this innovative community service and leadership development program, I would provide a ballpark figure of ten thousand students whom we have engaged in not just the notion but the action of giving back to the community over the course of twenty years. The program is designed to provide a teaser to students who may or may not have experienced any prior close-range exposure to the poverty and pervasive sense of helplessness that economically challenged communities and individuals face on a daily basis. Each section takes on a community service project for a day and is then given an opportunity to reflect on the root causes of the poverty not just of money but of spirit that they have witnessed, prior to developing a hopefully deeper commitment to remain engaged in global citizenship activities as they continue to pursue their business management graduate degrees. We have been gratified to find that, as a result of this introduction to global citizenship, as many as 80 percent do get involved with mentoring younger students in the community, or doing community development or environmental work that is more beneficial to the community than simply to themselves and the advancement of their own no doubt high-potential, large-opportunity careers. It is precisely this form of deep engagement on the part of our MBAs which in our experience creates a foundation for our next generation of organizational leaders to deepen their own personal commitment to global citizenship.

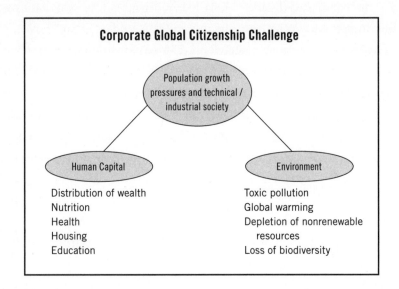

Apart from the MBA program, I have always built into our leadership development programs at global companies a strong global citizenship component. In fact, I have routinely made the incorporation of this element a condition of my willingness to accept the engagement. At CP in Thailand we have encouraged executives to participate in the adoption not just of orphans but of entire orphanages, including the provision of financial support but also, even more important, the commitment of volunteer hours to work with the children, mentoring them to foster their continuing education and even their qualification for jobs and careers.

At Grupo Salinas in Mexico, all of our leadership development programs executed across the various lines of businesses and subsidiaries include an emphasis on connecting senior and high-potential rising executives with community agencies and projects. One of the more creative ideas that we executed for this socially responsible corporation is to have trained several dozen executives in our action learning program to teach Peter Drucker's famous five precepts as a basis for improving the management and leadership practices at nonprofit community agencies and institutions, enabling them to do a much better job of strategic and resource planning. We teach the executives how to go out and run workshops for community agencies. It is a required part of their leadership development program, so there are more than forty agencies that get taught in half- to full-day workshops every time the executive program is run, at least once a year.

The critical issue here is that we operate from the deeply rooted assumption and commitment that leaders who do not embrace global citizenship as a core component of leadership will not survive, much less thrive, in tomorrow's world.

Trend 4: The Continuing Rise of Activist Investors

It has becoming increasingly clear even as I have been writing this book that activist investors like William Ackman of Pershing Square Capital—who was instrumental in ousting P&G's Bob McDonald and installing (before de-installing) JCPenney's Ron Johnson—or Daniel Loeb of Third Point LLC, who ousted a CEO at Yahoo and helped to install Marissa Mayer while taking on the management of Sony, thus far to no avail—are not going anywhere anytime soon. Of course, as more than one story told in this book illustrates, there are many occasions when the removal of a CEO due to pressure applied by activist investors is the right move for a company and a leadership regime that has been slow to force changes to unleash value. Other examples of boards' submitting to activist pressure may not present as clear-cut advantage or benefit to the long-term shareholder value of the company, often because the vast majority of activist investors actually exacerbate the tendency of the CEOs of public companies to feel pressure to short-change long-term investments to please the short-term and often myopic perspectives of industry analysts and fast-trade investors. Yet whatever the ultimate outcome may be, these pressures will not only continue to increase but are likely to dramatically accelerate as activist investors—and the investors in their funds—dig in for the long haul even as they hold CEOs and boards to short-term performance and results. While activist investors first gained prominence in the United States, they are widely predicted to soon start attacking established companies in Europe and Asia, where typically managements have been far more firmly entrenched and better protected by corporate governance restrictions, including the use of "poison pills" that prevent individual investors from amassing large enough stakes in a publicly traded corporation to threaten existing management.

With the inevitable spread of this trend across the globe, it is even more obvious than ever before that the only viable defense is a good offense, namely, performance. Different sectors may have different metrics to contend with, but whether it be an index of measures for university presidents to benchmark themselves against, including the selectivity of admissions, faculty publications, endowment, or the career success of graduates, or share price appreciation versus peers in publicly traded companies, in all spheres and in all sectors, the pressures of globalization and the speed of change will accelerate in the not-for-profit and global business arenas.

Since the only litmus tests of leadership are measurable results and performance, for all organizations there will be an ever-increasing demand for performance, carrying higher and higher risk for underperformance, as well as rewards for outperformance. The CEO role is in these turbulent times secure only if performance is rock-solid. The days when boards could tolerate CEOs whose performance gradually eats away at shareholder value—as was evidently the case with the failed leadership at Westinghouse over the course of more than a decade—are long gone.

Moving the Needle on the 80-20 Rule

The world of the present is so complex, and the world of the future will undoubtedly be much more so, that it will become increasingly difficult and therefore exceedingly rare for all of the traits required to succeed in the future to be found in a single person, as David Novak once told me. Although he seems to have found all of those traits in his own named successor, it is notable that the Office of the Chairman he established was publicly proclaimed as a triumvirate of leaders, with two long-standing top dogs coaching the next generation not from the sidelines but from the center of the court. All of this will inevitably make people judgments and team selection an even more critical core competence for all great leaders in the future. Arrangements like the current one at GM, where the CEO inherits structural limitations on building her own team, will make an already difficult job next to impossible. One of the core competencies of successful CEOs will be picking people who can pick people to build teams and organizations, and that has/will become the sine qua non for successful leadership.

Throughout this book I have frequently invoked the 80-20 role to describe a number of different circumstances and scenarios, including the fact that, as Jack Welch often assured me, only 20 percent of leadership development and training can take place in an institutionalized or formalized setting like Crotonville, while 80 percent takes place on the job. That is what makes it so critical to design HR systems and processes that take that 20 percent of formalized training and ensure that it radically transforms the 80 percent on-the-job training. That is the name of the game with CEO succession, in which arena my admittedly less-than-scientific empirical study leads me to believe that an 80-20 ratio of unsuccessful to successful assessments is probably a generous evaluation of the track record of even many of our most admired (or formerly admired) companies. The same goes for, as I described in the penultimate chapter, nonprofit companies. The single most important take-away of this book, if I had only one lesson to leave you with, would be this: CEO succession and executive transition is not, should not, and never will be only about selecting the best CEO from a pool of likely candidates. It must *always* be about building a continuously transforming succession pipeline carefully constructed and designed to grow truly transformative leaders on the inside. It is, in this sense, fundamentally about creating, coaching, and developing leaders at all levels.

If all of you who read this book truly and sincerely absorb that single lesson, I will judge my work to have been successful and worthwhile if it succeeds in moving that very sticky needle from 80-20 to 60-40.

CONCLUSION

Every question about leadership ultimately gets down to development. It's about creating crucible experiences that make others better as a way of making yourself better. It's about focusing on a task you don't think can be done where you are rallying people across cultures and functions, where you're challenged ethically, and where your integrity is going to be tested.

In my experience, you don't go searching for those experiences. They tend to find you. The older you get the more you learn that people decisions are the most difficult. They are emotionally difficult, and they are also the best measure of how well you are doing as a leader.

—James McNerney, chairman, president, and CEO, Boeing; lecture at the University of Michigan Ross School of Business

TECHNICAL
- The right CEO selected for future success of the enterprise
- A disciplined, data-rich process—looking to the future

POLITICAL
- Stakeholder alignment of board, CEO, HR, candidates
- Carefully orchestrated—high-integrity constructive conflict to arrive at the optimum succession decisions

CULTURAL
- Alignment of candidates with the values of the organization
- Problem-solving culture partnering key stakeholders

Getting It Right at Caterpillar: One Final Best-Practice Example

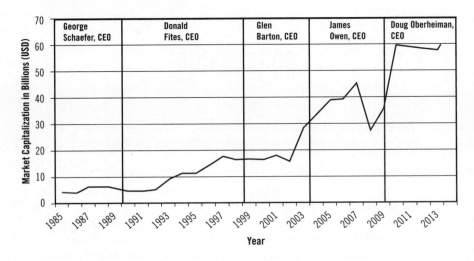

I will close with one final case study, which I believe exemplifies everything that this book is about: a series of seamless transitions from CEO to CEO whom I have known and worked with as they spent as much time tending to the construction of their leadership pipeline as they did building the world's pipelines, roads, bridges, dams, and other great civic projects from the Hoover Dam to the Alaska Pipeline to vast construction projects on every continent. They relied on the use of an iconic product that dates back to the days when the United States was a largely agricultural economy, and the productivity of the agricultural sector was boosted by the development of the tractor.

In 1989, accompanied by the eminent business consultant and my frequent colleague Ram Charan and the distinguished Harvard Business School professor and master of corporate strategy Michael Porter, I traveled to the headquarters of Caterpillar in Peoria, Illinois—the heart of the American farm belt and in many ways Tractor Heaven. The name Caterpillar is derived from the observation that the steam tractors—then often referred to as "traction engines"—developed by Benjamin Holt at the turn of the twentieth century were capable of crawling across soggy and muddy fields as consistently as a caterpillar. Founded in the mid-1920s through the merger of Holt's and a rival tractor company, today the company is a longtime member of the Dow 30 and the largest manufacturer of construction equipment of various kinds in the world.

The purpose of our visit was to consult with then-CEO George Schaefer, whose five years as CEO were the culmination of a four-decade-long career at the company, and his top thirty leaders to strategize about continuing his campaign to extricate Caterpillar from a period of unprecedented losses that had begun in the mid-eighties as the result of a global recession and fierce competition from its Japanese archrival Komatsu.

Over dinner as I conducted a spirited conversation with the executive seated on my left, I couldn't help eavesdropping on the conversation Ram was having with Schaefer. As Ram gently grilled Schaefer—employing his time-honored Socratic method of nearly continuous questioning—about the latest evolution in his strategy to beat Komatsu at their shared game, Schaefer grew increasingly animated in his responses to Ram's probing questions. Finally, all of us at the table perked up as Ram asked Schaefer his parting shot:

"Do you think the CAT leadership team is tough enough and smart enough to win this battle?"

To which Schaefer loudly replied, "Okay—I totally get it! We've got to get out there, go get 'em, and win this war!"

Learning from Best Practices

I put Boeing CEO James McNerney's quote in both the introduction and at the conclusion of this book because to my mind it captures the essence of everything this book is about more precisely than anything anyone has ever said. "Every question about leadership," he told me, "ultimately gets down to development . . . it's about creating crucible experiences that make others better." McNerney is crystal clear that the most important CEO responsibility is to grow transformational leaders from the inside so you will never need to go outside in search of one. It is incumbent upon the current generation of leaders to be proactive in designing and framing the right crucible experiences for developing the most promising high-potential candidates throughout their careers, so that when the current leader departs, voluntarily or not, there is no yawning leadership gap requiring the organization to go outside for a new CEO. The irony of McNerney's taking this position on internal leadership development is that he was a successful outside CEO hire at 3M and at Boeing, and therefore one of a very small elite group, including Alan Mulally at Ford, who have succeeded at transforming organizations from the outside. Note that once they positioned themselves at the top of their new companies, both McNerney and Mulally developed leadership pipelines to ensure the development of internal successors; rest assured, they will not go outside for the next CEO at Ford or Boeing. Like IBM after Gerstner, the leadership pipeline was fixed with an eye toward future success.

In describing how the leaders of organizations should proactively play a role in building succession pipelines and setting the stage for making good leadership succession judgments, with PepsiCo, DuPont, Intuit, and Verizon being among the best-practice examples, my point has not been to put myself forward as a tough professor, which I am, but rather to provide tangible evidence that despite the miserable overall succession track record, it can be done right.

That good succession planning and processes are the lifeblood of future organizational success is exemplified by Caterpillar, where I have participated in the succession process from 1989 up to the present.

By 1990, when he retired, Schaefer was halfway to winning the war. Over the five years he ran the company he took it from record losses to record profits, and he accomplished that in large part by forming a select group of eight up-and-coming two-deep executives to serve on a new Strategic Planning Committee. He deliberately populated this committee with people he openly referred to as "renegades" and "breakthrough thinkers." Working closely with the SPC, Schaefer effectively torpedoed the centralized system of general offices that had frustrated both him and his successor Donald Fites by dictating all pricing and strategy worldwide from Peoria, often thousands of miles away from customers in new and emerging markets, where Komatsu was killing them.

On January 1, 1990, Schaefer kicked off the decade with the general offices controlling everything from the center, but by the third week of that month, the general offices had all been killed off. As he and Fites strongly suspected, this move rapidly revived the company and set it on a growth trajectory it has maintained ever since. Having declared that uphill mission accomplished, Schaefer demonstrated exquisite timing by passing the baton seamlessly to Fites, who had served as his primary partner in spearheading the restructuring. Our dynamic triumvirate consisting of me, Charan, and Porter continued to work closely with Fites as the company dramatically reinvented itself around a series of strategic business units, continued its uphill battle with Komatsu, and simultaneously took on its once-mighty labor unions to make its U.S. operations more than marginally profitable.

After posting a loss in 1992, Fites gained considerable notoriety by threatening to replace eleven thousand striking workers if they failed to give in to his demands to free CAT from "pattern bargaining," a term used to describe a long-standing practice favored by organized labor of forcing companies, even if not necessarily in the same industrial sector, to meet the same terms they had negotiated with other companies. Determined to remain competitive with Komatsu and not to dent that competitiveness by caving in to the demands of the unions, Fites also took on his own internal bureaucracy. He faithfully followed the Welch playbook by laying off thousands of middle managers and instituting a structure of fourteen independent P&L centers whose leaders were obliged to win or lose in their own markets, just as senior leaders have had to do at GE, P&G, Honeywell, and other best-practice companies for decades. When his forklift P&L failed to measure up to the tough mandate he had imposed of a 15 percent return on assets, he unceremoniously dumped the unit into an 80-20 joint venture controlled by 80 percent owner Mitsubishi Heavy Industries.

During the Fites era, I worked with his human resources staff to share lessons learned from GE and Crotonville, with a special focus on restructuring succession planning to adapt the next generation of leaders to the newly created, more internally competitive and personally accountable P&L environment, a far cry from the old centralized functional organization. Now in productive retirement, Fites—a neighbor of mine in Naples, Florida—has continued to push forward a global citizenship agenda, supporting the Immokalee Foundation, an outstanding nonprofit focused on training migrant worker children to break the cycle of poverty through improved education and empowerment programs and working with his former employer to donate equipment and training so that those who want a career in heavy equipment as operators can be trained and get jobs in the booming southwest Florida area where construction continues to be a growth industry.

It is a testament to the strength of Caterpillar's succession planning process and leadership development culture that each generation of leaders I worked with succeeded not just in passing the baton but in selecting the right leader to take on the next challenge when the time came for power to be transferred. Under Fites's successor Glen Barton, Caterpillar's sales and revenues more than doubled from $23 billion in 2003 to $51 billion in 2008 while earnings more than tripled from $1.56 a share to $5.66 a share. But by the fall of 2008, as the global recession hit the worldwide construction industry hard, Caterpillar's global sales went into a tailspin, skidding nearly 40 percent by the end of 2009, forcing the board's instinct to select a leader who would prove capable of winning in both good times and bad was affirmed. Former CEO Jim Owens reluctantly yet rapidly cut more than thirty-five thousand full-time and contract jobs, his own pay was slashed by 50 percent, and he froze wages across the company. By the time he passed the baton to his successor Doug Oberhelman, the company had maintained its profitability throughout the downturn and, just as important, maintained both its dividend and credit rating.

Oberhelman, Caterpillar's thirteenth CEO, recently ascribed the company's ongoing success at succession to its "leadership development philosophy of promoting from within. We've never had an outside CEO or chairman in the history of our company," he stated proudly, noting just as proudly that "we've been public since 1925. Sometimes that brings great things, and sometimes that can bring an inward focus. But we've always done it that way, and I would say that CEO succession at Caterpillar is an outflow of the way we do succession planning throughout the year and over a long period of time. We really have a solid succession planning process, both internally and with our board."[1]

Oberhelman describes the process as follows, exemplifying the balance of power and equitable distribution of collaborative roles and responsibility between the CEO, board, and CHRO that I have long held up as the essence of best practice:

> We start from the bottom up. Every one of our officers sits down at least once a year with their management teams, and then as a group, and talks through all of their people and assesses their long-term potential. That's an active process—a minimum of once a year. We follow a similar process in the executive office. And that process takes most of the year to work its way through. By the time we get to the board in October, we—the eight of us in the executive office at Caterpillar—have a good understanding of the highest-potential candidates out of the top 3,000 positions within our company. And over a period of years we get to develop the people who are in these positions—whether they're in China, Russia, the United States or anywhere—we prepare them to be senior leaders. By the time we get to the board in October, we spend time mostly on our officer level, which would be about 35 people—who's going to retire, what's our succession plan for each of those jobs, including external hires, who are our functional experts, who are the best high-performers to serve in that leadership role. We talk a lot about developing diverse candidates to fill these roles, and I will tell you, that's a challenge for our company at the officer level and across the board in all facets of having a diverse and inclusive leadership team, but we really work hard on it. We brought together a process that I think will help us down

the road, but it's a continuing challenge—and by that I mean developing and placing Asian leaders in Asia, European leaders in Europe, U.S. minorities and females for positions everywhere we do business, and on and on.[2]

As an outside board member of among other organizations the pharmaceutical giant Eli Lilly, Oberhelman insists that every board of which he is a member "makes sure that when management is working on succession planning for the CEO, that it's a much deeper process, something along the lines of what I just described. I don't think enough companies really spend enough time on that. I think many companies do, but if you don't start from the bottom up and work it all the way through, it's going to be very difficult to do that at the CEO level as well. I think that's where a lot of companies get into trouble. Certainly one where the candidate can come from within—if it works within that organization—and sometimes it doesn't—can be healthy; sometimes change is needed."

As a best-practice CEO of a best-practice company that cares deeply about maintaining and sustaining its develop-and-select-from-inside approach, Doug Oberhelman and Jim Owens firmly agreed that, as Oberhelman later put it, "We believe it's most effective for Caterpillar to combine the Chairman and CEO roles," which, as we all know, is often erroneously characterized as a slam-dunk good corporate governance practice. As Oberhelman recalled, Owens—who remained chairman for a brief period to facilitate the transition—"was getting questions as chairman that he couldn't answer about the day-to-day operations of the company, and I was getting questions about governance and things he had responsibility for as chairman that I couldn't answer. For our company, the way we're managed, the way we have come down through the ages, I am an opponent, at least for us, of separating chairman and CEO." The solution? Appoint a strong lead director.

Some Great Leaders Enjoy Second and Third Acts: Bob McDonald Heading up the Veterans Administration

In May 2014, retired four-star army general Eric Shinseki lost his job as secretary of the Veterans Administration in the wake of a series of scandals, none of which was directly tied to his leadership but which had occurred on his watch. President Obama and his advisers came up with a brilliant if unorthodox solution to the enormous set of challenges facing a compromised federal agency with an annual budget of more than $150 billion charged with serving more than 8 million veterans a year: to nominate as Shinseki's successor former Procter & Gamble CEO Bob McDonald. McDonald is a West Point graduate, son of an Army Air Corps World War II veteran, and longtime staunch supporter of the military and in particular of the U.S. Military Academy at West Point, from which he graduated in the top 2 percent of his class in 1975 and has continued to strengthen for the future with the establishment of the McDonald Cadet Leadership Conference to address emerging global issues, where he frequently teaches cadets and conducts leadership workshops. To add to his sterling credentials as the nominee for this prestigious post, McDonald also served in the army, mostly in Vietnam, for five years, achieving the rank of captain in the 82nd Airborne Division before taking an entry-level job at P&G.

As the incoming leader of an organization historically run by retired generals like Shinseki, both the president and the Congress obliged to confirm his appointment made it abundantly clear that the expectation on the past of nearly all concerned parties would be for him to fundamentally transform the VA during a period of deep crisis. But what McDonald knows, and which his establishment of the leadership institute at West Point reflects, is that while he is actively tackling the transformation of the institution itself he will need to do what Bill Weiss so effectively accomplished during his final years at Ameritech: he will need to simultaneously transform the institution while building a vital and robust pipeline of future leaders. As is the case at nearly all government agencies, while the most senior leader is typically a political appointee, the leadership *pipeline* tends to be comprised of career civil servants. And it is at that level and indeed at every level of the organization where McDonald will be obliged to foster leadership skills and traits of the sort needed for the institution to adapt to changing times.

With increasing numbers of veterans from the Iraq and Afghanistan wars returning home to uncertain futures, and with millions of older veterans from the Vietnam, Korean, and Second World wars still in need of significant agency attention, the dual mission of the agency to provide not only medical and mental health support but also help in rebuilding their lives as civilians, including finding employment and embarking on productive careers, has been clearly stretched to the limit and beyond. In some ways, this should not be so surprising, because what makes the VA so fundamentally different from other medical and hospital systems is that its medical mission is so deeply intertwined with this far more complex adjustment and reintegration-to-civilian-life mandate. And what makes that dual mission even more challenging to accomplish is that nearly all postwar periods have historically been eras of profound societal change and confusion. Still, there have also been significant variations in the degrees to which returning veterans have been more or less enthusiastically welcomed back home and strongly supported by the broader society in their efforts to adapt and readjust to civilian life.

World War II, for example, saw nearly all able-bodied men in the United States drafted into the armed forces while millions of women played supporting roles in the arms buildup, as memorably captured by images of muscular women eagerly churning out planes, tanks, and trucks on the home front. In the context of total war, it's hardly surprising that the post–World War II period was one during which communities celebrated their returning "war heroes" and universities warmly welcomed them back onto campuses. At the University of Michigan, where I teach, as was the case at countless campuses from coast to coast, married veterans were provided with special housing and strong academic and social support. With rapidly expanding industry across nearly all sectors offering plenty of productive and well-paying jobs for veterans in the 1950s, and with a former five-star general and bona fide war hero in the form of Dwight Eisenhower occupying the White House, the extraordinary degree of respect for the military and the impetus to foster a rapid and lasting integration of veterans into the mainstream American life could not have been higher.

But if we fast forward to the 1970s, when thousands of veterans were returning from the Vietnam War, the atmosphere that greeted these young men and women upon their return was very different, and often profoundly discouraging. I was a graduate student on the Columbia campus when many veterans were earning their MBAs, and not only was their presence in the classroom and on campus definitely not celebrated, these young men—and some women—who had put their lives on the line for their country were actively ridiculed as "dupes" of an evil administration and, in effect, socially ostracized for having fought—for the most part by no choice of their own—in the wrong war. Not once from the time I entered my PhD program in 1968 until I left the Columbia faculty to head to Michigan in 1981 was there ever a positive formal or even informal recognition for the service given by these veterans.

Today, we face a very different postwar environment in the wind-up of the struggles in Iraq and Afghanistan. Both wars were fought by an all-volunteer military, not drafted forces—with the consequence that far fewer families have been personally touched by the conflicts while society in general is personally removed from the military as an institution to be proud of or even relate to. Yet unlike the post–Vietnam War period, Americans have felt generally supportive of the sacrifices these young people have been called upon to make in the wake of the never-ending war on terror that has occurred since 9/11. That is the good news, as reflected in the positive press veterans have received.

But the bad and possibly even worse news is that the VA is currently in deep disarray, even as demand for its complex set of services has never been higher, overwhelming a dysfunctional system. While General Shinseki was a good man and a straight shooter, he was not a transformational leader of the mettle required to fix a broken system. Bob McDonald's appointment was greeted by strong bipartisan support in Congress precisely because not just the president but also congressional leaders were convinced that he not only could and likely would be the truly transformational leader required to creatively destroy and rebuild the system in the Schumpterian sense of the term. McDonald's challenge in facing down and fixing an overblown bureaucracy grown wildly out of control was not unlike the one faced by Jack Welch as he struggled to reinvent and reimagine General Electric in the 1980s and 1990s. Much as I laid out in the *Handbook for Revolutionaries* that concluded my earlier book, *Control Your Destiny or Someone Else Will*, Bob McDonald will need to take a page out of the Jack Welch transformational agenda if he wants to succeed. And as I personally came to know and see McDonald in action both at P&G and at West Point, you can bet that he not only wants to succeed but that, more important, he will succeed.

Here's how he will. While a number of veterans and military leaders rightly pointed out that McDonald's laserlike focus during his nearly lifelong career at P&G on customer satisfaction would likely work to his credit in seeking to improve agency service for multitudes of deeply dissatisfied veterans, I believe that his greatest challenge, exactly like Welch's, will be to tackle, manage, and ultimately gain some degree of control over a bureaucracy gone wild. Fittingly for a corporate executive about to embark on the third act of his stellar career—the first one in the military, the second at a Fortune 500 company culminating in his leadership of it, and the third as a public servant fulfilling a sacred mission of caring for those who cared about serving society—Act One of McDonald's revolution will (as I described in Chapter Two of this book, in addition to Controlling Your Destiny) will need to be jump-started with a form of institutional shock therapy I long ago termed the Awakening. I have described this turbulent time as an emotionally wrenching and terrifying experience for most participants, even the leaders, when the protagonist and his or her most committed colleagues will need to effectively shake up the status quo to a degree sufficient to release the emotional energy within the institution that will create conditions ripe for the revolution.

As a critical first step, he will need to create a sense of urgency, a burning platform for change, which will require him to move both quickly and stealthily to wake up the organization. This need for speed is required for him and the organization to escape the "boiled frog phenomenon," when, like a frog in a hot pot, the organization perishes before it is revived. And as an equally critical second step, he will need to overcome deeply embedded institutional and organizational resistance, which will inevitably surface along all three dimensions of the technical, political, and cultural nexus. The technical resisters will provide, as would be expected, a series of highly rational and elaborately rationalized reasons to avoid change, including force of habit, prior investment in the old ways of doing things, and that bugaboo of all organizations none less than the Veterans Administration: inertia.

Political resistance will arise in direct response to the coming disruption of the existing power structure. As powerful coalitions are deliberately disrupted, the displaced will fight back against the limitations placed on the distribution of critical resources, and as former powerful leaders are forced to take blame for the institutional failures that have contributed to the admitted dysfunction. Prior investments go above and beyond traditional financial investments to encompass even more difficult to redistribute emotional investments in training and the way things are done. As for political resistance, the focus here tends to be on resource reallocation, which will call upon all of McDonald's tough skills honed over decades of rising to the top of a highly competitive institution, P&G, to foster innovation and creativity over stagnation and stasis. Threats to powerful coalitions will require the new leader, in some critical cases, to indict incumbent leaders and oblige them to take ownership and responsibility for their previous actions, and or inactions. And finally, cultural resistance—which in many cases is far harder to overcome than either technical or political because it is subtler and less consciously understood—will occur as threatened and frankly frightened people desperately cling to outmoded mind-sets hoping to grab hold of an emotional life preserver and somehow make it to shore without drowning. Like all revolutionaries, McDonald will be required to exert a greater degree of control over the police—in most institutions, including both GE and the VA, this is the audit staff, which most memorably broke down at the VA as hospital administrators and staffs proved successful in hiding their tracks as their deficiencies went unnoticed and brushed over for decades. He will need to gain control over the media in the form of all internal and external communications. And as a graduate of West Point and a veteran himself, he will need to reform and revamp the training systems, which serve as the institutional guardians of the culture, just as Crotonville did at GE.

I conclude with Bob McDonald's future challenge even before he formally takes it on not simply because it is an important drama in its own right, but because it also signifies the leadership challenge facing every successor as he or she inherits and takes charge of not just the domain itself but of the interlinked nodes of thinking, acting, and leading that distinguish and make it unique. For every leader profiled in this book who was at one time a candidate, at another a new appointee and successor, and at yet another point in time an incumbent charged with nurturing and fostering not just the next leader but the next generation of leaders, the ultimate challenge to be overcome remains precisely and immutably the same: to take the assets you are given when you take over, raise the value of those assets during the course of your tenure, and most critically of all, in my opinion, to help select a successor who does the same.

The Final Takeaway

The case has been made that nothing is more important than having the right leader at the top of any institution, whether business, military, university, or not-for-profit. Unfortunately we live in a world where this is done wrong around 80 percent of the time. Failed CEO succession is the single biggest destroyer of shareholder value, or in not-for-profits the future success of the institution. This book has provided diagnosis of what is wrong and what is right with current practice as well as practical guidelines for getting it right in the future.

This is the same approach I have taken with other organizations, ranging from Intel, Exxon, CP in Thailand, to Tata in India to Royal Dutch Shell in Europe, as well as not-for-profit organizations, school systems, and hospital systems. It is up to the CEO and top team to be fully involved in this exercise and keep the board fully engaged; the process cannot be delegated to consultants and human resources staff. The one lesson I ask you to take away from this book is that leadership development from the earliest stage of someone's career and succession planning, if and when conducted properly—which they infrequently are—are one and the same and should be a top priority for the CEO, board, and head of human resources.

ACKNOWLEDGMENTS

All of my books are based on field research, which means that the first thank-you goes to the leaders, CEOs, human resource heads, and other key players in the organizations we profiled as "best practice" exemplars. Your time being interviewed and your dedication to keep working on the text till it was right is much appreciated. This book is a tribute to all of you.

My life partner, Patricia Stacey, has been a key part of my writing journey for a total of eight books. Each time I am thankful for her leadership of our consulting firm. When I am consumed by research and writing she more than picks up the slack. She also sees to it that our children and ten grandchildren are not lost in the shuffle of work as they are the truly important ones when it comes to "succession."

This is the first book that Erica Hyman, my administrator, has been involved in from the beginning through the production end. This means the coordination of interviews, background material on companies, editing as well as all the coordination with many significant "egos" all handled with grace and respect. I look forward to our next book adventure to see her grow even more.

Colleagues are the best part of being an academic and author. They give you tough love coaching along the way. Michael Brimm, Professor Emeritus, INSEAD, has been there for me since the late 1980s when we worked with GE, Jack Welch, and John Trani. He is perhaps my toughest critic, who, on our calls early in the morning from anywhere in the world, gave me some of the most painful, but helpful coaching and feedback. For that, I am thankful. Chris DeRose, my coauthor on articles and *Judgment on the Front Line,* as well as consulting colleague, not only took the lead on the handbook but played a major role in helping shape the book. Chris was also there to cover for me with our clients.

The team at Portfolio / Penguin could not have been better. Adrian Zackheim and I have worked together since the early 1990s on five books. He is an incredible partner, always making me think, reframe, and make better what I started out to do. What is exciting about this book is a new partner, Emily Angell, who had the lead role from beginning to end in the editorial process. She deserves a great deal of credit for the final product. I am thankful for her perseverance and dedication.

Finally, my partner on this book, Stephen Fenichell, who deftly edited and gave my voice more than I could do alone, deserves a great deal of gratitude. Our almost daily dealings, editing, revising, and going over interviews and articles made this book better with each iteration. Thank you, Stephen.

SUCCESSION PLANNING

A Process Handbook

BY **CHRIS DeROSE** AND **NOEL TICHY**

WITH **DON PRYZGODSKI**

Succession Planning Introduction

This handbook will help you design your organization's succession planning process. Throughout this book, there has been repeated emphasis that identifying, developing, and selecting top talent is never solely a technical process. Human emotions, personal relationships, and organizational norms all play important parts. A well-designed succession process addresses such political and cultural realities but must be based on a systemic approach for appraisal and development planning for leaders at all levels.

Ultimately, succession planning will be successful only if it is embraced by the leadership as an essential element of an organization's future success. Transitioning to a companywide succession planning platform requires the cooperation and support of every business leader in an organization.

Additionally, individual and team activities must be carefully orchestrated so that data can be aggregated and assessments reviewed with the appropriate checks and balances. This requires calendar alignment across multiple divisions or work units.

This workbook will walk you through steps that serve as a launching point for building a world-class succession process. Although the focus is on the technical process as the foundation, additional discussion of managing political and cultural aspects is provided at the end.

ROLES AND RESPONSIBILITIES

Effective succession planning begins with a close partnership between line operators and human resources. HR is a frequent target of criticism in many organizations—and often deservedly so given the transactional, administrative nature of many HR departments. For succession planning to work, HR leaders must be capable, trusted partners. Succession appraisals and talent planning should incorporate operators' assessments coupled with an HR partner's appropriate challenges, reflective prompting, and supplemental data. Assessments used for succession planning should provide a composite picture based on multiple information sources and varied perspectives. Operators are an important source of such data, while HR should safeguard the overall process, ensuring that no single data point or individual opinion unduly biases the final judgment.

Working in tandem with their HR partner, each business unit head, and head of each corporate staff function, should be responsible for conducting succession planning within their own business units or functions using a standardized process. In this handbook, we will focus on planning from the perspective of a business unit leader, but the process outlined can easily be adapted to any department or team leader.

A STANDARDIZED PROCESS

Succession planning and talent reviews should be integrated with other mission-critical organizational tasks such as development of strategy, operating plans, and budgets. It is important that every unit operate on the same annual calendar of events so that data can be compared across units or teams. The optimal succession process should help to identify talent that can be moved across units, helping to ensure broader development and better preparation for senior leadership roles while concurrently focusing top talent on a business's key priorities.

The calendar will be different for each organization, and may be affected by an industry's seasonality, shareholder reporting schedule, board of directors schedule, or other factors. A sample time line is provided below. The remainder of the handbook will detail the information required and the assessment process to put such a calendar into action.

. . .

Table 1: Sample Calendar of Annual Succession Events

Month	Activity	Who's Involved
Early September	Official launch meeting with CEO, business unit (BU) heads, and HR leaders from each business unit. Succession planning begins with dialogue of key strategic initiatives for the following year and talent requirements for achieving operational goals.	■ CEO, business unit heads, corporate function heads, HR leaders. ■ Preparation work is likely to involve senior teams in each of the business units.
Mid-September	Each business unit head reports back to his/her direct reports and trains them to deliver the succession plan.	■ Business unit heads, direct reports from each business unit, HR leaders.
Early October	BU heads create preliminary candidate slate for their business unit, identifying 3 candidates for each top job and proposing at least 2 candidates for their role.	■ Business unit heads, HR partner. Business unit head may also seek advice/input from corporate HR leader.
Early October	360-degree feedback surveys of all employees on the candidate slate are completed.	■ Process run by HR; all salaried staff involved.
Mid-October	Business unit heads and direct reports conduct employee evaluations and complete nine-cells on each of their direct reports.	■ Business unit head, direct reports, HR leaders.
Mid-October	Candidate slate, employee evaluations, and 360-degree surveys are compiled into one document and reviewed by the BU head.	■ HR team, business unit head.
Late-October	BU heads follow up with direct reports if they have questions concerning their employee evaluations.	■ Business unit head, direct reports.
Late-October	Succession planning binder for each business unit is finalized by the BU head and HR leader.	■ Business unit head, HR leader.
November–December	Succession review sessions. The chairman/CEO will meet with each business unit separately. The meeting will be a dialogue between the chairman/CEO and HR leader. Your meeting date will be scheduled directly by the chairman/CEO's office.	■ CEO, business unit head, corporate HR leader, business unit HR leader.

PREPARATION

To implement a standardized process across an organization, particularly a multiunit business, preparation at every stage is critical. As units prepare, it is imperative that they remember succession planning should be in the long-term service of their organization's mission, vision, and operational objectives. The immediate goal of succession is to ensure continuity by matching talent to strategic priorities. No succession discussions should occur without candid dialogue about the organization's current strengths and weaknesses, and expectations about what will be required of leaders to win in the marketplace in the future.

For this reason, succession dialogues between the CEO and business unit head begin with a review of the unit's current performance and structure, along with an honest review of performance gaps and how these may relate to leadership talent or skill gaps in the unit. Once the context has been set for where the organization is and what will be needed in the future, only then does the discussion of individuals proceed.

In short, talent assessment, staffing, and development rotations can only be determined in the context of the organizational structure and objectives. Since we are ardent believers that form follows function, and structure therefore must be determined after strategy, the dialogue regarding talent should derive from a shared vision about what will be required of the unit and overall organization to succeed. Armed with this agreement, leaders can discuss the relative merits of each candidate for current needs but, equally important, replace incumbent leaders as they retire or move to other posts.

The discussion of each succession candidate begins with assessment based on that individual's performance and behaviors in his or her current role. Key questions include how the leader has fared in delivering his or her objectives and how well he or she has demonstrated the desired organizational values through his or her behaviors. (Although not the focus of this discussion, it should be noted that a clear and effective goal-setting process is an absolute requirement of assessment and succession planning.)

AGGREGATING THE DATA

Succession planning is an inherently comparative process. Whether looking at candidates in relation to alternate internal leaders for a post or potential external recruits, the decision about who is the "best" candidate for a job should always have a reference point. For this reason, and in order to get a composite view of the overall bench strength in an organization, the dialogue between CEO and business unit head (or manager and team leader) includes an ordering of talent.

Comparing individuals with one another can be emotionally combustible. The tool utilized below asks the assessor to rate each individual on a nine-cell matrix that evaluates an individual's performance as high, medium, or low. Values, which form the x-axis of the matrix, are assessed on a similar scale. A couple of critical points are in order:

◆ *How* the rating process is carried out is a far greater determinant of acceptance and usefulness than the specific elements that are assessed. Feedback should be the beginning of a dialogue process that allows for discussion of differing interpretations of an individual's behavior. It should ultimately lead to agreement about how an individual can grow and develop. This can happen only if there is a direct, honest, transparent process in place.

◆ Any succession process is inherently *subjective*. There are no perfect algorithms to which human behavior can be reduced and understood. Each person involved in the succession process will either consciously or unconsciously be biased by their personal history, worldview, values, and impressions of the person in question. Rather than fight this reality, the succession process must accommodate it by standardizing the criteria on which candidates will be assessed and then encouraging vigorous debate and exploration about the extent to which each candidate has fulfilled those criteria.

With these principles in mind, it is important for each business unit head to compile an aggregate view of the individuals on his or her team.

These individuals should be evaluated in terms of performance, leadership behaviors, and future potential. Their development needs should be detailed, including the types of development experiences such as job rotations or training required for their future success. All of this happens against the backdrop of what the organization needs to drive successful execution of its strategy.

In preparation for a discussion with the CEO or manager, each business unit head will assemble a data file outlining the following:

Preparation Required for Each Business Unit

1. 1-page overview of the business unit (BU) head's goals and results to date.

2. Organization chart showing from the BU head down 3 levels.

3. 1-page succession slate showing candidates for the BU head and all positions reporting directly into the BU head.

4. Nine-cell chart of the BU head's direct reports.

5. Preparation required for leadership judgment.

6. Performance evaluations of
   - the BU head's direct reports
   - each of the direct reports' direct reports (e.g., the CFO is a direct report to the BU head, so the CFO will need to conduct performance evaluations of each of his or her direct reports).

7. 360-degree feedback for each individual identified on the candidate slate of the business unit.

This data will be translated into a final format for dialogue with the CEO, HR leaders, and other operational leaders as appropriate. The following sections of this handbook follow this structure, providing you with the data requirements and selected examples to help you develop your own succession planning process. The sections are organized in the order in which they would be discussed in a typical discussion between the CEO and business unit head.

[Elements Required for Successful Succession Planning]

Section 1:	Business Overview/Summary
Section 2:	Organization Chart
Section 3:	Candidate Slate
Section 4:	Nine-Cell Chart
Section 5:	Leadership Judgment
Section 6:	Employee Evaluation
Section 7:	360-Degree Feedback
Section 8:	Managing Political and Cultural Dynamics
Appendix 1:	Teaching Instructions

[SECTION 1]

Business Overview/Summary

The business overview and summary you compile for your business unit should include the following elements: key facts and figures for the past year, leadership changes within the business, talent and training upgrades, and key initiatives. This should not be an exhaustive summary that includes endless details; your overview should be no longer than three or four pages so it is easily digestible as a primer for dialogue. Below is a step-by-step process for building your business's overview. Please remember that the examples and criteria are provided at the business unit level so you may need to adjust these to suit your requirements. Although space constraints limit our ability to discuss how each data point is used for dialogue, the intent is to provide an overview of how the business is performing and of key leadership changes.

Step 1: Key facts and figures—For this step, you need to insert (a) annual revenue, (b) revenue increase (decrease) from previous year, (c) profit margin, (d) profit margin increase (decrease) from previous year, (e) employee head count, (f) unplanned talent losses, and (g) employee increase (decrease) from previous year.

Step 2: Leadership changes within the business—Outline the leadership changes that occurred during the previous year in your business, focusing on the senior-level positions. For each change/transition, identify (a) position where there was a change, (b) employee who left, (c) planned or unplanned, (d) reason for transition, and (e) replacement employee.

Step 3: Talent and training upgrades, which includes identification of:
1. The number of new hires within your business, including (a) number of new hires with advanced degrees, (b) number of recent graduates, (c) number of experienced hires,

(d) number sourced from universities, and (e) global talent hiring.

2. Transfers into the business by area, including (a) number of transfers into the company, and (b) number with advanced degrees.

3. Training—for training, identify (a) courses/programs, (b) number of attendees, and (c) total number of years each program has been conducted in the business.

Step 4: Key initiatives—List the strategic initiatives your business unit focused on throughout the year. Identify the following for each initiative: (a) initiative name and short description, (b) results achieved/business impact, and (c) next steps.

Example of what the candidate slate should resemble when complete:

[COMPANY XYZ]

KEY FACTS AND FIGURES (STEP 1)

Revenue:	(a) $1,750,800,000.00	% Change from Previous Year:	(b) +15.6%
Profit Margin:	(c) 22.7%	% Change from Previous Year:	(d) +2.3%
Head Count:	(e) 65,000		
Turnover %:	(f) 15%		
Head Count Increase/Decrease	(g) +4,051		

LEADERSHIP CHANGES (STEP 2)

Position	Name	Planned (Y/N)	Reason	Replacement
(a) VP Marketing	(b) T. Smith	(c) Yes	(d) Employee was transferred to another business unit within the company	J. Authers
VP Asia Distribution	D. Whitman	No	Employee was terminated	A. Nunn
Dir. Food Services	A. Nuun	Yes	Employee was promoted to VP of Asia Distribution	(e) Currently open

TALENT AND TRAINING UPGRADES (STEP 3)

1. New hires added to business	2. Transfers into business	
(a) Advanced degrees: 44	(a) Total transfers	120
(b) Recent graduates: 1002	(b) Advanced degrees	12
(c) Experienced hires: 500		
(d) Sourced from university: 2567		
(e) Global talent: 867		

3. Training programs		
(a) Name	(b) Total Attendees	(c) Years in Production
Action Learning Program	36	3
Business Leader Program	100	3
New Leader Program	200	2
New Hire Program	4000	7

KEY INITIATIVES (STEP 4)

(a) Name and Description: Nine-cell chart/talent upgrade throughout the business:

This year, the business planned to upgrade the talent base throughout the organization by focusing on the development of our employees at all levels. Our goal was to move 15 percent of medium-level (satisfactory) performers to high performers.

(b) Results: We were able to move 9 percent of our employees to high performers. While we did not reach our target of 15 percent improvement, we were able to make a tangible impact, which had direct impacts on our financial results for the year.

(c) Next steps: Our talent upgrade initiative will continue next year. We will continue to invest in and develop our people to achieve this.

(a) Name and Description: Enter European market:

Enter European market with our new services product suite. The aim is to set up and staff three locations (Great Britain, Germany, and Norway) and attain $25 mm in revenue by close of the year.

(b) Results: European market entry was successful. Three locations were established and revenue targets for all collective locations were exceeded ($33 mm). We will need to look at our Great Britain operation as they have not performed to standards this year due to leadership and selection ailments.

(c) Next steps: Grow this segment by 140 percent next year and fix the GB operations by end of Q1.

[SECTION 2]

Organization Chart

A s you begin succession planning, the organization chart that you create should include two levels within your business. The first level will be your direct reports, and the second level will be the direct reports of your direct reports. For each item on the organization chart you should include both the position and name of the person currently in that position. (As your organization gains more experience with succession planning, it should be scaled to lower levels.)

A standard graphical representation of the organizational chart, such as the picture below, is typically the most efficient way to communicate your existing structure and staffing.

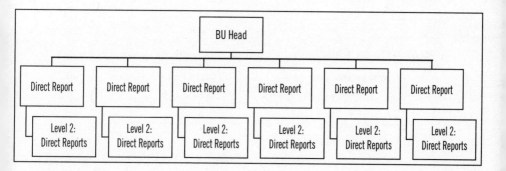

Any specific organizational needs, such as specific skill sets, along with vacant positions or impending moves and retirements, should be highlighted in this section.

[SECTION 3]

Candidate Slate

The candidate slate for your business is a tool used for organization and staff planning. The slate is a platform for displaying the top two levels in your business (business unit head and direct reports) and the potential replacements for each of these positions. The instructions for completing a candidate slate for your business are provided below:

Step 1: Enter (a) the name of your business unit and (b) the incumbent manager/BU head:

(a) Business Unit Name
(b) Name of BU Head

Step 2: For each direct report, fill in a chart that contains the following information: (c) title, (d) name, (e) position level, and (f) months in position:

(c) Insert Title	
(d) Insert Name	
(e) Position Level	(f) Months in Position

Step 3: For each title, (g) identify up to three potential replacements that could replace the existing direct report who currently holds that title. The potential replacements should be listed in order of preference. If you do not have three, provide as many as possible. Remember that a viable replacement can come from anywhere in your organization or include exter-

nal recruits. Also, if you have a potential candidate who is not ready to succeed the leader today but can be ready in less than 36 months, list the candidate's name followed by the number of months required to prepare him or her for that leadership position:

VP Sales and Distribution	
John Smith	
VP	16

(g) Insert #1 Preferred Replacement
(g) Insert #2 Preferred Replacement
(g) Insert #3 Preferred Replacement

Step 4: (h) Enter the name of the CEO the candidate slate was prepared by and the (i) date:

Prepared by:	(h) Insert Name	(i) Insert Date

Step 5: Following the review of the candidate slate with the Chairman/CEO, the Chairman/CEO should (j) write his name and (k) date stating:

Reviewed by:	(j) Insert Name	(k) Insert Date

Step 6: Candidate slate is complete and can be inserted into your succession planning book/binder.

The graphic below offers an example candidate slate when complete:

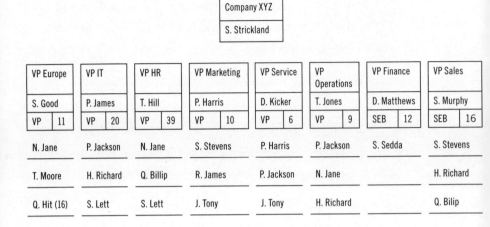

	Company XYZ
	S. Strickland

VP Europe		VP IT		VP HR		VP Marketing		VP Service		VP Operations		VP Finance		VP Sales	
S. Good		P. James		T. Hill		P. Harris		D. Kicker		T. Jones		D. Matthews		S. Murphy	
VP	11	VP	20	VP	39	VP	10	VP	6	VP	9	SEB	12	SEB	16
N. Jane		P. Jackson		N. Jane		S. Stevens		P. Harris		P. Jackson		S. Sedda		S. Stevens	
T. Moore		H. Richard		Q. Billip		R. James		P. Jackson		N. Jane				H. Richard	
Q. Hit (16)		S. Lett		S. Lett		J. Tony		J. Tony		H. Richard				Q. Bilip	

Prepared By: S. Strickland	Date:	10/2014
Approved By:	Date:	

[SECTION 4]

Nine-Cell Chart

The nine-cell performance and values chart was developed and popularized by General Electric and has been used extensively at a number of "academy companies," which are frequently hunting grounds for top talent. The purpose of the chart is for each manager to plot his or her direct reports in the nine-cell matrix based on only two variables.

The first variable, performance, is straightforward. It captures an employee's performance level as compared with their work goals, based on their manager's assessment. Some employees are high performers (those who exceed their goals), some are satisfactory (they meet the stated goals for their position), while others are low performers (they do not achieve their goals) in the company.

The second variable, values, captures the extent to which an employee demonstrates or *lives* the organization's values. The performance of an employee is systematically measured against observable outcomes or behaviors. For example, performance should be measured by analyzing employee scorecards or key performance indicators based on an individual's goals that are established on an annual basis. Values measure how an employee conducts himself or herself on a daily basis toward achieving his or her established goals based on interactions with coworkers or stakeholders.

Each business unit leader is required to complete a nine-cell chart that plots each of his or her direct reports on the matrix. The nine-cell chart should be an honest and candid assessment of each direct report through the lens of individual performance and values. All direct reports should not be considered high performers who rate high on values (or, conversely, low on performance and values). The goal is to provide meaningful differentiation through a distribution of ratings on the nine-cell chart. Our extensive experience using this tool suggests that, when completed with honesty and integrity, a nine-cell chart inevitably reflects a mixture of ratings on the matrix.

The direct reports below each manager are also required to complete nine-cell charts that plot each of their direct reports. HR and business leaders must take responsibility for teaching leaders at lower levels how to complete a nine-cell chart and reinforce the importance of the overall succession process.

The instructions below summarize the actions outlined above:

Step 1: Plot each of your employees on the nine-cell chart. Be sure your plotting of each employee honestly reflects both their performance based on hard facts and how their actions/ behaviors lend or don't lend themselves to supporting the organization's values. Note: the 360-degree feedback evaluations should be referenced when deciding which value rating to designate.

Step 2: Teach each manager's direct reports this process and inform them they are required to complete a nine-cell that includes each of their direct reports. (Reference the teaching guide at the end of this handbook for further detail.)

Step 3: Each manager reviews his or her completed nine-cell chart with his or her HR partner and makes adjustments where necessary based on additional input.

Step 4: Each manager reviews the nine-cells generated by his or her direct reports and conducts a dialogue to ascertain if any adjustments are necessary.

Step 5: Each manager finalizes his or her nine-cell chart and the business unit head/HR partner collect all nine-cells from the manager's direct reports.

Step 6: Nine-cell charts are complete and can be compiled as the basis for further development planning and dialogue with more senior leaders (or the CEO or board of directors).

The matrix on the next page provides an example of what the nine-cell chart should resemble when complete:

		Low	Medium	High
P **E** **R** **F** **O** **R** **M** **A** **N** **C** **E**	**High**	C. Sanders M. Jackson	S. Kiffen J. Anderson	G. Emmle N. Ussel J. Lof
	Medium	T. Sam B. Counters	J. Peterson P. Jackson E. Harvey S. Cupp V. Mott	S. Strickland N. Cooper B. Fellow
	Low	J. Trip	B. White N. Masson	P. Hart

VALUES

[SECTION 5]

Leadership Judgment

As leaders progress in any organization their effectiveness depends less on their ability to perform tasks. The ultimate yardstick of accomplished leaders is their ability to make good judgments and successfully drive them to execution. As part of the assessment process, you must consider the judgments that individuals on your team made in the past year, including whether these judgments led to successful outcomes and how effectively they engaged stakeholders in the process.

Leaders make judgments in three key areas: strategy, people, and crisis. The complexity and scale of these issues will increase at the more senior levels of the organization, but leaders at all levels must address these issues. For example, a senior executive may make strategy judgments that relate to new product launches or market entry, whereas a junior product manager may make judgments about competitive pricing or which suppliers to select.

A summary of the critical judgments you should consider in your review is provided below:

Strategy—What judgment calls did the leader make to position his or her business area, and ultimately the entire company, for success with customers in the market? This may include actions taken to enhance the business's offer, its operational effectiveness, or competitive actions.

People—What judgment calls did the leader make to build his or her team? This may also include judgments about the extended team of business partners or other stakeholders. This area encompasses identifying whether people the leader chooses to work with are capable, trustworthy, and placed in the right positions to be successful. Assessing people judgments includes examining the individual's hiring, promotion, and outplacement judgments.

Crisis—What judgment calls did the leader make to overcome unexpected difficulties and crises that inevitably happen in all businesses?

Remember that a "crisis" will be defined differently at various organizational levels, so it can be considered anything that threatened accomplishment of the goals in the leader's area or disrupted normal business operations.

In addition to looking at the judgment calls that a leader made, you will also be asked to gauge the success of the outcomes and the effectiveness of the judgment process. A judgment can only be considered "good" if it leads to desirable outcomes. Therefore, you will be asked to capture the quantitative or qualitative outcomes that resulted from the individual's key judgments for the past year.

Although we gauge judgments by their outcomes, the execution of leadership judgments rarely follows the expected path. Indeed, a measure of a leader's effectiveness is his or her ability to make adjustments to either execution or the judgment itself along the way. We call these "redo loops" because leaders are often forced to reexamine the assumptions or data used in their initial judgment calls and make changes during the course of execution.

When assessing an individual in the succession process, the recommended approach will ask you to review each of the following categories for every person you are evaluating:

Strategy Judgments

a. Describe the significant strategy judgments the individual made in his or her area in the past year.
b. What were the outcomes of these judgments?
c. How effectively did the leader engage his or her team and other stakeholders in both making the judgment call and adjusting execution?

People Judgments

a. Describe the significant people judgments the individual made in his or her area in the past year.
b. What were the outcomes of these judgments?
c. How effectively did the leader engage his or her team and other stakeholders in both making the judgment call and adjusting execution?

Crisis Judgments

a. Describe any significant judgment calls the leader had to make in response to a perceived crisis in his or her business area.

b. What were the outcomes of these judgments?

c. How effectively did the leader engage his or her team and other stakeholders in both making the judgment call and adjusting execution?

Leadership Judgment Process

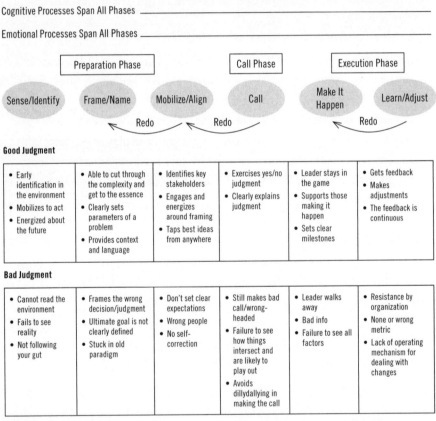

Cognitive Processes Span All Phases

Emotional Processes Span All Phases

| Preparation Phase | | | Call Phase | Execution Phase | |

Sense/Identify — Frame/Name — Mobilize/Align — Redo — Call — Redo — Make It Happen — Learn/Adjust — Redo

Good Judgment

• Early identification in the environment • Mobilizes to act • Energized about the future	• Able to cut through the complexity and get to the essence • Clearly sets parameters of a problem • Provides context and language	• Identifies key stakeholders • Engages and energizes around framing • Taps best ideas from anywhere	• Exercises yes/no judgment • Clearly explains judgment	• Leader stays in the game • Supports those making it happen • Sets clear milestones	• Gets feedback • Makes adjustments • The feedback is continuous

Bad Judgment

• Cannot read the environment • Fails to see reality • Not following your gut	• Frames the wrong decision/judgment • Ultimate goal is not clearly defined • Stuck in old paradigm	• Don't set clear expectations • Wrong people • No self-correction	• Still makes bad call/wrong-headed • Failure to see how things intersect and are likely to play out • Avoids dillydallying in making the call	• Leader walks away • Bad info • Failure to see all factors	• Resistance by organization • None or wrong metric • Lack of operating mechanism for dealing with changes

Not following gut can span all phases

© 2007 from *Judgment: How Winning Leaders Make Great Calls* by Noel M. Tichy and Warren Bennis.

Employee judgment is one of four components of an employee evaluation. Constructing a complete employee evaluation is described in the following section.

[SECTION 6]

Employee Evaluation

E stablishing a consistent evaluation format and standard process is foundational for encouraging productive dialogue and cross-unit talent reviews. This section provides a template that has been used successfully in diverse industries and across numerous geographies.

The leader—the business unit head for the purposes of our discussion—must take personal responsibility for completing evaluations for each of his or her direct reports. Evaluations of your direct reports *must not* be delegated to anyone in your business, including the person's HR partner. Similarly, the leader's direct reports will be responsible for personally completing evaluations for each of their direct reports. This process requires that each unit leader has three fundamental obligations: (a) completion of the evaluations for his or her direct reports; (b) teaching his or her direct reports to effectively complete evaluations of their direct reports; and (c) review and quality control of their direct reports evaluations. (As noted earlier, an instruction manual for training employees on this process is provided at the end of this guide.)

The employee evaluation can be divided into the following categories:

1. Demographic Information (name, current role, title, years of service in current role, and a three-year salary trend)

2. Performance Summary for this past year and performance trend

3. Employee Judgment Summary

4. Employee Appraisal
   a. Strengths
   b. Improvement and Development Needs
   c. Job/Career Recommendations
   d. Employee Potential

Required steps for completing each employee evaluation:

Step 1: Enter all of the demographic information for your direct report: (a) employee name, (b) current role, (c) title, (d) years of service at your organization, and (e) three-year salary trend.

Step 2: Enter the (f) performance summary of your direct report for the current year and identify the (g) performance trend (positive or negative). It should summarize your view of the person's accomplishments relative to his or her goals for the year.

Step 3: Summarize the individual's track record of significant (h) judgments in the past year, including your assessment of the leader's ability to drive successful outcomes and to effectively engage stakeholders or team members in the judgment process.

Step 4: Start the appraisal of the individual by first entering the (i) strengths of the employee. You should accomplish this by describing employee's strengths including how their actions align with the organization's values and how they have changed (developed, regressed, or remained unchanged) in the past year.

Step 5: (j) Identify the most critical needs for the employee, including leadership development and responsive action plans, and job expansion if appropriate.

Step 6: (k) Provide recommendations regarding this employee's job/career. If a job change is appropriate, identify alternatives and timing. Discuss your views of employee's potential and career path.

Step 7: (l) The final component of the evaluation is your assessment of the employee's potential. For this, you need to classify the employee in one of the following three categories: 1. Has the capacity to grow and move higher in the business; 2. Does not have the capacity to move to grow beyond current job/level; 3. Is not competent in current position and should be reassigned or removed from business.

Note: To facilitate dialogue and efficient review across the enterprise, employee evaluations should be limited to two pages. An example of an employee evaluation when complete is provided below:

Accomplishment Summary and Development Review

Name: (a) Samuel Good

Current Role: (b) VP Europe

Title: (c) Vice President

Years of Service: (d) 25

2011 Salary and Bonus: (e) $150,000.00

2010 Salary and Bonus: (e) $135,000.00

2009 Salary and Bonus: (e) $130,000.00

PERFORMANCE SUMMARY AND TREND (F AND G)

Last year was a particularly challenging year for Sam. He began his assignments in Europe with focus on Germany and France. This required multiple due diligence processes that Sam coordinated and eventually led to the business's newly established relationship of a strategic market leader whom Sam established and nurtured. The relationship continues to grow and develop, enabling the business to jointly work toward a major acquisition. Sam assumed leadership of an underdeveloped European operation in December and he has since worked tirelessly to recruit key people and scale our infrastructure to match business demands. He has made substantial progress in a short time period, demonstrating consistency in his approach and ability to deliver results. This upcoming year, Sam needs to deliver on the European promise, finalize our entry into Germany and France, and clarify our European strategy. Sam's targets in the coming year are challenging but achievable.

• • •

JUDGMENT TRACK RECORD (H)

Strategy Judgment

Sam's strategic judgment this year was on par with his impeccable judgment in his prior three years operating in Southeast Asia. To expand in Europe, he made a strategic judgment call to partner with a market leader in our industry. The call had substantial implications for our European market entry and without this partnership our projected expansion rate in Europe would have likely faltered.

At this time it appears that Sam properly framed the issues and mobilized the right stakeholders for supporting this judgment. What is not yet certain is how well he and his team will do on the execution of this judgment. Sam has a well-developed operational plan in place but it will require strong leadership and the ability to emotionally engage his young team.

People Judgment

Sam routinely exercises good people judgment, and when he finds that he missed a people judgment call he conducts a redo loop to correct the situation. Sam recently removed one of his direct reports who was a tenured employee as a result of a values issue. This judgment call was made without hesitation when it became clear the individual removed was placing personal success ahead of team success.

His other people judgments included promotions of three key leaders to new positions and demonstrated that Sam is able to evaluate potential and willing to make the decisions to support the future of the business with leaders in the right positions. Sam will need to continue working with these leaders, helping them to reinforce their teams and drive the necessary changes in our operations and marketing.

Crisis Judgment

The new product launch, which Sam inherited, had some serious quality problems that initially hurt our relationship with two key vendors. Had the problem escalated it could have caused long-term damage. Sam was a little slow to recognize the magnitude of the problem but once challenged to investigate, he quickly mobilized task forces to address the issues and made crisis judgments that addressed the problem within a reasonable time frame and led to its full resolution.

APPRAISAL

Strengths (i)

- Sam is tireless and passionate. All constituencies (internal and external) respect his dedication and know that his commitment is second to none.
- Sam keeps the customer at the forefront of all he does. His actions serve as a catalyst on customer responsiveness and quality issues.
- He has tremendous ownership for his team. He spends the time to coach and develop them, and helps everyone on the team commit to achieving stretch targets.
- Sam has tremendous knowledge of our business and industry.

Improvement/Development Needs and Plans (j)

- As evidenced in the 360-degree feedback, Sam's passion and ownership is both a strength and a weakness. He has protected himself and his team . . . sometimes to the point of appearing "paranoid" to peers from other departments. Sam needs to listen before defending his team, and strengthen his peer relationships as he deals with new counterparts after his job transfer.
- While Sam's judgments are typically good, his communication of action plans is not always clear and concise with stakeholders or his team. This can lead to wasted time and resources in execution. I have coached Sam to improve and expect to see focus in this area.

Job/Career Recommendations (k)

Sam has just assumed full responsibility for Europe less than one year ago. Successful implementation of the European strategy will determine future promotability. He should showcase his strategic and operational skill, and work commensurately on development needs in the areas of cross-functional peer coordination and clear communication of the action plan. I will work with him by continuing our dialogue on market development plans and support with stakeholder management as needed.

Employee's Potential (1)

Sam has the capacity to grow and move higher in the business. Europe provides an opportunity to demonstrate his ability to take a historically underdeveloped and underfunded business and grow it. If he is able to do so, it will demonstrate that his strategic alliance, marketing, and operational successes of the past are scalable and may be transferable to one day return to Asia to run the entire geography. With additional financial training, and likely a rotation through either finance or marketing, Sam could be a good candidate for one day assuming control of our largest market in North America.

Manager Signature and Date _____

[SECTION 7]

360-Degree Feedback

Facing reality is a critical trait of a transformational and winning leader. It is important to understand how and where to start when doing this. When facing reality, all great leaders perform a "mirror test"; 360-degree feedback is one of the best tools to help leaders face reality and learn about themselves. Further, it is a great tool to measure how well a leader lives the organization's values.

The goal of 360-degree feedback is to understand better how an employee's leadership affects other people and how he or she is viewed by others in the work setting. The methodology is used globally throughout the corporate world and provides a platform to assess individual leadership capacity. Oftentimes, leaders are insulated from feedback as a result of human nature. People always like to share good news, but difficult news is generally avoided and may never reach the leader. 360-degree feedback aims to break the avoidant pattern of human nature and not only share the good but share the emotionally challenging as well.

360-degree feedback is a central component of the succession planning process. Each employee who is listed on your candidate slate must go through the 360-degree feedback process. The outcome of the 360 will serve two purposes: 1. it will serve as a leadership development platform for the employee, and 2. it will allow you, as the business leader or HR partner, to have insight about the person's leadership traits from different perspectives at different levels in the organization. It will help you validate your perceptions of the individual or serve as a correction catalyst when finalizing direct report placement on the nine-cell chart.

The process for 360-degree feedback is simple. Employees on your candidate slate should be notified that they are included in 360-degree feedback for succession planning for the group. It will be their responsibility to identify a minimum of four subordinates, two peers, and their direct manager to take part in completing the survey to provide feedback. Once identified, that group of individuals should be sent details on how to complete the 360-Degree Survey for this individual.

The following page has an example of a sample online 360-Degree Survey for an organization that has the following values: 1. Speed, 2. Simplicity, 3. Innovativeness, 4. Adapts to Change, and 5. Integrity and Honesty. Please note that before the 360-degree feedback instrument was adopted in this organization, the senior leaders of each business unit defined specific behaviors associated with each of the values. These were in turn taught throughout the organization, and each work team developed its own set of working norms so that it could establish positive behaviors for each of the values.

[360-Degree Feedback Section 1]

For each of the organization values below, you will see two or three specific behaviors that relate to the value. Provide an overall rating of the person on this value using the following scale:

1 = the person exhibits none of the behaviors associated with this value

2 = the person rarely exhibits the behaviors associated with this value

3 = the person sometimes exhibits the behaviors but is inconsistent or may exhibit contradictory behavior

4 = the person more often exhibits the behaviors but is sometimes inconsistent for reasons that are not made clear to others

5 = the person typically exhibits this value, recognizing when he or she fails to execute at the required standard

6 = the person regularly exhibits the behaviors associated with this value

7 = the person always exhibits the behaviors associated with this value; the person is a role model who can teach others

After providing a numerical score based on the scale above, you will be asked to explain your rating with qualitative comments. Please provide as much detail as possible to help the individual understand your rating and what they may improve. If possible, please provide specific examples that explain your rating. Please note that you will not be able to continue to the next section until you have provided both a quantitative rating and qualitative feedback.

SPEED

The extent to which I see this person . . .

1. Set a pace for their team that equals or exceeds customer expectations.

2. Provide solutions that improve efficiency and effectiveness of our people and processes.

3. Focus and align people toward working with urgency while never compromising on quality.

4. Dedicate time and energy to development of the people with whom they work.

Rate this person on a scale of 1 to 7:   _____
Explain your rating:

_____

_____

_____

_____

SIMPLICITY

The extent to which I see this person . . .

1. Take actions that streamline work processes and communication.

2. Listen and learn from those who do the work in order to remove bureaucracy.

Rate this person on a scale of 1 to 7:   _____
Explain your rating:

_____

_____

_____

_____

INNOVATIVENESS

The extent to which I see this person . . .

1. Conceive of ideas that break with the status quo.

2. Challenge team to push beyond incremental thinking and adopt creative solutions.

Rate this person on a scale of 1 to 7:   _____
Explain your rating:

_____

_____

_____

_____

ADAPTS TO CHANGE

The extent to which I see this person . . .

1. Anticipate changes in customer or market needs.

2. Readily adopt new behaviors or outside best practices in order to improve results.

3. Motivate others to work in new ways in spite of resistance, obstacles, or setbacks.

Rate this person on a scale of 1 to 7:   _____
Explain your rating:

_____

_____

_____

_____

INTEGRITY AND HONESTY

The extent to which I see this person . . .

1. Lead the way by being truthful and authentic.

2. Act with integrity, always keeping his or her commitments.

3. Deal with conflict in an open, candid, and productive manner.

Rate this person on a scale of 1 to 7:   _____
Explain your rating:

_____

_____

_____

_____

[360-Degree Feedback Section 2]

1. What I appreciate most about this person is . . .

2. How I think this person can be even more effective as a leader for our business . . .

[SECTION 8]

Managing Political and Cultural Dynamics

This handbook has principally dealt with the technical aspects of organizing an effective succession process—evaluation criteria, review processes, assessment forms, and the like. As noted earlier, this is a vital first step, but the succession process must account for political and cultural dynamics that are unavoidable in any human endeavor. When not handled properly, evaluating people is a subjective process that can become tainted with the exercise of individual power or poisoned by unfair biases.

Managing the political and cultural dynamics is essential for creating a successful process that leads to real understanding of each individual and to long-term development. While space is limited, we will note some of the challenges to be addressed and describe the dialogue process that can help to overcome these.

POLITICAL DYNAMICS

Every organization has politics. While many rail against it, the fact remains that when resources, power, and opportunity are scarce, human beings will lobby, cajole, and even coerce. There are some obvious ways in which politics can affect evaluations:

♦ The crony: When a powerful individual provides an overly positive review of a person he or she likes, mentors, has personal history with, etc.

♦ The blackball: When a powerful individual is unduly critical or blocks a positive review of someone he or she dislikes, or even does so if that person is a potential competitor for a job that he or she would like to go to someone else.

♦ The inquisitor: When a powerful person asks questions ad nauseam, placing the assessor in a defensive position, challenging the assessor's self-confidence and leading others to question the assessment's veracity even though the minutiae being discussed have little relevance.

These are only a few of the most common and destructive ways that power can be used in the process. Ultimately, it is the leader's role, along with his or her HR partner, to facilitate dialogues and manage personal biases so that political dynamics are recognized and minimized.

There are three important checks and balances that help to regulate politics in the succession process. First, "two over one" approval is required. Simply put, an individual's manager does not have the final say on the evaluation. Instead it is the manager's manager who must sign off and edit the assessment as needed. Just as financial decisions in most organizations require escalation, final judgments on a company's most precious asset—its people—should not be relegated down the chain of command for fear that local prejudices and politics will seep into the process.

Second, there should be a peer dialogue. In most work teams, cross-departmental or cross-functional work is routine. In this way, senior managers from other areas—managers who are the peers of the person signing off on the individual assessments—come in contact with and form views of employees on other work teams. The business unit head, or appropriate leader, should hold a review with his or her team in which each individual talks openly about their assessments of their direct reports. Transparency and open dialogue will shine a light on political biases, enabling the leader to recognize and eliminate these.

Finally, involvement up the chain of command provides a subtle but powerful influence if the CEO or board of directors is appropriately involved in talent reviews. The assessments at the business unit level should not be publicly available but certainly should be accessible to the organization's top leader and HR partner. If these two leaders, possibly in conjunction with the board of directors, periodically review and discuss assessments of top talent with the business unit leader, it encourages fairness and careful monitoring of the assessments.

There are obviously numerous other ways in which politics can impact assessments that we do not have the space to explore here. It is critical that the leaders responsible for succession planning keep a watchful eye, constantly questioning themselves and others about whether politics has taken hold of the process.

CULTURAL DYNAMICS

Although cultural dynamics may distort the process and final evaluations to a lesser extent, they can be very difficult to spot. Presumably, most of the individuals involved in the succession process are part of the organizational culture, so subtle, ingrained assumptions about how evaluations should be conducted may not be obvious.

Some of the cultural biases that we have seen in multiple organizations include:

◆ "Only outsiders welcome" (or alternatively "only insiders need apply"): Sometimes ingrained notions of where talent should come from can tilt assessments toward the unjustifiably positive (or negative). In organizations that feel historical pressure to grow their own leaders—companies where people speak with pride about the long history of leaders' coming from within—this attitude can lead to rose-colored assessments and lack of good talent benchmarking in the external market. Conversely, when a board or incumbent leader sours on the team after a failed project or successive earnings misses, an unspoken assumption that nobody in the organization could be fit for a leadership job can creep into the evaluation process.

◆ "Let's all get along": Conflict can be discouraged or suppressed in public forums in many organizations. This leads to ineffective dialogue sessions in which people are reluctant to speak the truth and have candid discussions about development needs or a candidate's lack of qualification for certain positions.

◆ "Don't tread on me": Some organizations have strong boundaries between departments and strong personal ownership of one's team. In these situations you will often hear leaders talk about "my people." This cultural attitude can evoke defensiveness anytime there is disagreement with the direct manager's assessment.

Managing cultural biases can be difficult because they are hard to see when the leader is equally ingrained in the culture. We often suggest that leaders take time to outline cultural biases and habits that may interfere with the desired outcomes before they begin the process. A robust dialogue about norms and expectations for which cultural factors may be present and how these will be handled before the assessment process begins will help leaders at all levels anticipate and address these influences.

[APPENDIX 1]

TEACHING INSTRUCTIONS

Teaching Introduction

To complete the succession planning preparation for your business area you will need to enlist the support of your direct reports. Each of your direct reports will need to complete nine-cell charts that plot each of their own direct reports, as well as complete employee evaluations for them. To ensure uniformity in the approach and assessment criteria, you will need to teach your direct reports how to complete both the nine-cell chart and the employee evaluation.

This section provides teaching instructions for relaying the process and format described earlier to your direct reports. This introduction is a ninety-minute meeting with your direct reports that should be supplemented by individual coaching as needed.

The steps below will guide you through the preparation for teaching the succession process to your team.

STEP 1: CHECK LOGISTICS

Make sure that you reserve the necessary space and equipment to conduct your session. The checklist below lists all of the major components you will need for your room.

Meeting Room
- ✓ Adequate lighting
- ✓ Size; the room accommodates all of your direct reports
- ✓ Electrical outlets for a projector and computer
- ✓ Adjustable temperature controls

Equipment
- ✓ Projector for the PowerPoint slides
- ✓ Projector screen
- ✓ Computer
- ✓ Microphone and speakers (depending on group size)
- ✓ One flip chart at the front of the room

Supplies/General

✓ Paper, pens, and pencils

✓ One magic marker

✓ Participant materials (nine-cell chart and employee evaluation guide)

STEP 2: INVITE DIRECT REPORTS

Once you have established a meeting time and date you will need to invite all of your direct reports. In the event some employees are located in different geographic locations, you may need to hold a video conference with them to avoid travel expenses. Provided all direct reports have the materials, there should be no problem conducting this remotely.

STEP 3: REVIEW MEETING MATERIALS AND AGENDA

The agenda below will provide teaching points for your session. Your teaching should reflect your leadership style and be in your own words. The outline below will guide you through the key topics, but you will need to prepare diligently to make this session effective.

SUCCESSION PLANNING TEACHING	
TIME	**SUGGESTED ACTIVITY**
0:00	**Opening**
	• Your opening should set the tone for the importance of succession planning within your organization.
	• Note how development of a world-class leadership pipeline throughout your organization will be essential to achieving your business's vision and objectives.
	• Provide historical context regarding how this process may be similar to or different from what your team members have done in the past.
	• Explain the process. Note that each business unit head (or the role appropriate for your organization) will be responsible for conducting succession planning using the new, standardized succession planning process. Succession planning requires each business unit (or team) to produce a file that includes the following:

1. Business Unit Overview/Summary

2. Organization Chart

3. Candidate slate for their business unit

4. Nine-cell chart of the BU head's direct reports

5. Nine-cell chart created by the BU head's direct reports that include their own direct reports

6. Performance evaluations of (a) the BU head's direct reports and (b) each of the direct report's direct reports (e.g., the CFO is a direct report to the BU head, so the CFO will need to conduct performance evaluations of each of his direct reports).

7. 360-degree feedback for each individual identified on the candidate slate of the business unit.

- Enlist the support of your direct reports. Let them know how this process will impact them and their future within the business.

- Provide timing guidelines for when this process will begin and its completion date.

TIME	SUGGESTED ACTIVITY

0:15   **Values and 360-Degree Feedback**

- Note that a solid understanding of organizational values and expected leadership behaviors are required to complete the assessment (nine-cell chart, 360-degree feedback, development plans).

- If necessary, teach or remind your team of the values, with emphasis on how to link these to behaviors in your team or work area.

- Review your organization's values. Do not simply list the values but provide behavioral examples demonstrating positive behaviors of how team members in your work area demonstrate these, and negative examples that contradict the values.

- Teach the concept and methodology of 360-degree feedback to the audience.

- Explain that the goal of 360-degree feedback is to understand better how an individual's leadership affects other people. The methodology is used globally throughout the corporate world and provides a platform to assess individual leadership capacity. Often, leaders are insulated from feedback as a result of human nature. People always like to share good news; however, difficult news is generally avoided and never reaches the leader. 360-degree feedback aims to break the barrier of human nature and not only share the good but share the difficult as well.

- Explain the process for how 360-degree feedback will be completed in your organization and linked to succession planning. This will vary in your organization depending on, for example, whether you have an online or computer-based system, how that system is administered, etc.

- Note how respondents will be notified and by whom. (Again, this will depend on the system in your organization.)

- Explain how and when individuals will see their feedback report, and who will be involved in the process or have access to this data.

- Reinforce the importance and value of this opportunity by noting that you will also be going through the 360-degree feedback process.

TIME	SUGGESTED ACTIVITY

0:35   **Employee Judgment**

- Explain that the evaluations will also look at another critical dimension of leadership: judgment.

- Summarize why an important measure of leadership is the quality of judgments that person makes. Particularly at the senior levels, leaders are making decisions rather than operating. Our assessments of employees must also include the key judgments they have made in the past year that impact our company and the organization.

- Explain the three judgment domains leaders will be assessed on and provide examples of each from your own experience:

  1. People Judgments: These are judgments relating to whom the leader selects for his or her team, and how the leader engages with stakeholders.

  2. Strategy Judgments: These are judgments relating to the strategic direction that an individual sets for his or her area and quality of execution plans (for example, allocating resources toward one business function or project in favor of another).

  3. Crisis Judgments: These judgments hopefully don't occur on a regular basis; however, every business faces crisis and difficulties. Strong leaders must have the ability to make good judgment calls in times of a crisis.

- Note that when assessing judgment in the three domains, your people should consider the following for each when evaluating their own direct reports:

  1. People Judgments:
     a. Describe the significant people judgments the individual made in his or her area in the past year.
     b. What were the outcomes of these judgments?
     c. How effectively did the leader engage his or her team and other stakeholders in both making the judgment call and adjusting execution?

  2. Strategy Judgments:
     a. Describe the significant strategy judgments the individual made in his or her area in the past year.
     b. What were the outcomes of these judgments?
     c. How effectively did the leader engage his or her team and other stakeholders in both making the judgment call and adjusting execution?

3. Crisis Judgments:
    a. Describe any significant judgment calls the leader had to make in response to a perceived crisis in his or her business area
    b. What were the outcomes of these judgments?
    c. How effectively did the leader engage his or her team and other stakeholders in both making the judgment call and adjusting execution?

- Pass out an example (one can be found above) from a hypothetical employee (i.e., not real data) that demonstrates the application of judgment in your organization.

TIME	SUGGESTED ACTIVITY
0:50	**Employee Evaluations**

- Reinforce that assessment and development is a leadership responsibility. Each of your direct reports is personally responsible for completing evaluations for each of their direct reports. This is a responsibility that must not be delegated to anyone, including HR partners. Further, everyone will be responsible for personally completing evaluations for each of their direct reports.

- Note that the final information required to complete the employee evaluation can be segmented into the following categories:

1. Demographic Information (name, current role, title, years of service, and three-year salary trend)

2. Performance Summary for this past year and performance trend

3. Employee Judgment Summary

4. Employee Appraisal
    a. Strengths
    b. Improvement and Development Needs
    c. Job/Career Recommendations
    d. Employee Potential

- Review the required steps for completing each employee evaluation:

Step 1: Enter all of the demographic information for the direct report: employee name, current role, title, years of service, three-year salary trend.

Step 2: Enter the performance summary of the direct report for this year and identify the (g) performance trend (positive or negative). It should summarize your view of employee accomplishments as compared with goals in the past year.

Step 3: Summarize the individual's track record of significant judgments in the past year, including your assessment of the leader's ability to drive successful outcomes and to effectively engage stakeholders or team members in the judgment process.

Step 4: Start the appraisal of the individual by first entering the strengths of the employee, including how their actions align with the organization's values and how they have changed (developed, regressed, or remained unchanged) in the past year.

Step 5: Identify the most critical needs for the employee including leadership development and responsive action plans, including job expansion if appropriate.

Step 6: Provide recommendations regarding this employee's current assignment and overall career. If a job change is appropriate, identify alternatives and timing. Discuss your views of the employee's potential and career path.

Step 7: The final component of the evaluation is assessment of the employee's potential. This requires a classification of the individual's potential and growth capacity into one of the following three categories: 1. Has the capacity to grow and move higher in the business; 2. Does not have the capacity to move to grow beyond current job/level; 3. Is not competent in current position and should be reassigned or removed from business.

- Remind the group that to keep the process manageable each evaluation should be approximately two pages. This will be challenging because the assessments require great consideration and there is much to be said. The final analysis must be distilled and then will be supported through dialogue that will probe for details and further examples.

- Answer any questions as needed.

TIME	SUGGESTED ACTIVITY

1:10   Nine-Cell Chart

- Teach the nine-cell concept and process. Explain how this process allows an organization to evaluate the performance of their employees on both job performance and organizational values.

- Discuss why performance and values are both important.

- Provide instructions for completing the nine-cell:

  1. Plot each of your employees on the nine-cell chart. Be sure your placement of each employee honestly reflects both their performance based on hard facts and how their behaviors lend or don't lend themselves to supporting the organization's values. Note that the 360 review evaluations/surveys should be referenced when deciding which value rating to assign/designate. For both dimensions, multiple inputs should be used to make the final assessment.

  2. Observe that the matrix provides a grid with performance on one side (low, satisfactory, and high) and values on the other (low, satisfactory, high).

  3. Tell the group that they will all be responsible for completing a nine-cell chart that has each of their direct reports plotted. Explain the process for completing and submitting these reports (that is, manual, IT system instructions, etc.).

  4. Note that the nine-cell should reflect meaningful differentiation among the direct reports; not everyone will be in the high performance-high values box.

5. Explain that placement on the nine-cell is an iterative process and the leaders may need to reconsider placement once they have finished all the assessments of their direct reports.

- Check for understanding from the group and move to the closing of your meeting.

TIME	SUGGESTED ACTIVITY
1:30	**Closing**

- Reinforce the importance of succession planning for the sustained growth and success of your organization.

- Ensure that your personal enthusiasm for this is evident and explain how you and your HR partner will help and support them throughout the process.

- Thank everyone for their time and engagement with this critical effort.

ACTION LEARNING

Simultaneous Development
and Succession Planning
Handbook

BY CHRIS DeROSE AND NOEL TICHY

Selecting an individual for a leadership position can be a confounding task, particularly at the most senior levels of an organization. It is necessarily a subjective judgment based on innumerable variables, most of which are hard to quantify. This task is made all the tougher by the fact that there is rarely a perfect candidate. As long as the candidate pool is made up of human beings, each is sure to have his or her own unique strengths, notable flaws, and underdeveloped competence areas.

A strong succession process will use multiple sources of data such as, to name only a few, performance history, judgment track record, accomplishment analysis, and 360-degree feedback. An invaluable and essential tool that is often underestimated or thought to be only for training is an action learning development program.

"Action learning" is a development methodology that was originated by Reginald Revans based in part on his training as a physicist at the University of Cambridge (with a brief stay at the University of Michigan) and his educational work at the United Kingdom's National Coal Board. Revans wrote most extensively in the 1970s and 1980s, defining action learning as:

> [A] means of development, intellectual, emotional or physical that requires its subjects, through responsible involvement in some real, complex and stressful problem, to achieve intended change . . . (Revans, 1982)

As a methodology, it has been modified for both better and worse many times since Revans. Its corporate use arguably gained the most traction in the United States when Noel made it the standard methodology for General Electric's corporate training center, Crotonville (today known as the John F. Welch Leadership Center). Throwing out traditional lectures and case studies in favor of having GE executives work on real-world problems faced by the conglomerate's business units in diverse industries, GE has since developed thousands of leaders using action learning. Participation in the top two action learning programs has become a rite of passage necessary for further promotion and an important data point in a succession pipeline that has produced CEOs both internally and for many other companies.

MORE THAN DEVELOPMENT

Action learning is powerful as an assessment tool because it places people in uncomfortable and unfamiliar situations, forcing them to work with others to resolve a live challenge rather than a hypothetical circumstance or case study borrowed from another organization. In the process, individuals display their capacity in critical areas such as learning rate, teamwork, problem solving, vision, analysis, networking, and change management. Because action learning can be devised to create a microcosm of the types of challenges that executives will face—or need to face to foster their development—it can be used to test, assess, and develop an individual's readiness for a new job and greater responsibility.

We outline the methodology that we have used for simultaneous development and succession planning in the pages below. It is a refinement and evolution over more than twenty-five years since Noel popularized action learning through his work with GE. We will also outline many of the pitfalls that we have encountered with ineffective programs labeled as "action learning" but sorely lacking the needed structure to be successful.

Before we move on, we would like to address a question that we often hear: shouldn't training be safe and segregated from assessment? Our answer is an emphatic no! The reality is that despite best intentions, judgments are being made in every venue, so those who say they completely separate the two aren't being honest with themselves or those being assessed. Even if observations are not formally catalogued, the executives who participate form impressions they take into the succession process. We find it to be far more constructive to engage with executives when they participate in development programs, particularly action learning, to share and synthesize observations rather than to let individuals come to their own haphazard conclusions based on partial data.

More important, leaders, and particularly those who aspire to be top executives and CEOs, are constantly being assessed by multiple constituents as they learn, grow, and make mistakes in real life. Development should prepare people for the pressures and realities they will face. Informing participants and making them aware that they are performing "onstage" prepares them for the difficulties of the largest organizational roles, which are often played out in public forums in most major corporations today.

Finally, we argue that the data available from well-constructed action learning development is too precious not to be used in the arduous yet critical task of selecting an organization's leadership. As we will explain in more detail below, action learning is a treasure trove of data about an individual that can be used to foster further development and inspire reflection on each person's career trajectory.

ACTION LEARNING FOR SUCCESSION

When used effectively, action learning can simultaneously solve an organization's biggest challenges, foster individual development, and provide invaluable insight for assessment and succession planning in a compressed time frame. To successfully deliver all three objectives requires the following:

♦ *Real projects, real priorities.* The problems to which people are assigned must be real. In our application for corporations, the priorities are selected directly by the CEO and top team. Although not an immediate crisis, they are strategic business challenges that require resolution for the continued success and growth of the company, such as growing business in a new region, accelerating application of new technologies, or transforming internal processes to create new capabilities. These are issues in which the CEO has a direct interest, not a passing curiosity or a priority that a well-meaning training staff member imagines the CEO should have.

♦ *Nonexpert teams.* Teams of six to eight executives should mostly be composed of nonexperts who do not deal with the project issues on a daily basis. Action learning was originally based on Revans's realization that nonexperts are much more likely to offer breakthrough, unconventional solutions. Because these teams work together for approximately four to six months, the nonexperts are instrumental in catalyzing learning and new problem-solving routines among those who may have more experience.

♦ *Support structure for learning and process effectiveness.* Although action learning advocates a trial-and-error approach to learning, it is paradoxically most effective when there are strong support structures in place. The goal is for individuals to challenge themselves and for teams to independently resolve business or interpersonal issues. However, this is not a "sink or swim" environment. Executives remain involved, periodically supporting the teams while not providing the answers or directing action. In our consulting practice, we act as coaches checking weekly with teams to ensure that they are making progress on their project, working effectively with their teammates, and individually challenging themselves in new ways. When teams or individuals get off track and do not demonstrate the ability to self-correct, executives or coaches may intervene to ensure that the team is on a path toward meeting its collective and individual objectives.

♦ *Transparent assessment process.* Participants should know from the first day that assessment is a component of the program. When advising corporations, we conclude the program with an exhaustive review of each person. Throughout the program there are at least two face-to-face dialogues with the individual to discuss his or her strengths, career aspirations, and development needs. At the final session, data is shared among senior executives and executive coaches so that the individual can be placed on a nine-cell chart that rates the individual's relative project contribution and leadership behavior as low, medium, or high. Following the final session, an executive shares the assessment with the participant and discusses future career opportunities. The following provides an example of ratings for one team and abbreviated coaching notes for one person.

	Low	Medium	High
High			Melanie S. John B.
Medium	Mike L.	Tom G. Eric T.	
Low			Mary W.
	Low	**Medium**	**High**

Performance (vertical axis label)

Values / Leadership Behaviors

ABBREVIATED COMMENTS FOR MIKE L.

Observed Strengths	**Performance:** Mike made many contributions to defining the project scope, benchmarking our capabilities against competitors and identifying gaps that we need to fill. His greatest contributions came in accelerating the team's work during Phase 1 of their project plan.
	Values/Leadership: Mike is a diligent worker who maintains very high standards. He expected a great deal of himself and held the team to expectations of excellence. He repeatedly exhibited a commitment to learning, one of our core values.
	Performance: Mike contributed the most during Phase 1 when the team members worked independently. Although he participated actively in the later stages, he was less skillful at connecting solutions to individual gaps into a broader, coherent organizational strategy. Because Mike tends to lead through ideas, his leadership role diminished during Phase 2 and 3 as he was less able to contribute.
Observed Development Needs	**Values/Leadership:** As Mike's role changed and felt he had less impact, he noticeably withdrew from the team. This led to a period of relative isolation and frustration. When addressed by the team during one feedback exercise, Mike admitted his teamwork had not been effective and expressed a desire to change. In part due to his regular work responsibilities and in part due to his continued emotional difficulty with the situation, Mike showed little improvement. After a one-on-one discussion with his team's executive sponsor, Mike's resolve to improve his ability to play the role of "follower" when he did not have all the answers visibly improved. Although Mike concluded the program much better, this remains his most important development area. Mike needs to display more than an intellectual understanding that, as a leader, he will not have all the answers but must rely on team members or subordinates at times to drive success.
Coaching / Next Steps	Mike has spent most of his career as a team leader, first in research and the last 15 years in operations. To reach his full potential, he needs to be placed in more situations where he is outlining an integrated strategic response rather than implementing discrete initiatives. More important, he needs to be in a role that requires mobilization of multiple constituents to lead change and assemble different perspectives into a leadership plan with buy-in that he did not solely create.
	As an executive team, we feel an assignment as the leader for the upcoming Technology 2.0 task force would be an excellent first step for Mike. This will enable him to leverage his technical background but the technology changes will impact all of our business units so he will need to step outside his operations and assemble a team that can represent the multiple business units and product lines that will be impacted by the change.
	Mike's career could progress several different ways. The most likely path at this point would be for Mike to assume the Director role of Operations Strategy and Quality en route to perhaps becoming VP of Operations for our core business. Before Mike is prepared to oversee Operations at the Corporate level, he would also benefit from a geographic director position which would develop his capacity for getting ideas and formulating strategy by mobilizing others.

DEFINING ROLES AND RESPONSIBILITIES

Developing an action learning platform that provides detailed insights about each participant, offering useful insights for succession planning and development while concurrently delivering solutions to some of the organization's biggest problems, requires active involvement of senior executives and faculty. There must be a carefully orchestrated process in which each actor understands and plays his or her important role.

Ownership for the overall process must rest with the CEO and senior executives if the program will truly inform succession at the topmost levels. This does not mean that the program exists only for the aggrandizement of the CEO's legacy or as a symbolic act to promote the organization's reputation for development. On the contrary, participants must be genuinely committed to their own growth, while teams must take responsibility for resolving issues with both their team process and project resolution. Additionally, the faculty must aid the executives in providing a support structure. Faculty create the scaffolding by providing content expertise, process facilitation, and individual coaching that enables the teams to build toward their own success.

Some of the key responsibilities for each role include the following:

1. CEO and Senior Executives

- Preparation Phase: Selecting Participants and Projects

    Identifying and growing candidates to replace the top team members requires the active involvement of the existing leadership team. Business unit leaders, in partnership with their HR leaders, must identify the high-potential candidates who should participate and whose development will improve the organization. The individual participants should be carefully vetted and determined to have the possibility of becoming senior leaders given the right training and on-the-job experience. The time frame for succession will vary within each organization, but we typically suggest that the individual should be on the promotion path within three years and a potential successor for a top job within five to seven years. Ideally, the CEO and senior executives should identify the candidates for an action learning program through a succession process or, if not, each person's submission should be discussed to ensure that there is clarity on the individual's strengths, development needs, and perceived potential for advancement.

In addition to nominating participants, project ideas are generated directly by the CEO and senior executives. Participants are assigned to each project based in part on their development needs.

- Program Phase: Coaching and Assessing

During the program, a senior executive is assigned to act as a coach for each action learning team. In the early phase, they will work with the team to ensure that the project has been framed properly and is aligned with the overall business direction. By meeting with the team on a semimonthly basis, the executive coaches can also offer advice to their assigned team if they feel that the team is unable to resolve issues or has failed to account for factors essential to the project's resolution. They also meet with each participant on two occasions to counsel the team members on their leadership development agenda and career plans. Throughout this process, however, executive coaches do not provide answers or explicit direction. Their role is to offer prompts that will provoke inquiry and further action by the team.

In the final workshop, the CEO and executives also play the critical role of decision makers. They determine which of the recommendations from each team will be adopted, who will be assigned follow-up, and provide feedback to the team on the quality of their final work product.

- Post-Program Phase: Developmental Feedback and Execution

Following the program's conclusion, each executive will provide individual feedback to the participants. As noted above, each person will understand conclusions made about his or her performance throughout the process and how leadership behaviors were displayed. Through dialogue the executive coach helps the individual participant process the feedback and consider next steps for his or her own development, including assignment to special projects, job rotation, or additional developmental experiences. These are communicated back to the HR leaders and integrated with the overall succession planning process.

Graphic: Integrating Action Learning with Succession Planning

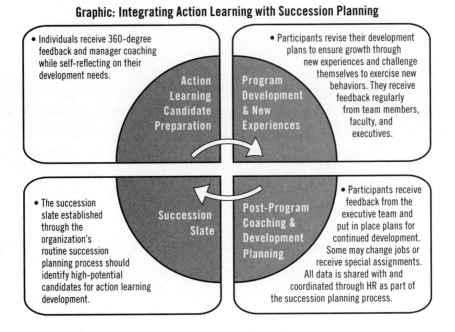

- Individuals receive 360-degree feedback and manager coaching while self-reflecting on their development needs.

Action Learning Candidate Preparation

- Participants revise their development plans to ensure growth through new experiences and challenge themselves to exercise new behaviors. They receive feedback regularly from team members, faculty, and executives.

Program Development & New Experiences

- The succession slate established through the organization's routine succession planning process should identify high-potential candidates for action learning development.

Succession Slate

Post-Program Coaching & Development Planning

- Participants receive feedback from the executive team and put in place plans for continued development. Some may change jobs or receive special assignments. All data is shared with and coordinated through HR as part of the succession planning process.

2. Participants

- Preparation Phase: Preparation Assignments, Reflection, and Contracting

    Prior to the start of the program, participants need to prepare themselves, their work teams, and their families in addition to completing some preparatory reading. Each person is asked to reflect on his or her development needs and career goals, followed by a sit-down discussion with his or her direct manager. Participants also discuss with their manager and work team how they will handle the added time commitment, preparing for more delegation and empowerment of their work teams (skills they will be taught during the first workshop). Finally, individuals must contract with their families or friends to establish realistic expectations for how the impact of added responsibilities will be managed. Juggling the demands of multiple priorities alongside family and personal commitments is stressful but also a realistic preview of what life is like at the top of most corporations.

■ Program Phase: Developing Self and Team, Delivering Results

The project team members will commit an additional 25 percent to 50 percent of their time each week while maintaining their regular responsibilities and workload. The added work requires participants to grow the capability of their direct reports to cover responsibilities in their absence. Participants also focus on delivering results while demonstrating their learning capacity. Individuals are encouraged to learn skills and practice new behaviors outside their comfort zone. On a technical level, this means for example that someone with a finance background will be encouraged to contribute in a different area such as marketing. At the same time, those who have the requisite skills act as coaches to other team members, thereby enhancing their teaching capability. Participants also receive feedback at frequent intervals from team members, executives, and faculty encouraging them to remain open to new learning opportunities.

■ Post-Program Phase: Finding New Ways to Grow Self and Work Team

Following the program, individuals return to their full-time work assignment. Having delegated and repurposed 25 percent or more of their calendar during the program, they are encouraged to find new, more meaningful ways to contribute to their organization's success while continuing their own development. Many participants will rotate positions or be assigned to special projects within a year of the program's conclusion.

3. Faculty

■ Preparation Phase: Business Partner and Program Designer

The faculty plays varied roles throughout the process. They are a business partner to the CEO and top executives in planning the projects and selecting the participants. They act as an organizational development specialist in identifying project goals and mapping the root causes of the existing business challenges. They also help to prepare executives and participants for their upcoming roles.

- Program Phase: Facilitator, Coach, and Teacher

   They will teach, facilitate, and coach each of the workshops and carefully track progress between each event. Faculty often are able to see connections between projects before participants, encouraging strategic cross-team linkages and information sharing for the organization's benefit. A faculty coach also holds a one-on-one discussion with a member of each team on a weekly basis to ensure that the team is functioning well, there is progress on the project, and the individual remains committed to self-development.

- Post-Program Phase: System Integrator

   Although the faculty play no formal role in project execution or individual career counseling, they help to ensure that tracking and implementation systems are in place. If projects are not implemented as agreed or individuals do not receive clear feedback, the program credibility will be damaged.

PROJECT SELECTION

As noted earlier, the projects are selected by the CEO and top team members based on real challenges that are facing the organization. We have encountered situations where the CEO arrives at the final workshop only to hear a report-out by teams that have been diligently working for months on projects in which the company's leadership has little interest and no emotional investment. In one situation, a leading pharmaceutical manufacturer and Fortune 100 company, the CEO politely nodded at each team's recommendations and thanked them for their effort—and then went on with his day. The senior leaders had learned little about the participants, project implementation was unlikely, and the CEO's role had been reduced to that of a ceremonial figurehead on graduation day.

To ensure that projects are truly organizational priorities, each senior leader should be required to submit ideas for review with the entire leadership team. Ideas should percolate up from the levels immediately below the senior team and be informed by any significant shifts in a company's industry or strategy.

Linking the projects to the future direction of the organization, or to an area of perceived competitive weakness, helps to build new capabilities among the participants while also providing an assessment center to understand each individual's adaptability, learning speed, and strategic vision. Over the course of the program, participants will be required to benchmark externally, speak with industry contacts, talk to financial analysts, and take many other actions to learn, assimilate, and apply new knowledge in a vital area. As the top executives and faculty watch and learn alongside the participants—albeit at a distance—it becomes easy to see an individual's propensity for identifying, framing, and resolving key issues.

Once the project topics have been selected, defining the deliverables and providing background information requires careful preparation by the faculty and executives. The project statement and supporting documents should give the participants a running start at understanding the problem and current state. A synopsis of the areas that should be covered in the briefing is provided below.

1. Background: Provide a brief explanation of the history and case for change.
   a. What is the issue?
   b. How long has it been an issue?
   c. What is the financial/operational/cultural impact currently?
   d. What have we attempted?
   e. What were the results?
   f. What have been the key inhibitors (technical, political, cultural) to our success in this area?
2. Vision of Success: Outline the operational and financial expectations.
   a. What are our financial and operational targets in two to

three years? What market knowledge or other data do we have that leads us to believe we can attain these?

b. What additional information do we need in order to develop or verify our targets?

c. What do we believe our financial and operational targets *this year* should be? What market knowledge or other data do we have to support this?

3. Deliverables: Define the hard and soft deliverables required to achieve the vision.

a. What are the hard (e.g., operational, technical, systems design) deliverables that must be accomplished this year? Consider those specific activities required for implementation this year.

b. What are the soft (e.g., cultural, developmental) deliverables that must be accomplished this year? Consider those specific activities required for implementation this year.

c. What hard and soft deliverables are required to prepare the business for the next two to three years? Consider plans that must be developed, stakeholder dialogues required, negotiations, or pilot tests.

4. Decision Makers and Key Constituents

a. Do the issues above lie in one part of the business or organizational hierarchy, or do they span multiple functions/business units?

b. If technical systems are likely to change (processes, tools, IT systems), who has ultimate authority to authorize such changes?

c. Who is the ultimate decision maker(s)?

d. Who are key stakeholders that may influence the decision maker(s) or impact resource allocation as you work to solve the problem?

5. Resources Available to the Team

a. Who are the internal people/teams or other resources that the team should consult or utilize to better understand the issue and/or execute? For each resource, include a brief description of what you believe the project team should learn/do as a result of using the resource.

   b. Are there any internal or external documents the team should review to gain an understanding of the project topic area? For each document, who can provide the document?

   c. Are there any external experts or benchmarks that provide positive expertise or lessons learned related to the project topic? Are there any industry experts or analysts who can help the team? If you have a contact or relationship with the individual or organization, identify what help you can provide to facilitate a dialogue. For each person or organization identified, state what you believe the team can learn as a result of benchmarking.

6. Project Budget

   a. What are the funding limitations or other resource constraints as the team completes its work?

   b. Will team expenses (e.g., travel) come from your budget or another budget?

7. Team Coaching and Development Process

   a. How will team members be assessed and coached during the process?

   b. How will team members be coached after they have completed the project?

WORKSHOP STRUCTURE

The action learning process is divided into three workshops and two interim periods between workshops. Both the workshops and the interim periods provide rich opportunities for observation and assessment.

Preparation Phase

Prior to the first of three workshops, each participant undergoes a 360-degree personal assessment of his or her skills as a leader. Each person receives feedback comparing other people's perspectives of the individual with the person's own views of his or her talents and leadership ability. Individuals are also given reading material that relates to overall organizational objectives, industry trends, or new knowledge areas. They are not told which project they will work on as doing so encourages a great deal of unstructured, uncoordinated effort. If participants are informed of their project topic in advance they will likely undertake research in the hopes of getting a leg up on their colleagues. We have found that such efforts yield little return until participants discuss the project with senior executives and one another.

First Workshop

The first workshop lasts five days and is aimed at launching the teams, beginning strategic project work, and building new skills for each individual leader. Participants are exposed to innovative concepts in the areas of leadership, organizational change, corporate strategy, globalization, and shareholder value creation. Participants also examine their individual interaction within the newly formed teams and the team processes by which project tasks will be accomplished. As a component of this analysis, the teams spend a half day engaged in group activities so that team behavior can be practiced and new learnings immediately applied. Team activity culminates during the first session with the definition of a mission, vision, and work plan for each team. On a personal level, individuals consider how to reframe their leadership efforts and more efficiently work with peers and direct reports in their work area. In the process, they also construct personal development agendas for time both during and after the action learning process.

First Interim Period

Following the first workshop, participants return to their regular jobs while simultaneously working on their strategic projects. They are faced with the challenge of juggling multiple assignments, delegating work more effectively in their part of the organization, working collaboratively with peers, and communicating better via remote or asynchronous method.

Second Workshop

A midcourse, three-day workshop provides teams with feedback on their project work and individuals with feedback on personal leadership skills and behavior. Best practices are also shared during this middle workshop, and teams receive coaching support to better enable them to move forward with their strategic projects. Executives participate to review the project progress and understand how effectively teams are working together.

Second Interim

During the second interim, teams often work at a frenetic pace to complete their recommendations while lobbying for the needed commitment by senior managers. Teams become increasingly task focused and must work to avoid burying team conflict and to continue individual learning. Communication among the different action learning teams also increases if there are any interdependencies across teams or learning synergies, deepening the personal networks formed throughout the process. Finally, the teams have an opportunity to meet with members of the company's board of directors, a stressful exercise for some but an opportunity to hear another perspective and better understand organizational dynamics at the top. A sample board dialogue agenda for a ninety-minute session is included below.

Sample Agenda with Board Members

Day 1:
- Teams are assigned to present to one or two members of the board of directors.
- Teams prepare a twenty-five-minute overview of their project analysis and draft recommendations.
- Teams and executive coaches provide feedback to each group.
- Time is set aside for some rehearsal and revision.

Day 2:

- Each team meets with assigned board member(s) while the executive coach observes but does not actively participate (in order to provide feedback to team members in the future).
- Team provides board member(s) with an overview of the action learning process (5 minutes).
- Team members introduce themselves to board member(s), sharing their personal development agenda (15 minutes).
- Team presents project update (25 minutes).
- Dialogue and questions for board member(s) input (25 minutes).
- Board member(s) provide final feedback to team and ask any questions of individuals (15 minutes).
- Wrap-up (5 minutes).

Third Workshop

The final workshop is an intensive commitment process. Each team project receives two to three hours of focused attention from all participants, including senior management, to review team achievements, analyze recommendations, and commit to implementation. These project reviews are active dialogue sessions with full participation from everyone, debate, real-time compromise, and firm commitments to take action by the CEO and senior leaders. Time is taken throughout the session to assess individual learning and personal development and to establish individual leadership agendas for the future.

A graphical display of the process can be found below.

TYING ACTION LEARNING AND SUCCESSION PLANNING TOGETHER

As the psychologist Kurt Lewin once said, "no change without learning and no insight without action." Implementation of an action learning program provides a unique lens into each of the potential succession candidates' ability to learn, change, and convert insight into action. Because action learning lasts several months, involves real projects, and requires

Follow-up
- Ongoing monitoring of project implementation.
- Ongoing application of concepts, skills, and behaviors learned.

Workshop III
- Review team recommendations.
- Commitment process for implementation of team recommendations.
- Establish individual development plans for period after program.

Board Meeting
- Teams meet with members of the board of directors to review project areas and receive feedback on tentative recommendations.

Interim Period II
- Teams continue to meet while individuals fulfill ordinary job responsibilites.
- Teams conclude benchmarking, prepare final recommendations, and work to achieve commitment of senior management.

Workshop II
- Check progress of teams and receive input from all participants.
- Make midcourse adjustments to team processes.
- Review personal development agendas.

Interim Period I
- Teams meet to conduct project work.
- Individuals continue to fulfill ordinary job responsibilities, applying new concepts, skills, and behaviors.

Workshop I
- Learn new concepts: global industry mind-set, transformation leadership.
- Team/personal development.
- Project teams established and initial work plans set.

Prework
- Complete readings and collection of leadership feedback.

Start of process

close teamwork, it provides an environment in which to observe a potential leader's judgment and values. Simply put, it is impossible for someone to "fake it" for such an extended duration.

Along the way, the participant will be observed and provided feedback by fellow team members, executives, and faculty coaches. It is extremely useful to see how the individual processes such feedback and whether he or she becomes defensive and detached or embraces the opportunity to change and grow. There is no question that increasing self-awareness and the ability to modify behaviors and style are prerequisites for effective senior leadership. Nonetheless, even today some people make it close to the top of organizations through brute force or political manipulation that would poison teamwork and kill an organization's culture if exercised at the very top.

Most important, in nearly every organization in which we have conducted action learning, one of the biggest benefits has been the discovery of diamonds in the rough. Action learning provides an up-close perspective on leaders who were suspected to be outstanding but the jury was out due to insufficient data.

To cite only one example, in a Fortune 50 manufacturer one woman had joined mid-career and worked in a subsidiary. Although the senior executives who knew her imagined great potential, few others on the top team had been exposed to her and nobody felt they had a good assessment opportunity because her daily work was far removed from the organization's mainstream. After emerging as a leader on an action learning team and displaying remarkable interpersonal abilities, financial analytic capability, and a smooth operating style, she was recognized by each of the senior executives and CEO for her outstanding potential. Today, she occupies a top post in a core area for the company and is on the slate to succeed a senior team member when the time comes. Absent the action learning process she might have risen to a senior position in the subsidiary but likely remained undiscovered by the company's senior leaders.

Finally, exposure to the board of directors should not be underestimated. Although it is only a short session, typically lasting just two hours, it is an important opportunity to introduce top talent and hopefully better educate the board about the organization's bench strength. In this way, an action learning program should be a catalyst for building relationships that encourage ongoing development and assessment with board members, the CEO, and top leaders well beyond the duration of the program.

A MICROCOSM OF DATA

In summary, it should be reinforced that no single experience or data point should ever be the basis for a succession decision. Selecting leaders can only be addressed through diligent review of multiple inputs on performance, judgment, values, and potential. Action learning offers an extraordinarily useful microcosm in which to view each of these elements, challenges participants with experiences that may not be present in their careers so far, and adds to the succession data bank, helping to ensure more successful selection and promotion.

NOTES

Introduction

1. *Del Jones, "Some Companies Cheer When Alumni Move On and Up," USA Today,* January 8, 2008.
2. In Geoff Colvin, "How Top Companies Breed Stars," *Fortune,* September 20, 2007, the author credits my old friend professor Jeffrey Sonnenfeld of the Yale School of Management with coining the term some twenty years ago. "Sonnenfeld notes that academy companies offer more internal training to their executives, and their alumni often populate the leadership of other firms."
3. Noel M. Tichy and Mary Anne Devanna, *The Transformational Leader* (Wiley & Sons, 1986).
4. When Welch was shouldering much of the blame for laying off thousands of employees in the early eighties, the nickname "Neutron Jack," bestowed upon him for "vaporizing jobs while leaving buildings intact," as memorialized in a July 26, 1982, *Newsweek* cover story entitled "White Collar: The 'New Unemployed,'" by Susan Dentzer, stuck to him like glue but also stuck in his craw.
5. By the time *Fortune* crowned him "Manager of the Century" at the end of his twenty-year term and even before, the same publication that had branded him in 1982, *Newsweek,* felt obliged to concede the remarkable degree to which his reputational table had turned in twelve years. "The unions that once denounced Welch now sing his praises . . . strikes have been virtually eliminated and workers are delighted with their new powers, such as the right to review prospective managers." Daniel McGinn, "Scratches in the Teflon," *Newsweek,* October 2, 1994.

CHAPTER 1
Getting It Wrong: The Broken CEO Succession Pipeline

1. Readers will likely recall that in the best-selling study *Built to Last: Successful Habits of Visionary Companies* (HarperBusiness, 1994) by Jim Collins and Jerry Porras, HP was held up as an example of a "visionary" company that outcompeted rivals on the strength of its enduring culture, as enshrined in its legendary "HP Way."
2. Apotheker's appointment as CEO of HP was effective November 1, 2010.
3. Carly Fiorina's appointment as HP's first outsider CEO occurred in July 1999.

4. James B. Stewart, "Voting to Hire a Chief Without Meeting Him," *New York Times*, September 21, 2011.

5. Ibid.

6. In "GE Rethinking the 20-Year Chief," *Wall Street Journal*, April 15, 2014, Joann S. Lublin, Ted Mann, and Kate Linebaugh cite a recent analysis by executive search firm Spencer Stuart setting the average tenure of S&P 500 CEOs at 7.2 years, although estimates of CEO tenures vary.

7. Noel M. Tichy and Warren G. Bennis, *Judgment: How Winning Leaders Make Great Calls* (Portfolio, 2007).

8. Noel M. Tichy, *Managing Strategic Change: Technical, Political, and Cultural Dynamics* (Wiley & Sons, 1983).

9. The Conference Board, *CEO Succession Practices: 2012 Edition*, April 2012.

10. SEC Staff Legal Bulletin 14E (CF), SEC Division of Corporate Finance, October 27, 2009.

11. Monica Langley, "Ballmer on Ballmer: His Exit from Microsoft," *Wall Street Journal*, November 17, 2013.

12. John Gapper, "Where the Buck Stops," *Financial Times*, August 24, 2013.

13. MIT professor Michael A. Cusamano, as cited in Michael J. de la Merced, "Anything-But-Ordinary Succession for Company at a Crossroad," *New York Times*, August 24, 2013.

14. David Goldman, "Microsoft Names Nadella CEO, Gates Out as Chair," CNN, February 4, 2014.

15. F. John Reh, "A Crack in the Glass Ceiling," About.com, July 26, 1999.

16. Peter Barrows and Peter Elstrom, "HP's Carly Fiorina: The Boss," *Bloomberg Businessweek*, August 2, 1999.

17. Ibid.

18. Stewart, "Voting to Hire a Chief Without Meeting Him."

19. James Bandler with Doris Burke, "How Hewlett-Packard Lost Its Way," *Fortune*, May 21, 2012.

20. Nathan Vardi, "Citigroup's Succession Disaster," *Forbes*, October 16, 2012.

21. Francesco Guerrera, "Citi's Weill Admits Flaw in 2003 CEO Succession," *FT.com*, May 28, 2008.

22. James Bandler and Doris Duke, "How Hewlett-Packard Lost Its Way," *Fortune*, May 8, 2012.

23. Stewart, "Voting to Hire a Chief Without Meeting Him."

24. Ben Worthen, "Larry Ellison 'Speechless' Over New CEO of HP," *Wall Street Journal*, October 1, 2011.

25. Stewart, "Voting to Hire a Chief Without Meeting Him."

CHAPTER 2

**Cultivating Transformational Leaders on the Inside:
The Theory of the Case**

1. This colorful quotation often attributed to investor Warren Buffett was first uttered by Texas attorney Robert L. Clarke, comptroller of the currency under Ronald Reagan, in reference to the savings and loan crisis of the 1980s.

2. "Remarks at the National Defense Executive Reserve Conference," November 14, 1957.

3. Peter F. Drucker, "The American CEO," *The Wall Street Journal*, December 30, 2004.

CHAPTER 3

**Getting It Right: Building a Transformational
Leadership Pipeline**

1. Matthew Boyle, "The Art of CEO Succession," *Bloomberg Businessweek,* April 29, 2009.
2. Ibid.
3. "Leadership in the Field: Interviews with Global Leaders, Interview with Bank of America Non-Executive Chairman Chad Holliday," RussellReynolds .com.
4. Boyle, "The Art of CEO Succession."
5. Claudia H. Deutsch, "Irving S. Shapiro, 85, Lawyer and Ex-Chairman of DuPont," *New York Times*, September 15, 2001.
6. "Leadership in the Field."
7. Diane Brady, "DuPont's Ellen Kullman on Her Risky Path to the CEO Job," *Bloomberg Businessweek*, September 15, 2011.
8. Boyle, "The Art of CEO Succession."
9. Carol J. Loomis, "Ellen Kullman's Quest to Make DuPont Great Again," *Fortune*, April 15, 2010.
10. Brady, "DuPont's Ellen Kullman on Her Risky Path to the CEO Job."
11. Noel Tichy and Christopher DeRose, "Roger Enrico's Master Class Executives Chosen for the Ultimate Pepsi Challenge Spend Three Months Learning How to Really Grow the Business," *Fortune*, November 27, 1995.
12. Ibid.
13. Katrina Brooker, "The Pepsi Machine," *Fortune,* January 30, 2006.

CHAPTER 4

**The CEO Role in the Succession Pipeline:
The Paradox of Power**

1. Elizabeth Ross Kanter and Matthew Bird, "Transforming Verizon: A Platform for Change," Harvard Business School Case, 2011.
2. Official Verizon Corporate Statement, September 20, 2010.
3. Ivan Seidenberg and Marc Reed, interview with the author, September 12, 2013.
4. Katrina Booker, "Can Procter & Gamble Change Its Culture, Protect Its Market Share and Find the Next Tide?" *Fortune*, April 26, 1999.
5. Emily Nelson and Nikhil Deogun, "Change Was Too Fast at P&G; Jager Goes, Pepper Is Reinstalled," *Wall Street Journal,* June 9, 2000.
6. A. G. Lafley, "The Art and Science of Finding the Right CEO: Lessons from P&G's Obsession with Succession,"; foreword by Noel M. Tichy, *Harvard Business Review*, October 2011.
7. Ibid.
8. Ibid.
9. Ibid.
10. Robert Berner, "P&G: New and Improved," *Bloomberg Businessweek*, July 6, 2003.
11. Ibid.
12. Lafley, "The Art and Science of Finding the Right CEO."
13. Interview with the author.
14. Lafley, "The Art and Science of Finding the Right CEO."
15. Ibid.

16. Jennifer Reingold, "CEO Swap: The $79 Billion Plan," *Fortune*, November 20, 2009.

17. Lauren Coleman-Lochner and Carol Hymowitz, "Lafley's Comeback at P&G," *Bloomberg*, May 28, 2013.

18. Lafley, "The Art and Science of Finding the Right CEO."

19. Alan F. Lafley, Review of *The Succession Planning Handbook for the Chief Executive* by Walter Mahler and Stephen J. Trotter, *Human Resources Management* 26/1 (Spring 1987): 129–34.

CHAPTER 5
The Critical Role of Human Resources in CEO Succession

1. Noel M. Tichy and David O. Ulrich, "The Leadership Challenge—A Call for the Transformational Leader," *MIT Sloan Management Review*, October 15, 1984.

2. This dichotomy was originally articulated by one of the true heroes of leadership studies, the Pulitzer Prize–winning political historian James MacGregor Burns, whose landmark work *Leadership* impressed me when published in 1978 as one of the most penetrating analyses of leadership ever achieved. In Burns's formulation, transformational leaders succeed by aligning the mission of the organization with the motivations of their people.

3. *Peter Elkind and Jennifer Reingold*, "Inside Pfizer's Palace Coup," *Fortune*, July 28, 2011.

4. Ibid.

5. Ibid.

6. Carol Hymowitz and Sarah Frier, "IBM's Rometty Breaks Ground as 100-Year-Old Company's First Female Leader," *Bloomberg Businessweek*, October 26, 2011.

7. Randy MacDonald, interview with the author, October 2, 2013.

8. Brad Power, "IBM Focuses HR on Change," HBR Blog Network, January 10, 2012.

9. Ibid.

10. Kristen B. Frasch, "An HR Icon Reflects on Retirement," *Human Resources Executive*, May 30, 2013.

11. Ibid.

12. "Accenture Partners Take the Cake," *Bloomberg Businessweek*, July 8, 2001.

13. Scott S. Smith, "Private Consultation," American Way, http://hub.aa.com/en/aw/joe-forehand-accenture-customer-relationship-management-andersen-consulting.

14. Melissa J. Anderson, "Voice of Experience: Camille Mirshokrai, Senior Executive and Director of Global Leadership Development, Accenture," *The Glasshammer.com*, October 18, 2010.

CHAPTER 6
The Role of the Board

1. At year end 2013, ExxonMobil vied with Apple as the world's most highly valued publicly traded company, with a market cap of approximately $400 billion, as compared with Shell's roughly $200 billion, on equivalent revenues.

2. Janet Guyon, "Why Is the World's Most Profitable Company Turning Itself Inside Out?" *Fortune*, August 4, 1997.

3. Warwick Business School professor Christian Stadler, cited in David Whitford, "Shell's Big Surprise," *Fortune*, July 9, 2013.

4. Guyon, "Why Is the World's Most Profitable Company Turning Itself Inside Out?"
5. Bank of America repaid $45 billion in TARP funds to the federal government on December 9, 2009, so by retiring on December 31, he kept his commitment to stay on until he got TARP off the bank's back.
6. Pallavi Gogoi, "CEO Succession Plan a Mystery at Bank of America," *USA Today*, November 12, 2009.
7. Tom Saporito and Paul Winum, *Inside CEO Succession: The Essential Guide to Leadership Transition* (John Wiley & Sons, Canada, 2012).
8. See Greg Farrell, *Crash of The Titans: Greed, Hubris, the Fall of Merrill Lynch and the Near-Collapse of Bank of America* (Crown Business, 2010).
9. William J. Holstein, "What the Merrill Debacle Teaches Us About CEO Succession," *CBS/Money Watch*, October 31, 2007.
10. Ibid.
11. Bruce R. Ellig, *The Complete Guide to Executive Compensation*, cited in Tim McGlaughlin, "Merrill Lynch Succession Plan Under Scrutiny," *San Diego Union-Tribune*, October 30, 2007.
12. Farrell, *Crash of the Titans*, 94.
13. Irving L. Janis, *Groupthink: Psychological Studies of Policy Decisions and Fiascoes* (Houghton Mifflin, 1982).
14. This is a phrase popularized in Phil Rosenzweig's excellent book *The Halo Effect: And the Eight Other Business Delusions That Deceive Managers* (The Free Press, 2007).
15. Adapted from Ram Charan, Dennis Carey, and Michael Useem, *Boards That Lead: When to Take Charge, When to Partner, and When to Stay Out of the Way* (Harvard Business Review Press, 2014).
16. Adrian Cadbury, "Boardroom Roles," in *Business: The Ultimate Resource* (Perseus Publishing, 2002), 220.
17. Saporito and Winum, *Inside CEO Succession*, 61.

CHAPTER 7
The Insider/Outsider Dilemma

1. "J.C. Penney Apologizes to Shopper Via Social Media," Reuters, May 2, 2013.
2. Mary Buffett, "Why Did JC Penney Stumble So Badly Under Ron Johnson? It's Culture, Stupid," *Huffington Post*, April 18, 2013.
3. "JC Penney Ousts CEO Ron Johnson, Ullman Returns," Associated Press, April 8, 2013.
4. Jennifer Reingold, "Ron Johnson: Retail's New Radical," *Fortune*, March 19, 2012.
5. James Surowiecki, "The Turnaround Trap," *New Yorker*, March 25, 2013.
6. Kat Ascharya, "Ron Johnson: From Apple Genius to JCPenney Outcast; Where Did JCP's Anointed Savior Go Wrong?" 2machines.com, April 30, 2013.
7. Reingold, "Ron Johnson: Retail's New Radical."
8. Ibid.
9. Ascharya, "Ron Johnson: From Apple Genius to JCPenney Outcast."
10. Reingold, "Ron Johnson: Retail's New Radical."
11. Max Nisen, "It Was All Over for Ron Johnson When Bill Ackman Shredded Him on Friday," *BusinessInsider.com*, April 8, 2013.
12. Surowiecki, "The Turnaround Trap."
13. Stephanie Clifford, "Chief's Silicon Valley Stardom Quickly Clashed at J.C. Penney," *New York Times*, April 9, 2013.

14. Betsy Morris, "He's Smart. He's Not Nice. He's Saving Big Blue . . ." *Fortune*, April 14, 1997.

15. David Kirkpatrick, "Breaking Up IBM," *Fortune*, July 27, 1992.

16. Ram Charan, Dennis Carey, and Michael Useem, *Boards That Lead: When to Take Charge, When to Partner, and When to Stay Out of the Way* (Harvard Business School Press, 2014).

17. Louis V. Gerstner Jr., *Who Says Elephants Can't Dance?* (HarperBusiness, 2003), 73.

18. Micheline Maynard, "From Driver to Passenger," *New York Times*, September 10, 2006.

19. Monica Langley and Jeffrey McCracken, "Ford Taps Boeing Executive as CEO," *Wall Street Journal*, September 6, 2006.

20. Scott Hamilton, a managing director of aviation analysis firm The Leeham Group, as quoted in Maynard, "From Driver to Passenger."

21. Ibid.

22. Alex Taylor III, "Ford's Smooth CEO Succession—Plus a Few Bumps," *Fortune*, November 1, 2012.

23. Maynard, "From Driver to Passenger."

24. Diane Brady, "Alan Mulally on Ford's Amassing Debt in the Downturn," *Bloomberg Businessweek*, September 20, 2012.

25. Ibid.

26. Bill Vlasic, "European Cloud over Ford," *New York Times*, January 29, 2013.

27. David Kiley, "Alan Mulally: The Outsider at Ford," *Bloomberg Businessweek*, March 4, 2009.

28. Claudia H. Deutsch, "3M to Select G.E. Executive as Next Chief," *New York Times*, December 5, 2000.

29. Online Extra: "The Hard Work in Leadership," *Bloomberg Businessweek*, April 11, 2004.

30. Stanley Holmes, "Cleaning Up Boeing," *Bloomberg Businessweek*, March 12, 2006.

31. Carol Hymowitz and Thomas Black, "McNerney Tested at Boeing as 787 Inquiry Raises Costs," *Bloomberg*, January 22, 2013.

32. Interview with the author, November 11, 2012.

33. Thomas A. Stewart, "Allied-Signal's Turnaround Blitz," *Fortune*, November 30, 1992.

34. Noel M. Tichy and Ram Charan, "The CEO as Coach: An Interview with AlliedSignal's Lawrence A. Bossidy," *Harvard Business Review*, March 1995.

35. Larry Bossidy, "The Job No CEO Should Delegate," *Harvard Business Review*, March 2001.

36. Ibid.

37. Michael Elliott, "The Anatomy of the GE-Honeywell Disaster," *Fortune*, July 8, 2001.

38. Claudia H. Deutsch, "A Former Boss Tries to Put Honeywell on a New Path," *New York Times*, December 13, 2001.

39. Joseph L. Bower, "Solve the Succession Crisis by Growing Inside-Outside Leaders," *Harvard Business Review*, November 2007.

CHAPTER 8

Building a Succession Pipeline in Family Organizations

1. www.iefamiliar.com.

2. Devin Leonard, "The Bronfman Saga: From Rags to Riches to . . . ," *Fortune*, November 25, 2002.

3. Andrew Carnegie, *Triumphant Democracy; or, Fifty Years' March of the Republic* (Scribner's, 1886), 366.
4. Brian Milner, "The Unmaking of a Dynasty," *Cigar Aficionado,* March–April 2003.
5. Leonard, "The Bronfman Saga: From Rags to Riches to . . ."
6. Amy Chozick, "The Man Who Would Be Redstone," *New York Times,* September 22, 2012.
7. Merissa Marr, "Redstone Daughter Still in Succession Mix," *Wall Street Journal,* October 26, 2012.
8. Christian Caspar, Ana Karina Dias, and Heinz-Peter Elstrodt, "The Five Attributes of Enduring Family Businesses," www.mckinsey.com, January 2010.
9. Nicolas Kachaner, George Stalk, and Alain Bloch, "What You Can Learn from Family Business," *Harvard Business Review,* November 2012.
10. www.iefamiliar.com.
11. Aveek Datta, "Ratan Tata: A Journey in Four Stages," *Live Mint & The Wall Street Journal,* December 20, 2012.

CHAPTER 9
Building a Succession Pipeline for Nonprofit Organizations

1. Michael D. Cohen and James G. Marsh, *Leadership and Ambiguity: The American College President: Report to the Carnegie Commission on Higher Education* (McGraw-Hill, 1974).
2. Ibid., 42. Note the absence of "his or herself"—four decades ago, there were so few women university presidents as to not even be worth noting in a study of the class.
3. Robert H. Ferrell, ed., *The Eisenhower Diaries* (W. W. Norton, 1981).
4. Andrea Gabor, "Leadership Principles for Public School Principals," *Strategy + Business,* Winter 2004.
5. Noel M. Tichy, *Managing Strategic Change: Technical, Political, and Cultural Dynamics* (Wiley & Sons, 1983).

CHAPTER 10
Leadership 20/20: Framing and Facing the Future

1. Scott Cook, "Entrepreneurship for a Disruptive World," Leadership in an Agile Age, The Economist Conference Innovation 2011, April 20, 2011.

Conclusion

1. Jeff Cunningham, "How Caterpillar Chairman and CEO Doug Oberhelman and the Board Transformed the Company," *NACD Directorship,* December 8, 2011, www.directorship.com/strategy-at-caterpillar/Strategy at Caterpillar.
2. Ibid.

INDEX